ARTISTS AMONG US

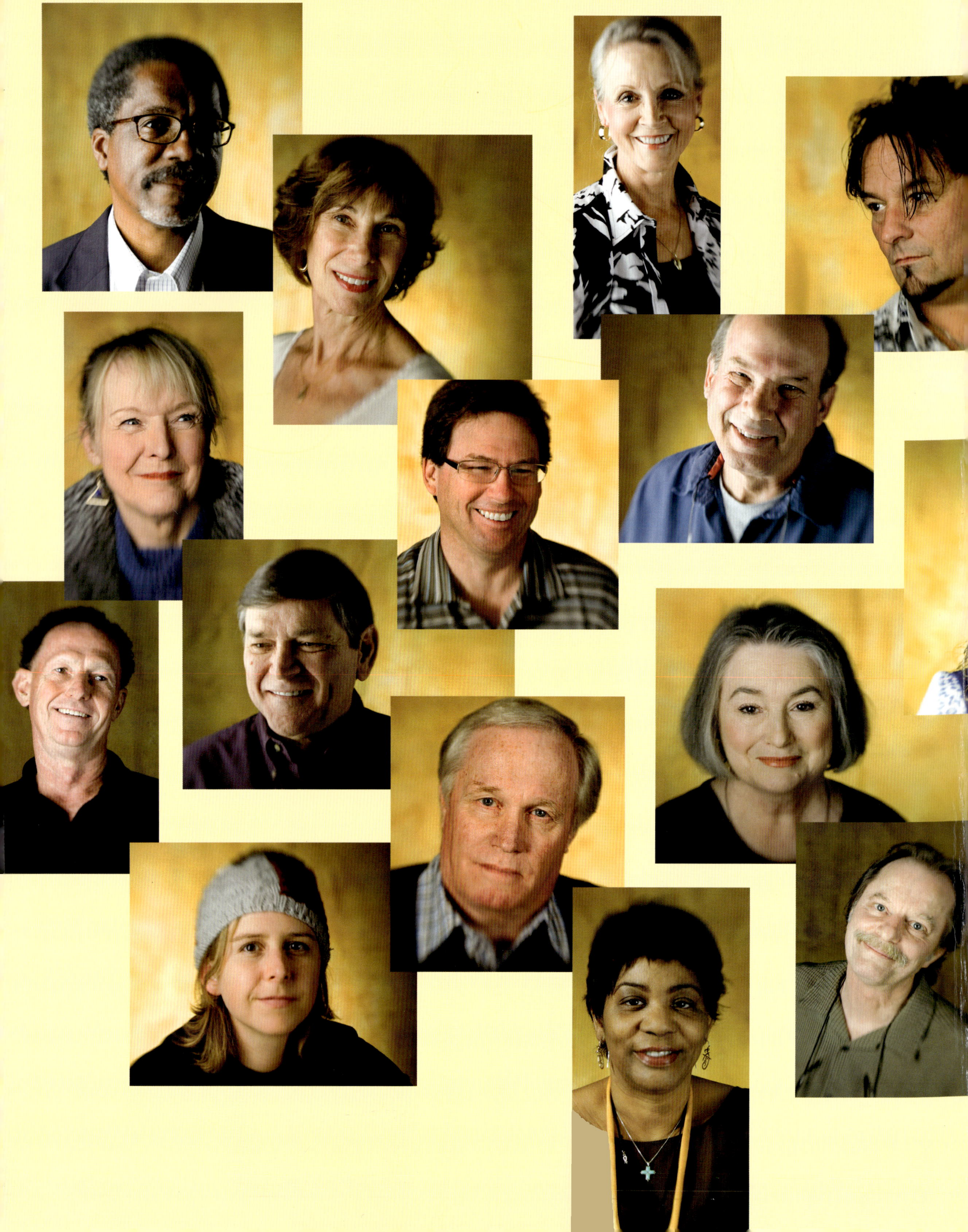

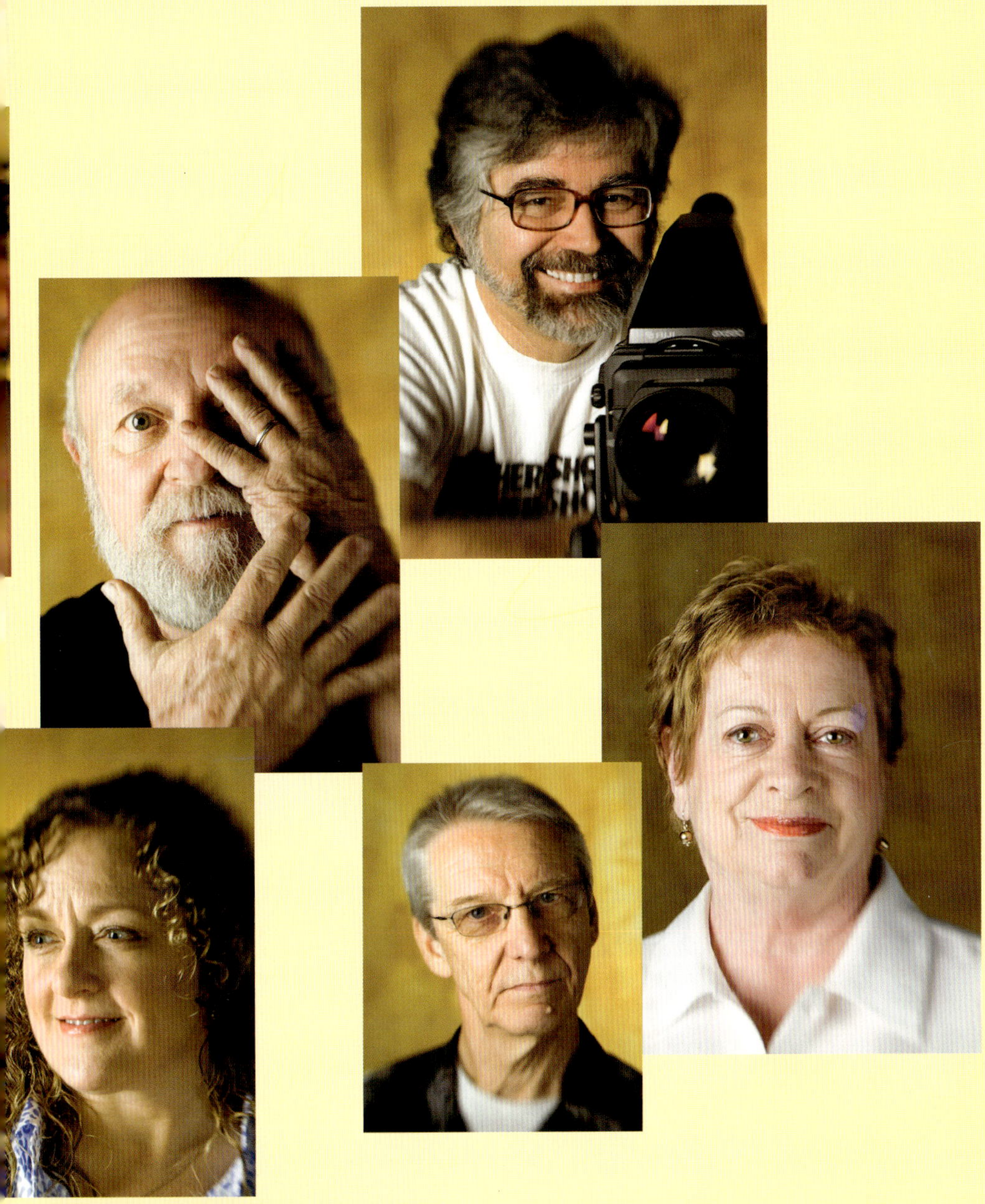

100 Faces of Art in Spartanburg

ARTISTS AMONG US

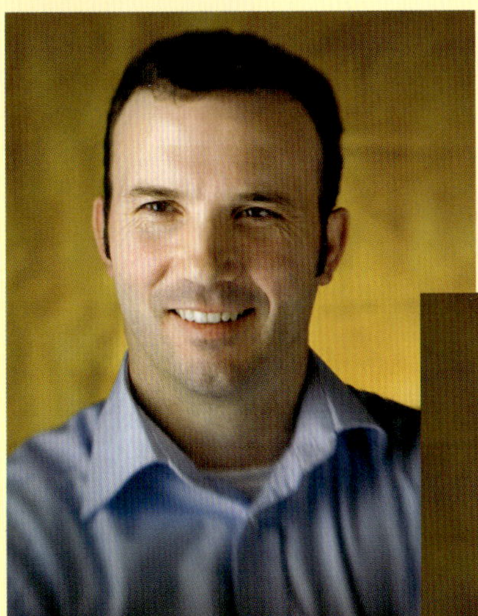

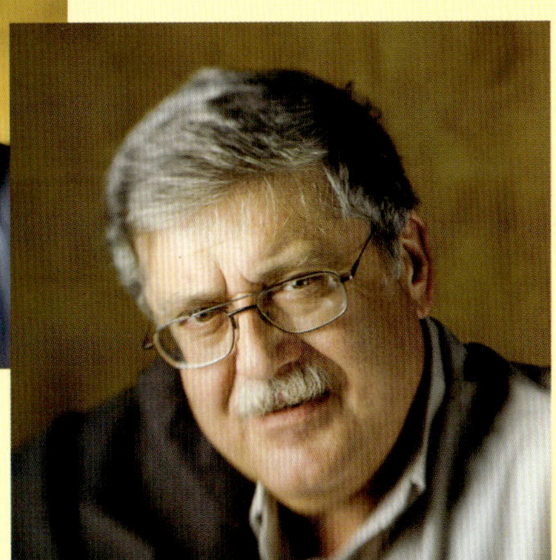

EDWARD EMORY AND

STEPHEN STINSON

Hub City Press

Spartanburg, SC

First printing, November 2011
Editor: Betsy Wakefield Teter
Front cover image: Stephen Stinson and mystery guest
Book design: The Midnight Oil Design, LLC, Nancy Cutler
Proofreaders: Kari Jackson, Jan Scalisi, Tammy Whaley
Printed in China by Everbest through Four Colour Imports

ISBN: 978-1891885-86-0

This project is funded in part by the Arts Partnership of Greater Spartanburg and its donors, the City and County of Spartanburg, and the South Carolina Arts Commission, which receives funding from the National Endowment for the Arts.

HUB CITY PRESS

186 West Main Street
Spartanburg SC 29306
864 577 9349 www.hubcity.org

The Hub City Writers Project thanks its friends who made contributions in support of this book and other Hub City programs:

The Arts Partnership of Greater Spartanburg
The South Carolina Arts Commission
Valerie and Bill Barnet
Bea and Dennis Bruce
Marsha and Jimmy Gibbs
Elizabeth Fleming
Sara, Paul, and Ellis Lehner
Stacy and John McBride
Liz and Dwight Patterson
John Lane and Betsy Teter
Betty and Walter Montgomery
QS/1
Anne Marie and Dennis Wiseman
White's Pine Street Exxon
Catherine Woodard

Paula and Stan Baker
Carol and Jim Bradof
Margie and Mac Cates
Sally and Jerry Cogan Jr.
Colonial Trust Co.
Anna and Justin Converse
Nora Beth and John Featherston
Wickie Fort
Dorothy and Julian Josey
Lib and Rick Orr
Norman Powers
Nan and Tom McDaniel

Carolyn Alexander
Bob and Ruta Allen
Mitch and Sarah Allen
Mack and Patty Amick
Monta and Ken Anthony
Tom and Ceci Arthur
Daingerfield Ashton
Robert and Susan Atkins
Carol Augthun
Dianne R. Bagnal
Vic and Lynn Bailey
Bailie Studios
Susan Baker
John and Isabel Barber
Jessica Barnes
Tom and Joan Barnet
William Barnet & Son LLC
Michael and Judith Battaglia
Charles and Christi Bebko
Libby Bernardin
Patricia Black
Clarke and Martha Blackman
Shirley Blaes
Mayo Mac Boggs
Joyce Bond
Susan Bottone Boscia
Theresa M. Bowles
Betty Jane Bramlett
Mary Nell and George Brandt, III
JoAnn Brasington
Bob and Sheila Breitweiser
Susan Bridges
Mellnee G. Buchheit
Jack and Myrna Bundy
Chris Bundy
Julia Burnett
William W. Burns
Fred and Joan Butehorn
Fritz and Lori Butehorn
Brant and Judy Bynum
Linda Hyatt Cancel
Katherine and Marvin Cann
Mike and Vivianne Carey
Jay and Renee Cariveau
Terry and Janis Cash
Beth Cate
Chuck White and Ruth L. Cate
Randall and Sarah Chambers
John and Lisa Chapman
Chris Fletcher and
Marshall Chapman
Lacy and Rob Chapman
Nan and Tim Cleveland
Robert and Janeen Cochran
Jay Coffman
Rick and Sue Conner
Paul and Nancy Coté
Tom Moore Craig
Ophelia Crain
Dick and Ann Crenshaw
John and Kirsten Cribb
Daniel and Becky Cromer
Garrow and Chris Crowley
Nancy Rainey Crowley
Scott Cunningham
Betsy Cox and Mike Curtis
Ted and Becky Daniel
Jane Dempsey
Mr. and Mrs. Magruder H. Dent
Fredrick B. Dent
Paul and Tara Desmond
Georgie and Bill Dickerson
Toney W. Dillard
Chris and Alice Dorrance
Anne and Bernie Dunlap
Susan and James Dunlap
Kathy and Ray Dunleavy
Kirsten and Levon Eastin
Coleman Edmunds
Betty and William C. Elston
Edwin Epps
Janet Estes
Alex and Jennifer Evins
Henry and Phyllis Ann Fagen Jr.
Andy and Lynne Falatok
Ted R. Fansher
George and Mildred Fields Jr.

Donor list continued on the next page

Christine Lawrence and Trey Finney
First South Bank
Lib Fleming
Kimberly Anne and Ashley Fly
Jill Jones and Clif Flynn
Beth Cecil and Isabel Forbes
Will and Liz Fort
Caleb and Delie Fort
Lorelei Foster
Donald L. Fowler
Steve and Abby Fowler
Melton and Lisa Francis
Denise Tatum Frazier
Ken and Jean Frick
Sidney and Lenna Fulmer
Louise and Stephen L. Garrell
Joan Gibson
Judy Goldman
Jan and Larry Goldstein
Barney and Elaine Gosnell
Ben and Carter Graves
Margaret and Chip Green
Lucy H. Grier
John Morton and Susan Griswold
Jim and Kay Gross
Carlos and Barbara Gutierrez
Roger and Marianna Habisreutinger
Lee and Kitty Hagglund
Benjy and Tanya Hamm
Bob and Barbara Hammett
Tracy and Tom Hannah
Robert and Carolyn Harbison, III
John and Lou Ann Harrill Jr.
Peyton and Michele Harvey
Mark Hayes
Rita and David Heatherly
Steve and Denise Heeren
Gary and Carmela Henderson
Peggy Henderson
Mike and Nancy Henderson
Laura Beeson Henthorn
Patricia and Marvin Hevener
Marie C. High
Stephanie Highsmith
Mary Lou and William Hightower
Susan Hodge
Katie Adams Hodge
Max and Tom Hollis
Myrta and David Holt
Audrey and Christian Hope

Doug and Marilyn Hubbell
Mr. and Mrs. Kenneth R. Huckaby
Jim and Patsy Hudgens
Linda Page Hudgins
Joe and Elsa Hudson
Lawrence and Margaret Huey
David and Harriet Ike
Mr. and Mrs. James W. Ivey
Dr. William A. James
Dr. and Mrs. Vernon Jeffords
Mr. and Mrs. William Jeffords, Sr.
Anne Chapman and Al Jeter
Tom Johnson
Stewart and Ann Johnson
Wallace Eppes Johnson
Betsy and Charlie Jones
Frannie Jordan
Elizabeth and Bill Joyce
Mr. and Mrs. Daniel Kahrs
Jay and Pam Kaplan
Peggy and Greg Karpick
Ann J. Kelly
Wendy and Dan King
Mary Ann and Monty Kirby
Beverly Knight
Bert and Ruth Knight
Nancy Kochenower
Mark and Sharon Koenig
Mike Kohler
Mary Jane and Cecil Lanford
Jack and Kay Lawrence
Janice and Wood Lay
Brandy and Eric Lindsey
Francie and Lindsay Little
George and Frances Loudon
Brownlee and Julie Lowry
Robert and Nancy Lyon
Ed and Suzan Mabry
Nathaniel and Gayle Magruder
John and Becky Manatis
Zerno E. Martin, Jr.
Dan and Kit Maultsby
Bill and Wendy Mayrose
John and Jill McBurney
Connie McCarley
Gail D. McCullough
Edward T. McLean
Stanford McMillan
Ed and Gail Medlin
Lucia and David Meeks
Larry E. Milan
Don and Mary Miles

Boyce and Carole Miller
Karen and Bob Mitchell
John and Belton Montgomery
Peter A. Moore
T. Craig Murphy
John and Susan Murphy
Doug and Maxine Nash
Kam and Emily Neely
Kris and Patrice Neely
Kirk and Clare Neely
Missy and Nick Nicholson
Pamela Nienhuis
Margaret and George Nixon
Walter and Susan Novak
Oakbrook Preparatory School
Walter and Joy Oates
Jeanie and Patrick O'Shaughnessy
Don and Erin Ouzts
Geneva F. Padgett
Keith and Joan Parris
Richard Pennell
Carolyn Pennell
Pat and Ann Porcher Perrin
Bob and Dixie Pinson
Melissa and Bryan Pittman
Andrew Poliakoff
John and Lynne Poole
Jan and Sara Lynn Postma, Jr.
Perrin and Kay Powell
Harold B. Powell
Phil and Frances Racine
Kelly Lowry and Rebecca Ramos
Eileen Rampey
Karen Randall
Ron and Ann Rash
Allison and John Ratterree
Naomi Richardson
Nancy and Robert Riehle
Rose Mary Ritchie
Elisabeth and Regis Robe
Martial and Amy Robichaud
Renee Romberger
Dwight Rose
Steve and Elena Rush
Mary Ann and Olin Sansbury
Anne Sapp
Kaye Savage
Garrett and Cathy Scott
Sara Dame Setzer
Rosa Shand
Ben and Kathi Shoaf
Mr. and Mrs. John W. Simon Sr.

Danny and Becky Smith
Lee and James Snell, Jr., Esq.
Betty B. Snow
Howard Solomon
Sylvia Spears
Shelley Sperka
Hank and Marla Steinberg
B.G. and Sandra Stephens
Brand and Laura Stille
Kay B. Stinson
Tammy and David Stokes
Eliot and Michel Stone
George and Sissy Stone
Phillip Stone
Brenda and Ed Story
Mary Ellen Suitt
Christine and Bob Swager
Ed and Sydney Taylor
Jess and Allene Taylor
Nancy Taylor
Carol and Peter Theiler
Frank Thies III
Ray E. Thompson, Sr.
Bob and Cheryl Tillotson
Bill and Martha Tinder
Thomas A. Tucker
Doris Turner
Garry Turpin
Robert M. Urban
Robbie and Miriam Vannoy
Jean Souther Vaughn
Charlotte and John Verreault, III
Mary Helen and Gregg Wade
Chuck Reback and Melissa Walker
Bill and Winnie Walsh
Lawrence and Jerri Warren
Billy and Lindsay Webster
Mary Ellen Wegrzyn
David and Kathy Weir
Ann and Fred Wenz
Tammy Whaley
Karen and John B. White, Jr.
Mary K. Wilborn
Alanna and Don Wildman
William and Floride Willard
Mary G. Willis
Kathy Zimmerli Wofford
Bob and Carolyn Wynn
Susan Young
Steve and Charlotte Zides
Kurt and Nelly Zimmerli
Suzanne and Jon Zoole

Introduction

By Edward Emory

This book is an outgrowth of the Artists Among Us photography project. Photographer Stephen Stinson and I began our collaboration more than three years ago to raise awareness in Spartanburg and across the region of the importance of our community's visual arts. We originally intended to photograph three hundred artists in Spartanburg, Greenville, and western North Carolina. When Hub City Press saw our work, we were asked to pare the number down to one hundred Spartanburg artists and to create a colorful coffee-table book.

The artists included here make up a group who, day-in and day-out, contribute to our collective efforts in visual arts in Spartanburg. They are our citizen-artists, those whose civic spirit has helped build our local visual arts community. To select them, I began by creating a list of twelve questions to serve as a scoring method. If artists in our community scored at or above sixty percent

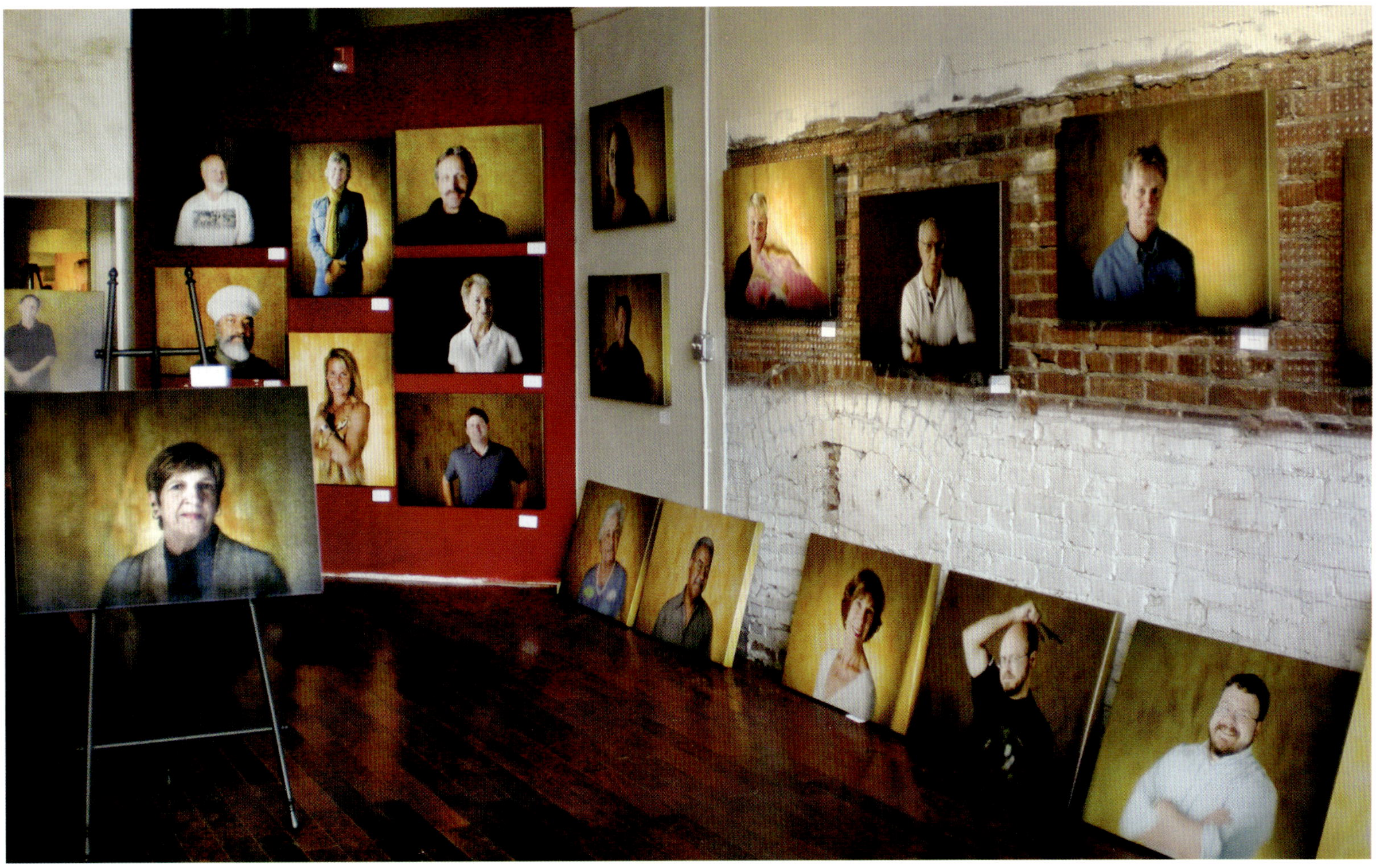

An early Artists Among Us exhibit on Main Street in Spartanburg, by Stephen Stinson

in relation to these questions, I tried to include them in the book. I asked such questions as, Are you a member of the Spartanburg Artists' Guild? *Are you a member of the Spartanburg Museum of Art? Do you exhibit on a continuous basis in Spartanburg? Do you teach art in Spartanburg? Do you contribute to philanthropic efforts in Spartanburg via your artwork? Do you encourage, support, and collaborate with other artists in this community?* This book could have easily included three hundred artists in Spartanburg alone. For those whom I have overlooked or failed to acknowledge, I apologize. Perhaps at some point in the future, if we are successful in our mission, we will follow this book with the *Thousand Faces of Art in Spartanburg*.

Some of the artists included here are professionally trained, full-time, working artists, and some are not. I often feel the need to educate the public about the difference. In most cases, but not all, professional artists have attended an art college that can—as it does for many professions—include four, six, or eight years of intensive education within a field. They usually attend workshops, collaborate with other professionals, and continue to hone their skills throughout their careers in much the same way doctors, attorneys, and other professionals do. Like most people who have dedicated their lives to a particular profession, they usually can charge more for their efforts and are highly respected among their peers. Other artists in the book are self-taught but are included because of their talent, their body of work, and their hyper-involvement in our community's arts scene.

I have also selected several professional photographers for inclusion in this book. Often painters, sculptors, ceramicists, and other artists reject photography as a true fine arts skill. Without exception, the photographers included in this book possess all the attributes stated above. They are capable of abstract thought that allows them to document what so many of us see but fail to grasp. They also can arrange themes, create effects, and take advantage of their understanding of light and depth of field that very few novice photographers can even imagine. All the artists in this book have the capability to perform at a professional level if they choose.

My original vision for the Artists Among Us project was to create black-and-white photographic portraits of the artists, mat and frame them in simple black frames, and exhibit them during Art Walk Spartanburg, which takes place monthly downtown. I asked Stephen Stinson to be my partner, and after seeing his first twenty images, it was clear that his creative vision and expertise in capturing the personality of each artist would be better conveyed in color and on canvas. We decided that Carolina Gallery would Giclee-print them on 22" x 30" gallery-wrapped canvasses. Stephen is a gifted Spartanburg photographer who made the artists feel comfortable enough to show their true artistic personalities. Without his creative gift this project would not have taken on the prominence and exceptional visual impact that it ultimately has. Stephen participated faithfully in Art Walk month after month, adding to the gallery of artists and exhibiting them in empty storefronts. Each third Thursday, he hosted a reception, donating wine, food, and effort to selflessly honor and promote our visual arts community. These artists and our community owe a great debt to his efforts.

One night as I was standing in a downtown gallery during one of the first Spartanburg Art Walks, a woman approached me and expressed her thanks for this project. She said she had several pieces of original Spartanburg art in her home that she had purchased without knowing who the artists were. Until seeing one of the portraits in the exhibit, she didn't realize that one of the artists lived down the street from her. She told me that she had waved at the woman frequently as she passed by on the way home, never knowing the woman had created one of the pieces of art that she loved so dearly. If she encountered any of these artists at the gas station, the grocery store, or the dry cleaners, she said, she planned to approach them and express her gratitude for her artwork and for their contribution to visual arts in Spartanburg. This wonderful sentiment has been repeated numerous times over the past few years and certainly validates this project.

When Stephen and I were invited to develop this book, I was asked to write an introduction that would include a very brief history of more than one hundred years of visual arts in Spartanburg. I reluctantly agreed, knowing there are many others who are more knowledgeable, more qualified, and more talented at conveying this information. I have relied heavily on those individuals to help me communicate this history. Those include but are not limited to: Suzanne (Zan) Schuweiler, associate professor of art history at Converse College; Scott Cunningham, associate director at the Spartanburg Art Museum; Nannie Jefferies, administrator of the Spartanburg County Regional History Museum; Dr. Betty Jane Bramlett, who served four decades as coordinator of fine arts for Spartanburg County School District 7; and Mary Ellen Suitt, founding member of the Artists' Guild of Spartanburg. I also leaned heavily on the work of Martha R. Severens, who has written the definitive biography of Helen Dupré Moseley. Much of the information here has been collected by these individuals and others. In addition, stories and information has been passed down verbally over the years.

It is our sincere hope that this book will bolster a sense of pride in the local arts community and among Spartanburg citizens, those currently pursuing art careers, and people serving in our city, county, and state governments. I believe strongly that by showcasing the extraordinary visual arts talent we have in Spartanburg that we will encourage others to come to Spartanburg and participate in our collective effort. Many cities across the country that boast an abundance of visual artists—as Spartanburg does—have discovered that by supporting and collaborating with these artists their own communities have prospered. Go to the Internet to see what visual arts have done for places such as Paducah, Kentucky; Pittsfield, Massachusetts; Fairhope, Alabama; Chattanooga, Tennessee; Beaufort, South Carolina; and myriad others. In these communities, local governments, entrepreneurs, developers, and other supporters have collaborated with the visual arts community to create inexpensive—sometimes free—gallery and studio space. In many circumstances, they have aggressively sought out visual artists to join them in urban revitalization by offering low interest loans for housing and studios. They also have partnered with artists in repopulating and improving blighted areas.

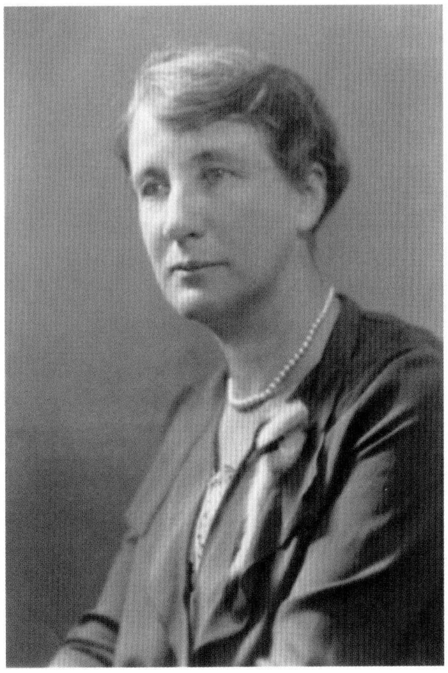

Margaret Law
Spartanburg Art Museum

I'm often asked what drew so many talented artists to Spartanburg. It's a process that has been unfolding for more than a hundred years. In the 1880s several railroad lines converged here, bringing people and businesses from all over the region, nation, and world. In 1895 the Spartanburg Opera House, considered one of the most beautiful in the country, sat at the present-day location of the Hub City Bookshop. Its limited capacity of seven hundred seats resulted in the need for multiple performances. In 1899 Twichell Auditorium, with a capacity of 1,500, was constructed on the campus of Converse College as an alternative. By the beginning of the

Robert Henri
The Girl with the Red Hair
Oil on canvas
31" x 25"
Spartanburg Art Museum

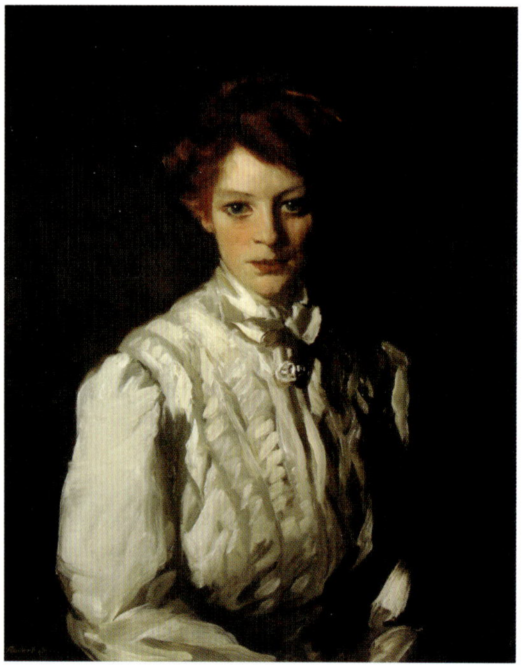

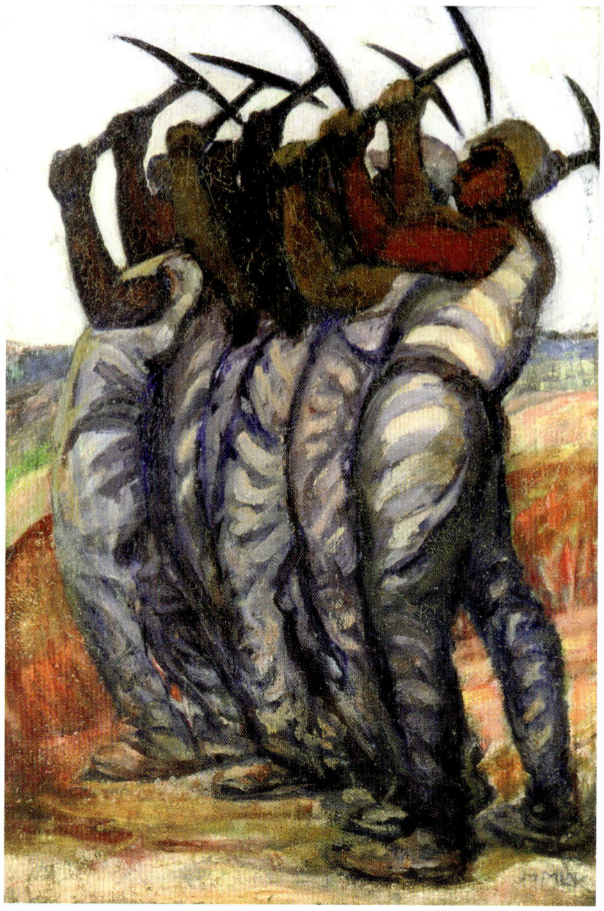

Margaret Moffett Law
Chain Gang
Oil on canvas
36" x 24"
Spartanburg Art Museum

1900s, Spartanburg was becoming a cultural center in the South. Next came U.S. Army camps in World War I and II, bringing newcomers from all over the country. At mid-century dozens of international businesses began moving into our county.

Two forward-thinking women artists, Josephine Sibley Couper and Margaret Moffett Law, were responsible for the establishment of the visual arts community in Spartanburg. In 1907, they conceived the idea of an art exhibit to entertain visitors and locals during Spartanburg's nationally renowned May Music Festival at Converse College. They formed the Arts and Crafts Club to bring exhibitions of fine paintings to Spartanburg. The first exhibit had more than one hundred paintings by some of America's leading artists: Robert Henri, William Chase, Elliott Dangerfield, F. Luis Mara, and Anna Hayward Taylor, as well as works by Mrs. Couper and Ms. Law. The paintings, which came from galleries in New York, were hung in a large hall upstairs over what was the Tom McCann shoe store, at the southwest corner of South Church and Main streets. (The store has since been demolished.) Visitors were asked to vote on the painting they preferred, and at the end of the exhibit, Robert Henri's painting of "The Girl with the Red Hair" was selected. The club set out to raise $500 to purchase it by asking for donations and selling coupons—for as little as five cents—on the street.

In a letter to the editor of the Spartanburg daily newspaper in 1907, a citizen wrote, "The appeal to civic pride, the having a genuine work of art the property of the community, is not unworthy by any means, but the better thought is that the money thus invested will for all time bear splendid interest in the elevation of the popular taste in such matters. ... It is a fact that Spartanburg will be a better place, better for those even who never see it (the painting) because such a painting is before the eyes of our children."

Time ran out on the fundraisers, though. With only $400 in hand they dispatched a telegram to Henri, asking for a two-week extension. He responded, "That you have liked my picture of the girl with the red hair gives me much pleasure, and I appreciate the honor that will be mine if you expect to make it the beginning of your city's art collection." Two weeks later, with a large contribution from Nicholas Trakas, a Greek immigrant fruit merchant, the money was raised. The painting now permanently hangs in the Spartanburg Art Museum at the Chapman Cultural Center.

Law and Couper continued to nourish Spartanburg's fledgling arts community, sometimes from afar. Born in Spartanburg to a prominent textile family, Law had chosen to pursue her artistic training in the Northeast rather than settle down in her hometown. She studied at the Pennsylvania Academy of Arts in Philadelphia and in New York at the Cooper Art School, the Art Students League, and the Chase School (later called the New York School of Art). Her teacher, William Merritt Chase, was a significant influence on her work. An impressionist painter, he has been called the "most important teacher of his generation, perhaps in all of American art education." Although Chase's teaching is apparent in Law's style, Law herself credited Robert Henri as the central influence on her art. Unlike Chase, Henri abandoned the impressionist style by the mid-1890s in favor of a darker palette. The belief in the dignity and worth of common folk became the focus of Law's paintings, many of which featured men and women in the fields. Law's work is full of slightly caricatured and formal studies of average people, and it is characterized by rapidly executed, expressive brushwork. From 1923 to 1924, she furthered her studies in Paris, France, under the direction of the Cubist painter Andre' Lhote, whose Cubist style painting briefly influenced her. To support herself, Law taught art throughout her career, first in Baltimore at Bryn Mawr College for women and Montrose Academy (a correctional school). Then in 1936 she taught in Spartanburg, becoming the

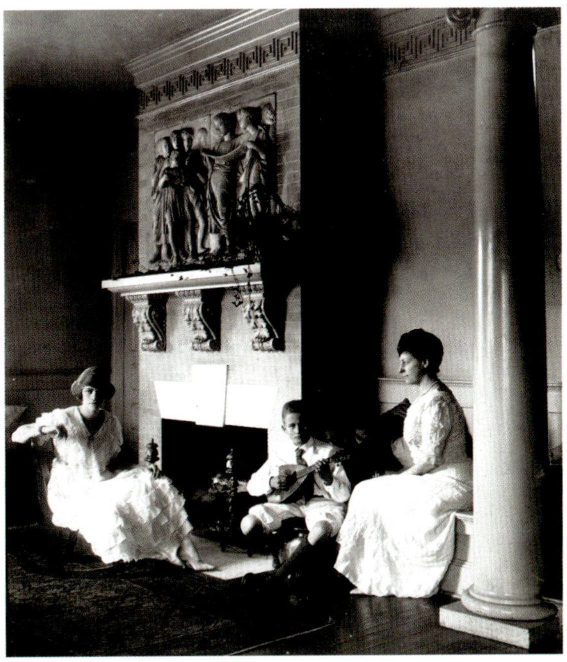

Josephine Sibley Couper is pictured on the right, with family members, in the entrance hall of her home.
The Spartanburg Art Museum

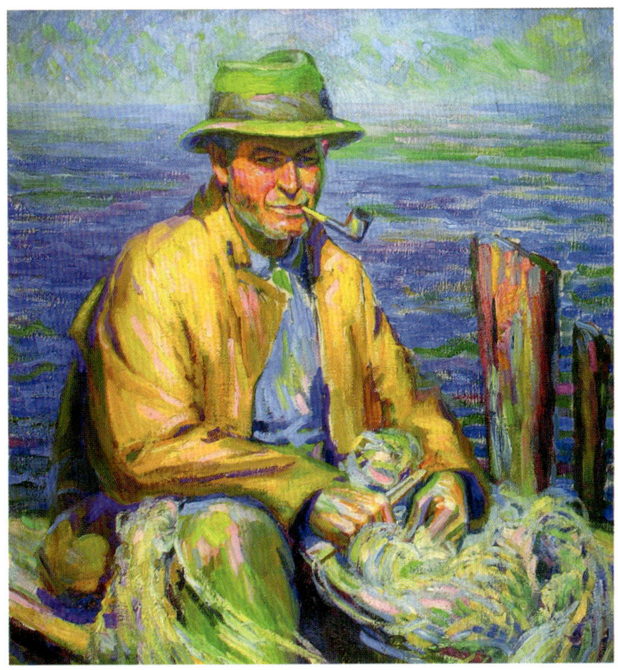

Josephine Sibley Couper
Mending the Nets
Oil on canvas, 1925
Spartanburg Art Museum

art supervisor for the Spartanburg school district. Law shared her independent thinking with her students, encouraging them to use their imagination instead of copying a realistic style.

Born in Augusta, Georgia, to a genteel and aristocratic family, Josephine Sibley Couper (1867-1957) showed an early interest in art following a trip to Europe at the age of twelve. She began with art lessons in a Charleston art school, and her interest in studying art led her to enroll at the Art Students League in New York. Beginning in 1888, she took classes with William Merritt Chase, Frank Vincent DuMond, and Kenyon Cox. In 1890, she went on a grand tour studying art of the old masters in Europe. In 1891, she married Butler King Couper, a cotton broker in St. Simon's, Georgia. They moved to a house on Pine Street in Spartanburg in 1900, where she raised her family and painted upstairs in a room with "a special northern light." The art she produced in Spartanburg was primarily portraits of her family and friends in a traditional style. After the death of her husband, she moved to Montreat, North Carolina, in about 1920 and continued to dedicate herself to painting, joining the Rocky Neck Artist's Colony every summer in Gloucester, Massachusetts. Her work included more landscapes, using light and color as never before. In the mid-thirties she moved to Western North Carolina and opened a gallery and studio in Tryon.

Couper and Law repeated their art exhibit the following year (1908), and afterward their club raised $700 to purchase Birge Harrison's "Early Lamplight" and "Home at Evening" (now known as "After Lamplight") to add to the local fine arts collection. The pictures, along with ones by Couper and Law, hung in the Kennedy Free Library on Magnolia Street.

The Spartanburg Arts and Crafts Club suffered its demise with the coming of World War I, and a new group of citizens devoted to art appreciation created the Spartanburg Art Club in 1923. The club took its turn in caretaking the collection that was alternately stored in attics when the library fell into disrepair during the Great Depression and returned to the library after its restoration in the 1950s. Ultimately, many of these pieces were donated to the Converse College permanent art collection and to the Spartanburg Art Museum, housed at the Chapman Cultural Center.

On August 7, 1939, one unlikely Spartanburg artist made national news in *Life* magazine, which at the time was read by more than a million people. Local residents were shocked and scandalized by the inclusion of photographs of Henry Bernhardt's nude yard sculptures. Many had traveled past the home of Henry and Nancy Bernhardt on West Main Street and had wondered about the life-size, nude female statues on the lawn. The magazine featured a five-picture, half-page presentation of the sculptures, including a large bust of Henry's own likeness among the female figures. In his note to Life pictures editor, photographer J.E. Whisenant noted there had been much local discussion about the nudes. Every time the neighbors complained, Whisenant said, Henry added another figure. The artist carved the figures from blocks of gypsum, and each one was encased in a glass box. The former Bernhardt home still stands at 582 West Main Street—though without the nude figures—and now is adjacent to the West Main Artist Cooperative. A small building behind the residence housed Henry's sculpture studio. His daughter, DeViolette, was a painter and noted photographer. A second daughter, Leonne, also was a painter.

Two other major art figures of the twentieth century in Spartanburg were August and Irma Cook, who moved to Spartanburg in 1924 after their college graduation. August became the sole faculty member of the fledgling art department at Converse College. Ten years later, he convinced the college to establish art as a

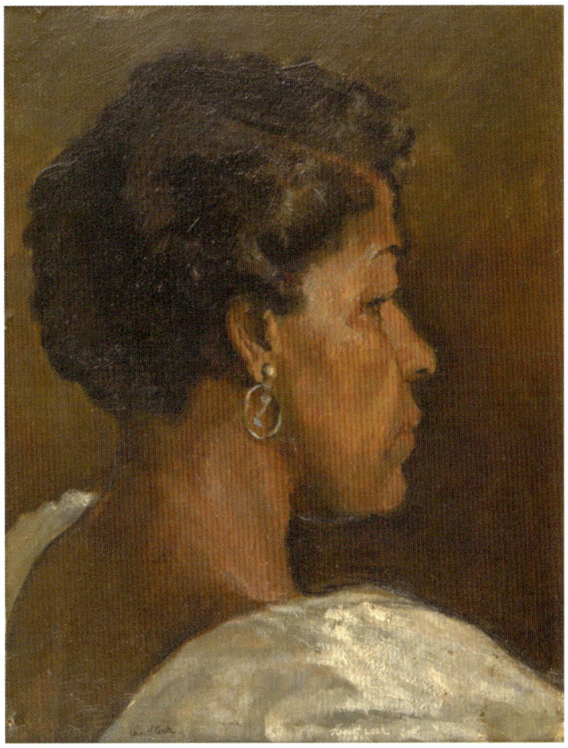

August Cook
Pearl
Oil on canvas
Spartanburg Art Museum

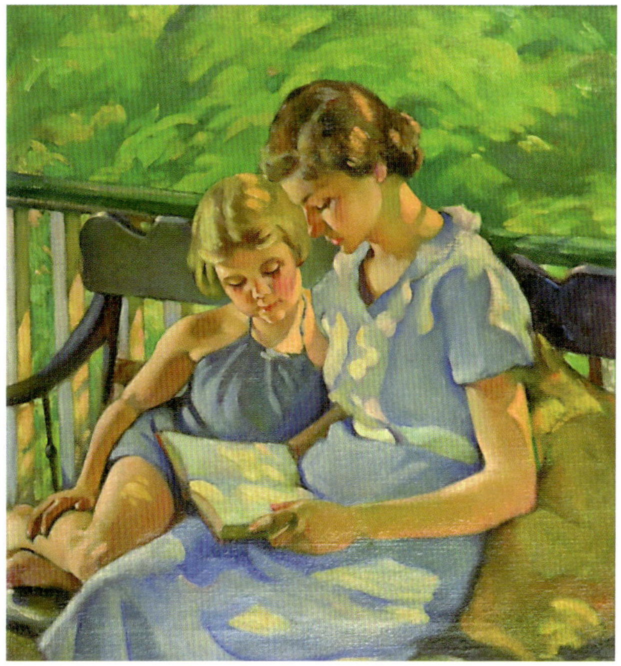

Irma Cook
Reading on the Porch
Oil on canvas
26" x 24"
Susan H Hayes &
Virginia H Wood Collection

major, the first college in the state to do so. Artists and teachers, the Cooks left a legacy of lifetime devotion to their art and to fine teaching. "Generations of artists in Spartanburg and beyond owe their fundamental training to the Cooks—to August who taught at Converse College for forty-two years and for many years at his Chesnee studio, and to Irma, who taught in the basement of their South Fairview extension home," according to an article written by Jan Scalisi for a Cook retrospective at the Spartanburg Art Museum exhibit in fall 2000. "But their impact upon Spartanburg, as significant as their artistic contribution was, is overlaid with the memory of two strong personalities whose passion for their work inspired the devotion of their students. Fiercely talented and independent, the Cooks, though wedded for a lifetime, made their marks individually and in their own unique ways."

Their approach reflected their early training of Philadelphia's Pennsylvania Academy of the Fine Arts, where they were schooled in the fundamental elements of design, such as line, space color, space texture, and form. "He frightened me at Converse because he seemed a strict disciplinarian," said the late artist Curtis Harley in an interview for Scalisi's article. Harley studied with August at Converse and later at his Chesnee studio. "But once you got to know him, he was gentlemanly, sweet, and kind to his students." Skilled in many disciplines—from pottery to oil, watercolor, egg tempera, and sculpture—August was particularly renowned for his wood engraving, a highly technical art he taught himself after receiving a set of tools from a friend.

Both August and Irma were known as colorists. "Irma had an incredible sense of color," remembered artist Ann Stoddard, who took art from Irma as a high school student. "Her emphasis was on looking. I have found myself quoting her: 'Look, look, look! That's the way you're going to learn, by looking.' I value that."

In the early 1960s, August bought ninety acres in Chesnee that would serve as the site of his full-time studio after his retirement from Converse College in 1966. There, in a former bootlegger's roadhouse that he rebuilt, he taught students eight hours a day, five days a week.

"'Action, proportion, composition!' He'd preach," remembered Katie Hodge in an interview in 2000. "'Get up there and make it turn!' He was very much the professor." Mary Ellen Suitt said, "They were so influential. They had followers, more than anyone before or since. They were the first really strong teachers in Spartanburg."

The Artists' Guild of Spartanburg began on the evening of October 7, 1957, as a coffee group to critique each other's work. It soon became much more. Charter members were Dorothea Baskin, Hazel Bobo, Betty Jane Bramlett, James "Buck" Buchanan, Lois Cantrell, Frank Coleman, Frank Collins, Irma Cook, Al Fleck, Murray Havens, Thomas Kendrick, John Mabry, Helen Dupré Moseley, Francis Riser, Marianna Smithson, Mary Ellen Suitt, Elizabeth "Libby" Taylor, Lucille Wallace, and Charlotte Wheeler.

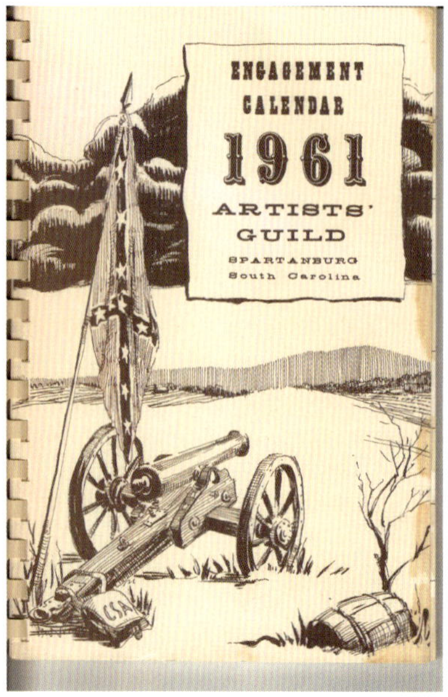

The calendar was produced in 1961 to raise money for the Artists' Guild.
Spartanburg Art Museum

Current Artists' Guild member Jill Jones interviewed several of the founders for an April 2004 article about the early years. She wrote that the fledgling Artists' Guild was committed to being a "serious organization" and agreed on tenets such as a rigorous jurying process for members, mandatory attendance at monthly meetings, and the production by each artist of a yearly body of "good quality" work. To this end, photography, crafts, printmaking, and even sculpture weren't allowed, and abstract art was discouraged. "It was 1957, it was the South, and abstract art was frowned upon," recalled Mary Ellen Suitt, who served as treasurer of the Guild in its inaugural year and was responsible for collecting the three-dollar yearly dues. Lois Cantrell recalled the group as having been very demanding, working by day and painting by night and willing to dismiss anyone who failed to live up to its rigorous standards. There were few opportunities for artists in Spartanburg in 1957, and the Guild was committed to changing this through a professional—if exclusive—organization. Membership was limited to twenty-five, with each new inductee requiring the approval of the entire organization. They met at the Spartanburg County Library and later at First Federal Bank, critiquing each other's work to become their own worst critics and best supporters.

Some members taught art classes for the Guild, fulfilling one of the organization's primary goals of bringing art to the Spartanburg community. Others focused their efforts on the production of the Artists' Guild of Spartanburg calendar—the organization's chief fundraising tool. Featuring pen and ink drawings of major historical sites in the Upstate, the calendars provided money toward the establishment of the Spartanburg Arts Center in 1975.

Helen DuPré Moseley was particularly active during this period. Born in 1887, the whimsical Spartanburg artist grew up on the campus of Wofford College, where her father was on the faculty. She was educated at Converse College and served as postmaster of Spartanburg from the mid-1930s to the mid-1950s, finally beginning to paint when she was sixty years old. Her life was captured in the 2001 book *Helen Dupré Moseley,* by art historian Martha R. Severens. "She developed her own artistic language," Severens wrote, "using largely figurative subjects—colorful and challenging images that are extraordinary for an amateur artist painting in the South during the middle years of the 20th Century." She drew Dr. Seuss-like hybrid creatures—animal forms with human characteristics, which often were dancing, singing, and parading. Many people in Spartanburg believed her creatures were satirizing local residents, though she always denied that. Instead, "Her hobbies may have indirectly influenced her art," Severens wrote. "She was a passionate reader, sampling a variety of subjects, including history, biography, and children's classics. She formed an extensive collection of stereographs, a popular parlor pastime in the late nineteenth century. Through her stereographs, Moseley saw and learned about places, buildings, and people far beyond upstate South Carolina." Moseley never achieved critical acclaim or genuine understanding for her art during her lifetime, though her art has been collected and celebrated fifty years later. Her work was chosen to inaugurate the Spartanburg County Museum of Art.

As the Spartanburg art community moved into the 1960s, many new art teachers and mentors began to inspire a new crop of talented artists. Art educators of unparalleled aptitude have taught and continue to teach in every public and private school in Spartanburg County. While working hard as educators, these individuals also remain practicing artists who seek inspiration for their creative process as well as their teaching methods. As talented students rise through art education toward careers, art teachers guide and nurture their development. Spartanburg boasts a wide range of public and private art programs with dedicated instructors for young artists from every age level and background.

Many of the artists in this book have credited those art teachers who pushed them to discover their own artistic voices. MacArthur Goodwin, Betty Jane Bramlett, Thomas L. Willis, Susan West, David Benson, Doris Turner, Carol Augthun, Nancy Corbin, and many other devoted art teachers have tirelessly dedicated themselves to inspiring the next generation of important Spartanburg artists. Opportunities for artists have exploded over the past few decades as a result of these teachers' support and instruction. From out of this mix came Johnnie Lee Gray (1941-2000), an African-American artist whose work was discovered by national art critics shortly after his death. *The Wall Street Journal* called him a "hitherto unsung folk artist" and "country cousin" to Nobel Prize-winning novelist Toni Morrison. Backed by New York Life Company, thirty-five pieces of his work toured the country in 2003-2004 as a part of an exhibit called "Rising Above Jim Crow: The Paintings of Johnnie Lee Gray." The child of sharecroppers, Gray graduated from Spartanburg's

Helen DuPre Moseley, untitled, n.d.
Collection of the Greenville County Museum of Art
Gift of Cynthia, Carlos, and Daniel Moseley, Spartanburg, SC

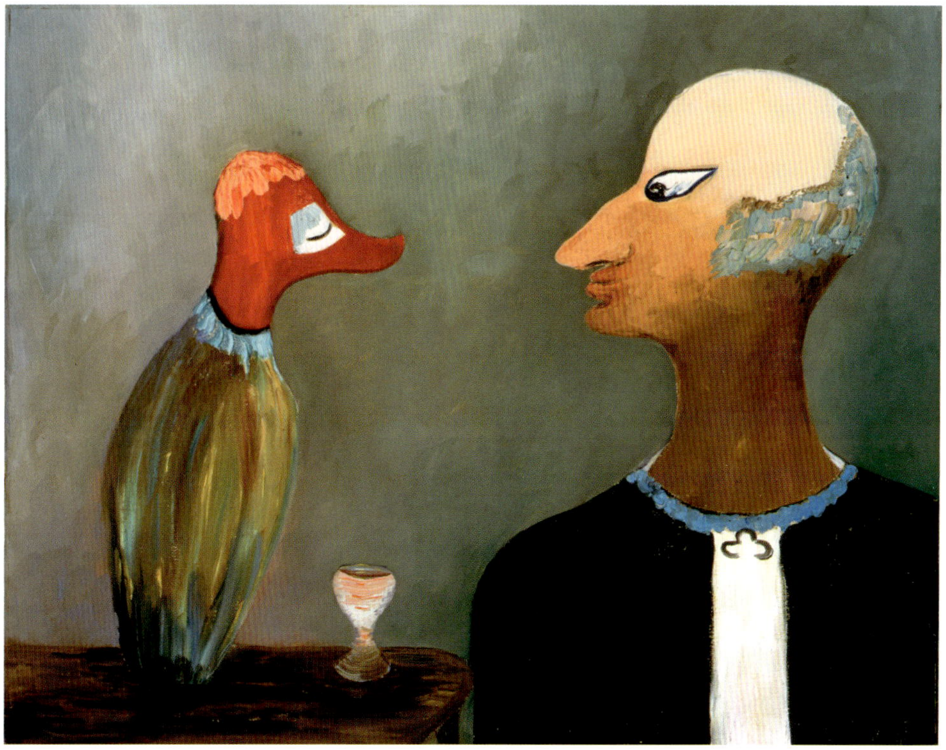

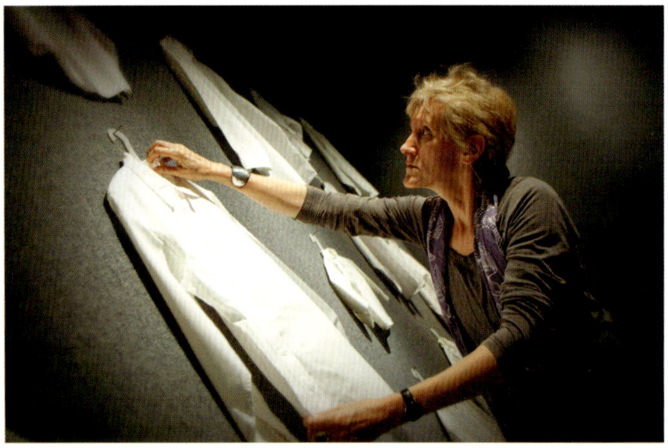

Jane Allen Nodine sets up for a show at the Curtis R. Harley Gallery at USC Upstate.
USC Upstate

Lincoln High School, served in Vietnam, and was encouraged to pursue art by local teachers Thomas Parham and Raymond Floyd and by his wife, Shirley Lee Gray. His colorful work on plywood and canvas addresses social change in the South through landscapes, devotional images, and events from his own life.

Spartanburg's colleges and universities include world-class art programs—and galleries—and have played a big part in the professionalizing of the visual arts community here. Converse College has produced many significant visual artists over the past century. Berry Bate, a 1975 Converse graduate and sculptor who helped restore the Statue of Liberty in the mid-eighties, has worked on a display in Morgan Square, in Glendale, and other public places around Spartanburg. Anyone interested in visual arts should investigate the work of each art professor at Converse College. Without exception this arts faculty, which includes Mayo Mac Boggs, Teresa Prater, Andrew Blanchard, and others, is respected regionally, nationally, and internationally. The University of South Carolina Upstate has equally impressive credentials. Jane Allen Nodine, professor of art and director of the Curtis R. Harley Gallery at Upstate, was named in 1999 by the South Carolina State Museum and the South Carolina Arts Commission as one of the top one hundred most important artists of the twentieth century in South Carolina. Oakley Coburn, dean of the library at Wofford College, has nurtured and supported students and local artists through exhibits for many years. Fabric artist Ann Wenz, now retired from Spartanburg Methodist College, was instrumental in the dedication of the Mary Ellen Suitt Gallery on the SMC campus. A number of public and private schools, including the Spartanburg Day School, have galleries.

Visual arts are obviously important to Spartanburg citizens. It seems as though public art is on display all over this incredible city. Our hospitals have continued to acquire and exhibit original works of art from important local artists. Banks, corporate headquarters, law firms, accounting firms, and commercial spaces of all varieties have amassed important original art collections. The citizens of Spartanburg raised in excess of $30 million to construct the Chapman Cultural Center in downtown Spartanburg. This beautiful campus houses nine funded organizations under the auspices of the Arts Partnership of Greater Spartanburg, including the Spartanburg Art Museum and the Artists' Guild of Spartanburg gallery.

Spartanburg is also home to one of the largest private collections of important historical Southern visual art. The inspiration for the Johnson Collection

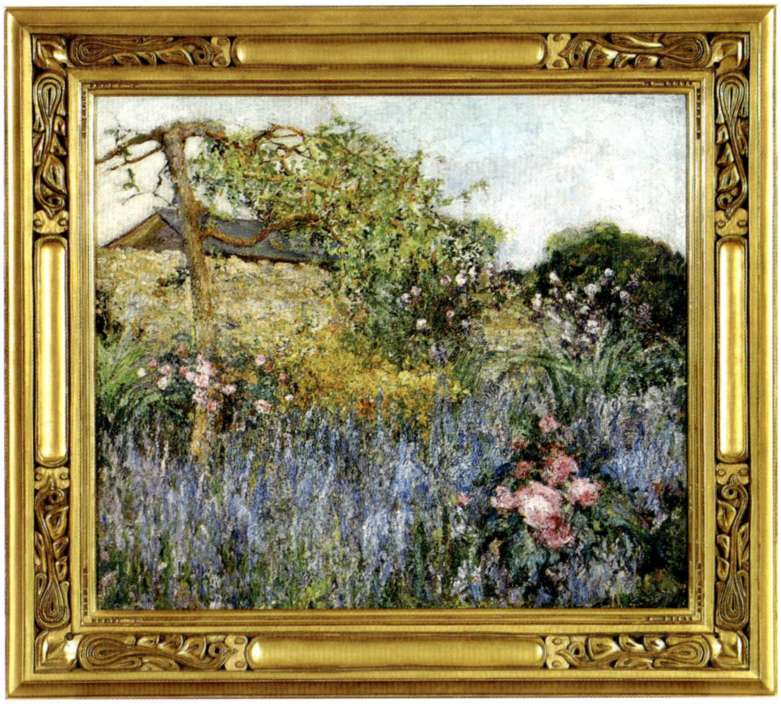

Blondelle Malone
(1877-1951)
Garden Stone
Oil on canvas
26 ¼" x 30"
The Johnson Collection

is the idea that works of art capture a moment in time and convey a shared history. The collection aims to provide a balanced view and to invite new interest and investigation into the complex and dynamic story of the American South. Paintings are on display in multiple businesses and colleges in Spartanburg. The citizens of Spartanburg owe a tremendous debt of gratitude to the Johnson family for sharing their collection with our community. Spartanburg is fortunate to have many citizens who have dedicated themselves to enriching lives by supporting visual arts in our community. Among the many are Kurt and Nelly Zimmerli, Mike Kohler and his late wife Lucile "Snooky" Kohler, Katie Hodge, the late Graves Jones, George and Susu Johnson, Bill and Valerie Barnet, Billy and Lindsay Webster, Fred and the late Millie Dent, Les and Betty McMillan, the late Roger and Nita Milliken, and countless others.

One of the best ways to experience the visual arts in Spartanburg is to attend the monthly Art Walk. Each third Thursday patrons of visual arts from all over the region have the opportunity to enjoy the fruits of local visual artists' efforts. The Showroom at HUB-BUB routinely exhibits emerging young artists, in addition to supporting a nationally recognized artists-in-residence program that annually draws applications from hundreds of young artists from all over the United States. The new West Main Artists Cooperative is home to thirty-six artists' studios with painters, sculptors, ceramicists, jewelry makers, and printmakers creating and exhibiting their work. The Artists' Guild of Spartanburg gallery at the Chapman Cultural Center features members' work each month. Selected pieces from the Johnson Collection are on display in downtown Spartanburg. Private galleries cluster around Morgan Square.

Stephen Stinson and I love Spartanburg and its talented visual artists. We are very proud of this project, and our dream is to see Spartanburg become THE visual arts destination it so rightfully deserves to be. We invite any artists searching for a place where they can feel welcome, supported, challenged, appreciated, and encouraged to join us all in making this dream a reality. You can't spell Spartanburg without ART!

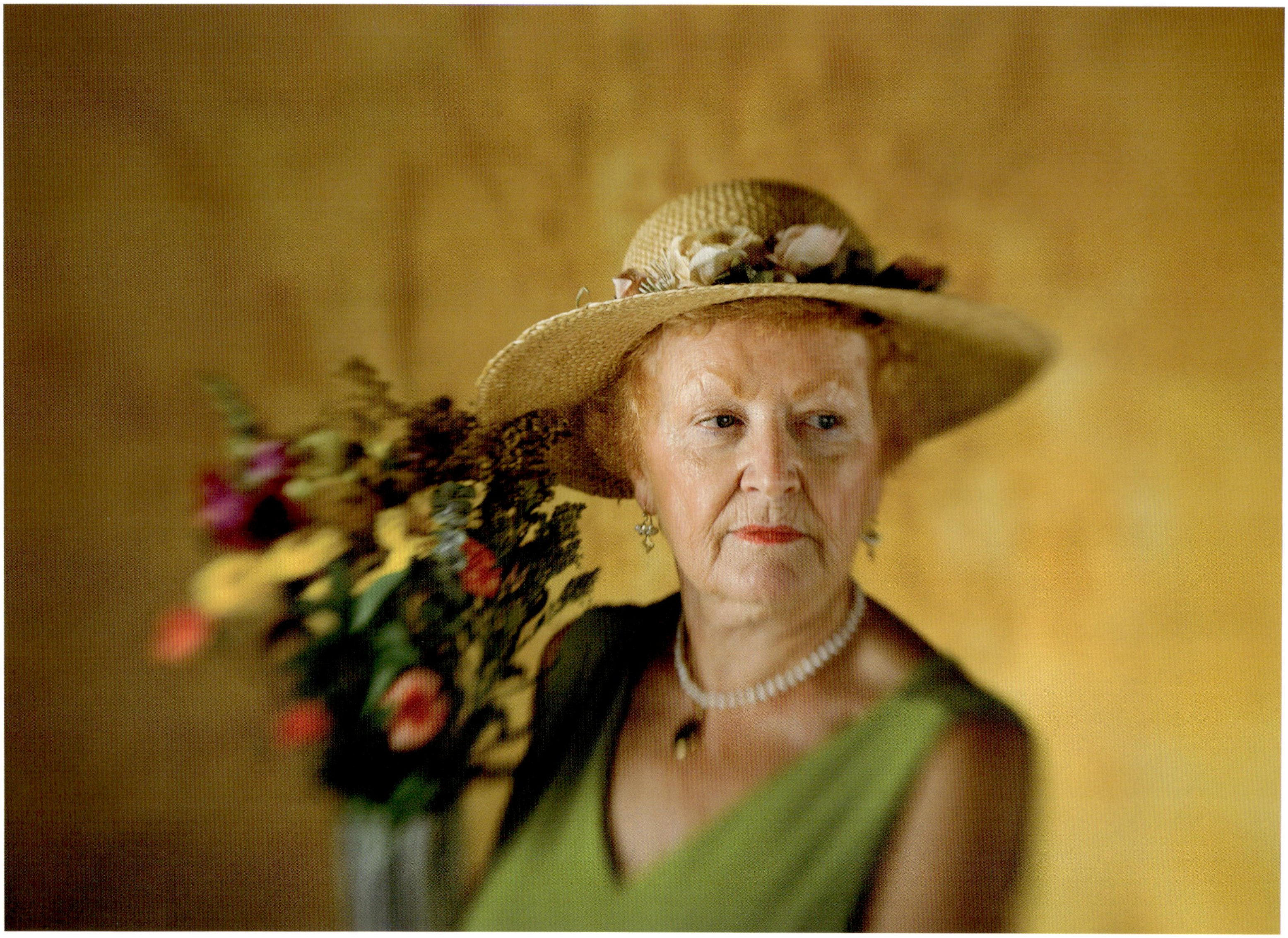

Carolyn Fulmer Alexander

The desire to draw and paint occurred very early in my life. One of my earliest recollections of making art was at age five when I drew crayon pictures on the wall of our hallway—much to the dismay of my mother. When she showed the "mural" to my father, he gazed at the scene and quietly said, "That's the prettiest picture I have ever seen." To little me, those golden words spoke *YOU'VE GOT TALENT!*

A Converse College graduate with a BA degree in English, I gained training for my art hobby from private lessons, workshops, simple practice, and perseverance on my part.

Subjects for my works reflect an enduring fascination and emotional response to people both young and old, to pets I have loved, and to the many roads I have traveled both here and abroad. My pictures perhaps serve as a window on these scenes so that viewers can put their imaginations into the work and, I hope, can feel some of the same emotion and joy as I do. The particular subjects that I choose for my pictures dictate the medium used. In a realistic manner, I create with pastels, watercolors, colored pencil, oils, and acrylics.

As a native of Spartanburg, living most of her my here, I have witnessed a growing interest and respect for art and the many talented local artists. Art galleries, museums, art boards, exhibits, workshops, and classes all reflect a community seriously devoted to the arts. I believe that opportunities for local artists compare favorably with those in many larger cities.

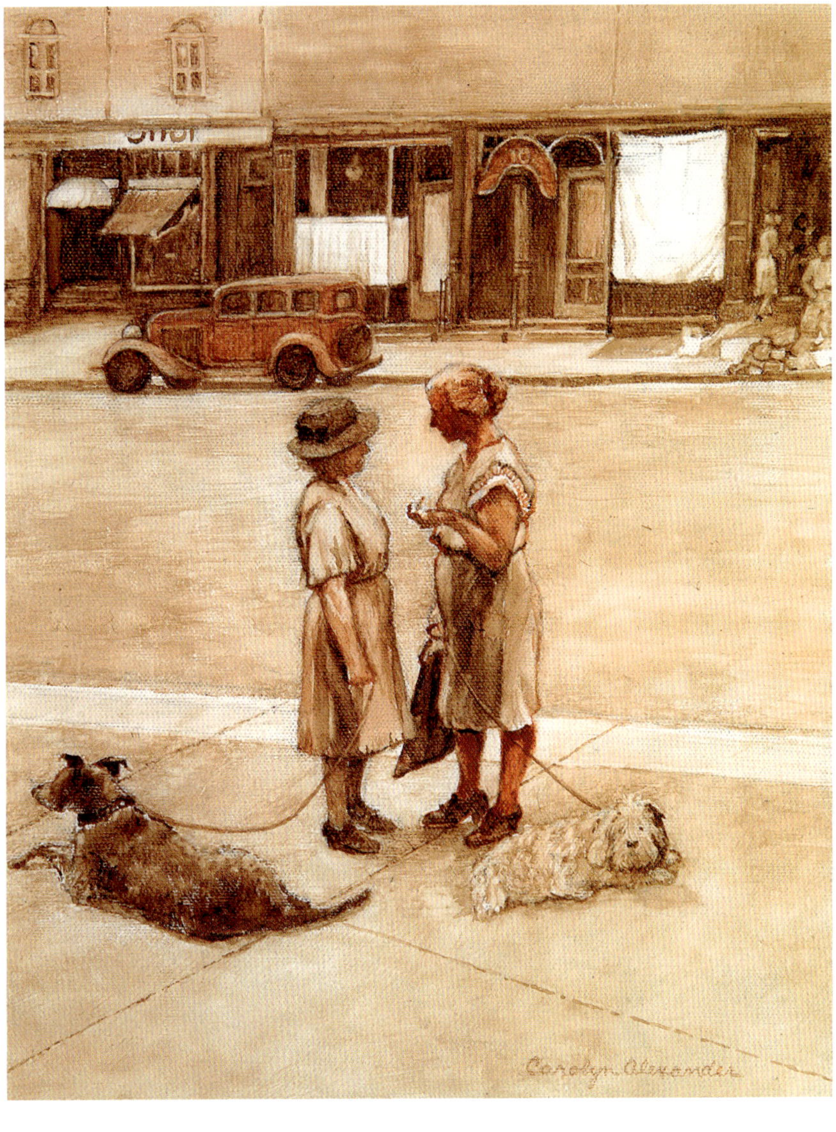

Two Ladies...Two Dogs

Watercolor

10.5" X 13.5"

Lisa Anderson

Memory

10" X 12"

Mixed media

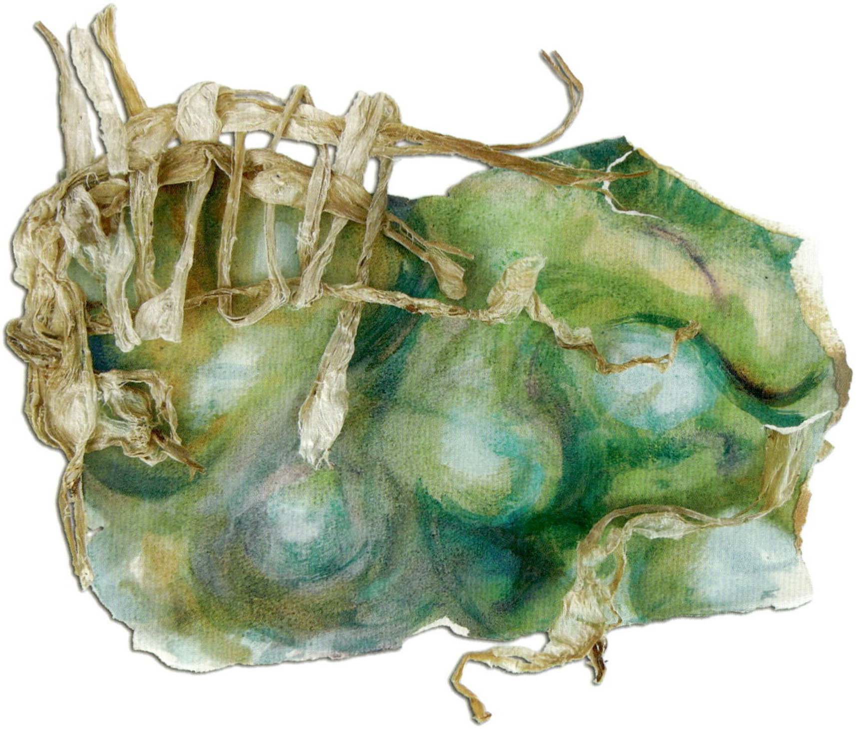

Originally from the Northwest, I made Spartanburg my home over ten years ago. Admittedly, while the position of professor at the University of South Carolina Upstate brought me here, I continue to be proud of this thriving and growing community that supports the arts, diversity, and global perspectives.

Noticing a simple occurrence became second nature as my grandfather taught me to pay attention to moments. He urged that if noticed, they became extraordinary. Untrained and uneducated in the arts, Grandpa could carve magic into pieces of wood. Other family members have manifested his influence in media, from painting to architecture and from graphic design to auto design. His sensory visions still permeate my work and life. The idea of capturing an experience and inviting participation continues to be a focus of my work.

Recent work includes intimate depictions and visual stories of occurrences informed by science and my perception. Small multi-media constructions and artist books narrate and illustrate these natural moments or phenomena. Handmade paper, photography, pastels, color pencils, wood, fabric, and other natural and plant materials combine and are collectively designed into two- and three-dimensional works. Some share common themes or ideas; others form a series of events, sequentially describing the phenomenon. Many stand alone as single moments.

The process of making work often transcends both the idea and the end result. Process is important in my exploration of experiential/interactive work, period design, typography, literary and musical themes, and commissioned graphic design or illustration. Process becomes the structure, the armature or grid, and the support of the idea. Making the best use of interactive relationships, including research, materials, elements, audience, and my interpretation, becomes the most satisfying part of the art-making experience. This symbiosis fuels the process and provides the stratagem for idea communication. The final iteration symbolizes the culmination of the process, documenting the journey and delivering the message.

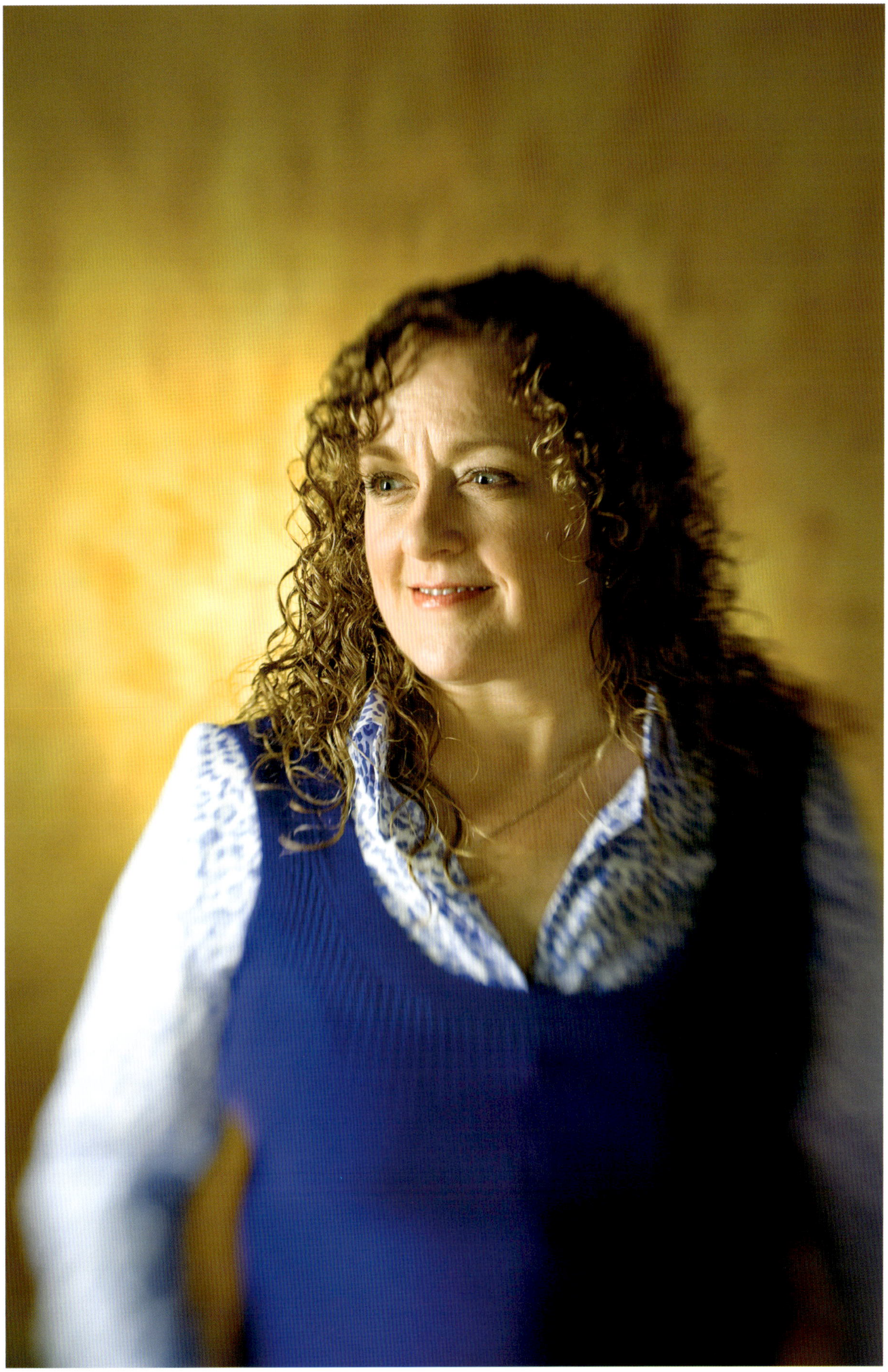

Monta Anthony

I grew up in Chester, Virginia, a small town just outside Richmond, as the third child (oops) of Lorraine and "Mizzerable" Moody. My mother had a huge book of the Old Masters in the basement that my friends from the neighborhood liked to sneak and look at. While they were tee-heeing at the nudes, I remember marveling at "The Birth of Venus" and wondering, "How did he paint that?"

I took and enjoyed art classes in middle school, but my mother wanted a music major, so I wound up at Converse College majoring in piano. While there I took a print-making course under Jan Sundean and, while I finished my degree in music, from that point on art was my passion.

Having found something other than Converse and art in Spartanburg that I liked, I settled down with my husband, Ken, and soon met Marianne Jansen, a Belgian artist living here who taught me art and pottery. My husband kept signing me up for art classes while we were raising our four children, but it was hard to find time for painting while also sculpting those four other works of art. As they left home I found more time and was able to take some classes but mostly think, relax, experiment, and enjoy.

I have done watercolor, pottery, sculpture, and large-scale murals, but I found my true love in oils. Colorblind (got that from Mizzerable), the colors I paint are my interpretations of whatever catches my eye as a thing of beauty, from Lowcountry marshes to Airstreams.

The Spartanburg visual arts community is a large, supportive family. It has been a great joy to be part of this movement, which has grown in recent years. I have been privileged to serve on the board and be involved with HUB-BUB and Hub City Writers Project, as well as various art shows and activities, and to share and enjoy art with so many encouraging and talented artists.

Cuban Sicar
Oil on canvas
24" X 36"

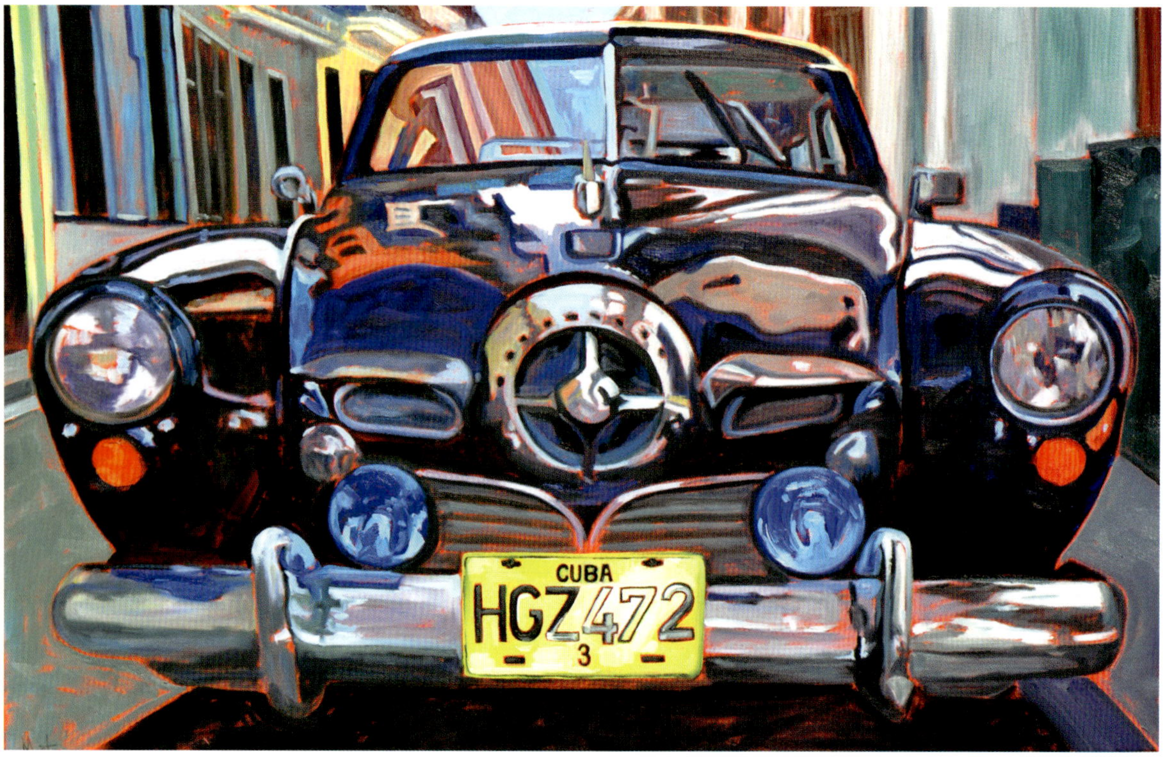

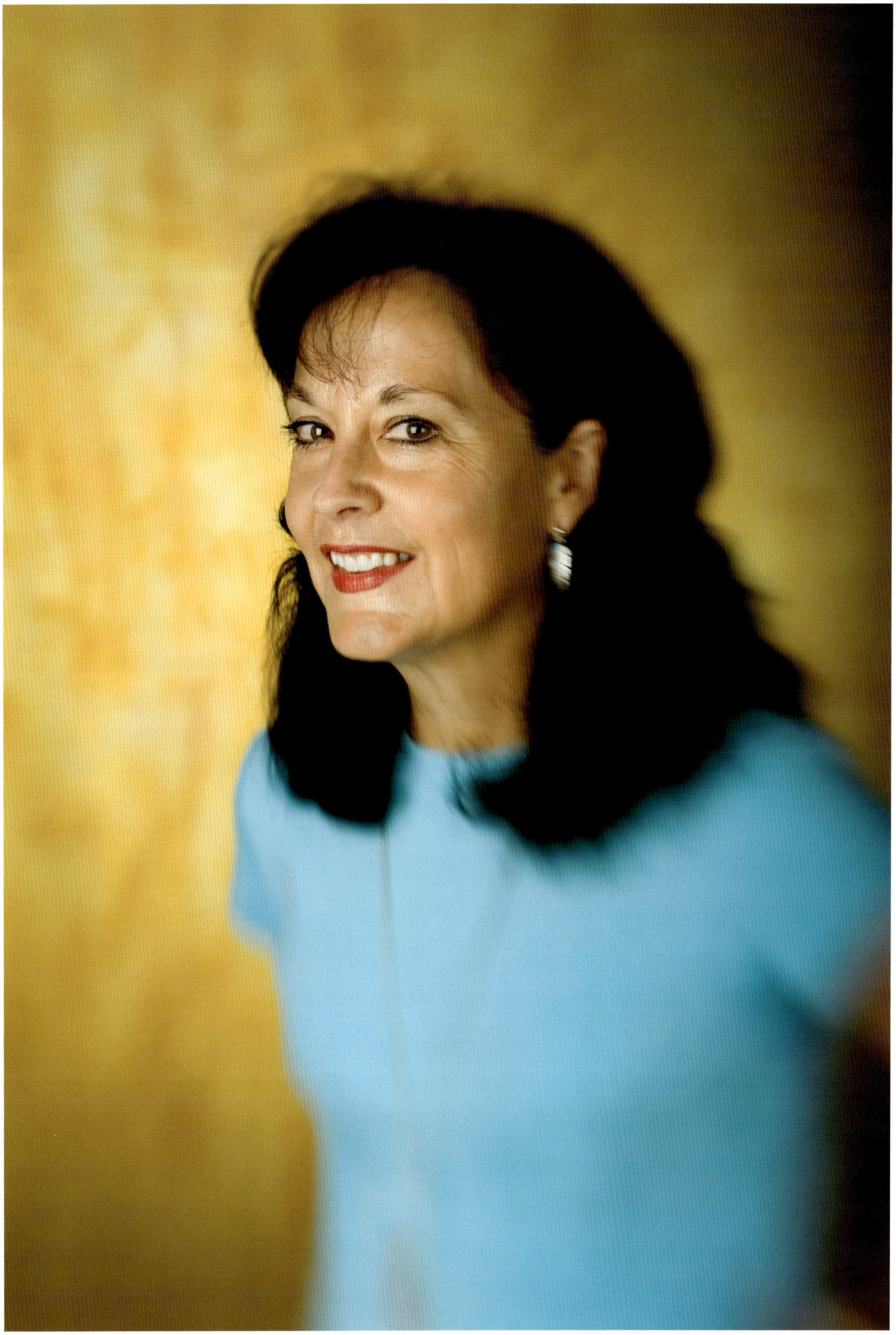

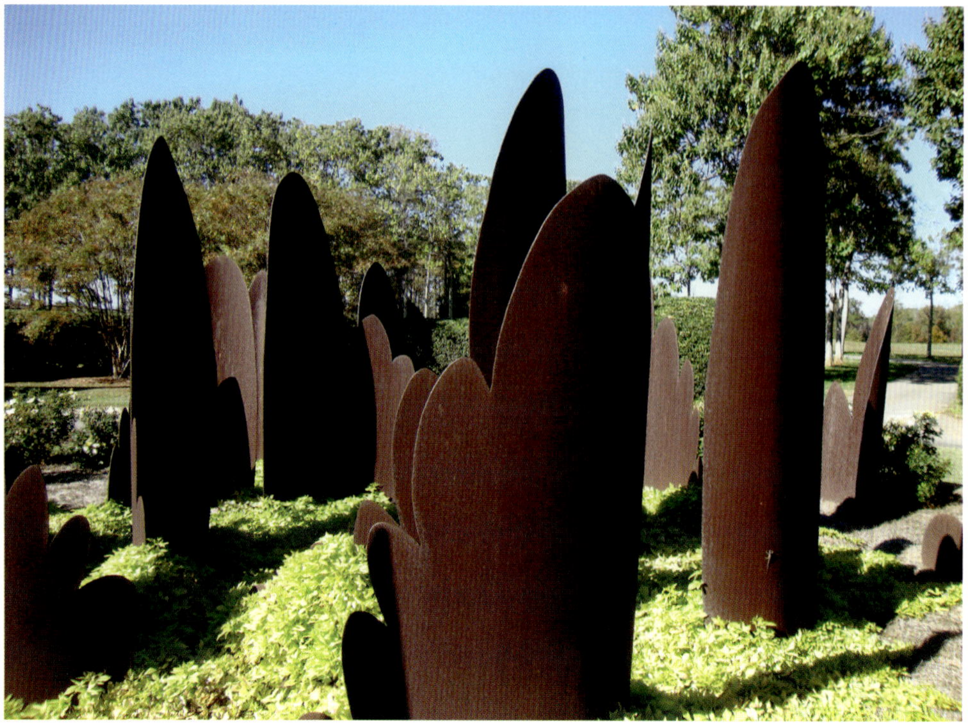

Untitled

30' X 12'

Corten steel

Growing up in Alexandria, Virginia, I spent many hours at the galleries in Washington, D.C., and took children's art lessons at the Corcoran Gallery through the generous help of my Quaker grandmother. She and I spent many hours wandering the Corcoran, the Phillips Collection, the Smithsonian Museum, and the National Gallery of Art. Those experiences, plus my elementary teachers, influenced me in my own artistic pursuit and fostered my curiosity and wonder.

I worked in Washington, D.C., as a commercial artist and at a local frame shop and art supply store, where I had mentors who encouraged me to pursue formal education in art. I attended Richmond Professional Institute, which became Virginia Commonwealth University, and finished at New Mexico Highlands University.

I came to Spartanburg in 1971 and taught at the Spartanburg Day School for thirty years. During that time, I completed an MFA at Winthrop University. My colleagues who taught in the public schools and the fine arts programs at Converse, Wofford, and USC Upstate have been an integral part of an exciting and vibrant community over all these years. We were members of the Artists Guild, and we showed together, in groups and individually, growing and encouraging each other in our own unique directions.

My media, as such, begins in the classroom with my students and then includes almost every two-dimensional and three-dimensional technique. Currently, I am primarily a sculptor, printmaker, and jewelry designer. I really consider my teaching an extension of all my art, and I remain a student of creative expression.

I create primarily because of the process, the problem solving, exploration, material, and wonderful equipment and toys. I like to say, "I dance not to express myself, but because I love to wear my tutu." I intend for my audience to experience the same wonder and curiosity of form and material that I do in its creation.

Daingerfield Ashton

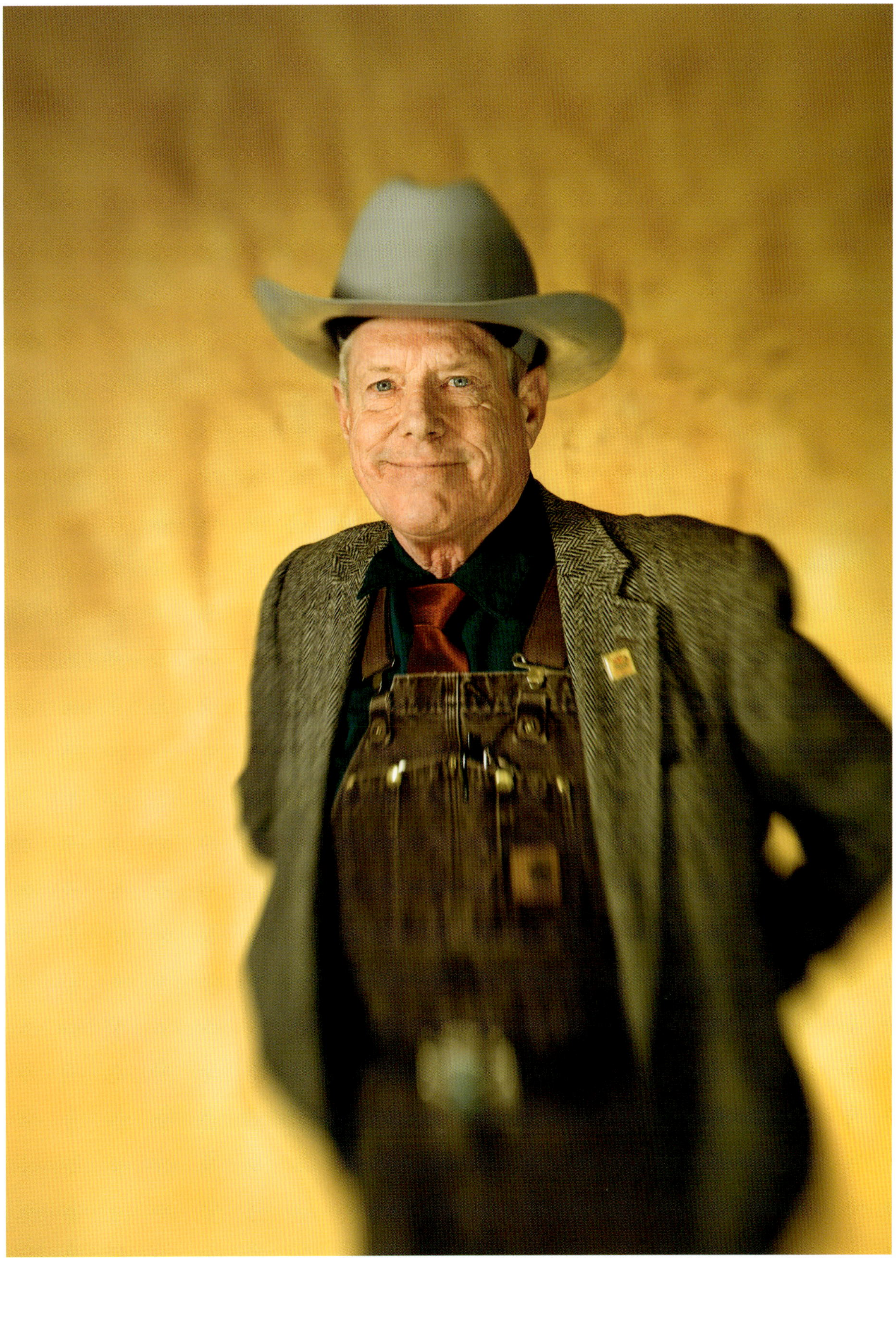

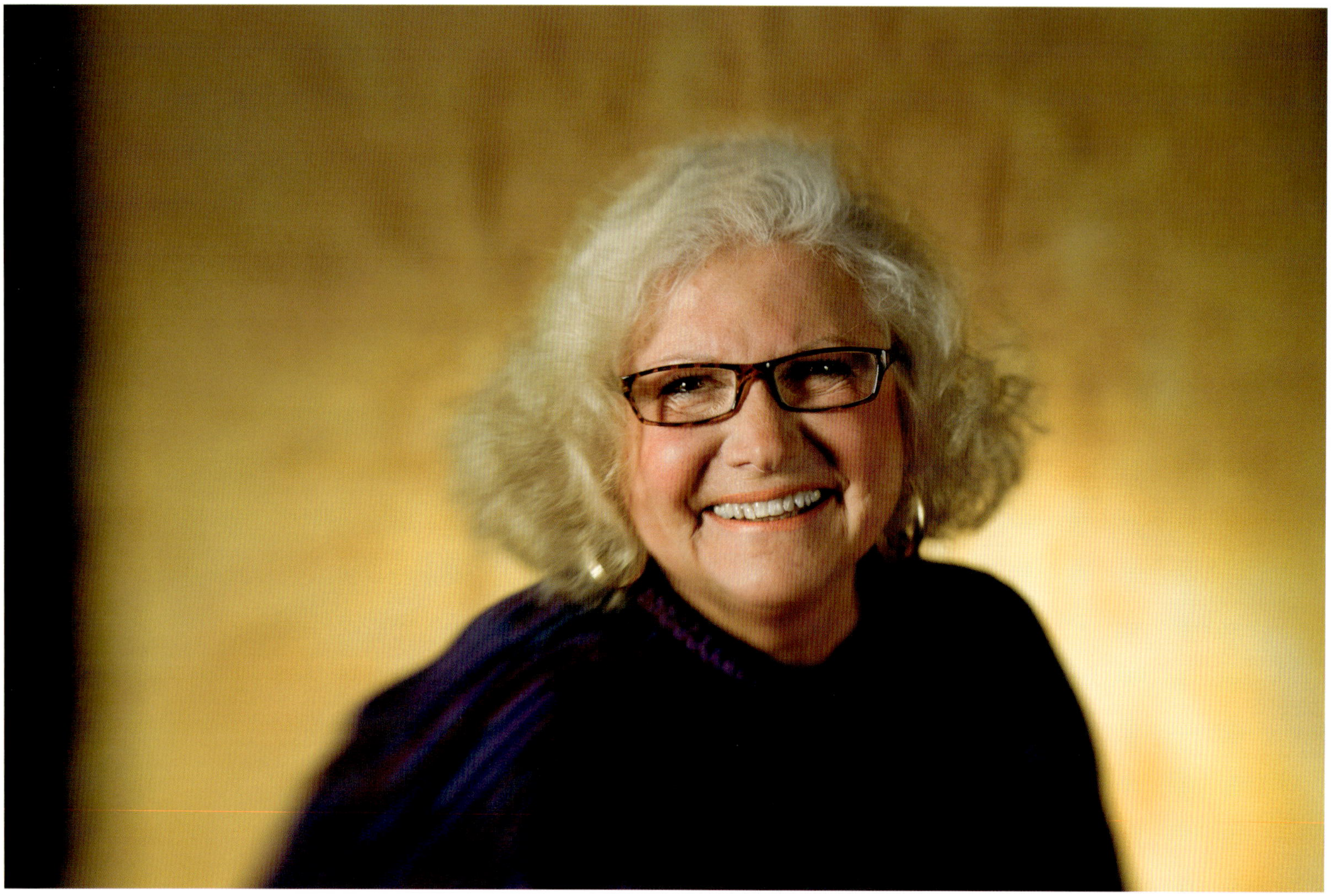

Carol Augthun

Centuries ago, when I was an art major in college, my area of emphasis was printmaking. The early part of my life as a professional artist focused on serigraphy. Silk-screen printing at that time required long stretches of unbroken studio work and also used materials that were not particularly healthy.

After I started teaching art full time in 1977, I no longer had the luxury of extended days in the studio, so I had to adapt my printmaker's mentality to other art forms that could be approached in small time increments—hence, my ten-year quilt-making phase that allowed me to layer colors and patterns in much the same way as a screen printer would layer images. During these quilting years I was considered a fiber artist, although very little, if any, textile products were involved. As demands of public school teaching increased, I had to abandon the quilted wall pieces that had defined my art. I started to explore drawing, printmaking, mixed media, and painting, and all combinations of these disciplines.

My "day job"—teaching—exposed me to the severe conditions of life that many young people face, as well as the economic and social disparities in our local economy. My work took on nuances of social commentary, and that continues to this day. Perhaps this is not the spirit of "art for art's sake," yet it is what I do and most likely will continue to do. My ultimate goal is to strike a balance between images that are aesthetically interesting (notice that I did not say "pleasing") and that have some type of meaning that is important to me.

Lately I have returned to acrylic and oil painting with some watercolor thrown in. My ultimate desire is to take all of my experienced techniques into retirement with me and someday create the perfect piece of art!

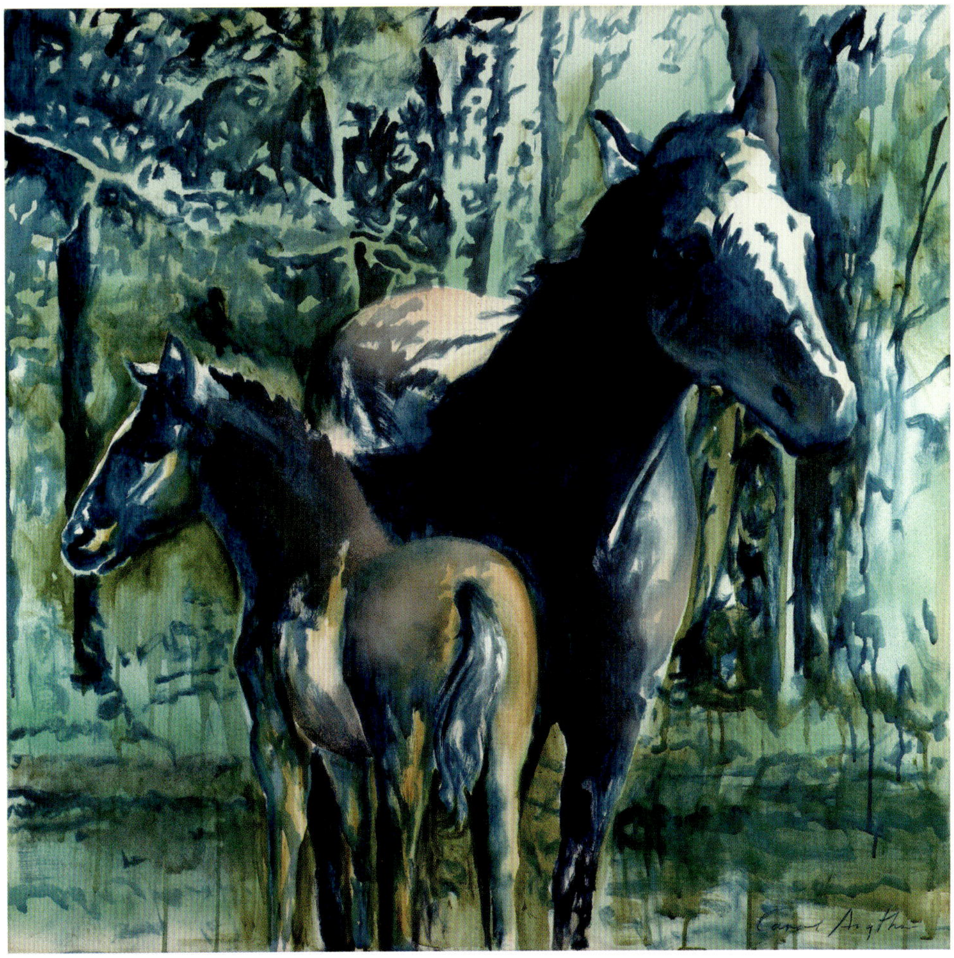

The natural order of things: a mare and her foal

30" X 30"

Oil and acrylic on canvas

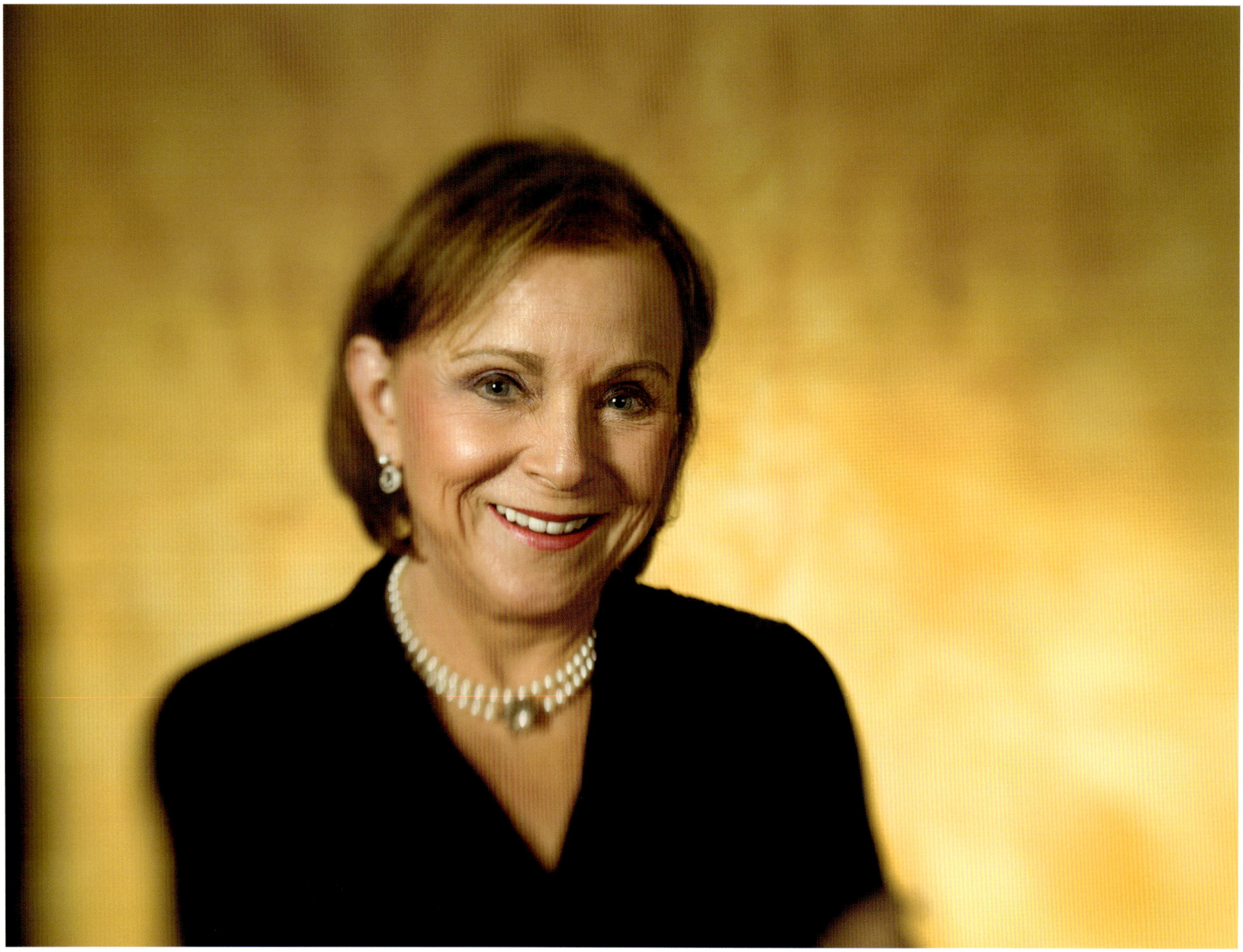

Dianne Rash Bagnal

I grew up in Mooresville, North Carolina, with a passion for art, and I wanted to teach. During my public school days, art instruction was just beginning to be a part of the schools in the Carolinas. My father's sister, Aunt Verla Mae, was a portrait painter and basically self-taught. She fueled my joy of all forms of art and nature. I asked her recently (she's 90) where she got her first art materials. She said her father worked in the cotton mill and brought home pieces of chalk used for marking fabric. Those were her first art supplies.

I graduated with a BS degree from East Carolina University and began teaching art. I first taught in Charlotte in the 1970s under the wings of Elizabeth Mack, director of art in the Mecklenburg County schools and one of the most admired art educators in the country. In 1978, I moved to Spartanburg with my husband and our three daughters. The public schools here had some of the finest art teachers, many hired by Dr. Betty Bramlett. I am proud to have taught many years in the public schools and at Converse College.

I currently work in watercolors and mixed media. I used to lose touch with sounds, smell, taste, and even pain when I created. Then I traveled to Winyah Bay off the coast of Georgetown to an area called North Island, accessible only by boat. I took my camera and bug spray. The sandy areas were covered by what seemed like millions of biting, tiny flies. The smell was salty and a bit earthy. The tide was low, and shells covered the beach. But the real art was the washed-up tree trunks and wind-sculpted trees. The sun had white-washed and smoothed the limbs. I wanted to touch everything, to visit in my mind the storms, the sea, the beauty. That day was the groundwork for my current images, a mysterious adventure in play. I continue to focus my work on the forms of nature that are often passed over. And I hope to pleasure your senses.

Driftwood from North Island
20" X 28"
Watercolor

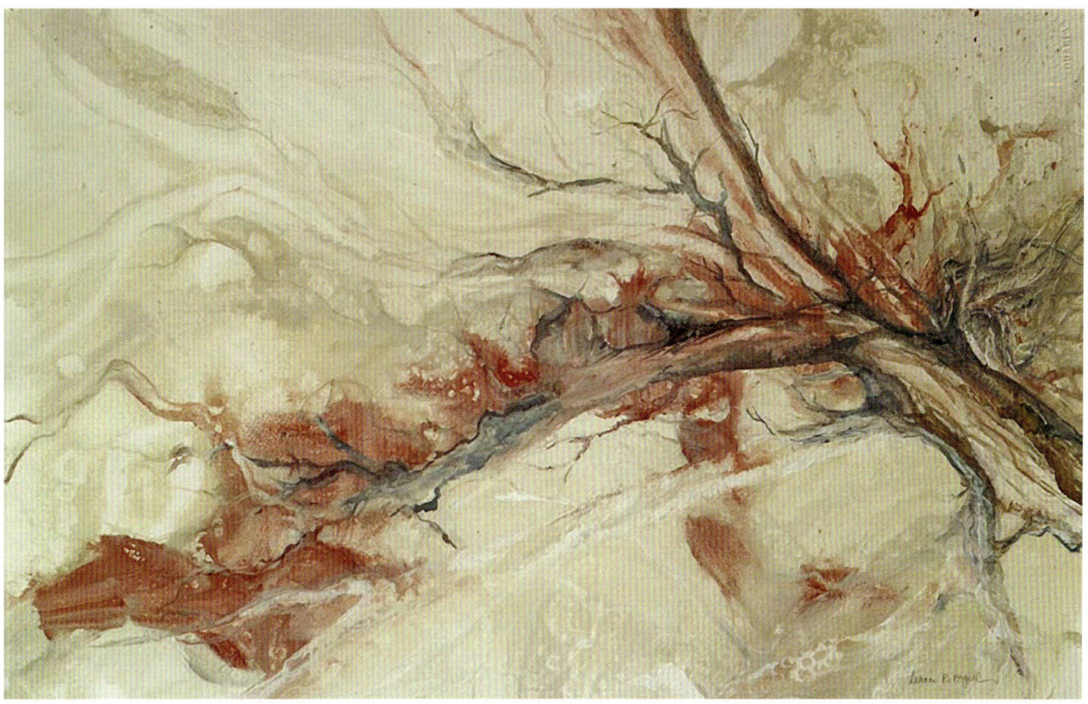

Bailie

As a professional artist, I am always impressed with the amount of talent we have in our community. Bailie Studios, which offers such services as graphic design and sculpture, constantly needs a network of artists who are able to take on projects. Between the Artists Co-Op, HUB-BUB, the Artist Guild, and others, there is never a lack of talent to be found.

I started drawing when I was a child because, honestly, my brother's art was getting all the attention, and I did not like being outshined. My earliest influence was the Gustave Doré etchings in my great-grandmother's Bible. They fascinated me and filled me with emotion. I have been drawing all my life but learned to paint as an adult when I met my mentor, Thomas Parham. I worked with him for eight years painting murals and learning in "master-student" style all of the ins and outs of the world of art. With this knowledge, I eventually started my own company, Bailie Studios, and have been making a living as an artist/educator for over ten years in this area. Making a living at what I love to do is the best job I could ever hope for.

My style, medium and subject matter vary. I never do the same thing twice. I believe my style is "believable surrealism." It is somewhere between fact and fantasy. Lack of inspiration does not seem to be an obstacle, as I am always starting something new. Whether it be making stop-animation, building a wall of balloons for a backdrop, or recording video from a remote control car, I am always creating.

Ultimately, I create to feed a hunger inside. I create to satisfy myself, and I hope my audience experiences emotions or thoughts they would not have had otherwise without seeing my work.

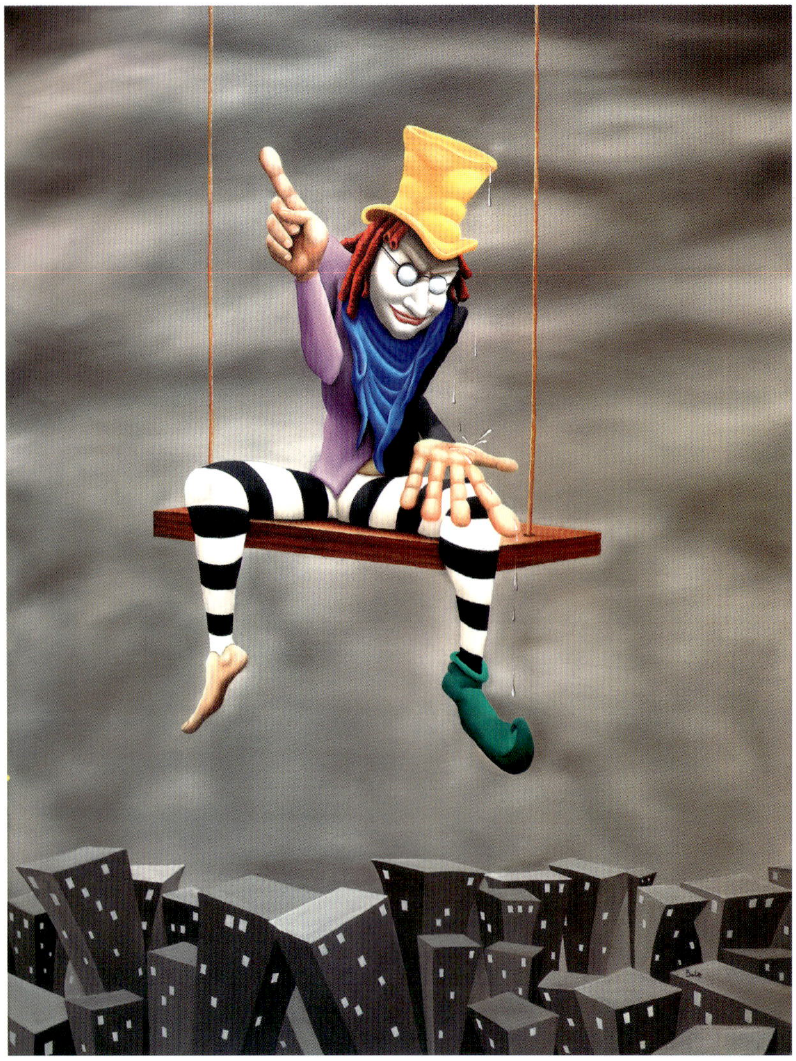

The Sandman

Oil on canvas

48" X 36"

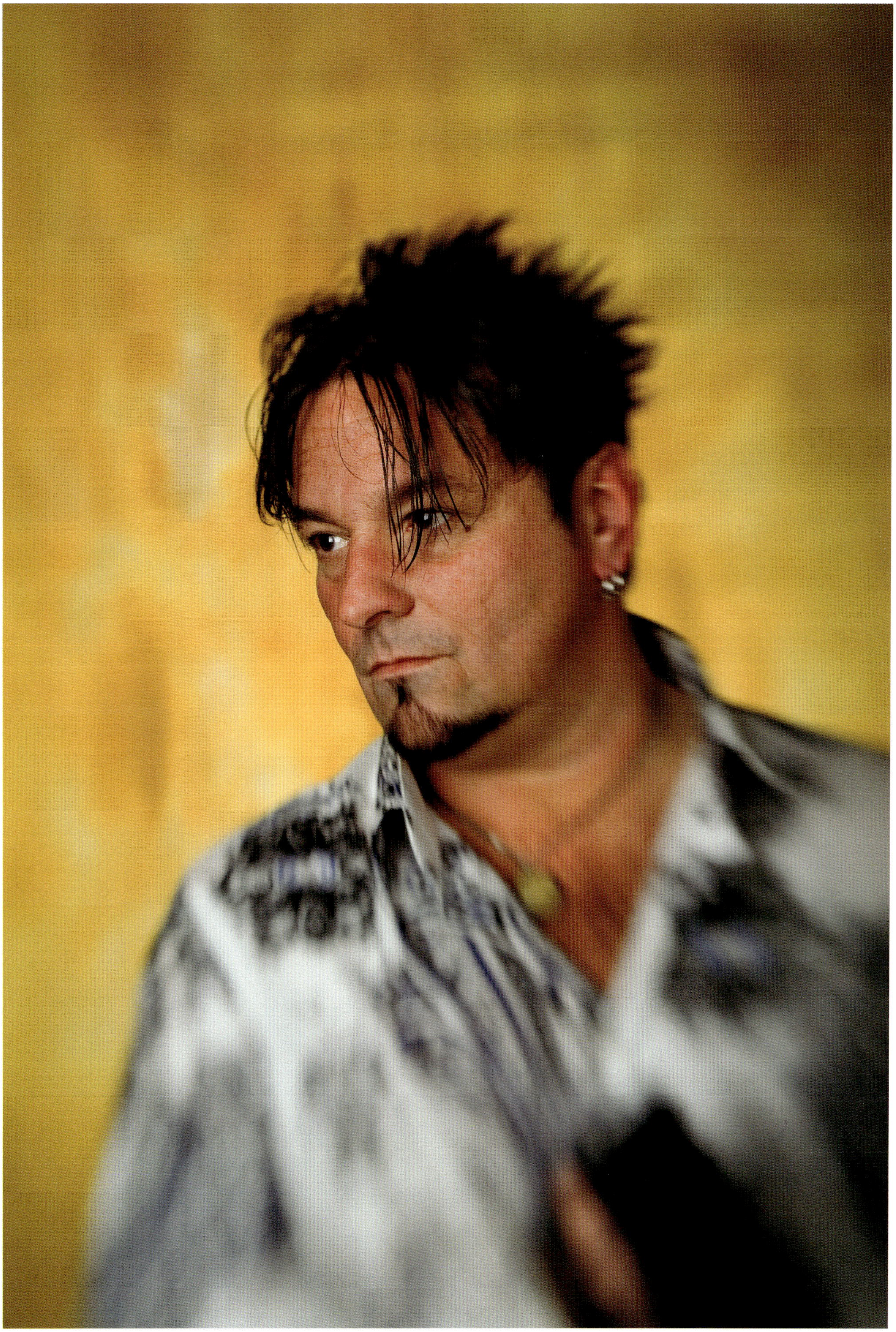

Jessica Barnes

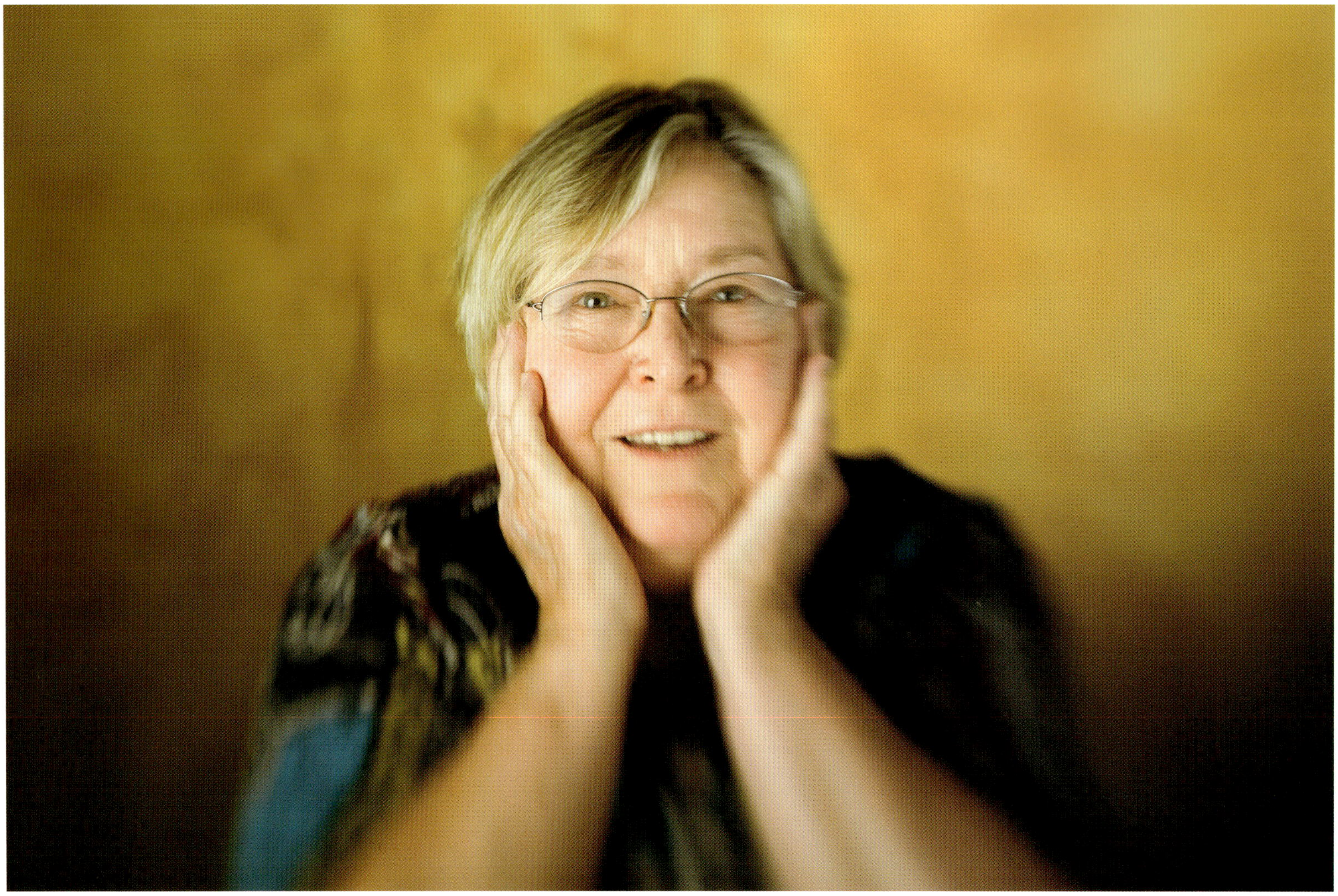

I am inspired by landscapes, structures, people, mountains, and surprises. I like to paint but also have been crazy about sculpture. My father was a construction engineer, so we traveled all over the United States. I have only met one other person who has been in as many places, and her parents were trapeze artists!

My mother used to drag my brother and me around to museums wherever we were, but the real deal was when she started painting. I was blown away that a person could make something that looked like something.

My parents had built a home in South Carolina as a touchstone from our travels. I attended the University of Hawaii, moved to Boston, and then came back to South Carolina in my forties because my mother gave me land to build on. Life in Boston had become very expensive and looked to become even more expensive in the future. People there thought I should stay and retire from teaching. At that time I was very excited about making sculpture, and I thought I might regret having never really used my education as a studio artist. When I first arrived in the Upstate, a friend was showing his work at the Greenville Museum of Art, and I was so excited to see such a wonderful space for art!

Now I work in oil and have never concerned myself with style. I consider what emerges is my style.

I used to be considered rustic in style, but I never really knew what that meant. I also don't have any concern for how the viewer sees my work, but I do love it when it is interesting or exciting to them.

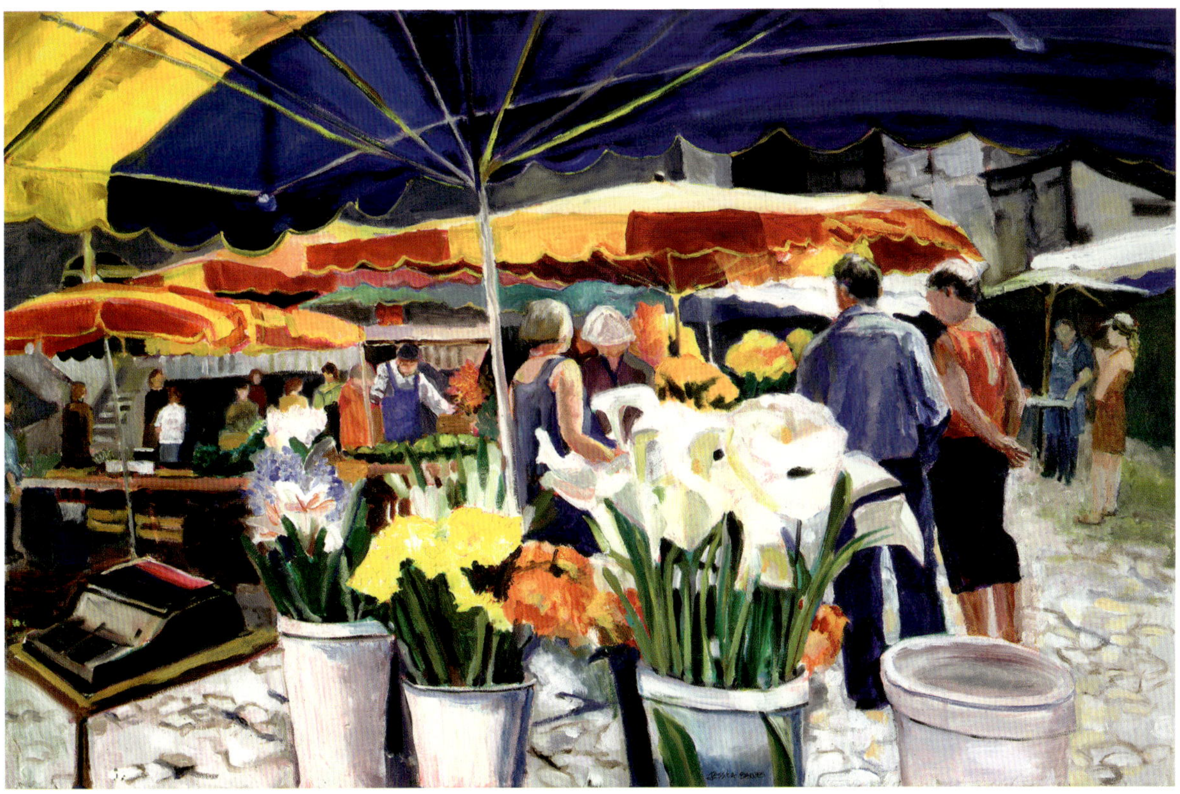

Flower Market,
Villefranche de Rouerque
Oil on canvas
24" X 36"

Judith Battaglia

I am one of those fortunate people who knew very early that I wanted to be an artist. From kindergarten on, I can remember enjoying projects that involved visual solutions. If I could draw something to explain an idea, I was happy.

Born in Schenectady, New York, I grew up in a rural setting in the foothills of the Adirondack Mountains. This environment influenced my love of the outdoors and helped me to develop an eye for the landscape. I am grateful to my mother and grandmother for introducing me to the world of art. My mother provided the technical means—she studied commercial art for a brief time while I was growing up—while my grandmother instilled a sense of wonder through sharing her travels and literature on great works of art. At the impressionable age of sixteen, my grandmother took me to see the Hyde Museum art collection in Glens Falls, New York. In 1964 I got to see Michelangelo's Pieta at the World's Fair. Both of these events help to cement my love of art and my desire to become an artist.

I studied at the State University of New York College at Buffalo. After a break to start a family, I finished a BFA and MFA in painting at Rochester Institute of Technology in Rochester, New York.

Currently my medium of choice is photography. The immediacy of the medium is a powerful draw. Color and light and composition are main concerns, whether the subject is natural or manmade.

The community of Spartanburg provides a diverse cultural heritage that invigorates the mind and body with many an image source. From the historic to the preserved lands, there is an endless resource for imagery.

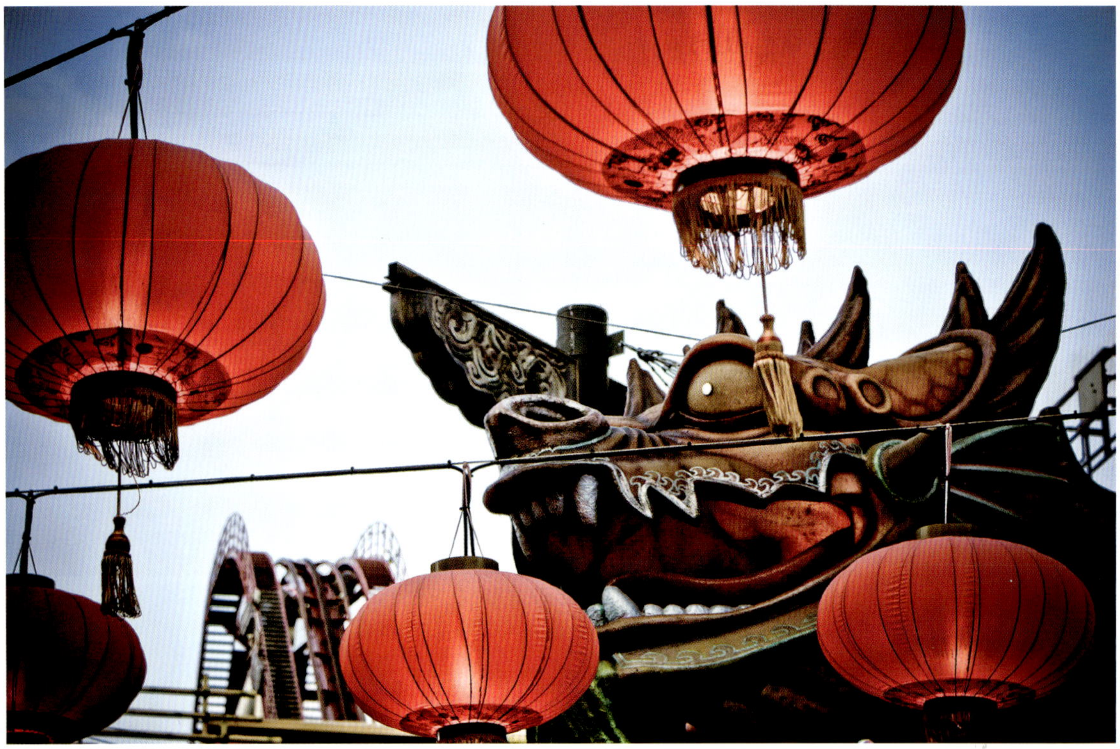

Beware the Dragon
Photograph

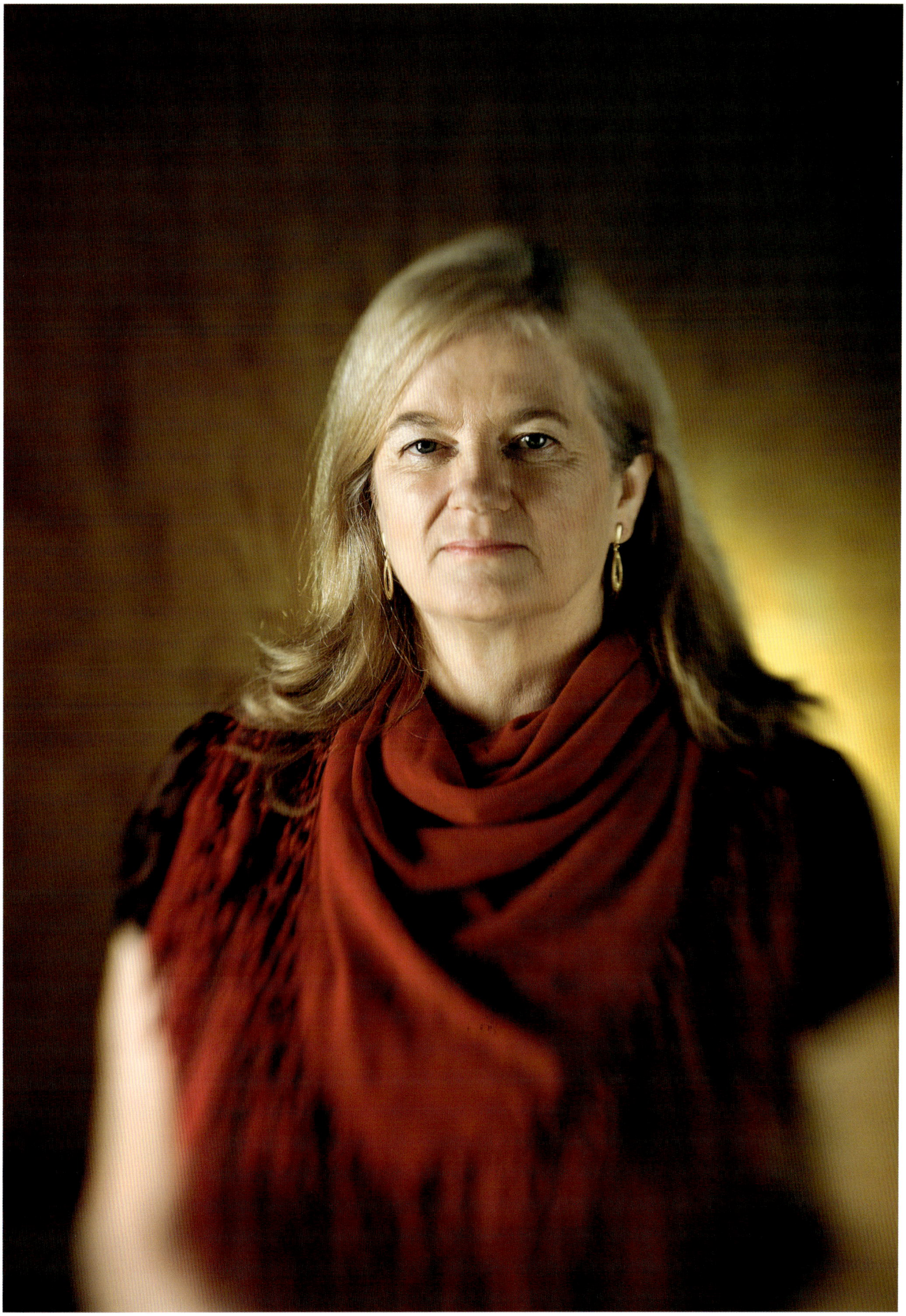

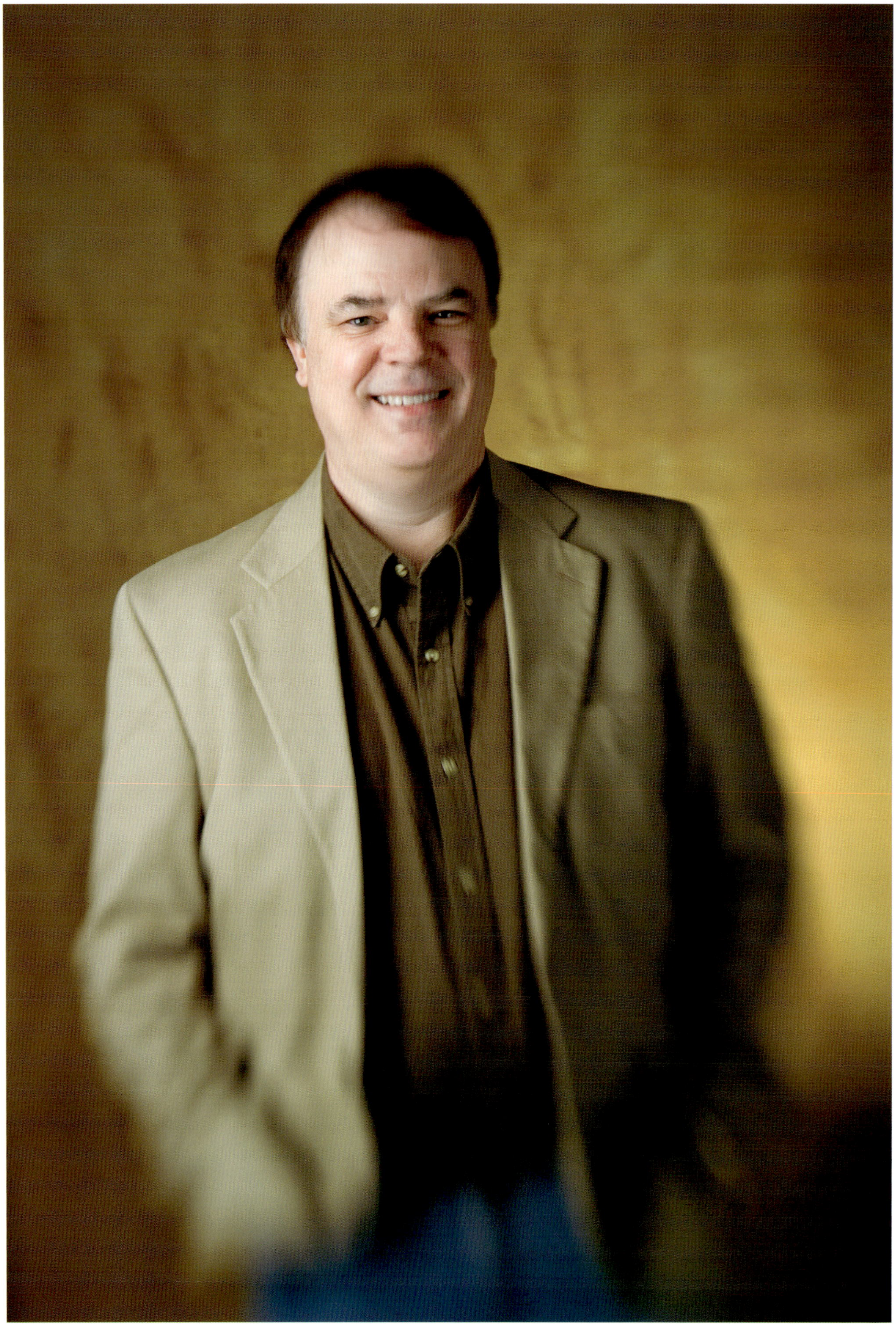

David M. Benson

During my early school days, I was characterized as the bashful, odd child, choosing to play alone rather than allowing myself to interact with other children. I was the last chosen for competitive games when teams were selected. Art class became my sanctuary and my refuge.

The subject matter of my work rarely strays from the familiar. Unless given an assignment or commissioned work, I stay with a subject that I am most comfortable with. I like art that tells a story and encourages the viewer to get actively involved. My objective is to start the story and then let the observer form the climax and closure. If the experience is intimate and spiritual, then the work can be classified as successful.

When someone tells me that my figures are distorted and my perspective is off, I just tell them that I will throw in a compass for their benefit. Mark Twain once sent a publisher a whole page of periods, commas, and question marks when the publisher complained about his punctuation. Twain told them to place those devices wherever they saw fit. I feel much the same about distortions and perspective.

My interest in Rauschenberg, Jim Dine, Max Ernst, Andy Warhol, and a handful of Impressionists are clearly evident. Someday I expect to be slapped by Leonardo da Vinci for the way I've abused Mona Lisa in my works. I use little color, opting for mostly achromatic and monochromatic palettes. I do love to use lots of contour lines, and I believe the more bizarre the media, the more opportunity for discovery and expression.

Most of my success as a developing young artist in this town is attributed to the strong support of the Spartanburg visual arts community. Organizations like the Spartanburg Artists Guild and Southern Exposure gave me the opportunity to exhibit work and to socialize with other artists, young and old. The strong art support is there for anyone who chooses to seek it out.

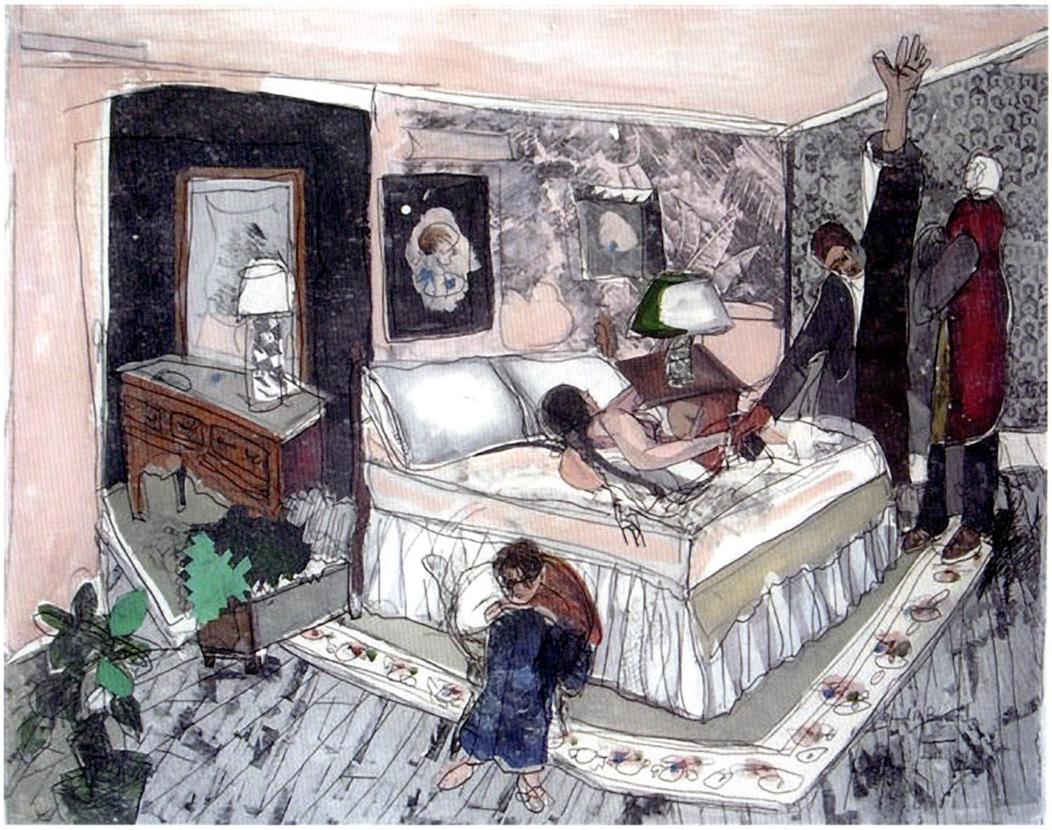

Sin Eater #5

Mixed Media

40" X 47"

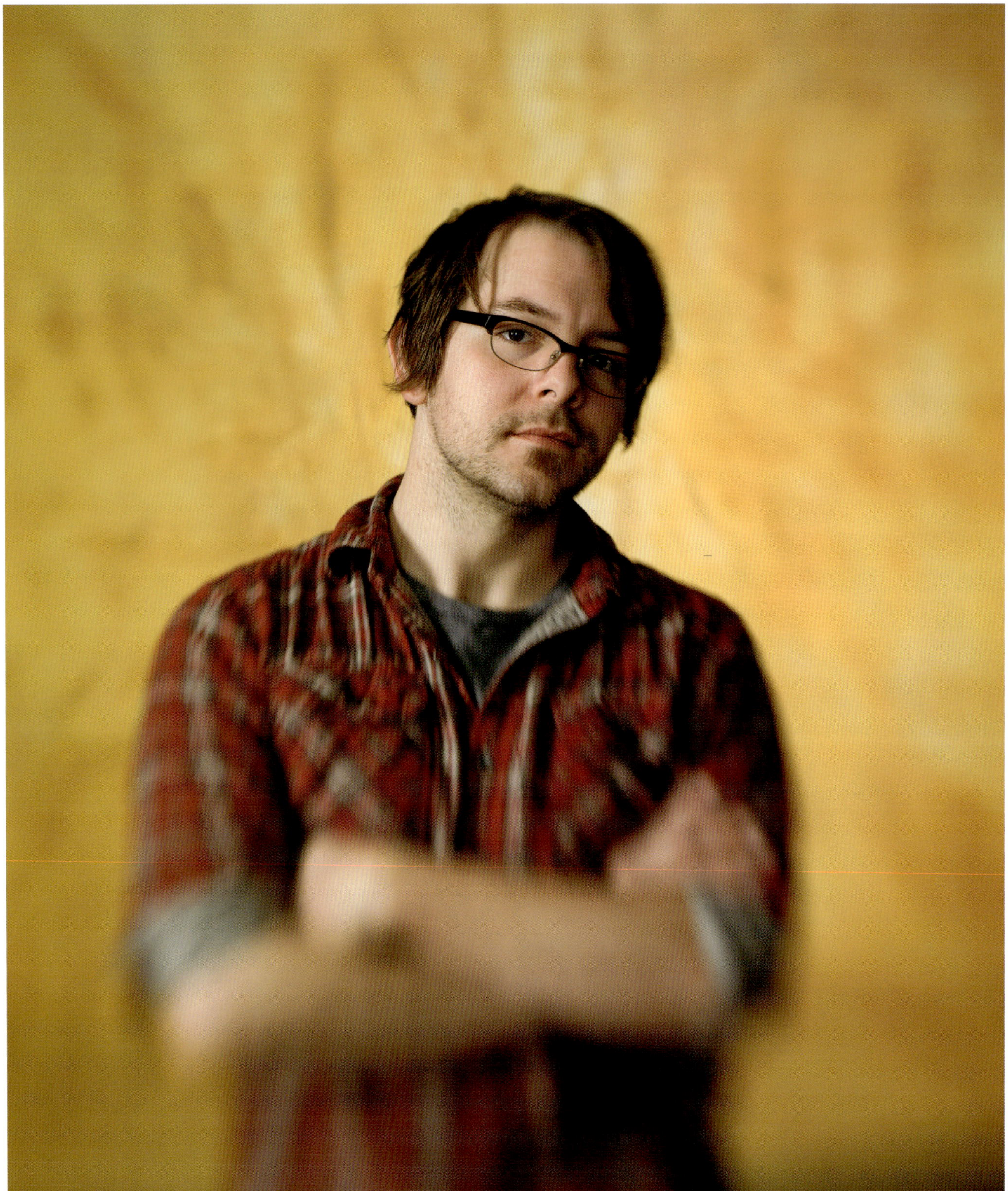

Andrew Blanchard

"Y'all Come Back Now, Ya Hear"

Screen print and graphite on mounted panel

48" X 72" X 3"

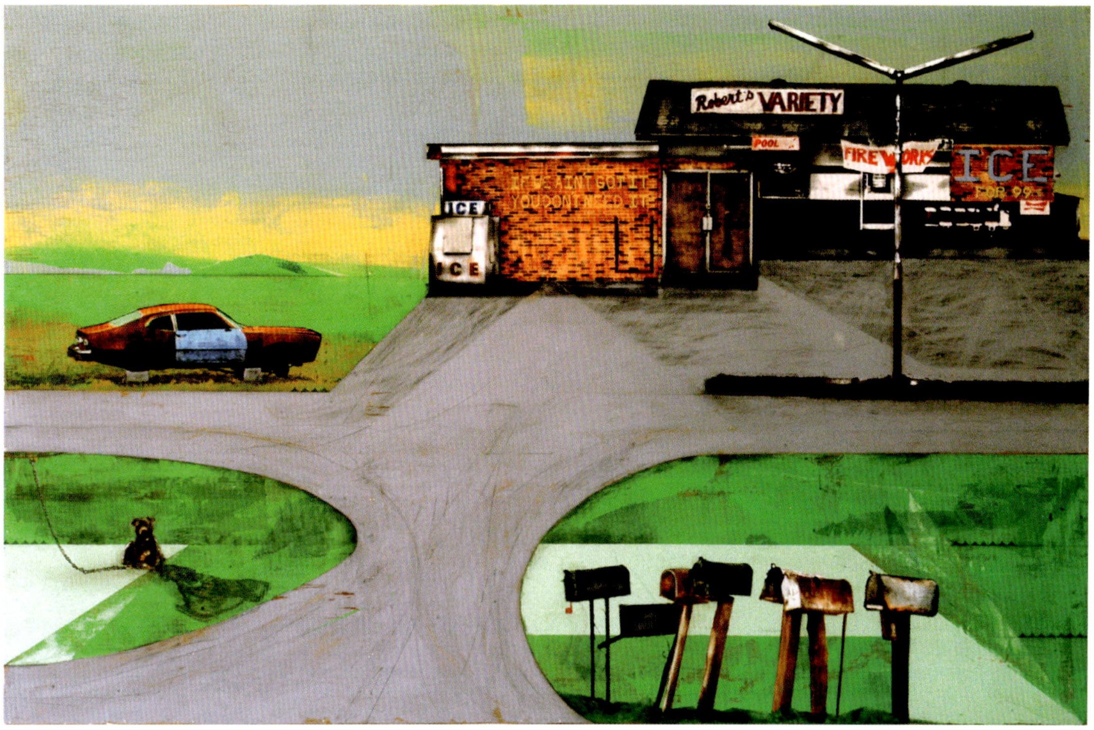

I have lived in Spartanburg for the past six years, teaching printmaking and photography at Converse College. I find the Spartanburg community is a very inexpensive place to live and create art, and one that nurtures its younger artists just as well as its already-established ones. Upon moving here at the age of twenty-eight, I was embraced by a wide gamut of locals that quickly made me feel like one of the crowd.

I was born in the wild swamps of Louisiana but was raised in Waveland, a small beach community on the Mississippi Gulf Coast. Like most boys who grew up close to a beach, I fished and swam until the ring of the dinner bell. At a young age, I became fascinated with the bold, curvilinear woodcuts of another Gulf Coast native, Walter Anderson. From this early inspiration, along with having an illustrator for an aunt and a French Quarter portrait painter for a father, I established my love for art, particularly printmaking.

I earned a BA degree with an emphasis in printmaking from the University of Southern Mississippi in 2000 and an MFA from Ole Miss in 2004. My current subject matter delves into the psyche of the American Gothic South. Inspired by innocently misspelled hand-painted signs, daily trips down Southern back roads, and serendipitous personal interactions, my present concept presents the viewer with identifiable monuments that explore socially-induced issues, revealing the cultural character of the American South. Though not one to categorize my artwork into any genre, I feel my work tows the line between urban and rural expressionism.

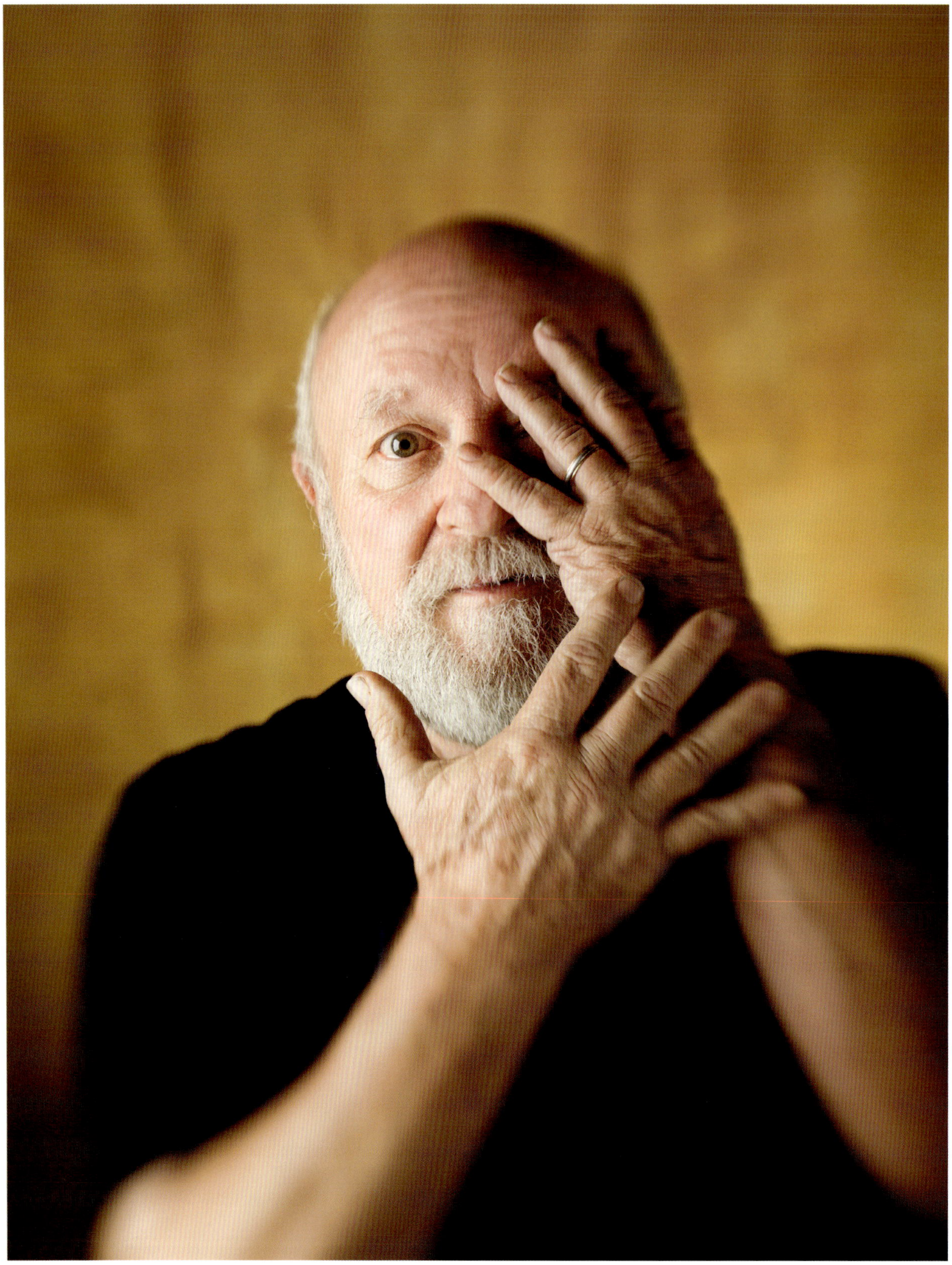

The Talisman

Collection of Lillian Jackson Braun

Powder-coated steel and copper

5' 8"

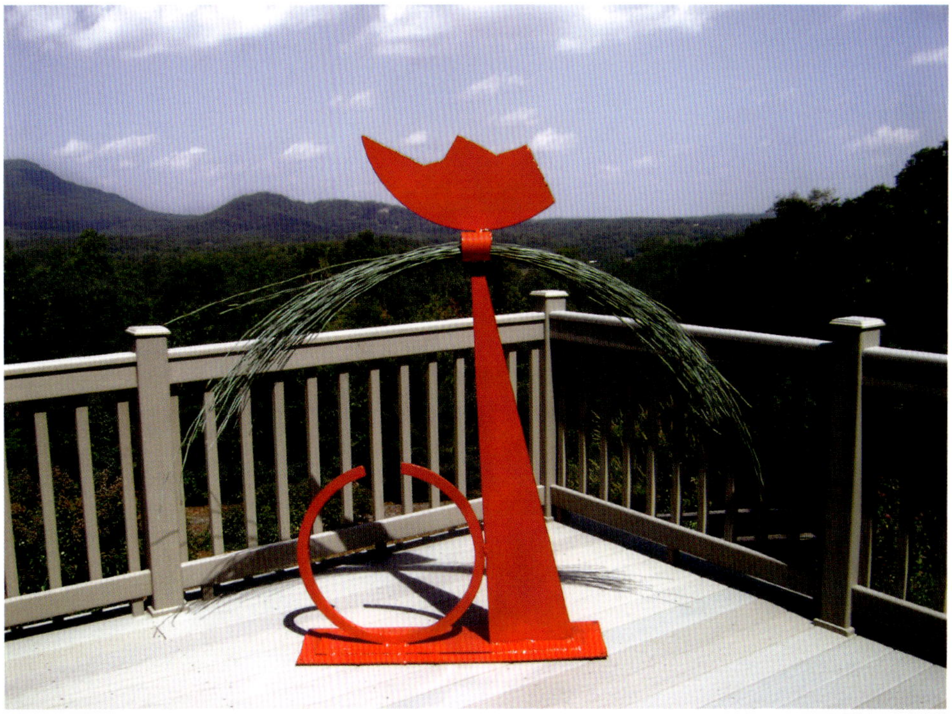

The welded steel sculpture has remained a constant as my medium of expression. My great-grandfather was a blacksmith in Kentucky; both my grandfathers and my father were welders and steelworkers. I grew up watching steel pouring from the blast furnaces and the nightly spectacular display of slag being dumped from huge railroad-sized crucibles, producing a red and yellow night sky over the town. I walked the railroad tracks and picked up scrap metal that had fallen from freight cars. The ironworker's material and process were an everyday part of my childhood. I have taken this material and its process and made art, thus continuing a family tradition of ironwork.

Over the past forty years, my sculpture, painting, and digital art have been concerned with an observation of the world existing as "strata." I was raised in a small industrial town in northeastern Kentucky where coal, oil, natural gas, and iron were my visual reality. At an early age, I became aware that while I was walking on the ground above, people were working, eating, living, and dying underground in coal mines. These images were coupled with underground oil and natural gas pipelines, which made their existence known by periodically breaking the earth's surface in the form of expansion loops and pressure valves. These subterranean images were often in sharp contrast to the natural beauty of the hills, woods, and streams above. My work is a reflection of all of these visual experiences that were so much a part of my youth.

My experimentation with digital images is an example of my sculptural vocabulary freed from the restraints of physical limitations. The images enter the world of the metaphysical: the rigid rendered modeled and warped, the attached freed from their welds and supported suspension. Their environment becomes a stage for imaginative exploration into the world of the surreal.

There are many things one can do to occupy his time while on this earth. I prefer to have non-verbal conversations with my soul. My art is the residue.

Mayo Mac Boggs

Betty Jane Bramlett

I was born in Augusta, Georgia, lived in Charleston, and moved to Spartanburg in my teens, where I graduated from Spartanburg High School. I received a BA in fine arts from Converse College, an MA in fine arts and supervision from Columbia University, and an EdD from the University of South Carolina. For forty-two years I served as fine arts coordinator for Spartanburg County School District Seven. In 1989 I was honored to receive South Carolina's Elizabeth O'Neill Verner Award for my artwork and for outstanding service in art education in my community and state.

Due to many bouts with asthma as a small child, I missed school a lot. My father furnished me with paints and drawing materials to pass the time. I was in a "new world" and have never left my love of producing art. August Cook, the art teacher at Converse College, gave me the love of color, which has always been the focus of my artwork. Two artists whom I have always held in high regard are Romare Bearden and Vincent Van Gogh.

For many years, my focus has been on exploring water media through many forms of mixed media, including acrylics, Japanese papers, and watercolors. Almost all of my paintings are based upon the environment around my house, the creek, rocks, trees, grasses, and flowers that have produced my abstract works.

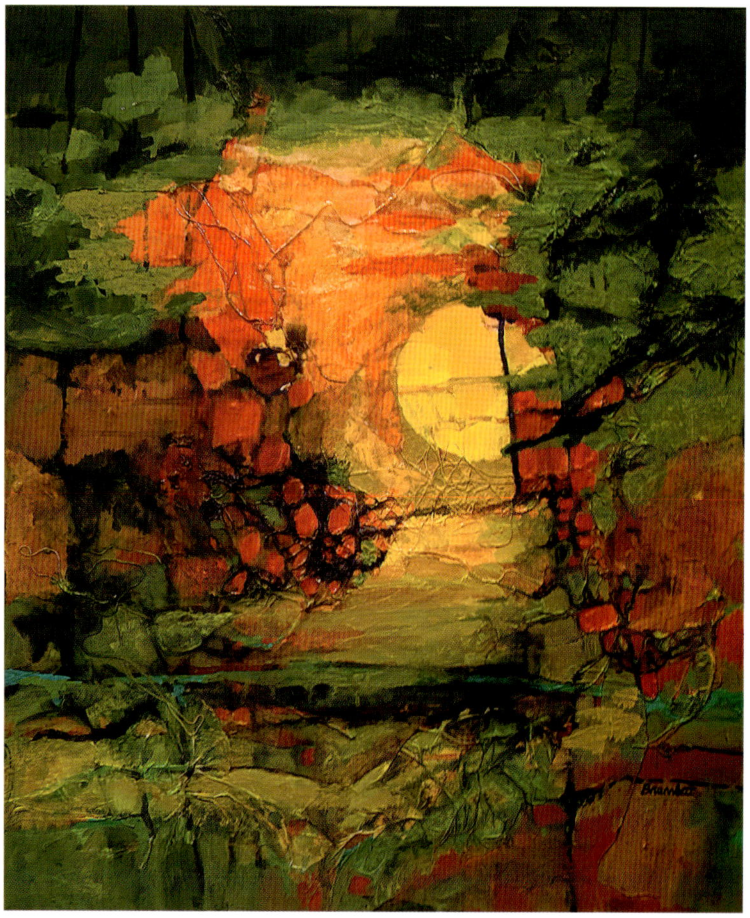

Same Old Sun

Acrylic on canvas

24" X 30"

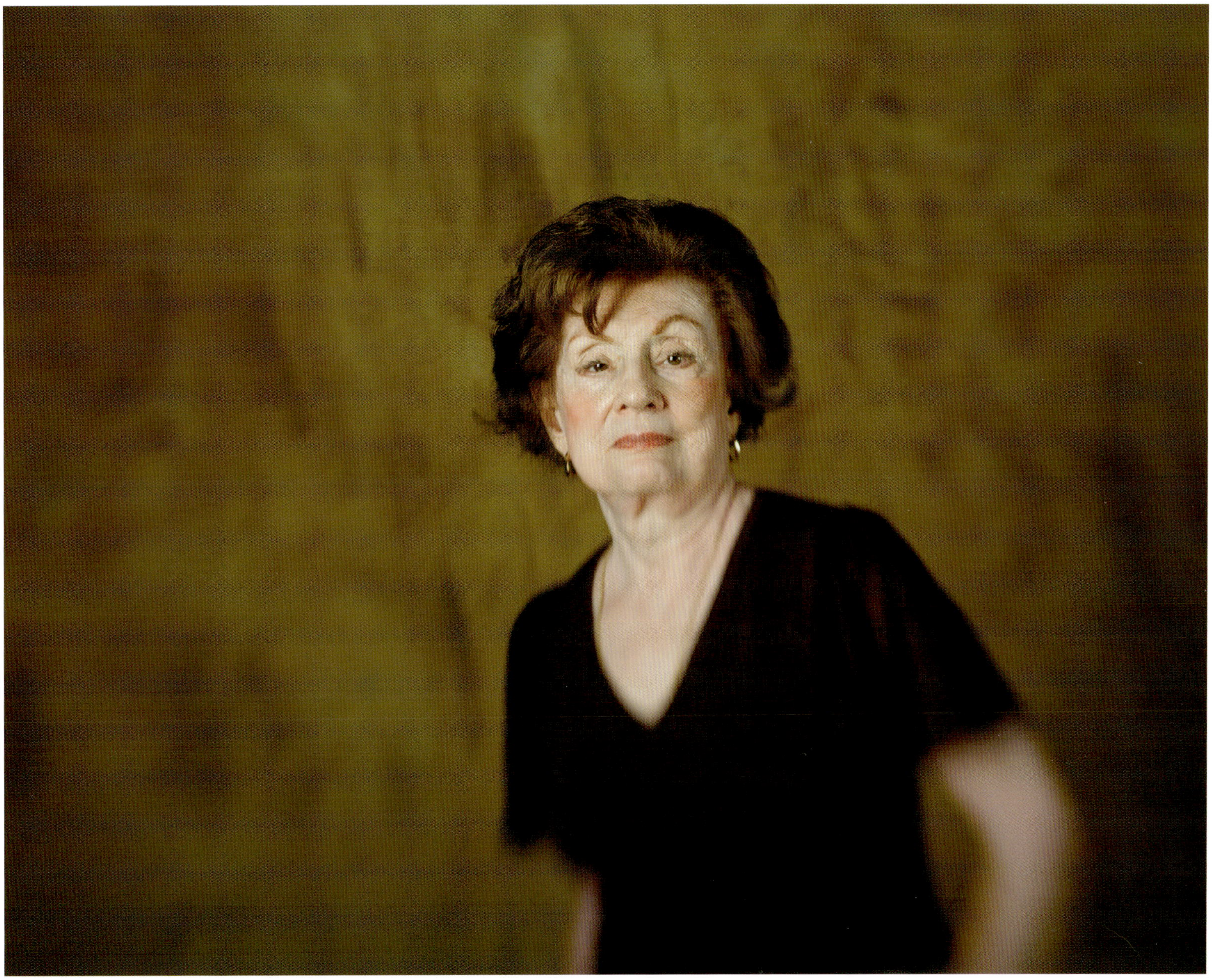

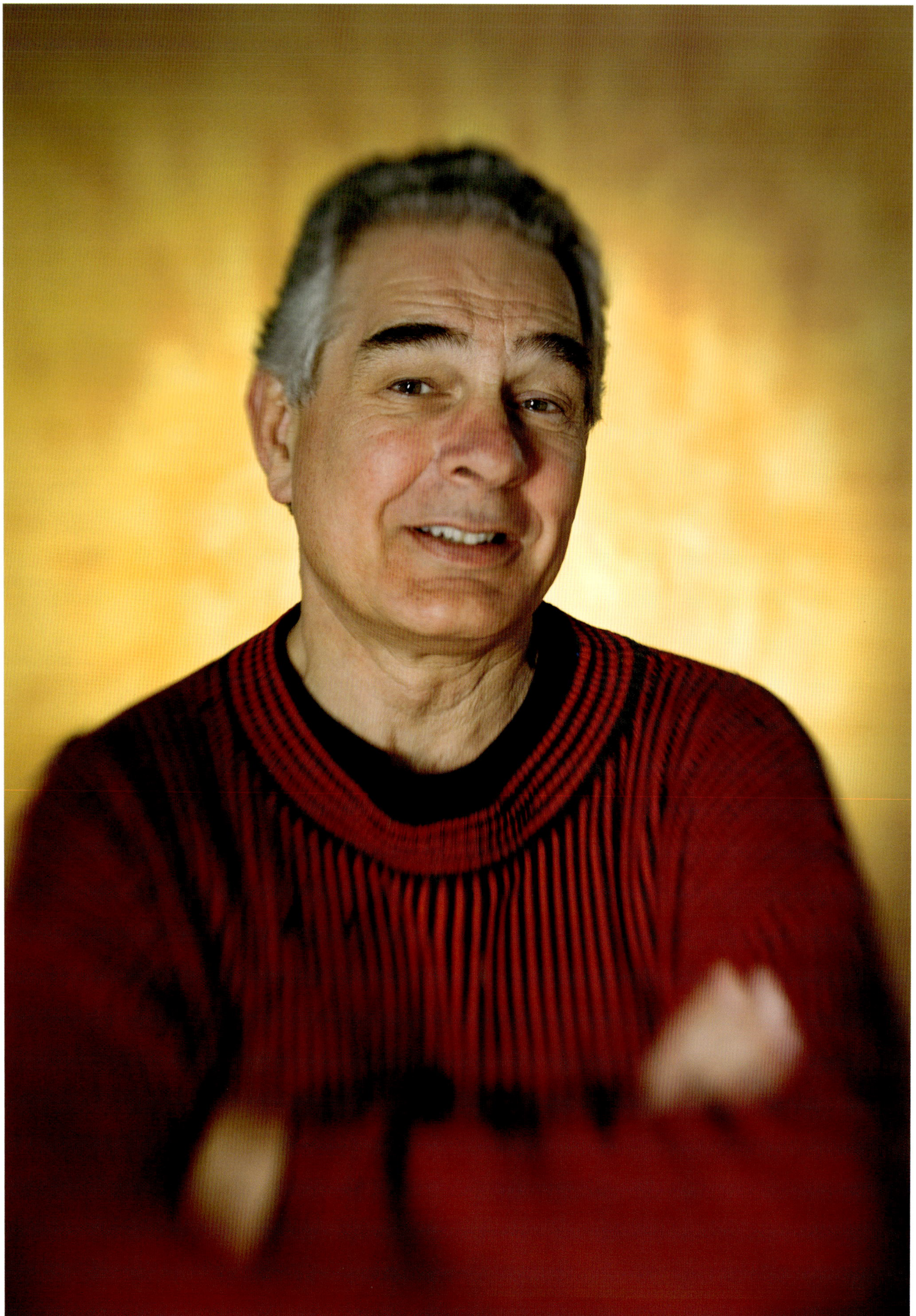

George "Buck" Brandt, III

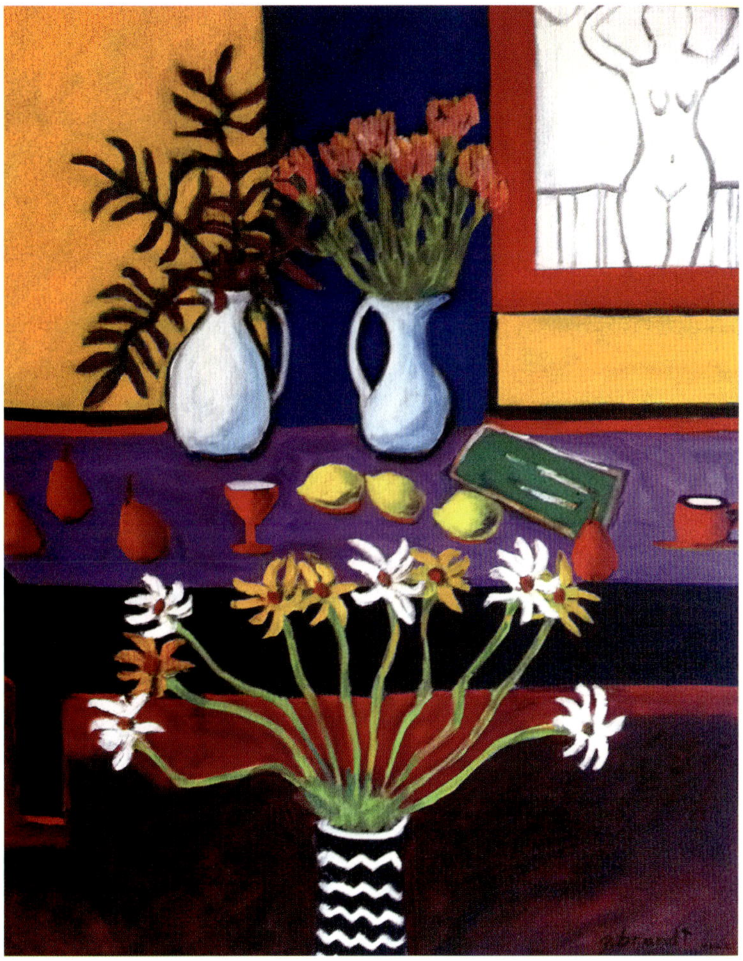

Still Life with Striped Vase
Oil on canvas
48" X 36"

I am an artist first and a lawyer second. I became interested in art as a result of taking an art history course offered by Constance Armitage at Wofford College in the early 1970s. Law school, a wife and four children, and a busy law practice interrupted my artistic inclinations until a friend gave me a copy of *Drawing on the Right Side of Your Brain* in 1989. After reading this book and performing the drawing exercises, I decided that I needed to paint, and I have been painting non-stop ever since. Although I am self-taught, I have been influenced by Matisse and the work of my great-uncle, Warren Brandt, who was an artist in New York City from the 1930s until his death in 2002.

Painting is my escape from the pressures of everyday life. It gives me time to focus on my art and to selfishly isolate myself with my work. I paint in oil. My paintings are color-driven. For some reason, which I cannot explain, I am most pleased when I am using vibrant colors that do not necessarily conform to the reality of the subject matter that I am painting. In other words, I paint the colors that I feel instead of the colors of the objects. This is not a neat and deliberate process. I go to my studio, turn on the music, and dance with the paints on canvas. I hope you like my work.

Jackson Bundy

As a child growing up in Cheraw, South Carolina, I spent hours upon hours creating roads in the dirt over mountains, across lakes, and into tunnels for the movement of my Matchbox cars and Army soldiers. Designing and building entire communities never ceased to excite my imagination. Toad and frog houses and castles turned an ordinary sandbox into dynamic new places.

After more than forty years in the non-profit world where I designed programs and implemented strategies involving people in addressing critical community issues, a childlike excitement returned when I put my first ball of clay onto a potter's wheel and threw my first clay pot. I then created a wonderland of bowls, pitchers, mugs, vases, and baskets, a few snowmen, and occasionally a funky piece of unknown origin. Every piece is an original—nothing is the same.

Having always enjoyed working with my hands, clay has followed furniture making, wood turning, wood carving, macramé, and painting. Most of my education has been local through teachers and special instruction at the Chapman Cultural Center and Spring Street, along with annual visits to John Campbell Folk School and Odyssey Center in Asheville.

Excitement comes from creating functional pieces, such as a bowl for holding fruit on the counter, a mug for coffee, a vase for flower arrangements on the dining table, and additional décor for a small living room table.

Inspiration comes from the finished pieces emerging from the kiln. Each opening is an adventure, as various colors emerge sort of like you thought but never exactly alike, for color combinations can yield new colors and different presentations of use. But the real joy is seeing the reaction of someone who truly likes your work when you give it away or sell it.

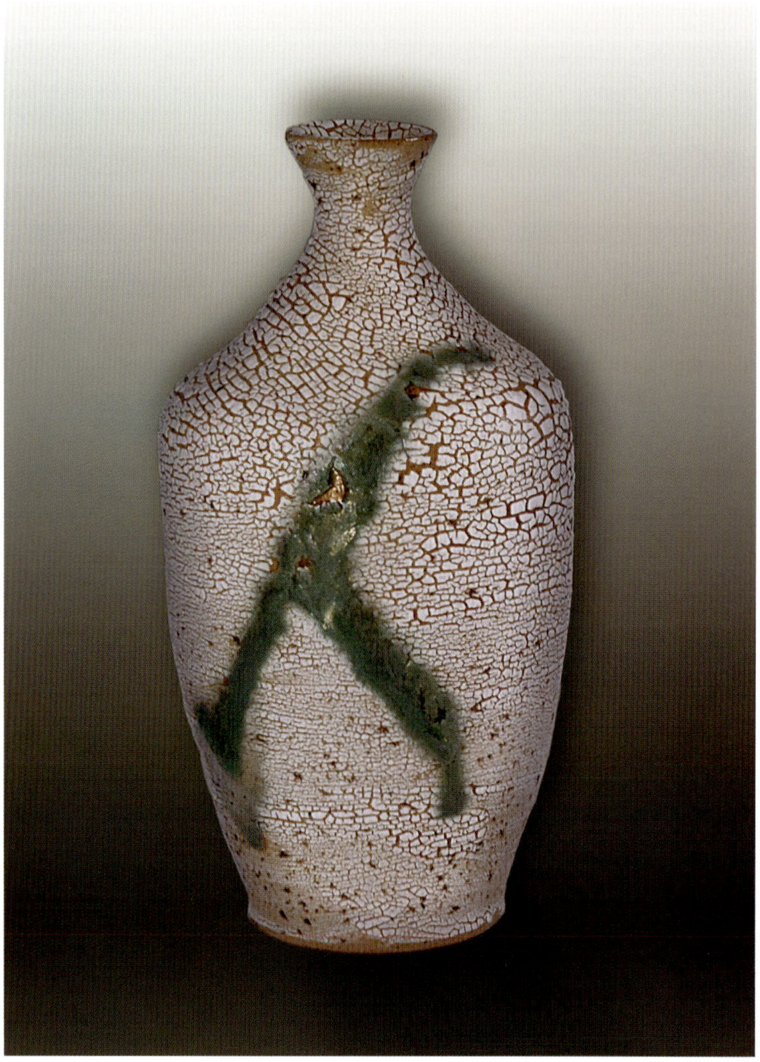

Tomorrow
Wheelthrown clay
9" X 4.5" X 4.5"

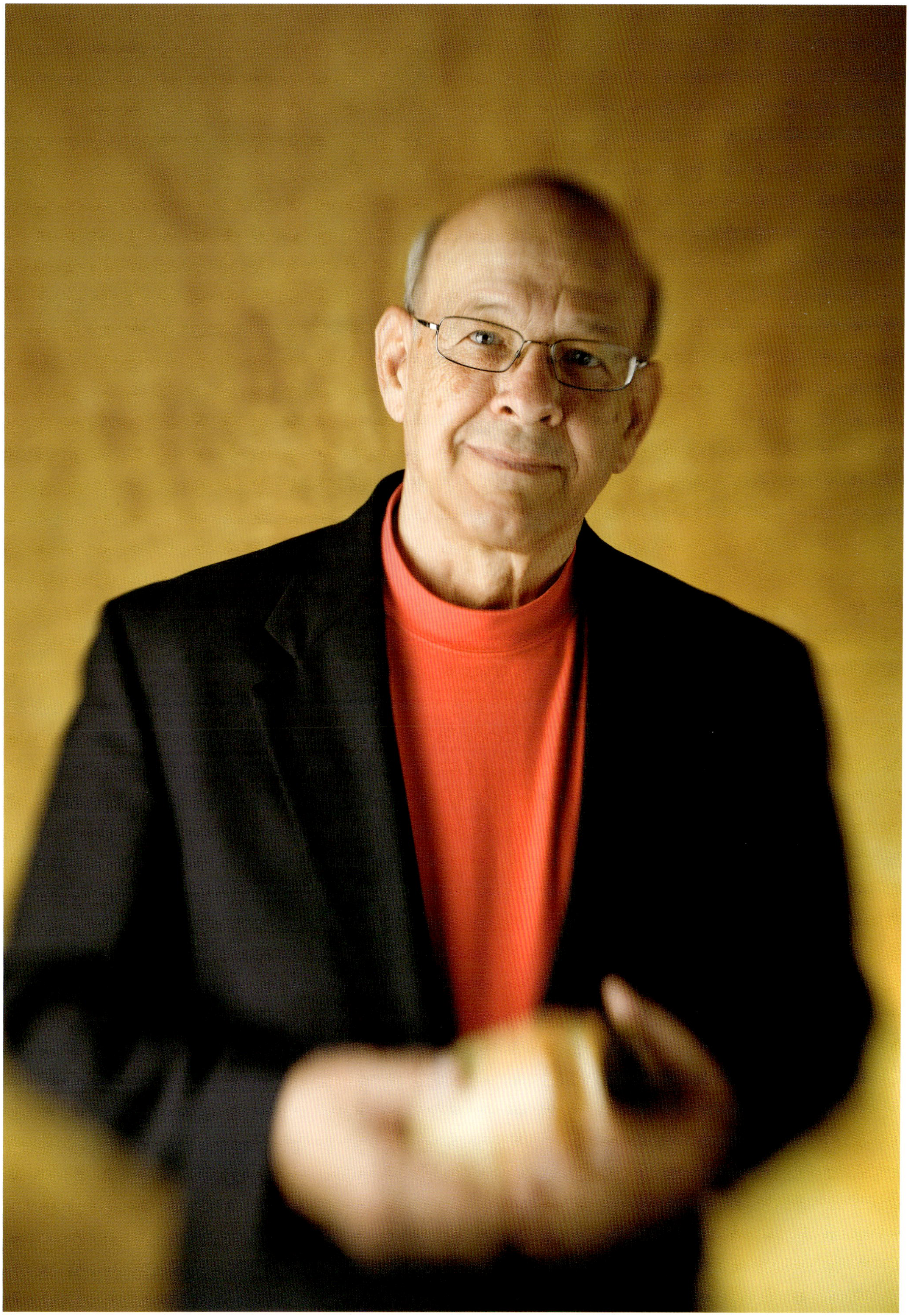

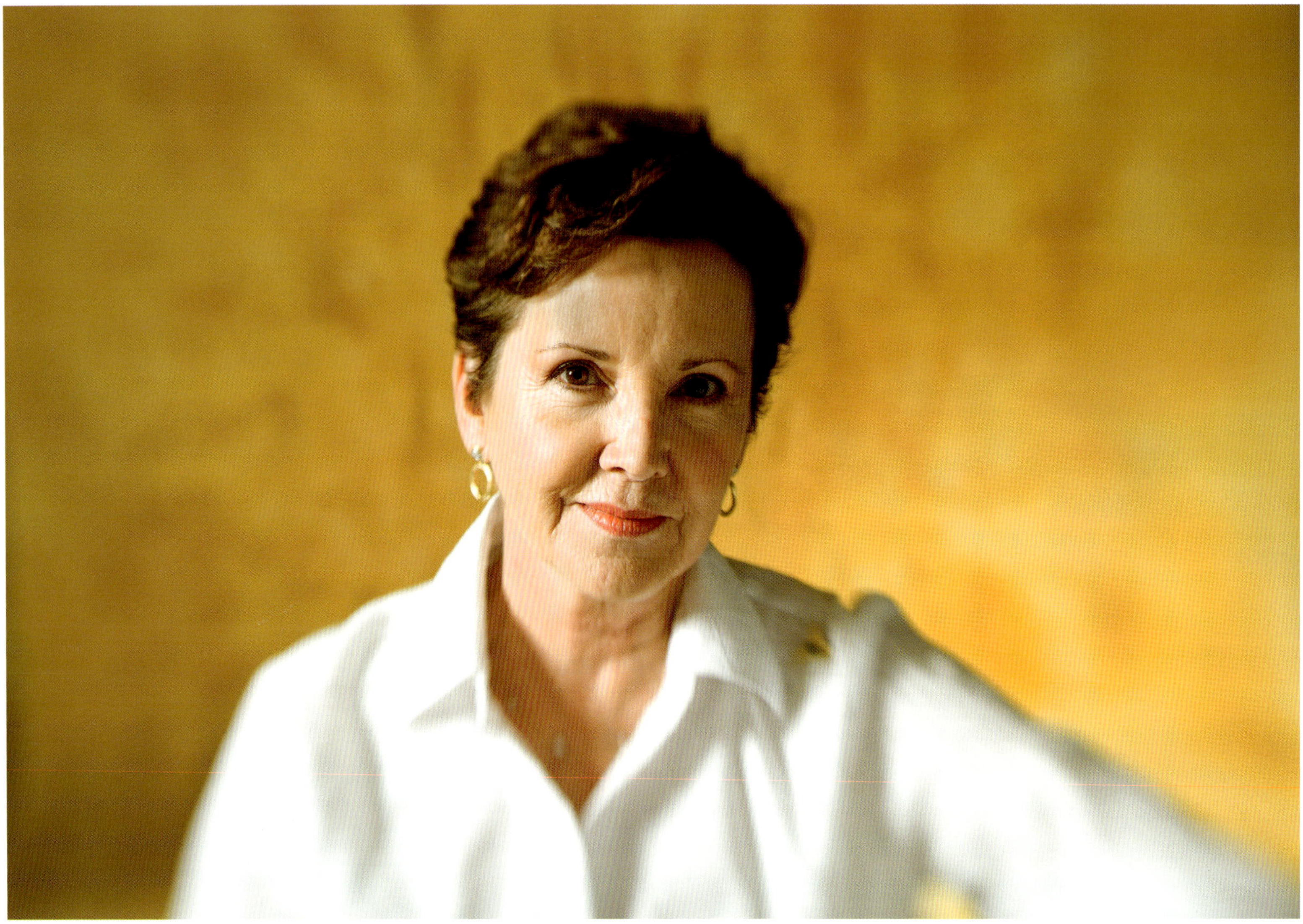

Julia Bowling Burnett

To me, the details of nature are too beautiful to leave out of my paintings. My mother taught me that. She taught me about wildflowers, birds, and the beauty of the world on the long walks we would take. There was a wonderful stream with white clay along its banks, and, excitedly, I would dig the clay up to take home and make tea cups. I left my family's Campobello farm long ago, but the deep-rooted love of nature blooms again each spring in my garden—and from the bristles of my paint brushes.

Today, my inspiration is only a few steps from my easel. My studio is a glassed room that overlooks a garden filled with plants, shrubs, and wildflowers. Bushes grown from 150-year-old plants that belonged to my grandparents occupy places of honor. Mountain Laurel and wild azaleas share space with shade gardens, Japanese maples, and a small pond.

My paintings begin with photographs I take. Not broad landscape pictures but hidden fragments of forest floor, a hummingbird's flight in search of the sweetest nectar, or a ground-level view of summer flowers. I did miniatures for years because I like the little details. Hummingbirds show up in many of my paintings; I call them my trademark.

I have painted all my life, but I've had almost no formal training. My watercolor works are a testament to other artists in my family, including my mother and uncles.

A painting of my father's hands wrapped around an old hat filled with a cluster of trailing arbutus is my favorite piece of work. The love story behind the painting gives it special meaning. Dad found the flowers and knew my mother would want to see them. He put them in his old, green hat and brought the flowers to the house. I've now added a painting of my mother's hands, holding a bouquet of wildflowers, to a wall in my home. It had to be flowers because she loved growing them so much, and she taught me to love them too.

Fathers Hands
Watercolor
21" X 30"

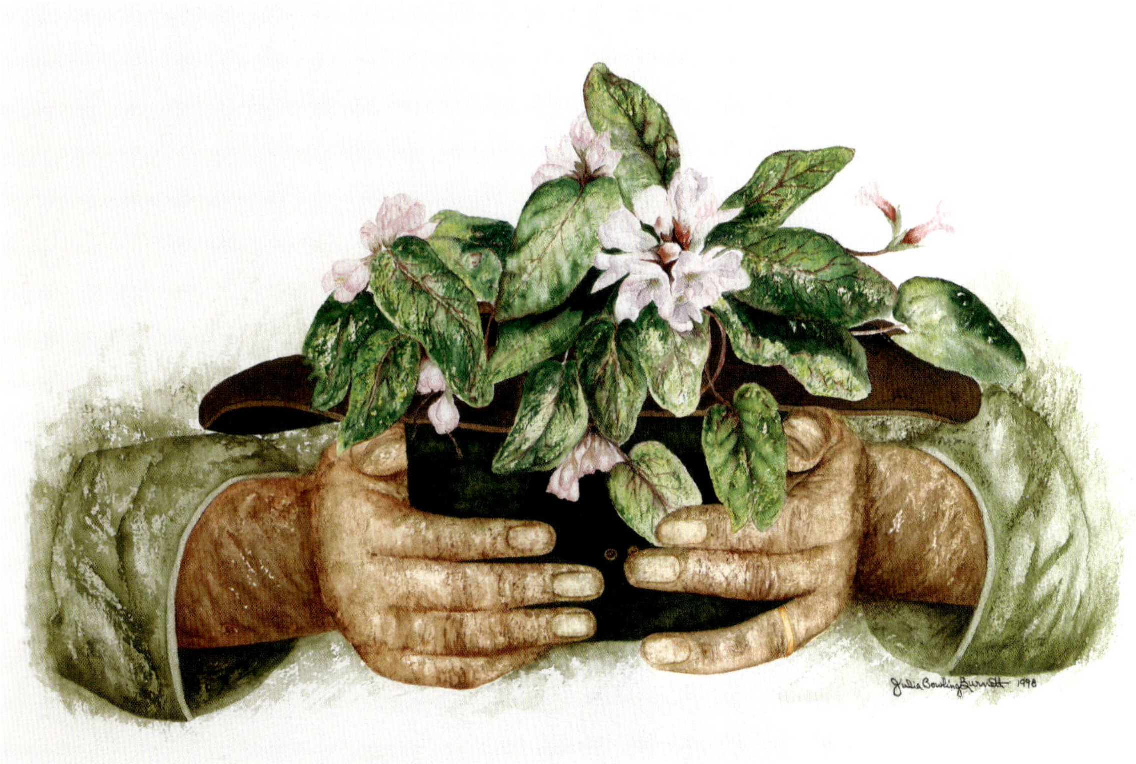

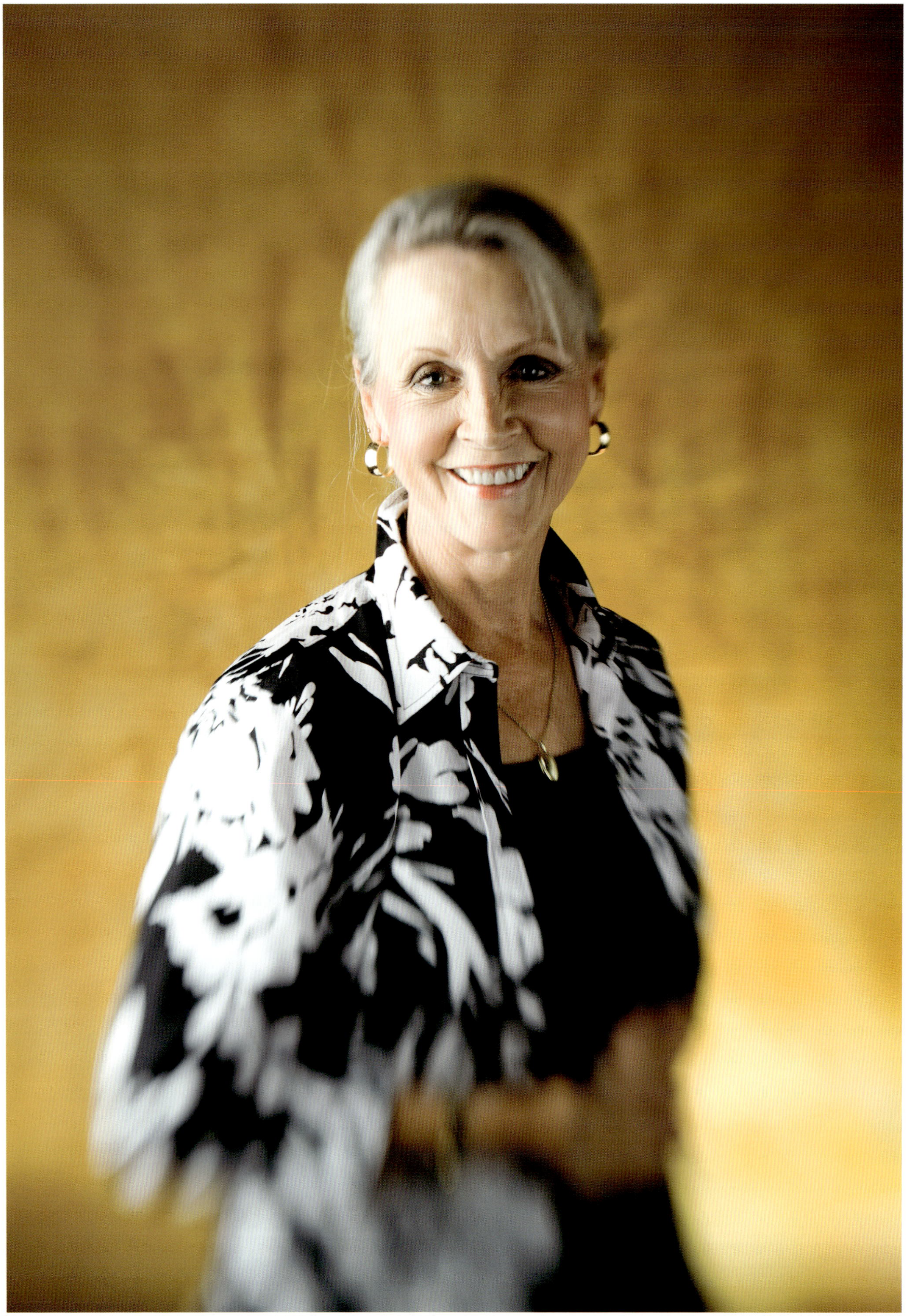

Pamela Brown Caldwell

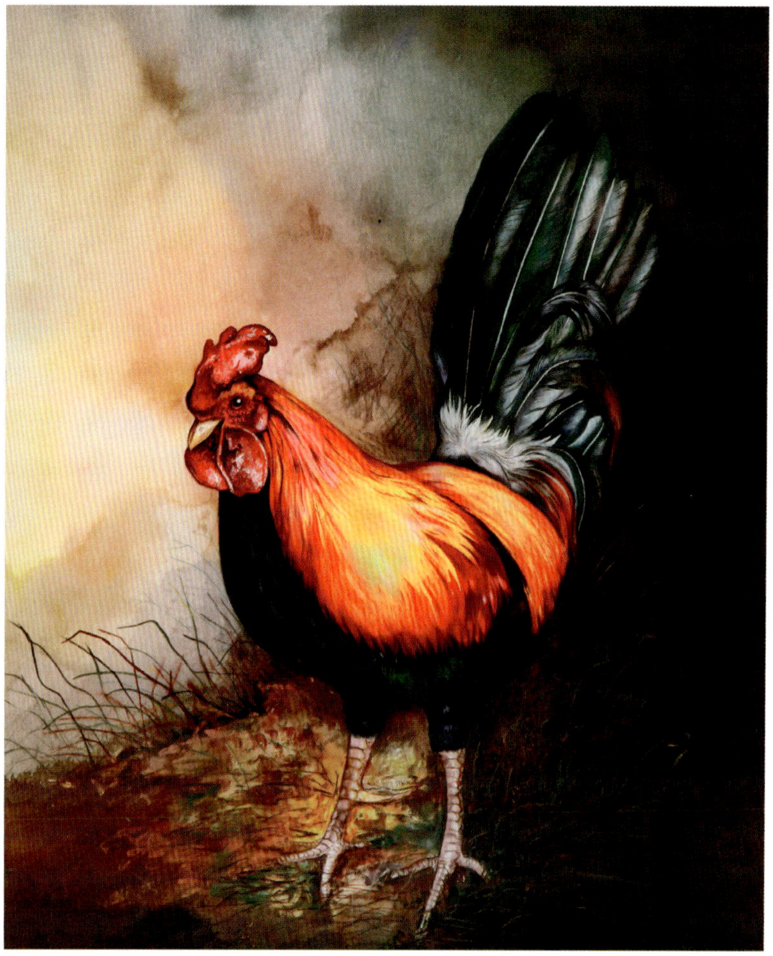

Ole Glory
19" X 24.5"
Watercolor

I am the daughter of a veterinarian father and floral designer mother. My eyes are constantly catching subjects for painting because I live in the Master Artist's world. I experience great joy as I attempt to capture a bit of the incredible beauty around me. Animals are a favorite subject, as are people and flowers; anything, when examined closely, will reveal God's brilliance. My painting style is realistic and is a celebration of what I see, not a painstaking task. I hold a deep and thankful love for the world God made ... all creatures great and small and the sheer beauty of the natural environment that each one inhabits.

I also paint portraits. My character studies take on a rare inner-perspective and are a reflection of my love and understanding of people. Collectors of my works can select from sixty-five favored watercolors that are available in limited edition, signed, and numbered prints. I continue to accept commissioned orders for original pieces of art.

I illustrated the books *Woodspirits* (Cairn Studio) and *The Charleston Coloring Book* (Tryon Publishing Co.) I was the first woman selected to paint "the print of the year" for the South Carolina Wildlife Federation and was chosen to paint the Harry Hampton print "Wild Palmetto Style" and "Coastal Visions" for the Tryon Fine Arts Center. In 1993 I was selected as "Spartanburg's Finest Artist" by *The Paper*.

I have been painting a series of Santas for nearly twenty years, always keeping in mind the true reason for the celebration. Each Santa is unique, ranging in character from playful to elegant.

I celebrate each day and invite others to join in.

Linda Hyatt Cancel

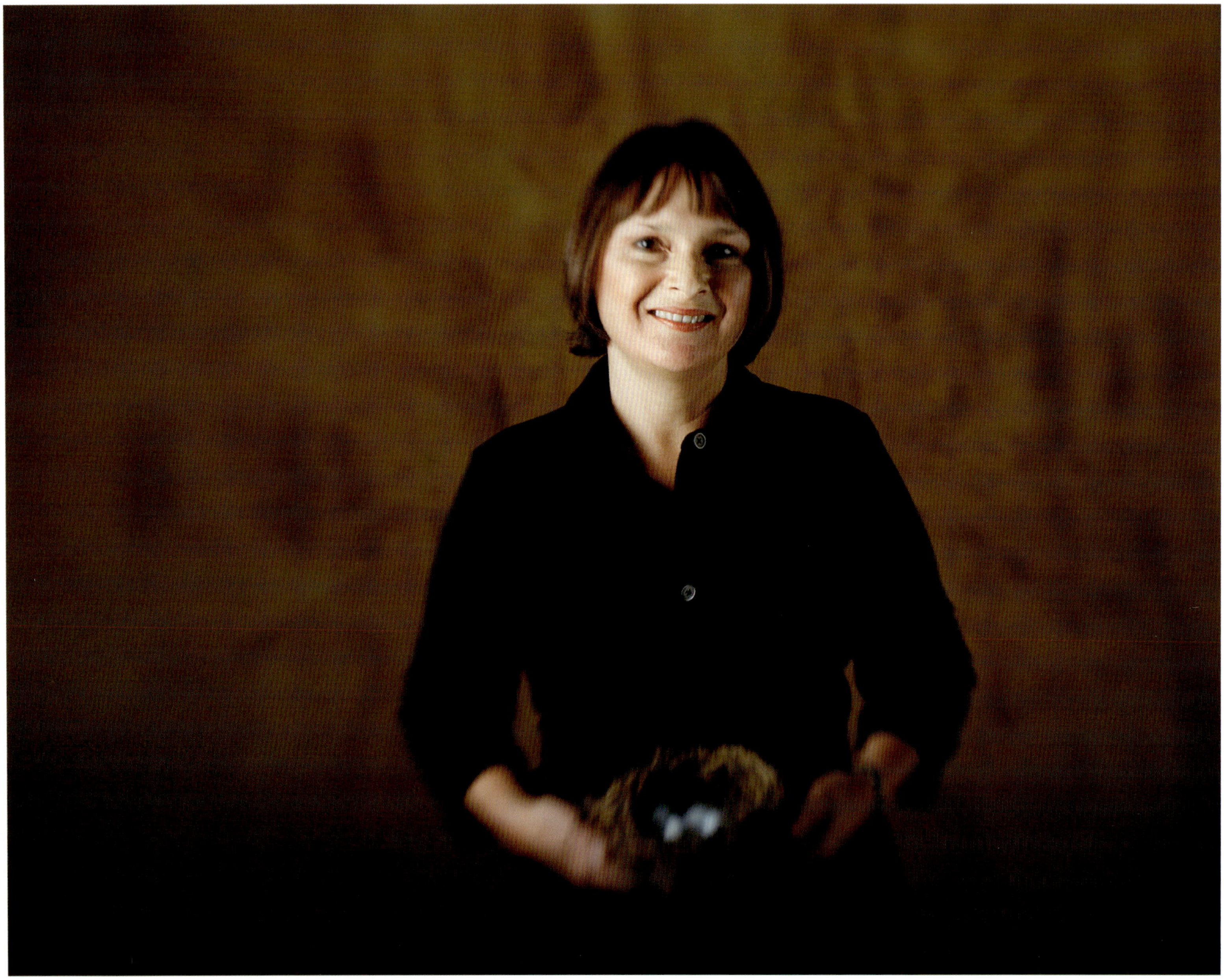

I was born in Moscow, Idaho, and raised in the Kettle Falls-Colville area of Washington State, several miles from Lake Roosevelt on the upper Columbia River. There my dad taught industrial arts, graphics, U.S. and world history. The drafting tools of the trade fascinated me, as well as the paintings of historical figures in his textbooks. As a family, we spent many weekends exploring the natural beauty and geologically diverse landscape of the Pacific Northwest. Dad was also a pilot, so wherever he traveled, he searched out the smaller airports in case he needed to land.

an actor or a casting or set director. But since I would rather be a quiet observer, the paintings themselves have become the performance. After careful consideration, subject matter is assigned an application, method, or style to bring out the highest level of dramatic effect. I enjoy painting for the audience, hoping to evoke strong emotion. It is a never-ending quest to capture the feeling of a moment and share it with the viewer, some who have termed my work "Poetic Tonalism" or "Spiritual Geographies." Painting is a way to distill all my interests into one place.

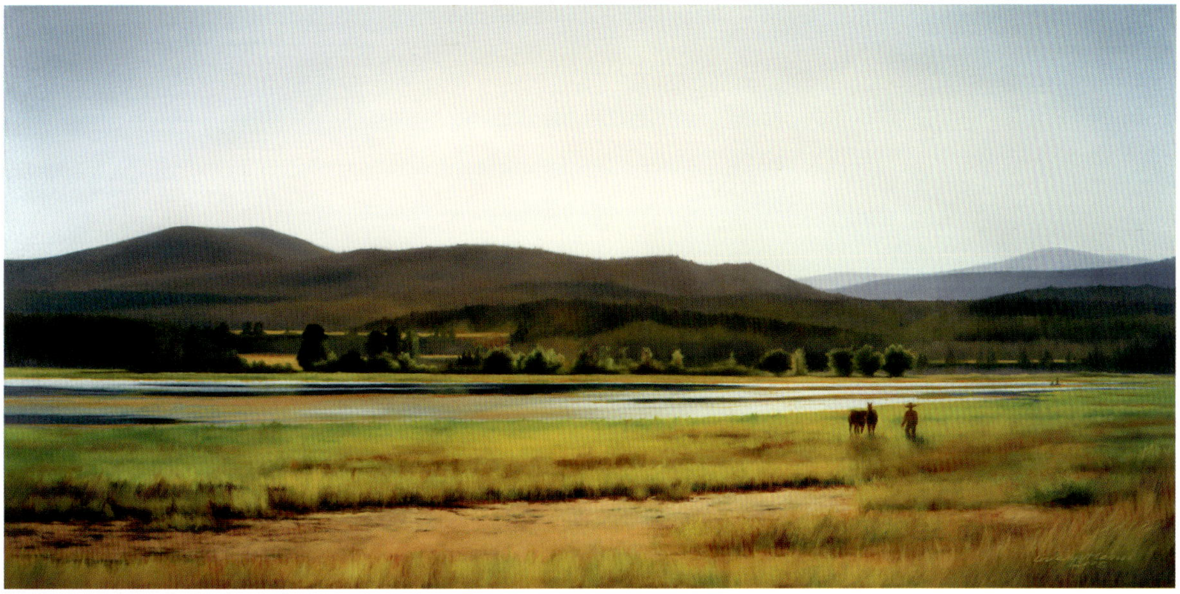

Sunday Evening
Oil on canvas
24" X 48"

Providentially, when I was twelve, my mother contacted noted artist William F. Pogue, who was teaching oil painting in his retirement, to see if he would consider teaching an adolescent. He was hesitant but agreed, so I studied in his classes for six years until enrolling at Spokane Falls Community College, majoring in visual merchandising and display design.

Architecture, photography, and films inspire me. If I were not a painter, I would gravitate to performance art as

My dad always said the weather patterns were most unstable in the mountainous region of the Southeast. Several years ago, I learned that my ancestors once lived in Laurens, Union, and Spartanburg counties. I have found the Spartanburg art community to be a wonderful, nurturing, respectful, inclusive, gritty, authentic, and magnanimous group of talented artists, musicians, writers, and educators. I have found a soft place to land.

Vivianne Carey

The art that I create is a reflection of my spiritual temperament. Most of the time, I strive for an atmosphere of worship and meditation. Is it foolish to say that I just listen to the little voice in my head while I work? God manifests his essence first in the natural world, then in the spiritual world; my feeble attempts are to portray his persona through mimicry of his natural creations. The results may be beautiful, sensual, exciting, or just simply funny.

As a Christian artist, it is important for me to enlighten and inspire, as my art is a reflection of God's essence and grace. God is speaking through my art. Through the manipulation of modest and sometimes clumsy mortal media I attempt to communicate love, hope, and joy by the images that represent the life cycle—birth, death, and rebirth.

I have lived in Spartanburg most of my life and have watched the city grow into an exciting metropolis that embraces the culture through the fine arts. Spartanburg is an artistically energized community and because sculpture adds so much to the visual impact of a city, garden, or park, the public spaces in which I have been privileged to place my work richly melds my style of outdoor sculpture to the natural environment. As I find myself sharing the vision of a revitalized Spartanburg and sense the obvious positive impact that the arts make in this community, I feel honored that I can contribute to it.

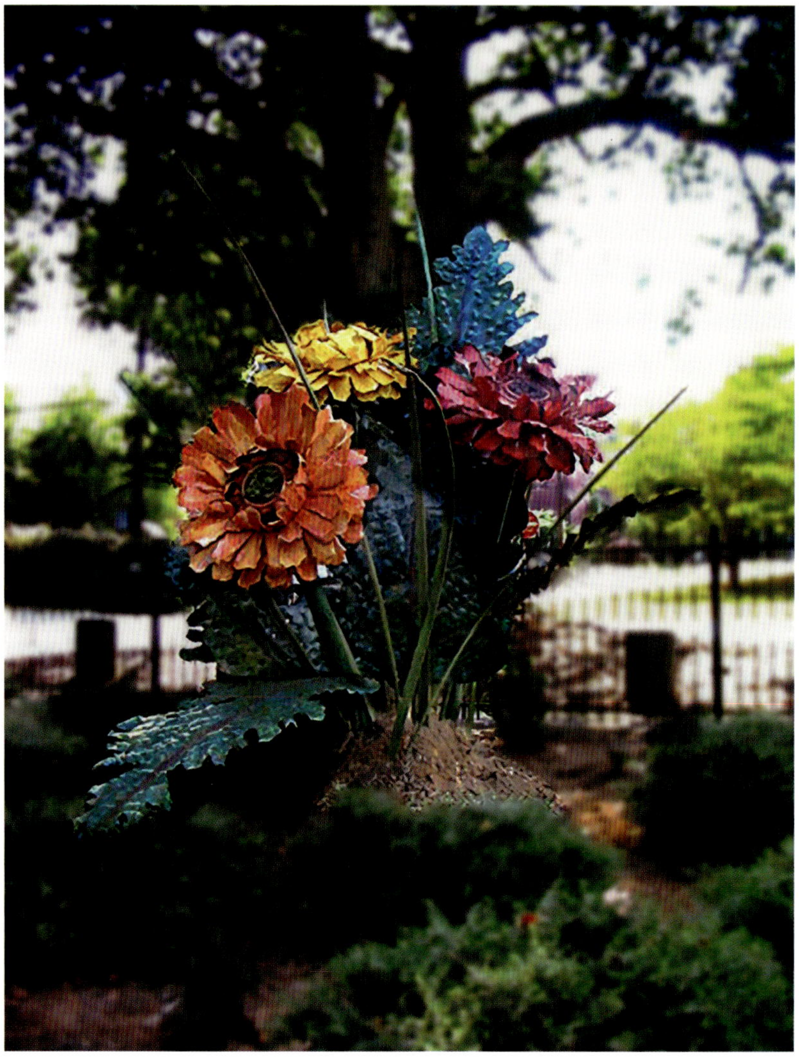

Magnified
Painted steel sculpture
6' X 11'

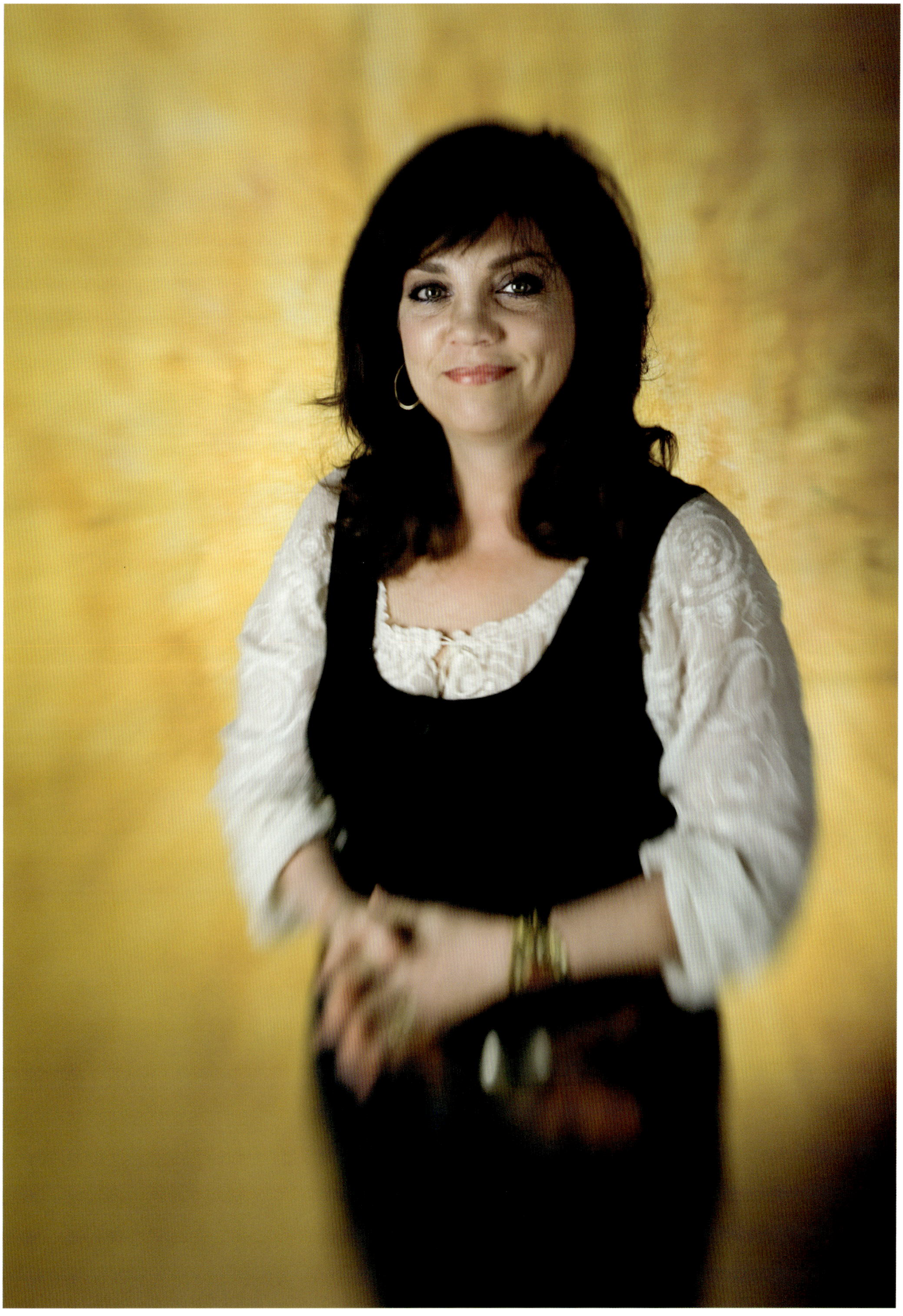

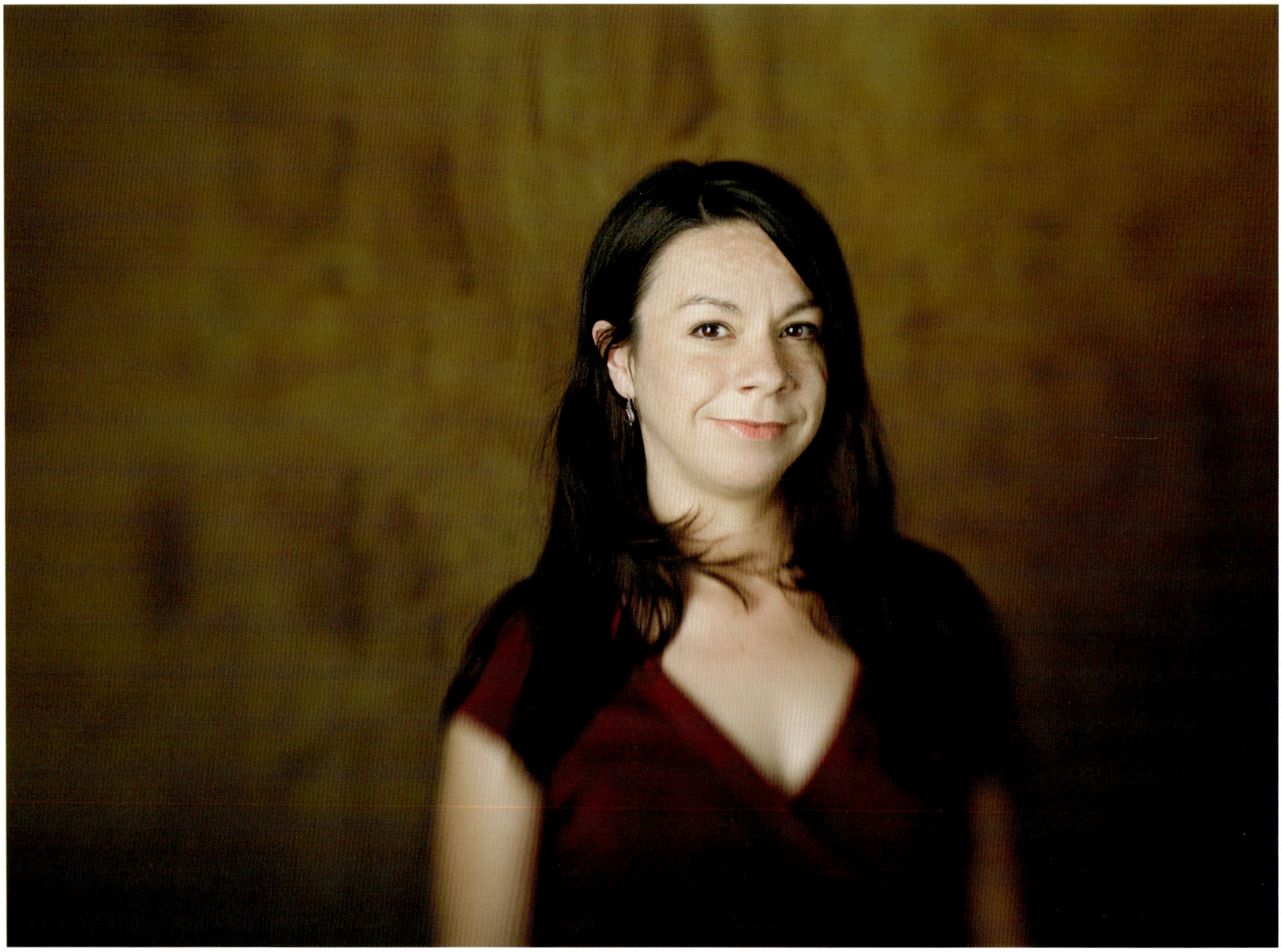

Nikki Caulk

My work addresses the oneness of existence: the connection between human beings and their environment, the connection between two souls, and the connection between humans and the divine. I believe that our best hope in healing ourselves, our environment, and our society lies in the recognition and acceptance of this interconnectedness. I intend for my work to inspire viewers to look deeper at their own connections with the Earth, their loved ones, their community, and the divine.

I delight in the beauty of the human figure in motion. Of particular interest to me is the body as a prayer tool, such as in the arts of yoga and ecstatic dance. In exploring these themes of movement and spirit, I draw reference from all of the sources available to me: live models, my own photography, and images I find on the Internet, including clips from YouTube. The square mark-making in many of my pieces is inspired by pixels in photography, by mosaic art, and by the work of the artist Chuck Close. It has become a symbol of the inherent oneness of the universe in my work, as all of the parts of the picture are composed of these squares. The squares inside of squares become windows through which the viewer can see deeper into the artwork, and ultimately deeper into his or her soul. The vibrancy and luminosity of oil paint and pastel allow me to portray what interests me most about my subjects—the spirit, the light, the essence.

I have always sought a connection to spirit through my work. This was difficult for me at the beginning of my career, as I had no spiritual practice or faith in a divine being. When I discovered the concept of the divine feminine in other traditions, I was delighted and soon began the Goddess paintings. After years of studying Eastern philosophy, I have recently returned to a study of Christianity, and for the first time I am painting women from the Bible. I look forward to exploring the integration of all of these spiritual traditions in my work.

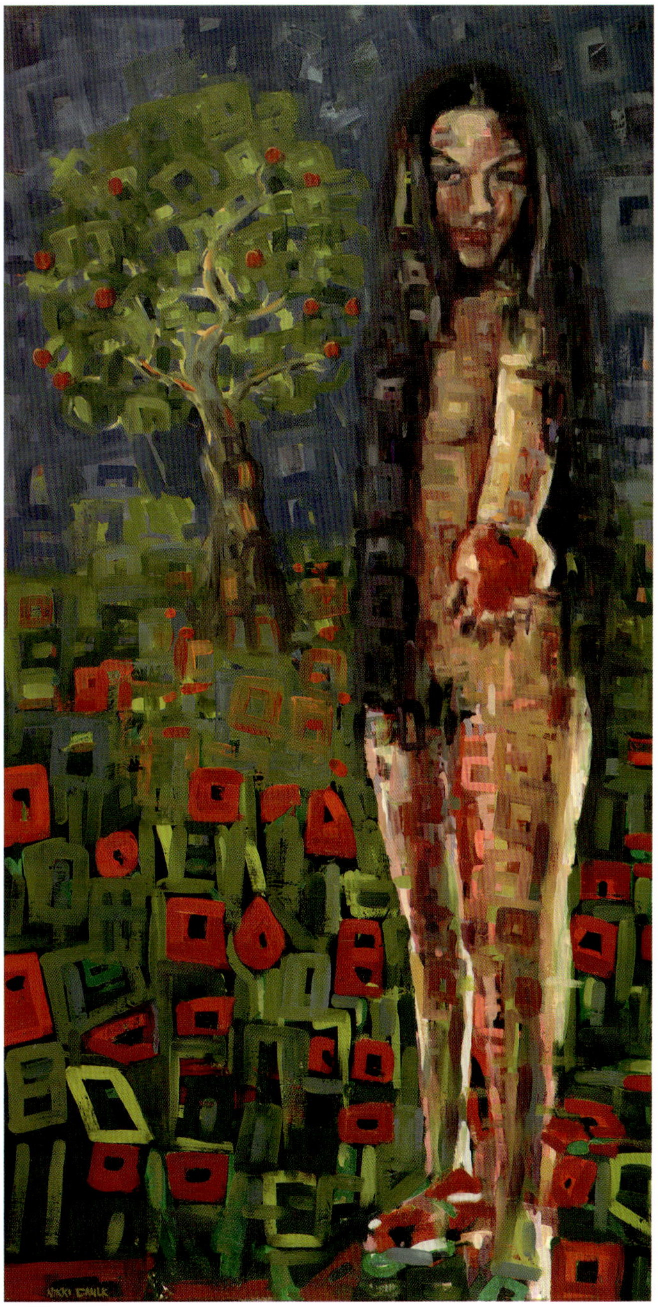

Temptation
Oil on canvas
24" X 48"

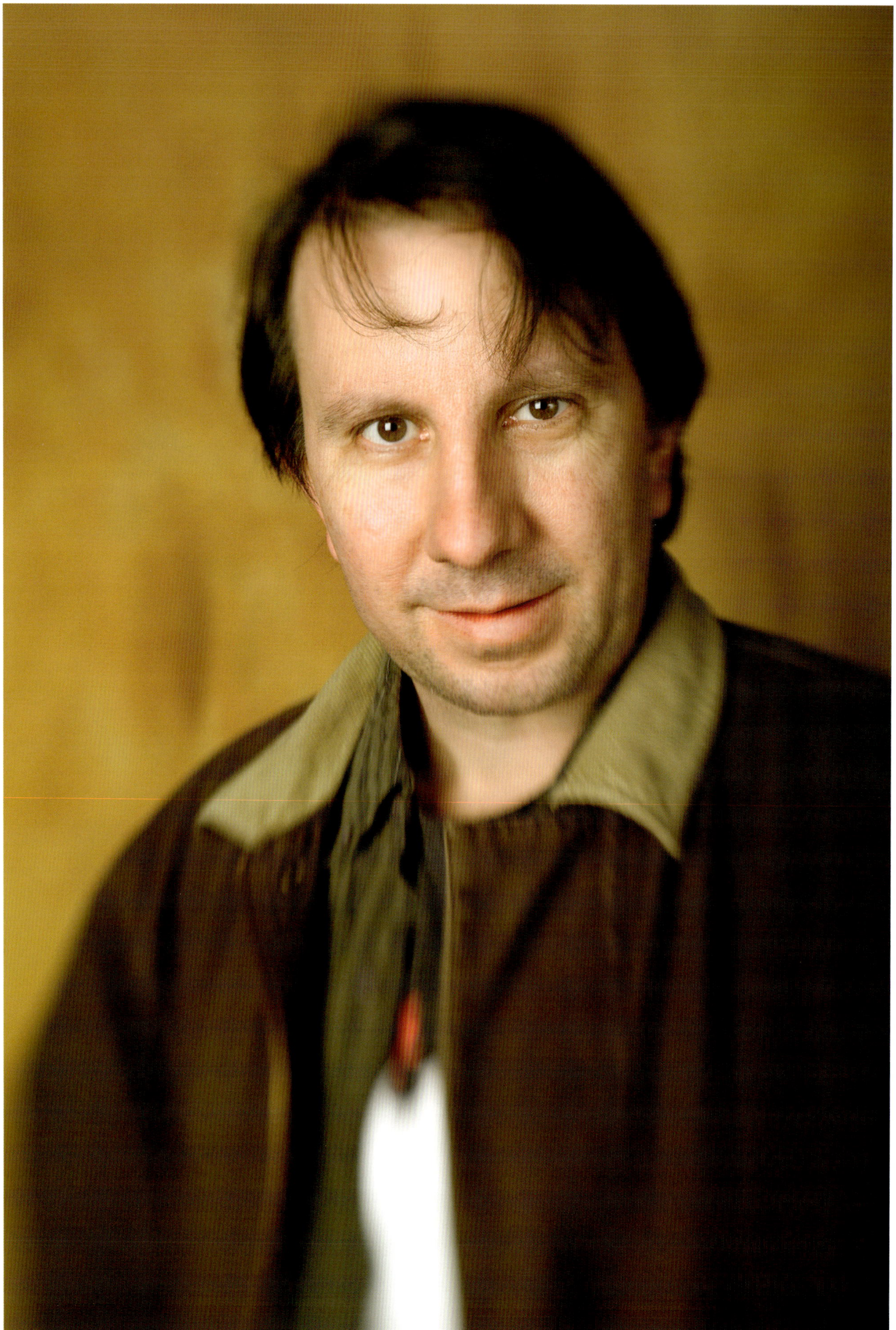

Richard Conn

Although I was born in Ann Arbor, Michigan, I spent the majority of my youth and early adulthood in Spartanburg. Over the years I have been witness to the changes, for better and for worse, which have transpired in our community. For me, the ebb and flow that occurs within the architecture of a town functions as traces of these changes. The layers of facade, vacant lots, and remnants of infrastructure are honest indications of the motivations of the residents and the stories they have left in their path.

My work is primarily oil paint on wood panels. Although I received my degree in graphic design at the University of South Carolina, I drifted into oil painting as an extension of a mural-painting endeavor. My work functions as records of an exploration of a place and of its depiction on the panel. Working from my own photographs, I select images that indicate a sense of fascination, a level of observation that comes from being in an unfamiliar place.

Although I am very familiar with the environment in which I'm photographing, I try to wander and observe as a stranger might. Once I have selected the image I wish to paint, I am no longer creating a painting of that place; I am making a painting of the photograph. By this process I focus on the act of painting and not on the illusion of the image. The paintings are very much about the surface of the panel. The shapes and colors, the blurred edges and distortions that are created by the degradation of the photographic process are the subjects of my work. Through this process, I seek to create paintings that are honest depictions of both place and process.

Saturdays Last Spin
Oil on panel
36" X 48"

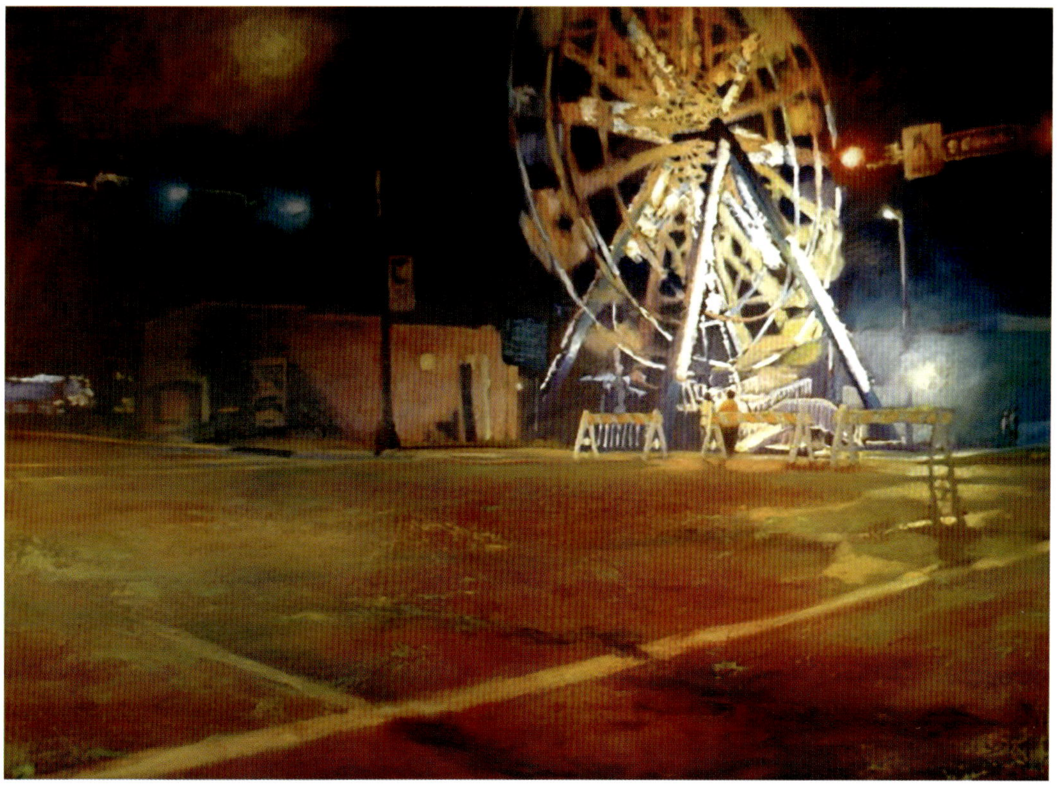

Mike Corbin

I grew up in the Midwest and attended the University of Cincinnati, where I met my wife, Nancy Linn. In 1976 we fled the Ohio winters and came to Spartanburg to teach art and raise our three sons. I retired from teaching art full-time at Carver Junior High School four years ago and now work part-time at Spartanburg Day School.

One of my earliest and clearest childhood memories is of a mural my mother painted on the bathroom wall above the big iron bathtub, a playful and fanciful depiction of Jonah and the Whale with many fish and birds. I remember watching my mother paint it, amazed. I wanted to do it too and began drawing and painting a lot after that.

In my early thirties, I rediscovered photography and began teaching it to my students in junior high. I became a little obsessed with taking pictures and built a series of darkrooms. Long-time Clemson University photography professor Sam Wang taught me one summer. I discovered that Spartanburg was home to a small but talented pool of photographers with shared enthusiasms: Mark Olencki, Carroll Foster, and Steve Stinson among them.

An interest in history and my past experience working in the peach industry as a state inspector led to my two-year documentation of the Cash family peach farm in Cowpens. This collection of photographs and history that was first exhibited in Spartanburg in 1997 and traveled to several locations around the country became the basis for the Hub City book, Family Trees: *The Peach Culture of the Piedmont*.

I have been fortunate to create several corporate collections of photographs over the years. The first one I did, for the Gibbs Cancer Treatment Center at Spartanburg Regional, is one of the more memorable experiences of my life. I got to meet and photograph people in five counties for two years. Thank you, Dr. Julian Josey and Tom Jennings. It was exhausting but exciting.

What has always amazed me about photography is how beautiful and moving it can be and in so many ways.

Harold Hatcher, Spartanburg, 1999 copy

Photograph

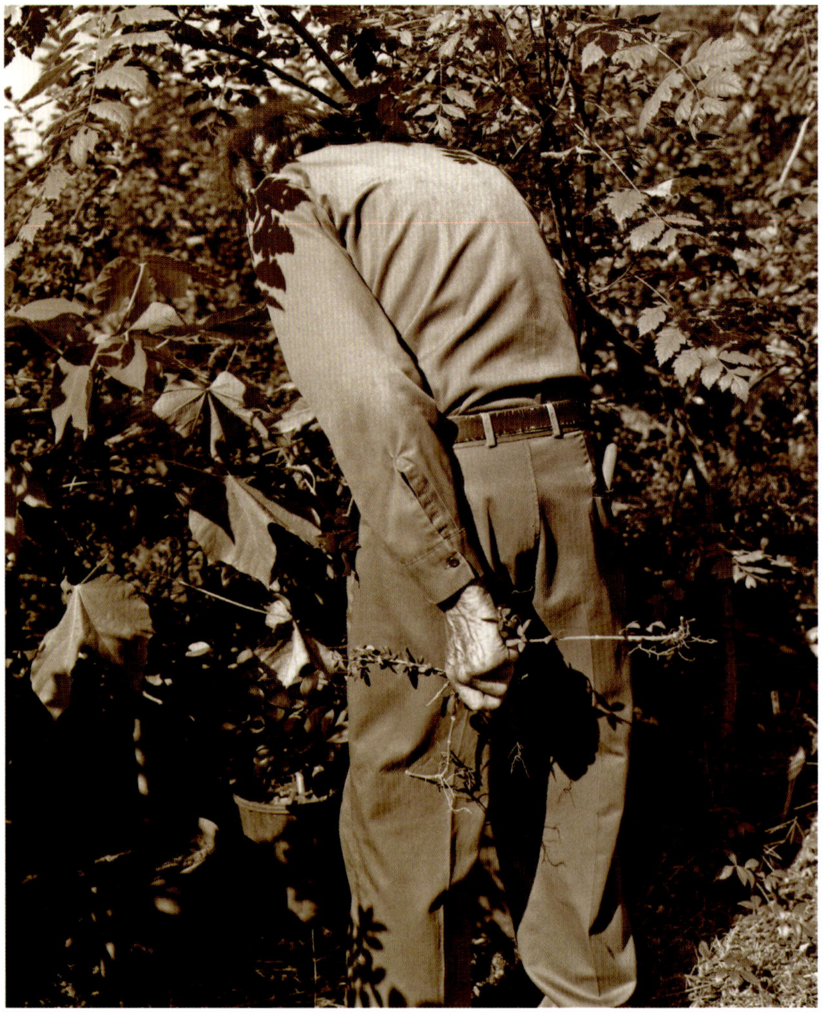

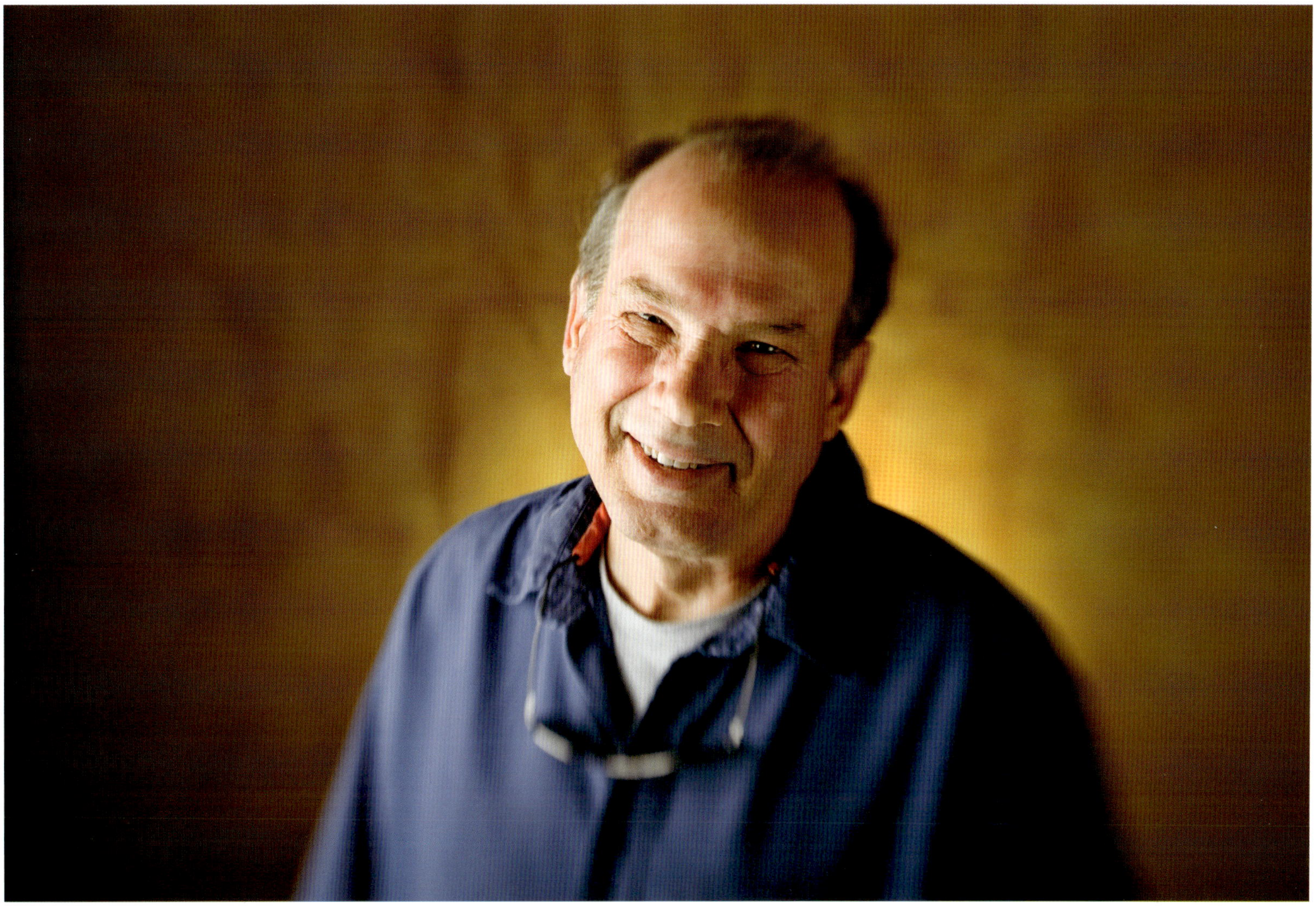

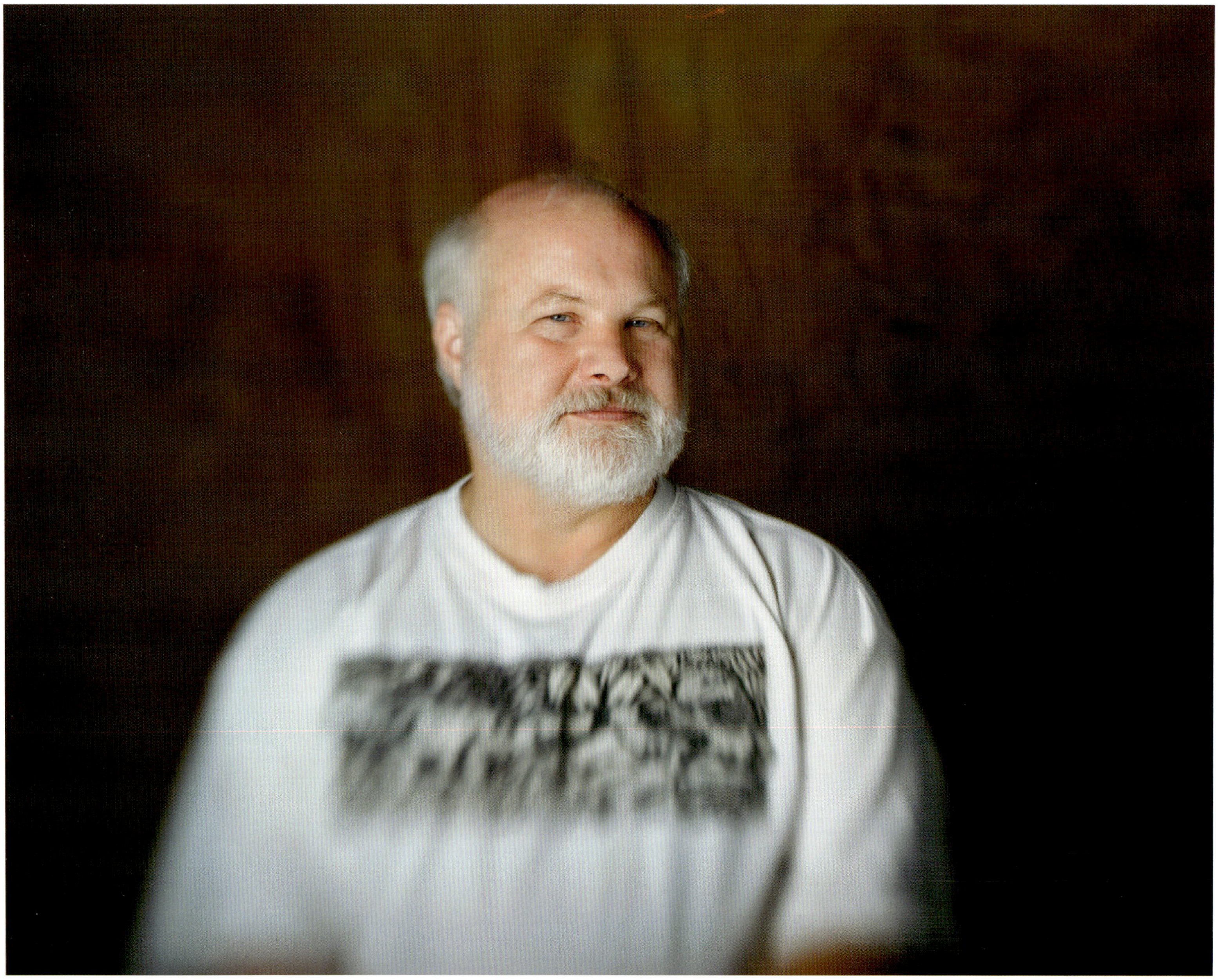

Jim Creal

I was born and raised in Spartanburg and got my lifelong interest in art from my family. When we traveled we often would go into the art museums. My father loved to draw cartoon-like caricatures in the margins of his work papers.

I have had a varied education and work history and have lived in many different places. I studied art at the University of Montana. In 1992, upon graduation, I moved back to Spartanburg and have been here ever since. I enjoyed getting to know the artists here, many of whom are not only quite talented but also are warm and embracing. I have had a great deal of support from this community and the institutions here, for which I am grateful.

I am engaged in the creation of cohesive bodies of work through select traditional print processes. I make landscapes, still lifes, and nonrepresentational images, and I develop these bodies of work through monotype (unique prints), lithography, and etching print processes.

I started out working in monotypes. I enjoy the fluidity and speed of this process and the crispness of the mark. Most often I work non-representationally, exploring combinations of texture, movement, and tone. I work to create strong formal abstractions with elegant gestural movement.

Many observers of my early monotypes thought they looked like lithographs, and I subsequently studied lithography briefly with Boyd Saunders at the University of South Carolina. In lithography I have found a love of the rich drawing possibilities it offers. In this medium, I create landscapes of our South Carolina coast.

My etched images develop in an evolutionary process involving many stages along the way. I enjoy building the images up through the addition of multiple steps to add line, texture, and tones. I love the richness and dimensionality of its printed surface.

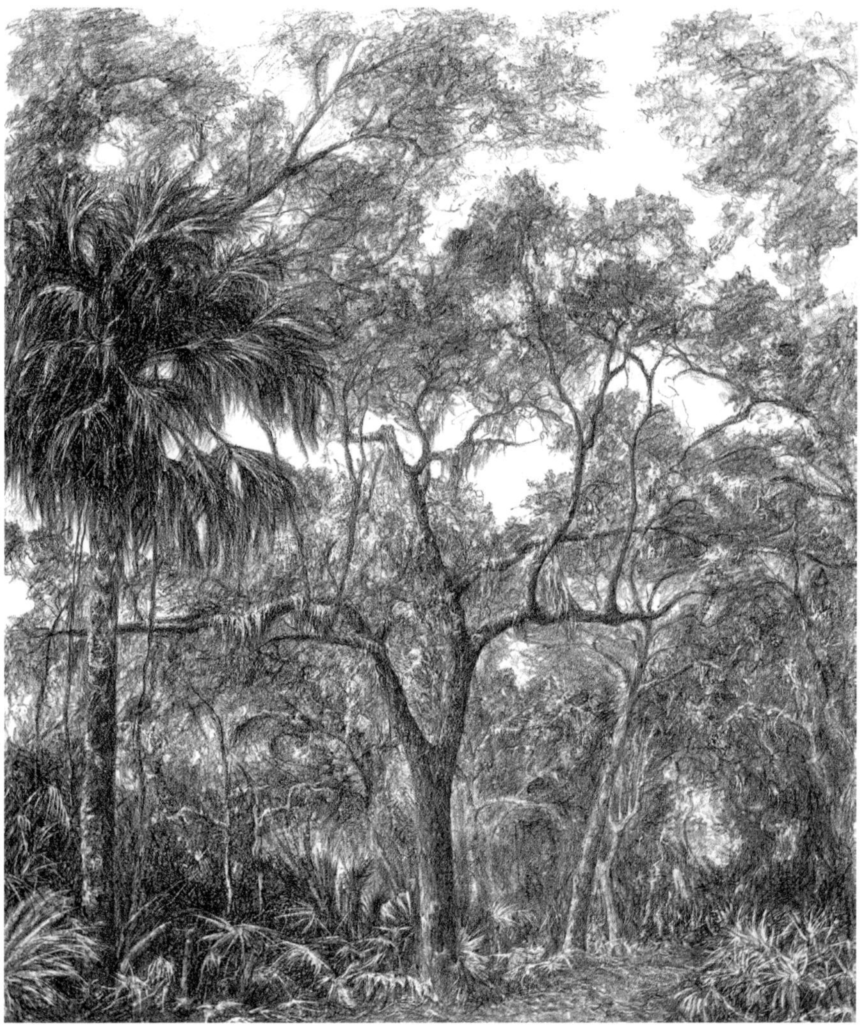

Forest Interior - Prichards Island Series

Lithograph

16" X 13"

Ann Richards Crenshaw

I was born and grew up in the farmlands of South Carolina near Florence. From my second-story bedroom window I saw my first canvas: I was just high enough to enjoy the views of beautiful expanses of land with patterns and colors of forest-rimmed fields. My love of landscapes was born.

Life later brought me visits to see my great aunts in the sand hills of the state. A beautiful painting hung in their home in Liberty Hill of their collie, Duster. The rendering was of "man's best friend," resting on their front porch. It was a peaceful painting and provided me pleasant memories of blissful times with Duster, warm summer evenings, and more. Those were moments, as a young girl, that nudged me toward a desire to artistically capture and recreate.

Florence also had a wonderful museum, and throughout my childhood I attended many shows and functions with my parents. On many days after school I would find myself engrossed in classes the museum sponsored. Rooms and halls of Egyptian artifacts, Chinese vases, and cultures of the world were ours to wander and imagine. I count this uninterrupted time to absorb it all as one of the building blocks of my art appreciation.

Although oil is my current medium of choice, I suppose it is my past that calls me back to venture in watercolors and, from time to time, pastels. In the end I guess I love it all. As for subject matter—who knows?—perhaps a landscape, or a Chinese vase, or maybe even a dog named Duster resting on the stoop.

Talented people abound in Spartanburg, and I remain impressed by the creative artists of all media. Our community is a lover of the arts, and I am always in awe of the number of participants who give of their time, talents, and encouragement of art in all forms. Most of all, I am grateful to be embraced by many, and glad to be counted among them.

Free to run
Oil on board
8" X 16"

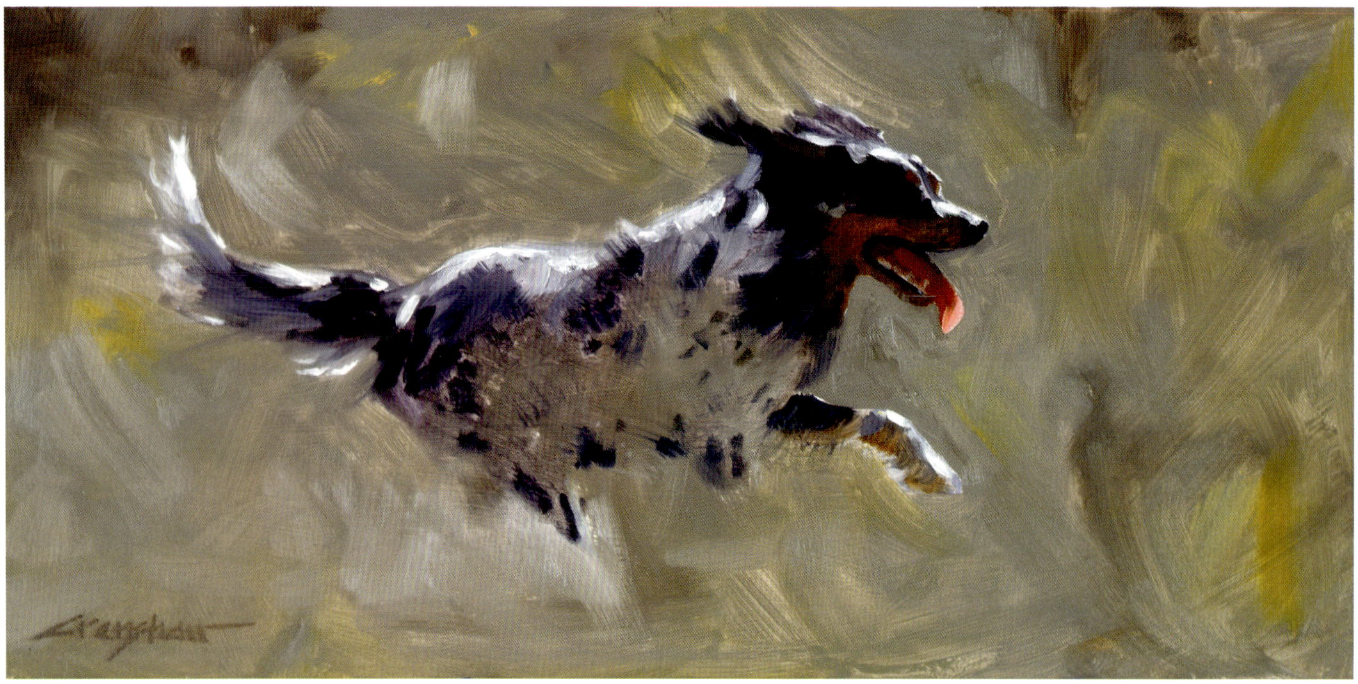

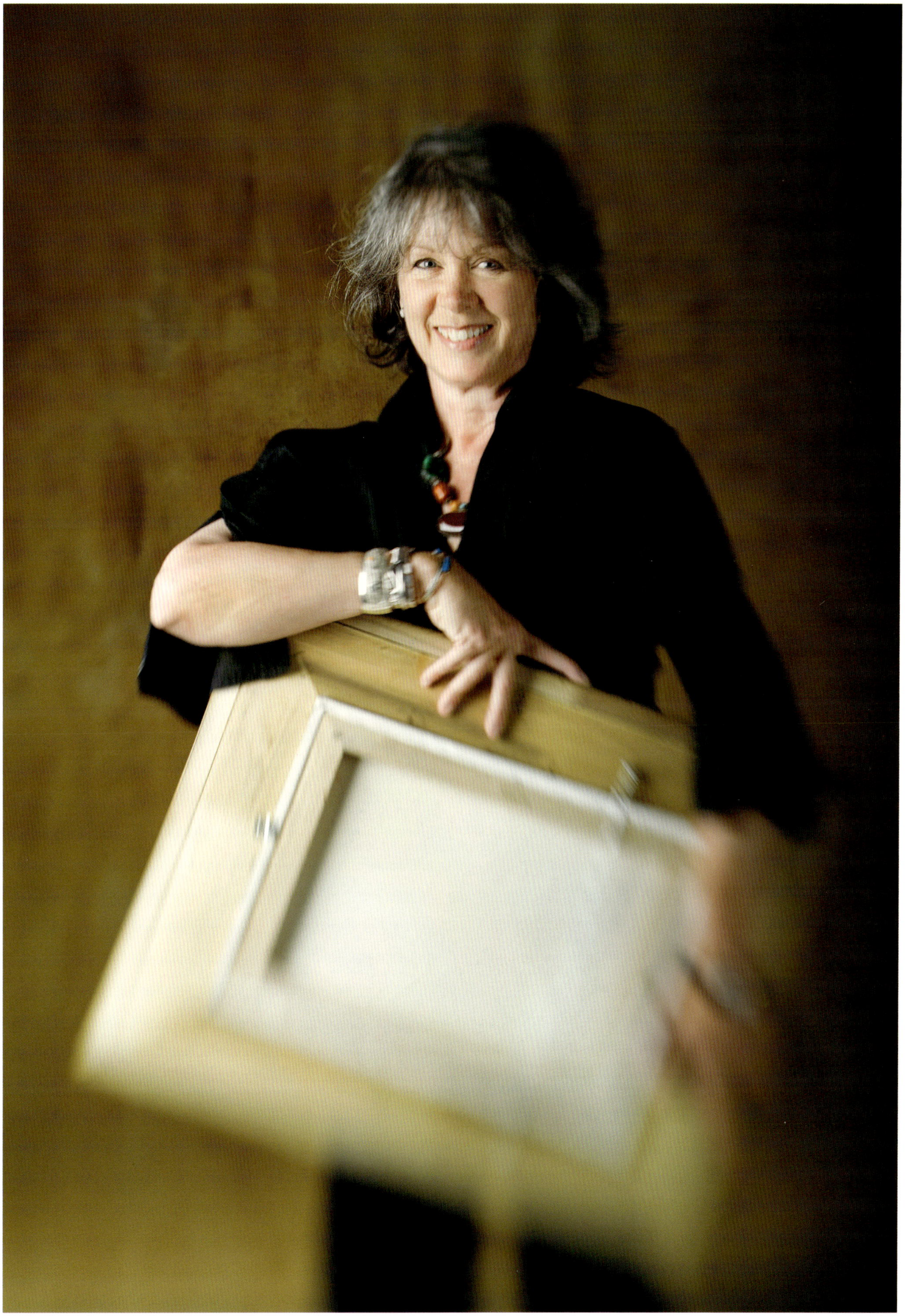

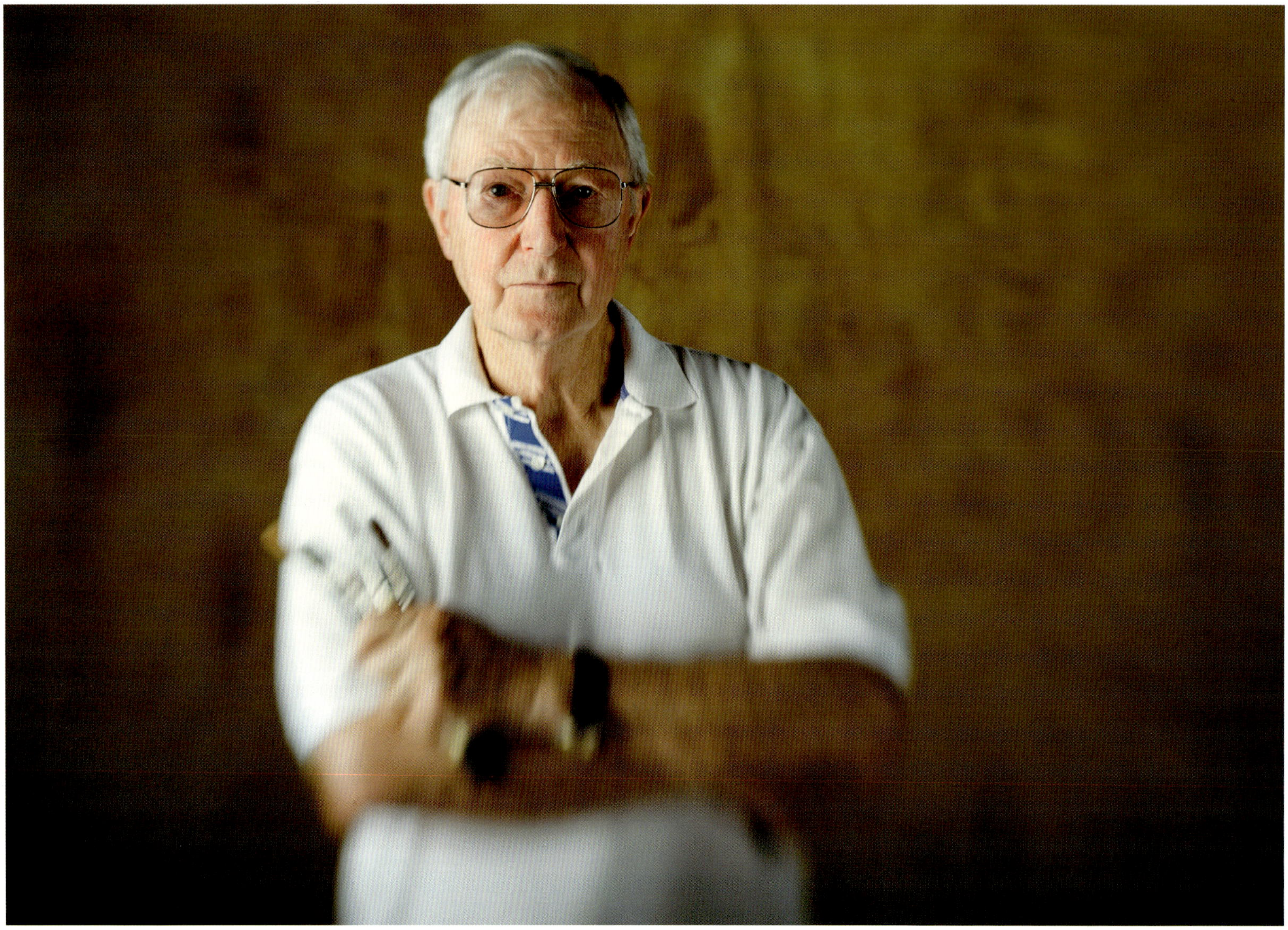

Daniel Cromer

Blue Train

Watercolor

30" X 42"

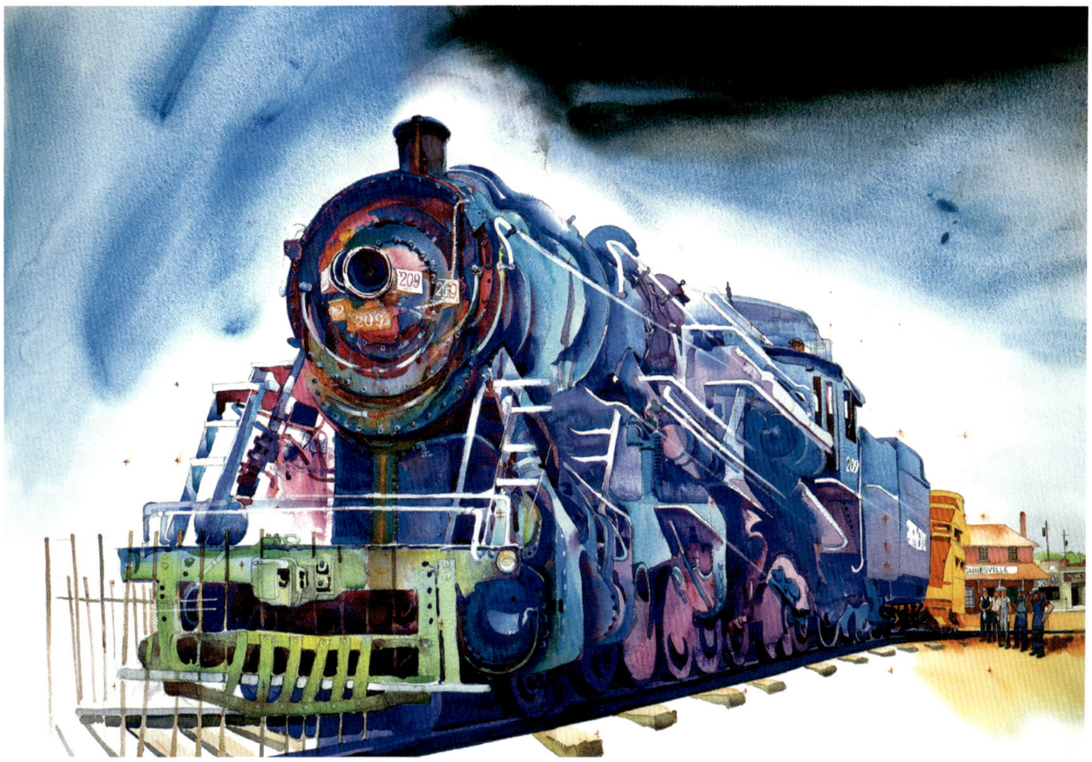

I grew up in Spartanburg, and from the day I could crawl, I have loved the outdoors and landscapes—from Hogback Mountain to the coastal dunes of Myrtle Beach. As soon as I could, I lived outside and began to hold onto everything I could see and touch and keep. As a child I knew nothing about "art" itself, but from time to time, my parents, family, and teachers gave me books, pencils, paper, chalk, colors—whatever was available in the 1930s and '40s.

After high school, my serious learning about "professional arts" began and led me to study at five art schools, ending at the Art Center School in Los Angeles. At graduation, I was offered a scholarship for further study, and the wonderful founder of the school personally set up introductions with key people in the exciting New York art world.

I lived in New York for six years, establishing a joint career as both a fine artist and a commercial artist. Then I went to live for thirty years in Europe, based in London. Part of my life was as art director, designer, and creative director for other people. The deep, interior part of me was an artist, working from a private studio, traveling from Scandinavia to Greece and Egypt to Africa, painting happily outdoors, capturing landscapes for the galleries in London and the walls of people who liked my work.

Finally in 1993 I returned home to South Carolina. You may ask, "Why?" And I will simply say, "Red clay does not wash off!" I have been happily astonished to find the streets of Spartanburg full of young and old artists—writers, painters, musicians, etc.—with their heads full of ideas and their hands full of notebooks of ideas, and everybody with those tiny hand-machines held against their ears talking to their pals and artist friends at the other end of Morgan Square or New York, or London, or San Diego!

Chris Crowley

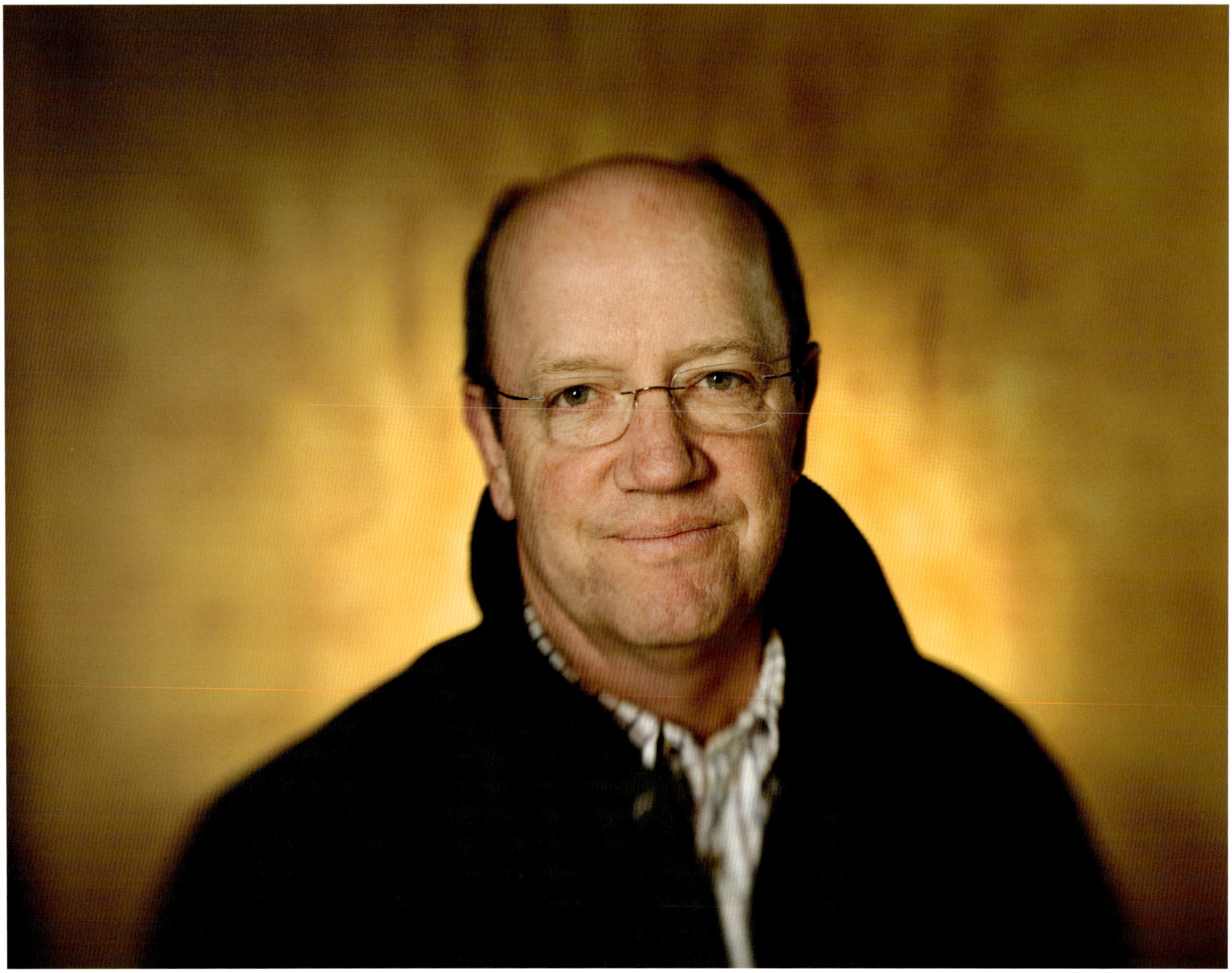

Spartanburg was a very different place when I grew up. It was a smaller, more rural community of screen porches and games of tag after supper, a place where everyone knew you and your family. The warmth and the Southern charm of the people are what have made Spartanburg home to me. The town has developed over the years, but I still love our little town.

Drawing was as natural as breathing to me as I grew up. Whenever I had a pencil in my hand, I drew things. I never really thought about it much; I just did it and still do. Linda Hudgins, my art teacher at the Spartanburg Day School, taught me how to interpret what I saw differently and encouraged me to keep sketching. The artist community of Spartanburg is like that. This vibrant, talented group encourages artists to persevere as they take those first baby steps in pursuit of their craft. Artists that I admire—like Dorothy Josey, Linda McCane, and Jane Nodine—are always encouraging me to keep painting. This community spirit is why so much is going on in Spartanburg's art scene.

My earliest interest in art was sparked by my mother and my older brother, Jerry. Jerry is an incredibly talented artist, and I learned a lot just by watching him paint. My medium is oil on canvas or board, and I have little formal art training. I am a representational painter, focusing primarily on still life and landscapes, and I find that natural light and the natural world provide all the inspiration I need to paint. I rarely look at things these days without imagining how I would paint them or what colors I would use. I love making the paintings, and I hope people enjoy them.

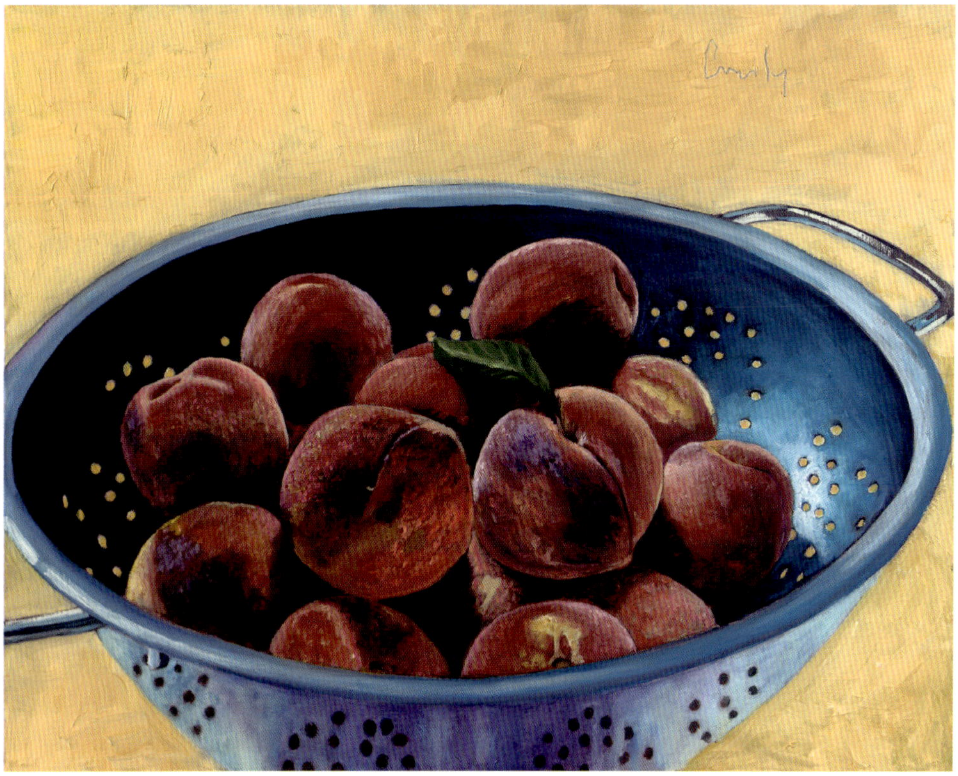

Peaches

Oil on canvas

16" X 20"

Jim Cullen

After thirty-four years in the film and video production industry in Chicago, I retired to a small area outside Campobello, South Carolina, called Little Chicago.

My art education began in high school, although I have drawn pictures since I could hold a pencil. I had great support from my high school art teacher, my industrial arts instructors, and my parents. I attended the Institute of Design at Illinois Institute of Technology in Chicago and studied commercial design and photography. After two years in Germany, compliments of the U. S. Army, I returned to Chicago to study motion picture and television production at Columbia College of Communications.

In 1976 I was introduced to clay; it was my hobby until I retired in 2003, and now it consumes almost all of my time, either teaching or making pots. Currently I'm teaching at the Spartanburg Art Museum Art School and at Tryon Arts and Crafts in Tryon, North Carolina.

My pots provide me a canvas, a surface on which I can paint or carve patterns, designs, or elements that convey my thoughts and feelings. For me, the making of pots is a form of meditation. Not until you have actually lifted a wall from a spinning lump of Mother Earth do you understand the Magic, the Quiet, and the Thrill of making pots. The decorating of pots is my form of communication. Until you have experienced the thought process involved with facing a blank canvas, not knowing what it is that you want to say or how to say it, do you understand the satisfaction, the exhilaration, and the accomplishment of making pots.

My pots are an extension of me, of my life, of my experience. They give me joy and relaxation. They speak to me in intimate terms, in undulations and responses without words. I give my pots shape and form; they give me untold moments of pleasure.

Grasslands #5
Wheelthrown clay
8" X 9" X 9"

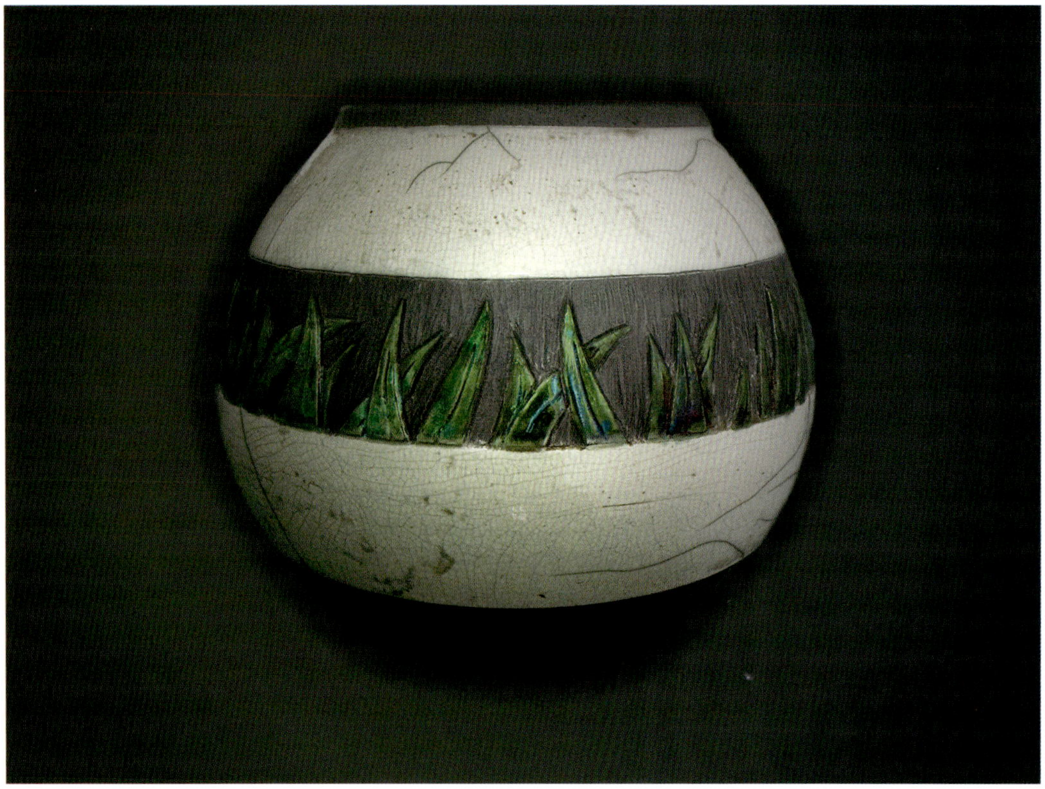

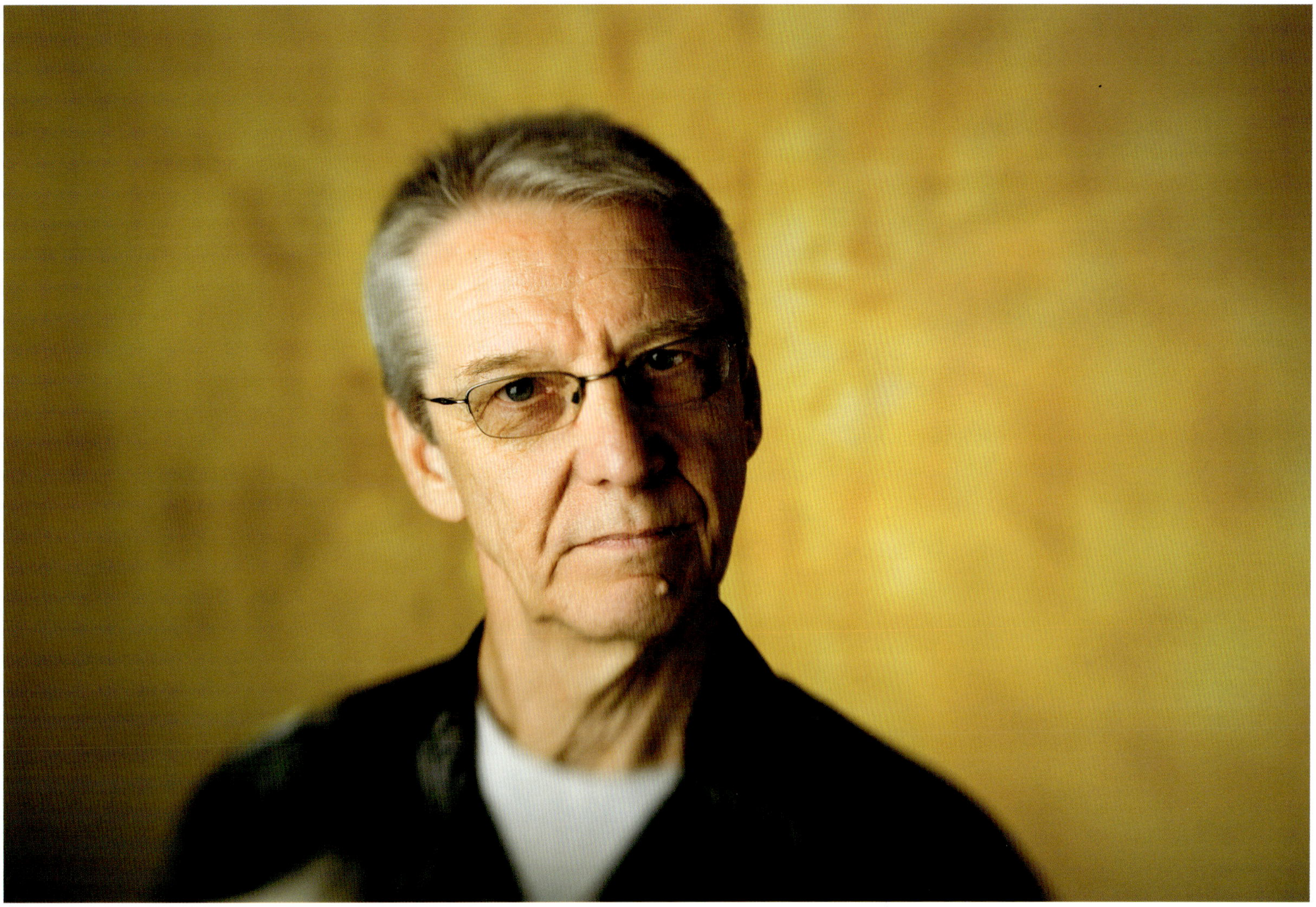

Scott Cunningham

The core values that have been instilled in me have been shaped by generations of folks who settled both sides of the Savannah River and the South Carolina Sandhills. As I have grown, family stories have taken on new significance, and the sense of place I instinctively had has evolved into a deep appreciation of the beauty and brutality of the land that my forbearers called home.

Spartanburg is in the heart of an area of that is blessed with an exceptional pool of artistic talent. A congenial spirit binds this talent into a community that is unlike any I've experienced elsewhere. The expected competitiveness is tempered by the unexpected support of numerous colleague-friends, each expressing encouragement that the other be the best that he or she can be. As a result, the fruit of this environment has a sincerity that seldom confuses pretentiousness with sophistication. It is at once cosmopolitan and provincial and reflects the enthusiasm and vitality of an artist community that continually reinvests its talents in itself.

I did study art, and for years I worked as a technical illustrator and graphic designer. However, it was several pieces of literature that I read during a stint as an art history major in college that were pivotal in my understanding of and approach to art. One of these was Heinrich Wölfflin's *Principles of Art History*. At that time, Wölfflin's five pairs of oppositional precepts provided me with a framework in which I would begin to understand and explore the formal elements of art.

Thematically, my work is about people, the environments in which they live, and how they relate to one another within those environments. Even in the absence of an obvious human element, the nature that I visualize reflects upon humanity; in the back of my mind, there is always an awareness of how man's ambitions impact nature and are ultimately frustrated by it.

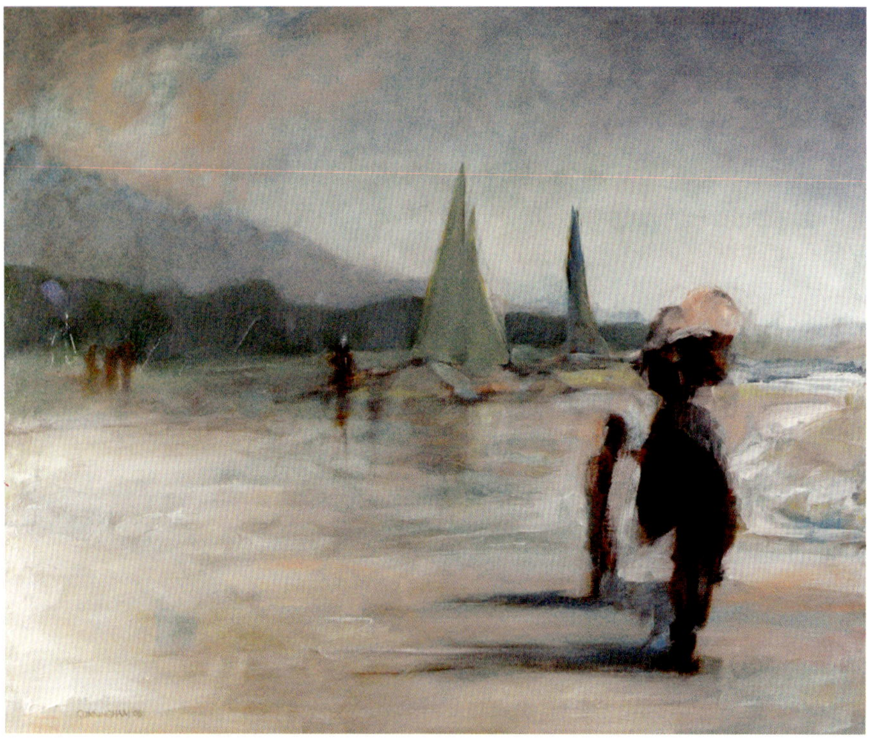

Marooned
Oil on board
30" X 36"

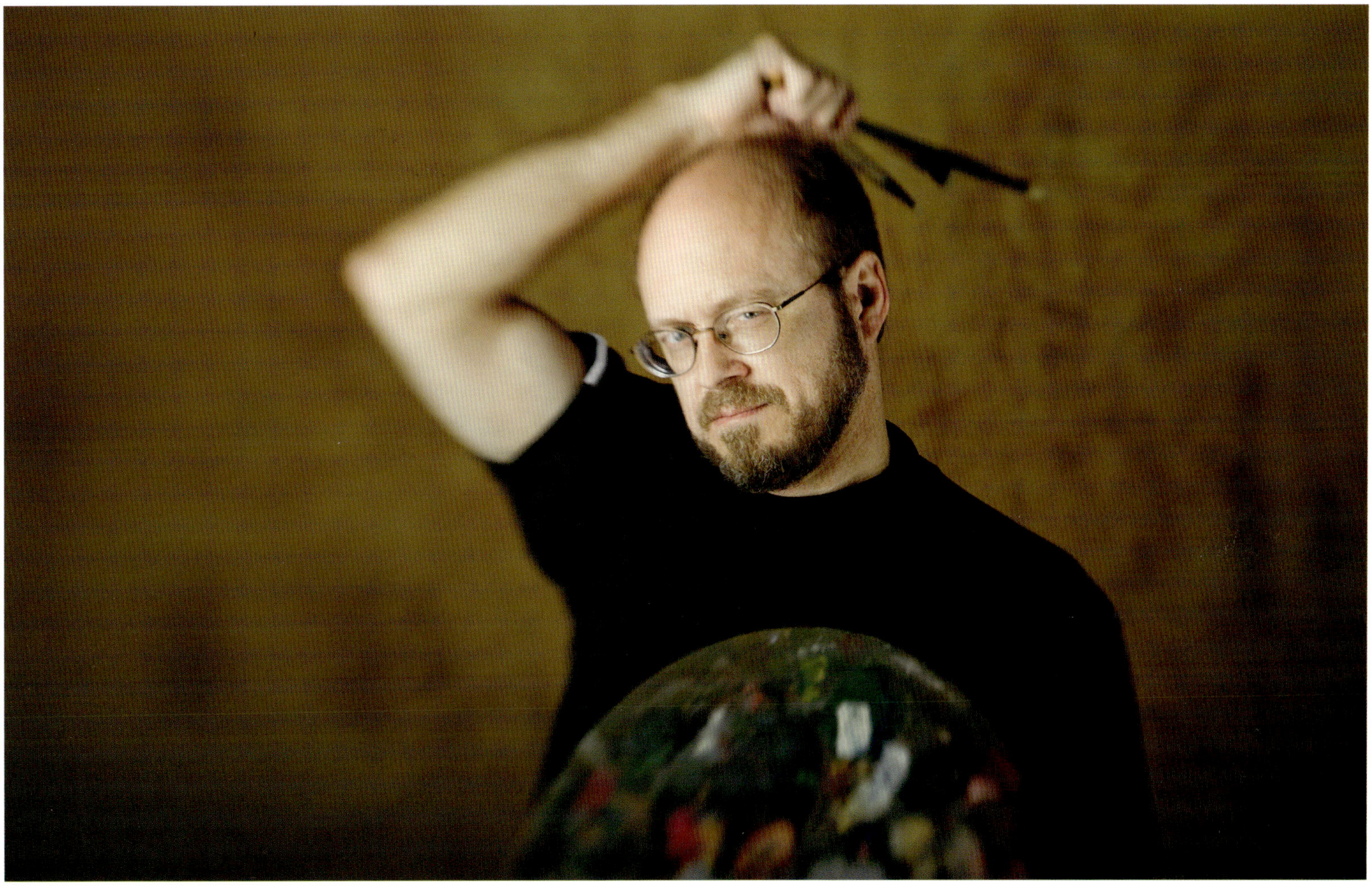

David Datwyler

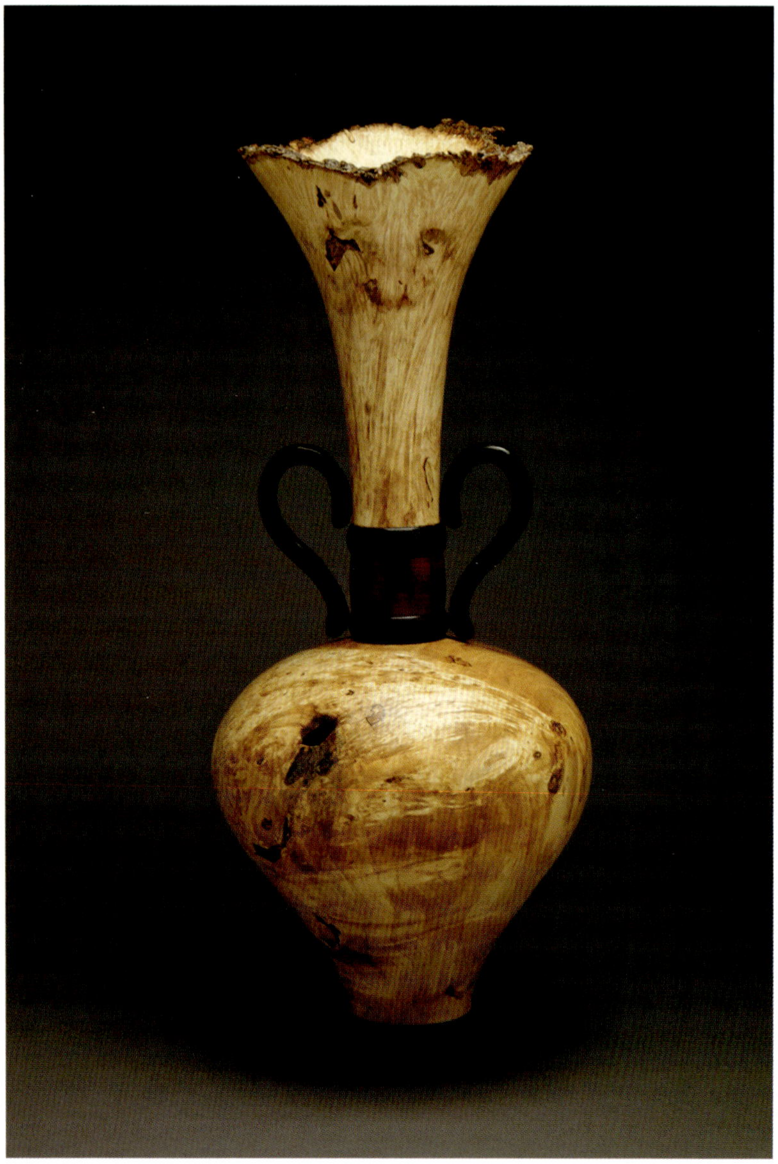

Loutrophoros
Elder burl, ebony and padauk
26" X 10" X 10"

I am a Utah native now living in Spartanburg and working full time as a certified registered nurse anesthetist. While working as a traveling nurse in the early 1990s, I gained an interest in art. My travels allowed for the opportunity to visit museums and galleries all over the country. During an assignment in the Carolinas I discovered wood-turning as an art form through the Southern Highland Craft Guild. Little did I know that fifteen years later I would take up wood-turning and become a member of that guild.

I have always been drawn to wood in furniture, architecture, and art. The natural beauty of the grain, the look and feel of different finishes, and the unique smell of each type of wood has always touched my soul. I have particularly admired the balance of manmade shapes with the beauty of the natural textures found in wood-turning.

With each piece I turn I aim to push the limits of my ability and vision while also reaching for the limit of the wood. Wood is a liquid medium—natural bark inclusions, the direction of the grain and knots, rot, fungi, cracks, and insect damage are all factors in the final form of a piece. Even when completed, the shape and the texture of the wood may continue to change as the piece dries.

As I shape wood, the process of turning shapes me. Therefore my art will continue to change and evolve as I experiment with new techniques, styles, forms, and shapes.

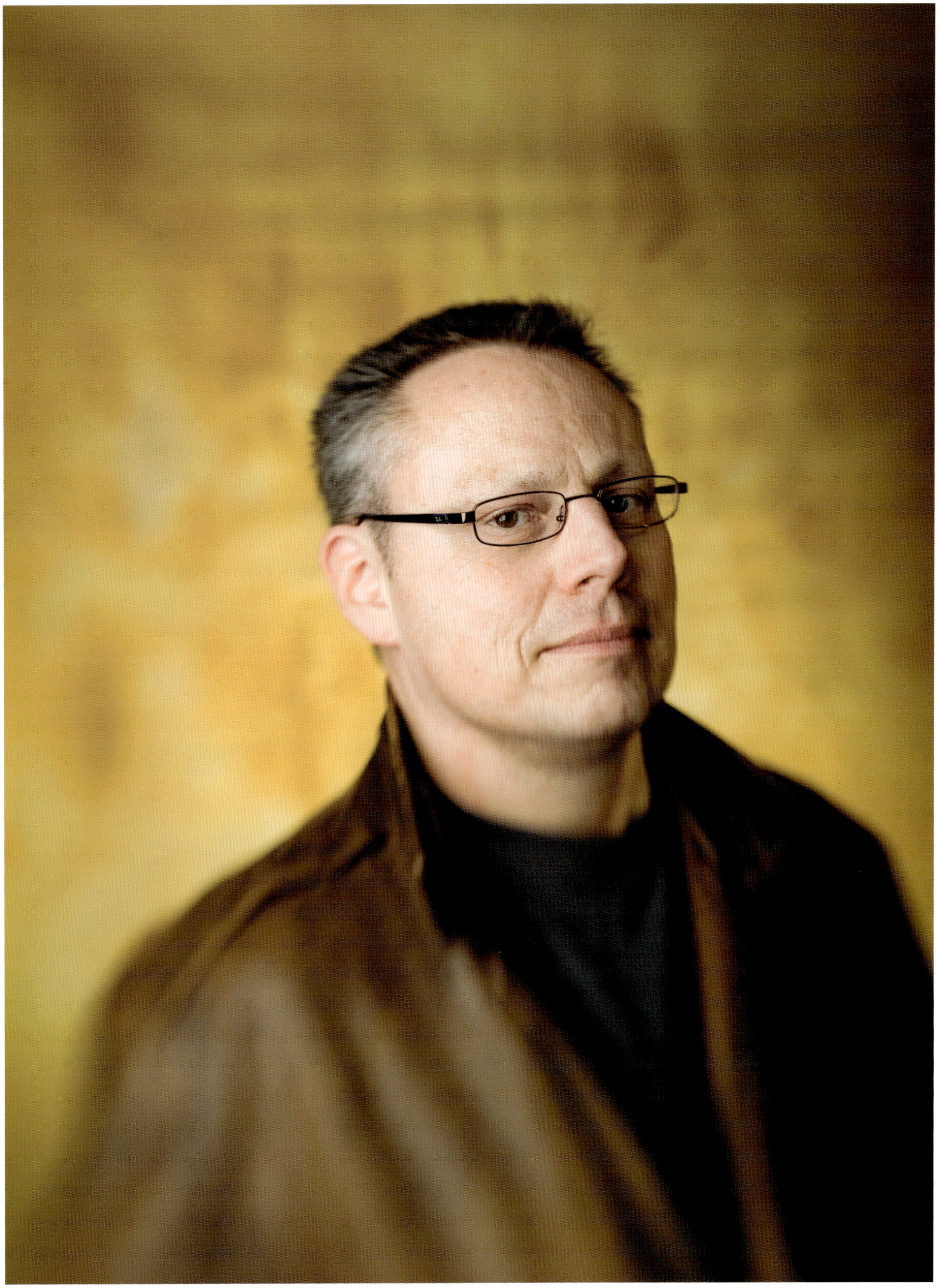

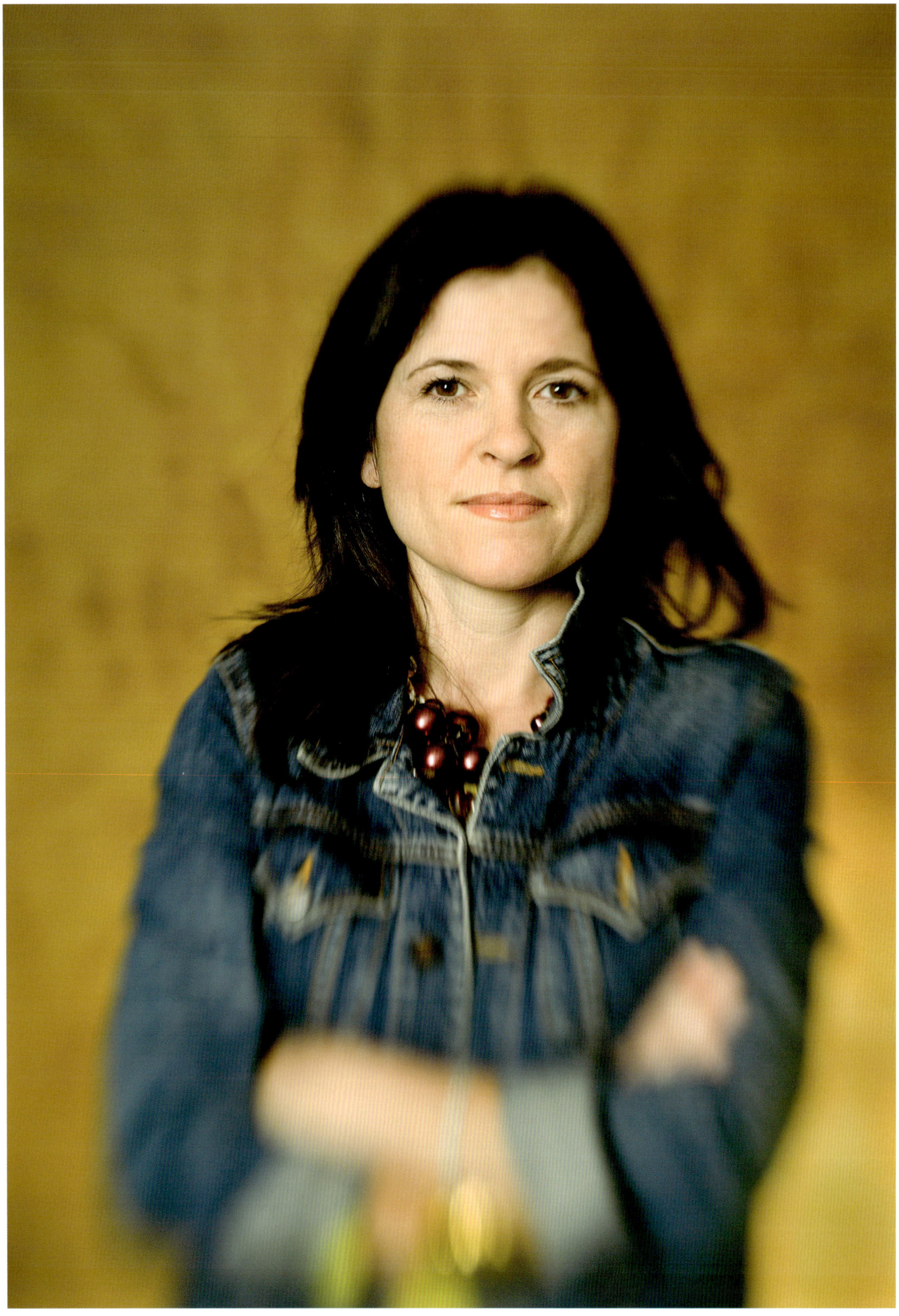

Page Jones Davis

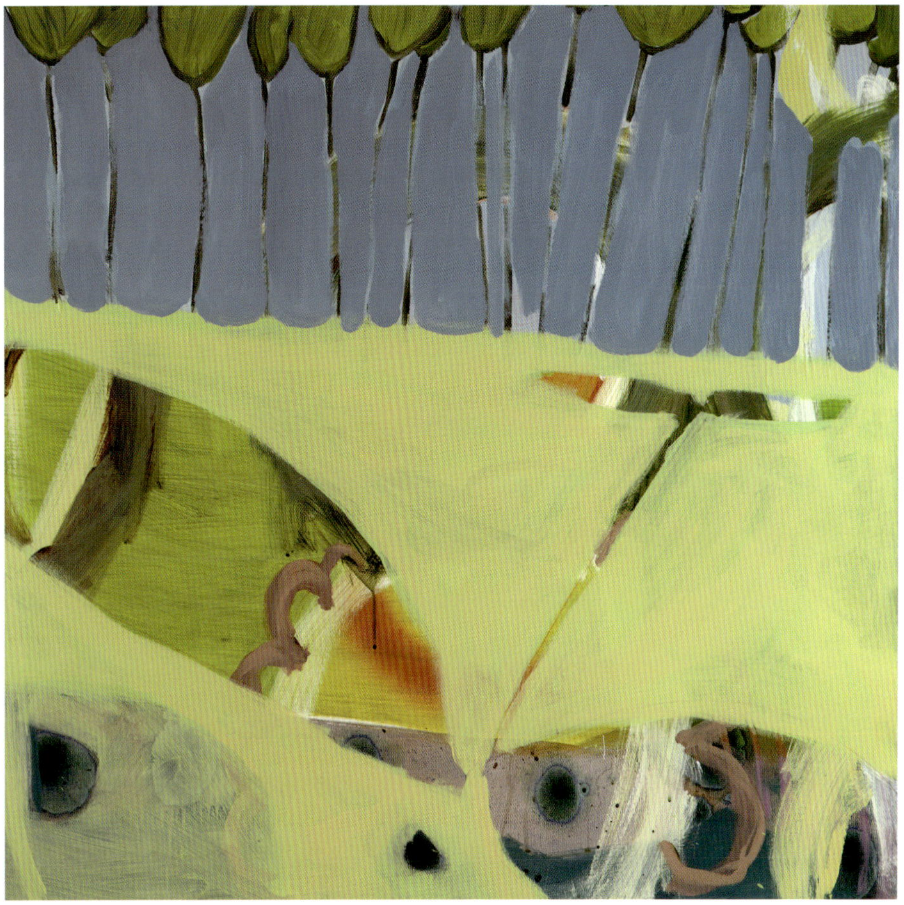

Heli
Oil on canvas
40" X 40"

I have been drawing and painting for as long as I can remember. Even at an early age, my interest in art grew from a feeling of accomplishment in art classes. Making art and teaching others to make art has been an ever-present and rewarding gift in my life.

I grew up in Spartanburg but lived in many places before returning to my hometown. Spartanburg has been incredibly supportive of my family and my work as an artist. It is so full of talented people who desire to create a vibrant art community.

I attended the South Carolina Governor's School for the Arts and Humanities, received a BFA in studio art from the University of South Carolina, studied abroad with the University of Georgia's Cortona, Italy program, studied with Boter-Santalo Tallier in Barcelona, and eventually received an MA in painting from Savannah College of Art and Design. I have been producing my own work and teaching in my studio for eighteen years.

In my studio I enjoy combining disparate images gleaned from memories, from my immediate surroundings, or sometimes from my children's drawings. I start each piece by layering pigment and varying textures onto the canvas. The process of responding to the results of the manipulation of the paint on the surface is what makes my work immediate. I let the composition evolve spontaneously, trying not to have a preconceived plan for the outcome. The game of improvisation never tires me: making marks, reacting, arranging, and re-arranging the images. Each painting builds layer upon layer until it reaches its own sense of balance. I study the form, line, and color, taking each into consideration as a dialogue takes place on the surface. I try not to take my artist-self too seriously—painting is a means of expressing my truest nature. I find that in front of a canvas I am my most honest, natural self.

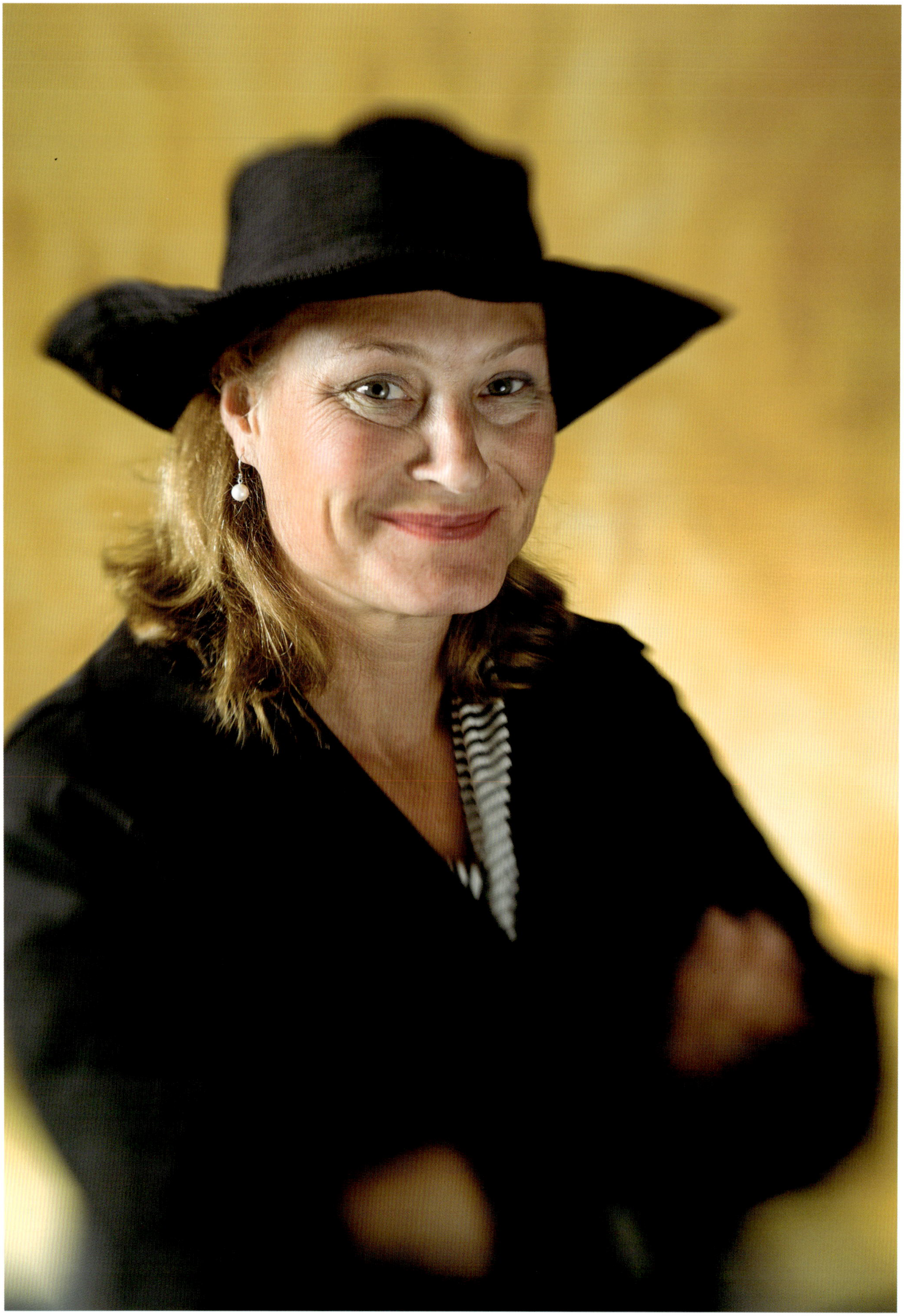

Jane Dempsey

Living and working in Spartanburg has been a gift. Converse College awarded me a BFA in 1991, and, having fallen in love with this art town, I never wanted to live anywhere else. My former professors, David Zacharias, Teresa Prater, Mayo Mac Boggs, and the late Judy Jones, encouraged me to trust my nature in all situations. Therefore, to this day I give the four of them credit for my overall survival.

Living in a small culturally rich community has given me the courage to be my own brand of smart. I lean on a support system of fellow artists here.

Gardening is my passion. I simply paint flowers that I grow, flowers I that tend to, and flowers that I imagine growing. Being humble is comfortable. Being small is safe. Being appreciative is the lynchpin, the facilitator—the water, if you will, for the garden and the flowers and the painting and ultimately the survival. We are so small, and yet there are smaller still creatures in our gardens. How do they view the colors? How do they interact with the smells, the textures, and the overall size? Their perspective is different, and I imagine so are their opinions. Different but valid all the same. When all is said and done, we are all nothing more than sunshine and water!

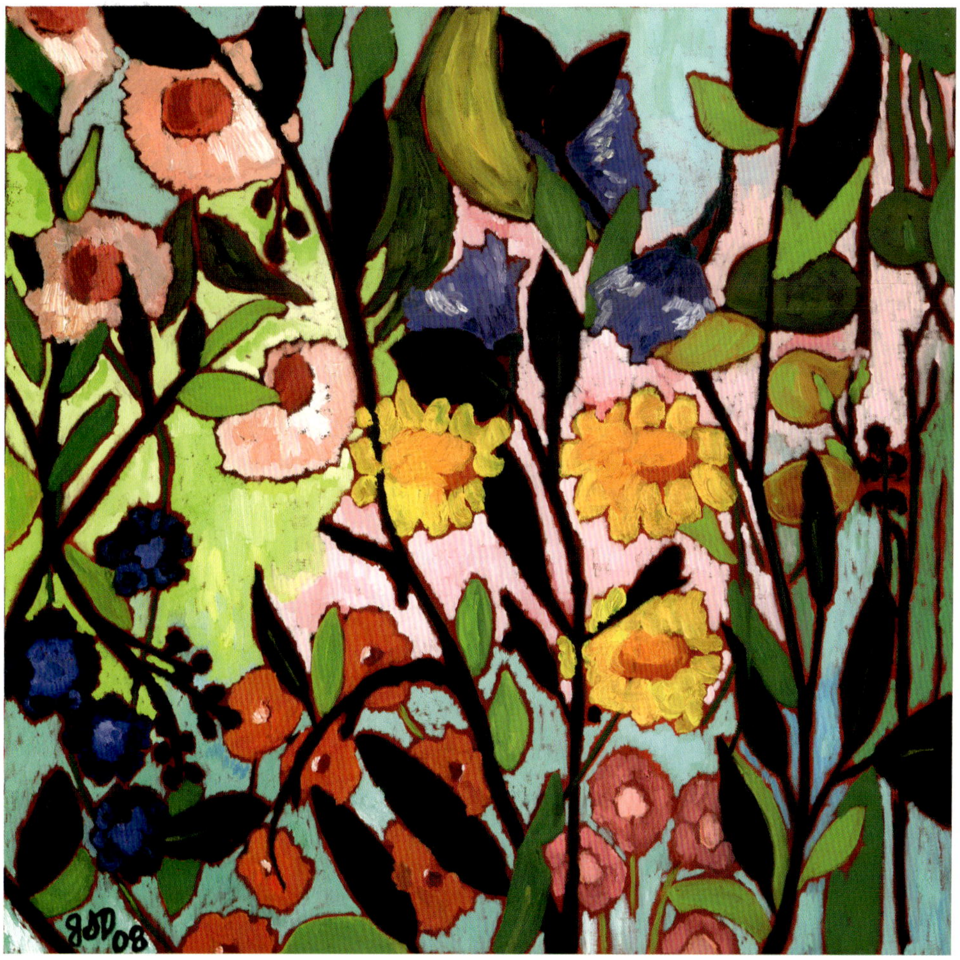

Small ... In the Garden
Oil on canvas
30" X 30"

Dottie Dillard

At a young age I studied ballet with Nina Stroganova and Lisan Kay at the Ballet Arts Studio in Carnegie Hall. Later, I was awarded a full scholarship with America Ballet Theatre, where I studied with Dimitri Romanoff, Alexandra Danilova, and other noted instructors. Between the ages of fifteen and seventeen, I was a member of the Ballet Company of Radio City Music Hall.

I received a scholarship to attend college, which subsequently changed the direction of my life. Graduating with degrees in English, French, and education, I was hired by the Department of Defense as a teacher in the school system for dependent military children in Germany. There I met my husband, Toney. With a love for travel, I have lived in two foreign countries and traveled in more than forty others.

A self-taught photographer—originally with an emphasis on nature photography—I photographed my first ballet performance in 1997 and subsequently embraced dance photography with a passion that reflects my knowledge and love of that art form.

Specializing in performance photography, I have photographed some of the greatest dancers in the world, including several gold medal winners. I worked as a company photographer with Ballet Internationale, which was under the artistic direction of Eldar Aliev, the principal dancer with the world renowned Kirov Ballet for thirteen years. Other ballet companies I have photographed include San Francisco Ballet, Atlanta Ballet, Ballet Arlington, and Washington Ballet, and some of my images have appeared in *Pointe* magazine.

My recent body of work includes close-up photographs of butterflies and hummingbirds in flight. These creatures mimic my most recent images of dancers as they hover, twirl, and pose in nature. I hope to present a sense of universal timelessness by recording the essence of a moment in time, creating images that are more like paintings than photographs.

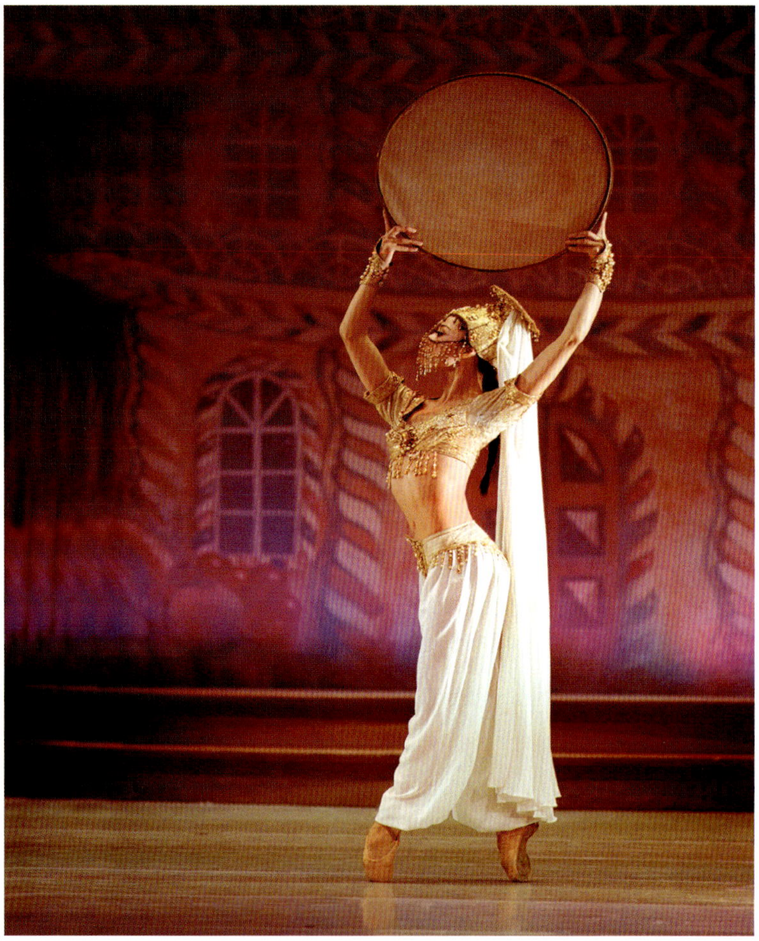

The Nutcracker #5

Photograph

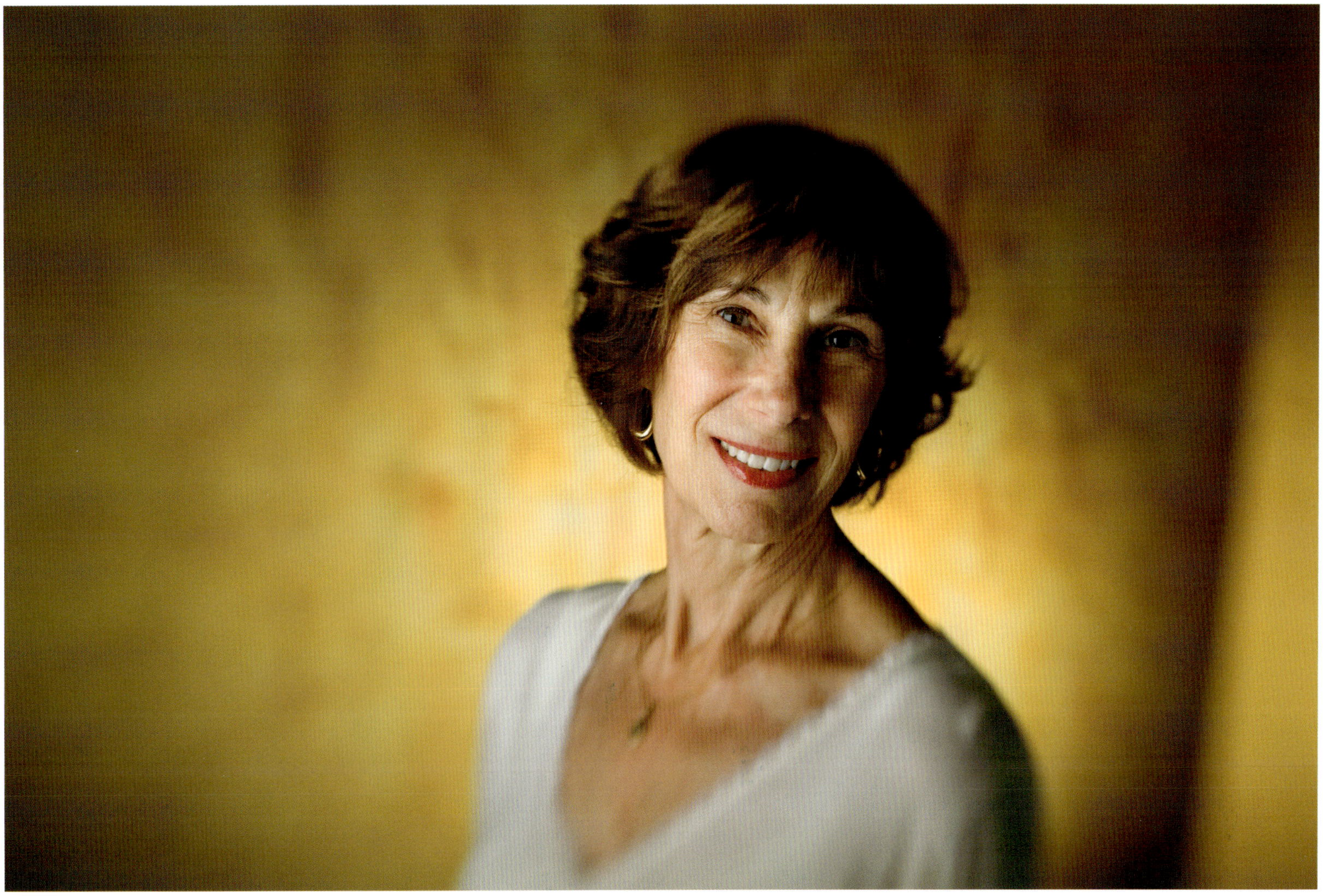

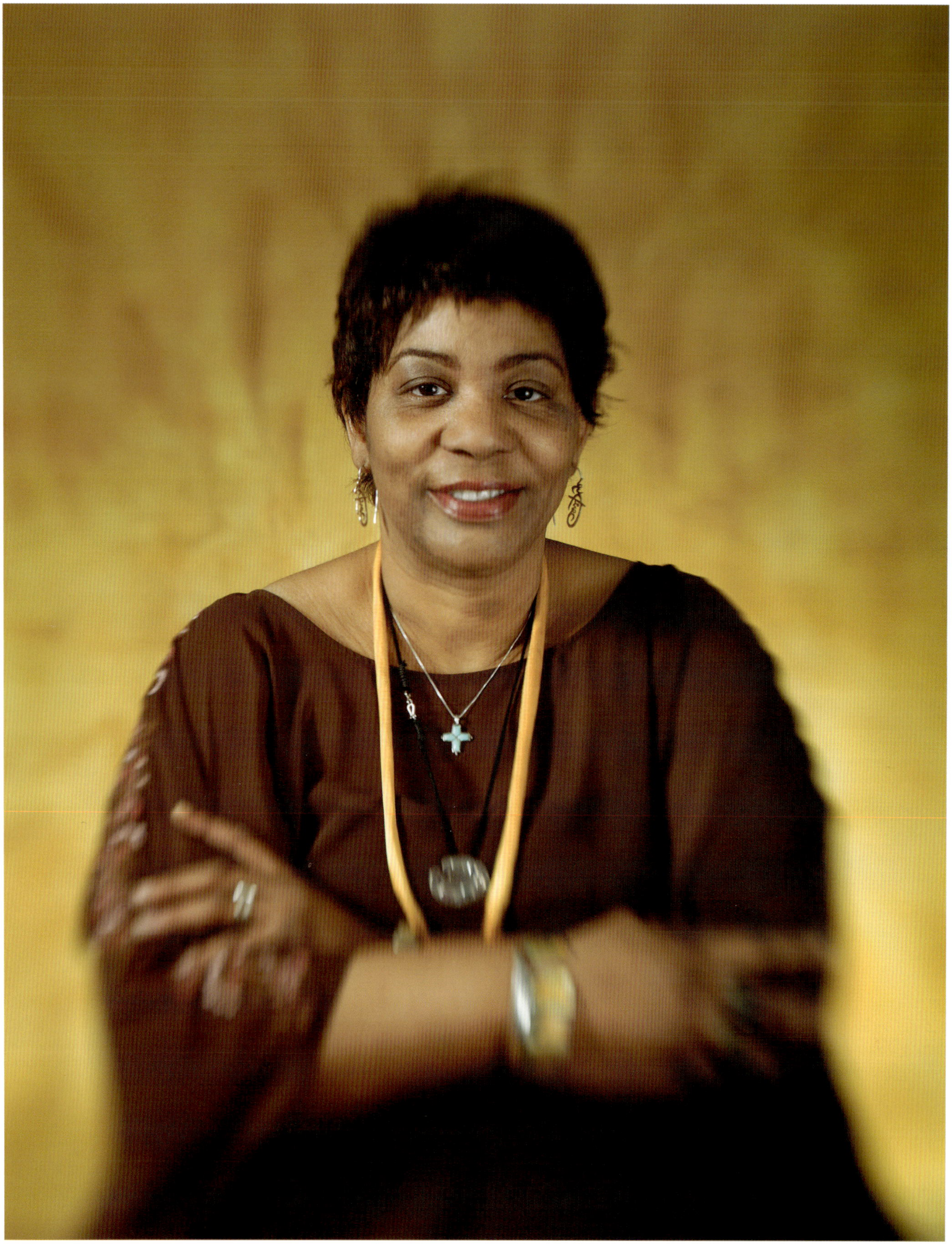

Geri Dye

I am a native of Spartanburg who moved away at the age of twenty-three. I define myself as a born-gifted artist who was discovered by my second grade teacher, the late Mrs. Willie Belle Tolliver. She enrolled me in the summer arts camp at Converse College when Spartanburg city schools were still segregated. At Spartanburg High School, MacArthur Goodwin and the late Tom Willis were my art instructors and were instrumental in awaking my hidden talents.

I moved north and enjoyed the array of arts in New York City at the Met and the SoHo arts district. I participated in many art events there, selling hand painted T-shirts and greeting cards. There I also indulged in learning graphic design, working in "slide houses" and graphic studios.

After the birth of my daughter, Liza, I returned to Spartanburg in 1992. I continued to make and sell my greeting cards and began painting. At the age of forty-five I left my job at a sign company because I was allergic to the chemicals, and I decided to pursue my artistic career at Converse College. There I was immersed in the arts like never before and taught by some of the best people I had ever met, including Teresa Prater and David Zacharias. I participated in the student artists' juried competition, and I won several awards.

Feeling that time was running out, I still had no idea what I wanted to do when I grew up. I then took two silversmith classes with Daingerfield Ashton and fell in love with the craft. I decided to teach it. Today I am a member of the West Main Artists Co-op, where I do silversmith and oil painting, as well as serve on two committees.

I would define my style of work as "historical" in that I love things from the past. I find inspiration all around me, in the corners of an old house or the top of a statue against the sky.

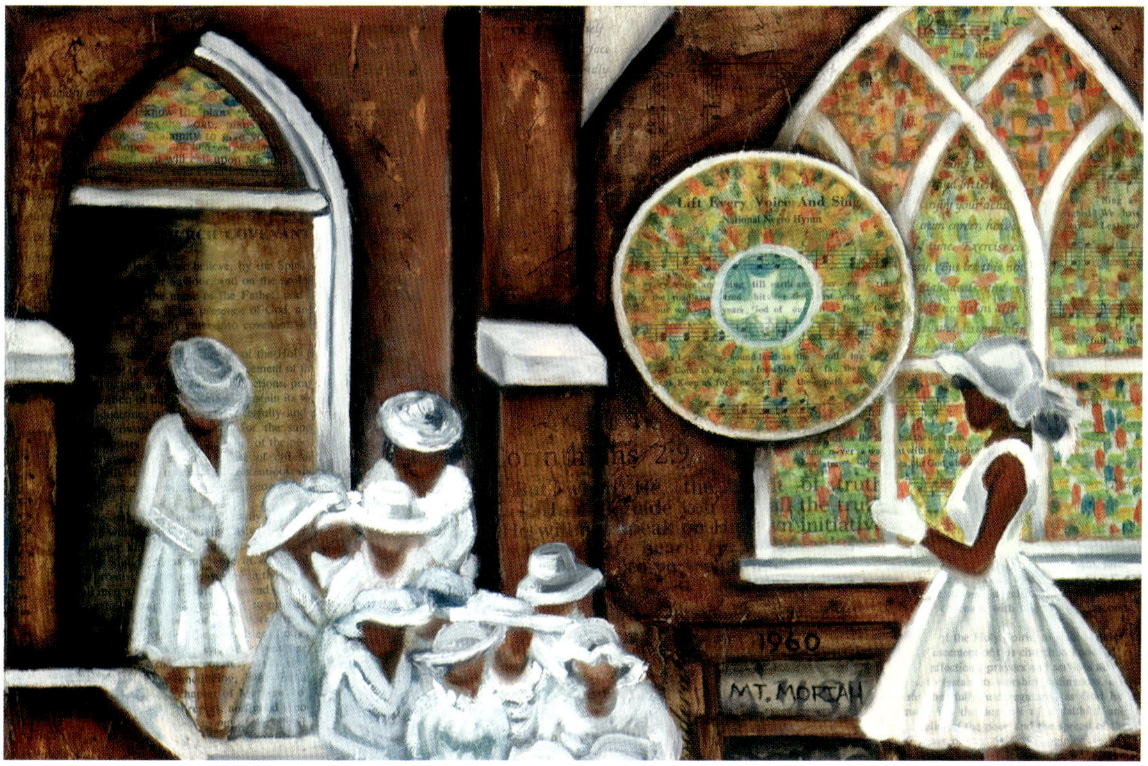

Missisonary Sunday

Mixed media

18" X 24"

Melissa Earley

I grew up all over the United States: up and down the East Coast, southern California and a couple states in the middle, from huge metropolitan cities to tiny rural towns. Since there were weren't many consistencies in my childhood, I relied a lot on the handful of people and things that stayed the same. Especially my mother and brother, and my records and crayons. I listened to music and drew constantly, and I think that art and music became a sort of therapy for me, a valuable way of expressing the fears and frustrations that I couldn't articulate. Today, art is still a way for me to take my ideas and emotions and transform them from electrical impulses into tangible images.

I usually start out sketching rather absentmindedly, and then flesh out my favorite images into paintings or even linocuts. Lately I have also been working with photographs, manipulating them in Photoshop. That early part of the process is spontaneous and emotional, and sometimes I repeat the image multiple times before it feels right. Then, if it's something that I think would be interesting in beads, I work out the pattern, select the colors and type of stitch, and then start weaving. This last part is rigidly organized and rather tedious but also can be quite cathartic, as it forces me to pay intense attention to every part of the image. In doing so I often discover that the image is revealing something to me as if I have tapped into my subconscious.

My hope is that others viewing my work will recognize a certain vulnerability and honesty in it, and that this will create a connection between us based upon our common human experiences of love and hate, grief and joy, fear and forgiveness.

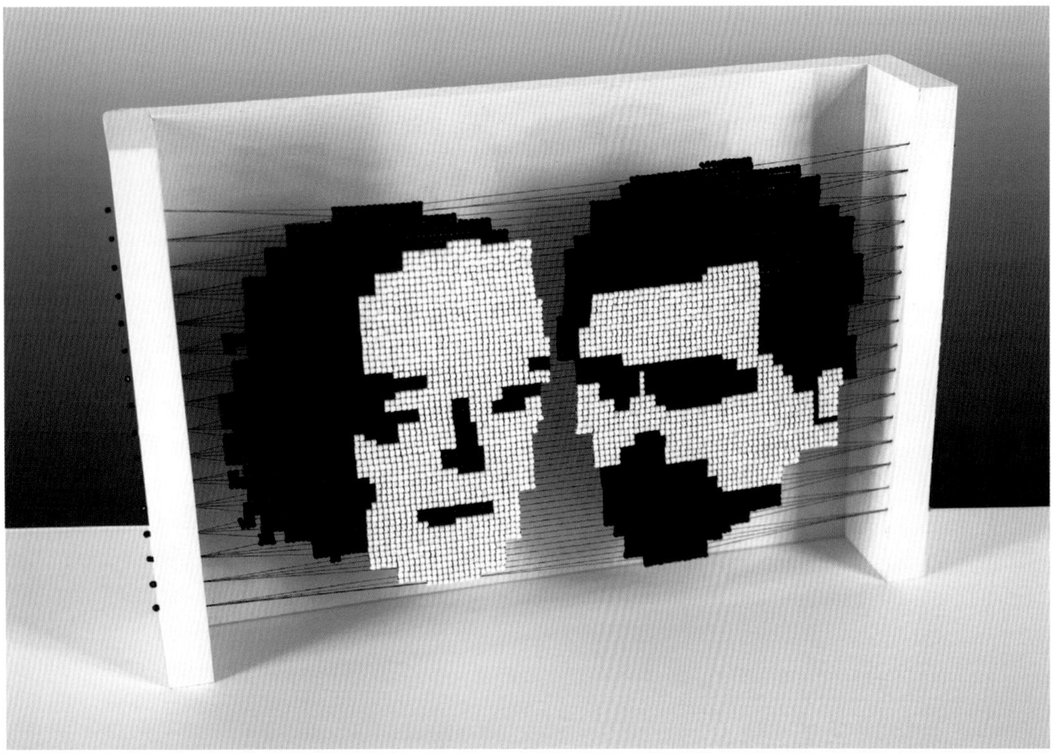

The Artists

Beadwork

12" X 16"

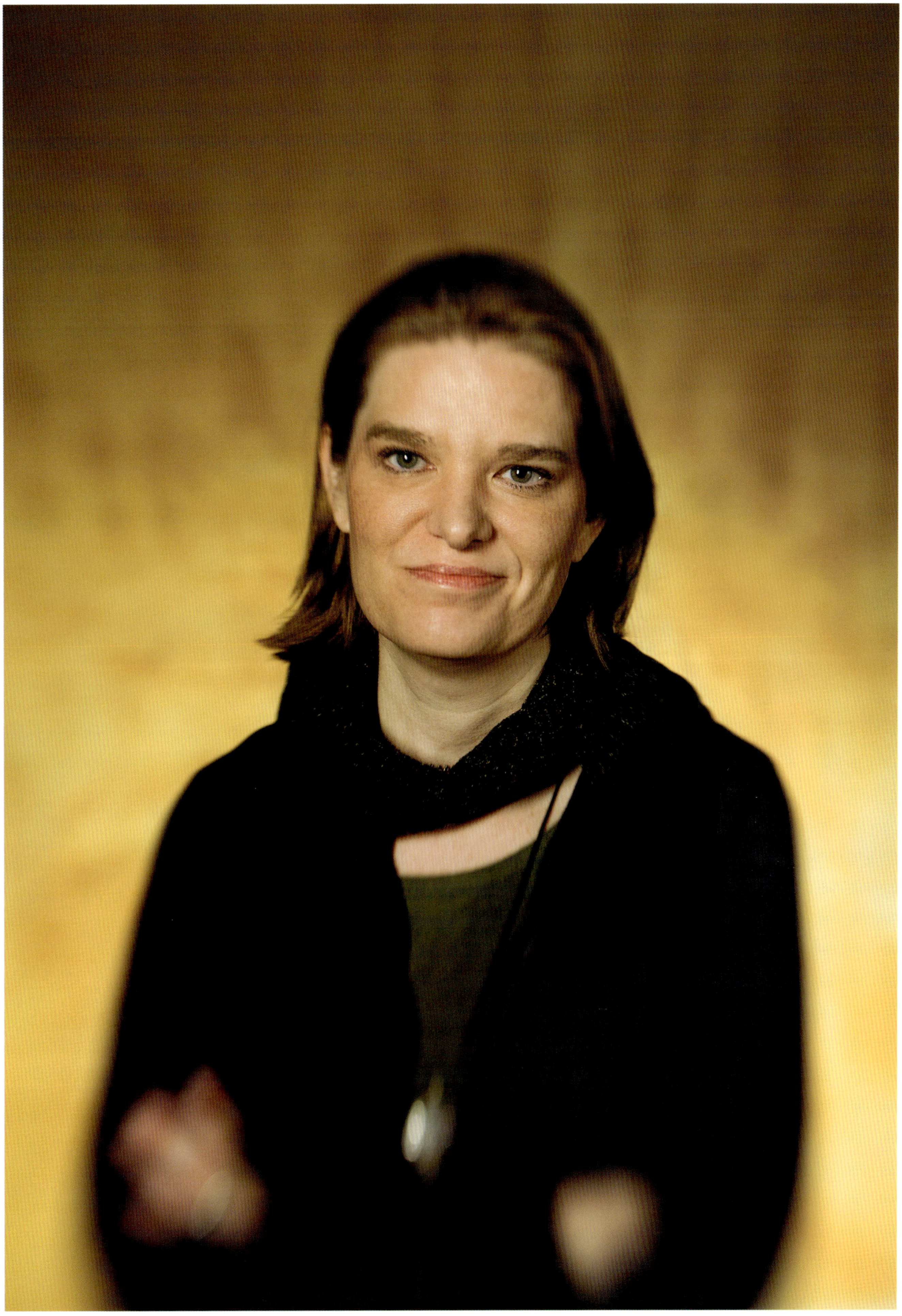

Rosa Eugene

I was born in the Colored People's Hospital in Spartanburg in 1949 and grew up on East Valley Street and Phyllis Goins Court. Being a native has given me enormous insights on the various aspects of life in Spartanburg. It has colored my world, shaped my ideas, and broadened my artistic reasoning. I've had no formal art education. I became interested in clay in 1996 because of my love for my husband and my desire to help him in our pottery business, Pottery by Eugene. My becoming a ceramic artist was born out of love and a need to express my ideas.

Living in Cowpens provides me with a great sense of peace and warmth. It allows me freedom of expression when I'm shaping the coiled clay, and it helps enhance my creative thought. My style is contemporary; my forms are strong but feminine. The shape is a woman expressing an idea of universal concern to all women. I am inspired by human existence and our place in this universe. When I create my pieces I am attempting to convey a message and answer a question. I hope to leave the viewer with some hope and more questions, and I want the shape and color of my pieces to give the viewer a sense of peace.

Being born in the South has given me strength and an unbiased conviction that as females we possess a powerful quality and a passion for whatever we wish to achieve. We can accomplish our goal no matter how hard it may be or how long it may take!

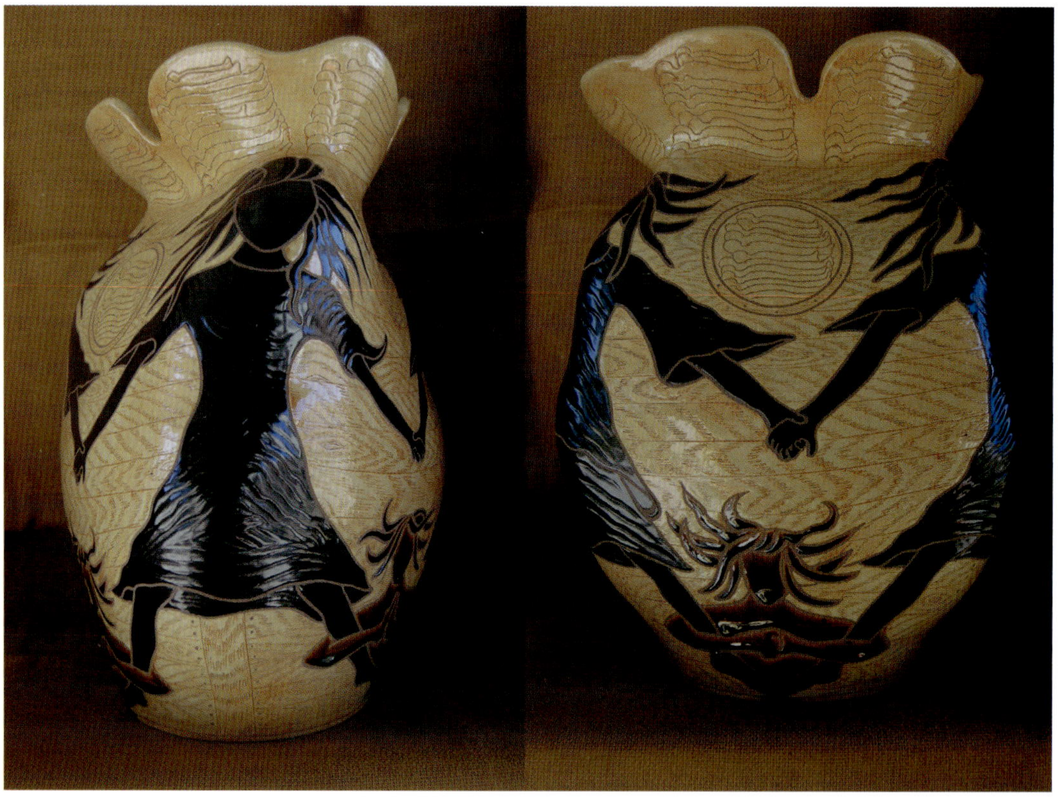

The Price/Freedom

Coil-built with carved & etched surface, tile grout, "mock mosaic"

18" X 13" X 18"

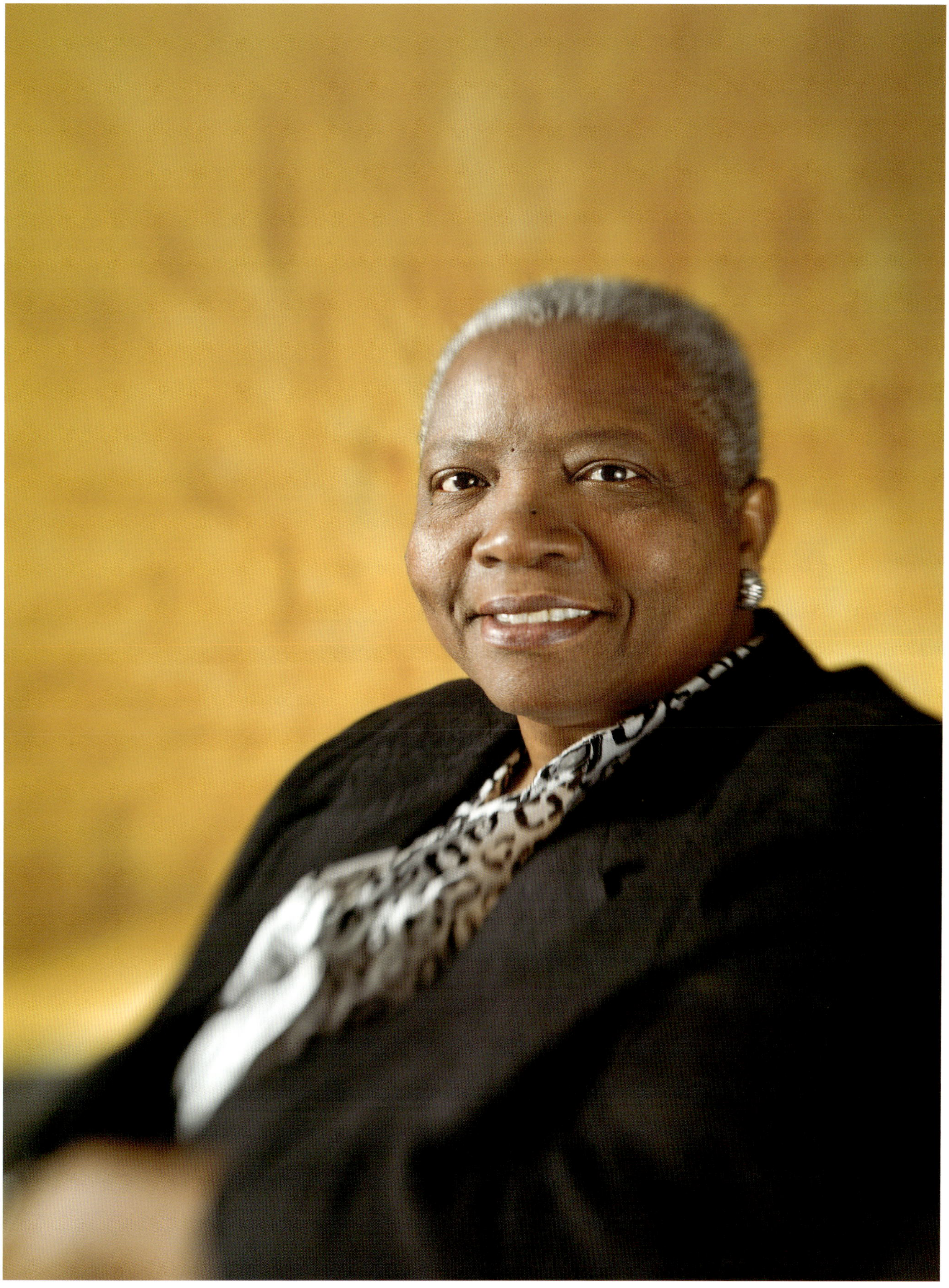

Winton Eugene

I grew up in Montz, Louisiana, a small rural town near a bend in the Mississippi River. As a boy, I liked to draw. In school I was always assigned to do the holiday drawings at Easter, Christmas, and Thanksgiving. During the Vietnam War I was stationed in Fayetteville, North Carolina, as a paratrooper in the 82nd Airborne Division. On a visit to a friend's home in Spartanburg, I met my wife. We married, lived in Chicago, then moved to Cowpens with our kids.

I've always had pictures inside my head that I needed to put on canvas. I've tried most mediums, but my love of oil paint is first and foremost. In 1985 I started to teach myself to turn on the potter's wheel. The clay placed me in a new dimension—everything around me didn't exist, just me and the clay. What a feeling of total contentment!

My forms are traditional, and they are made to accept the designs and paintings I place on them. I tend to be concrete; I want people to see and know what they are viewing, and I include a lot of details, so they can always see something new when they view the work.

Living and working in my studio in Cowpens and being able to participate in the Spartanburg visual art community has helped me grow as a potter. I am inspired by my surroundings. Living in a rural community, waking up to beautiful trees and flowers just gets my juices flowing. Then I am ready to start creating each day. One of my collectors said, "Your work is the essence of America." For me this says it all.

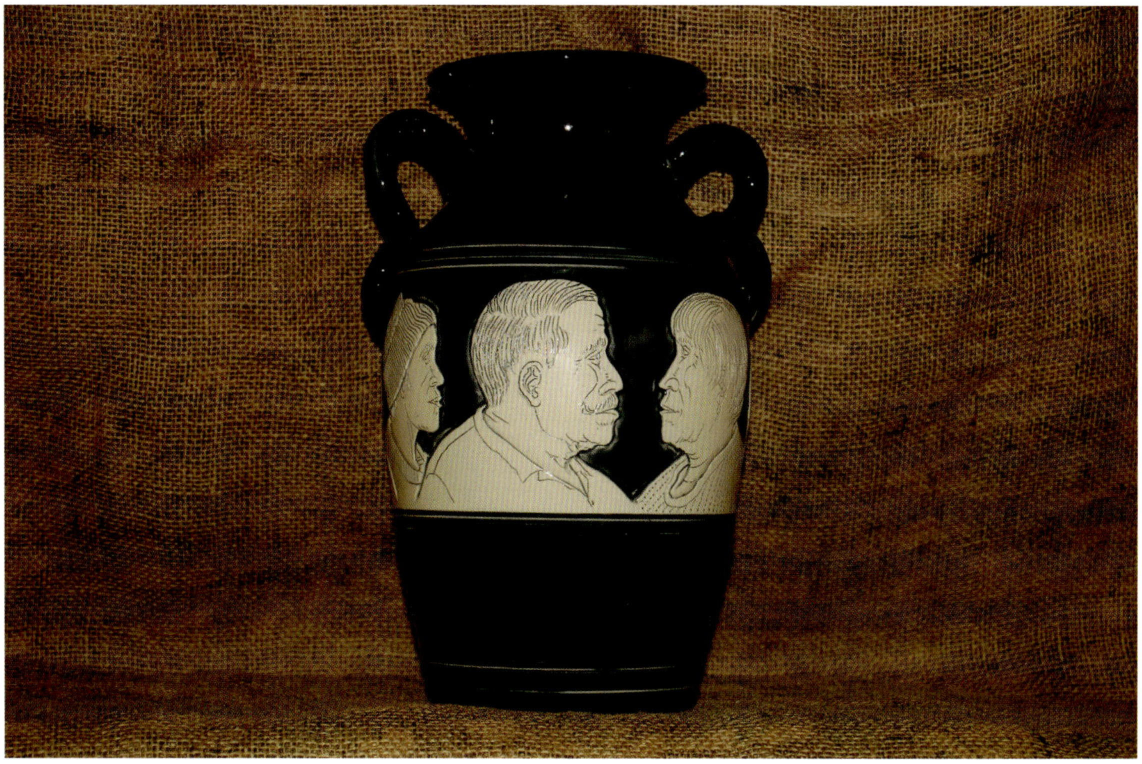

A Minority in Relief

Wheelthrown clay, low relief and carved faces, Chanjari blue glaze

13" X 9" X 12"

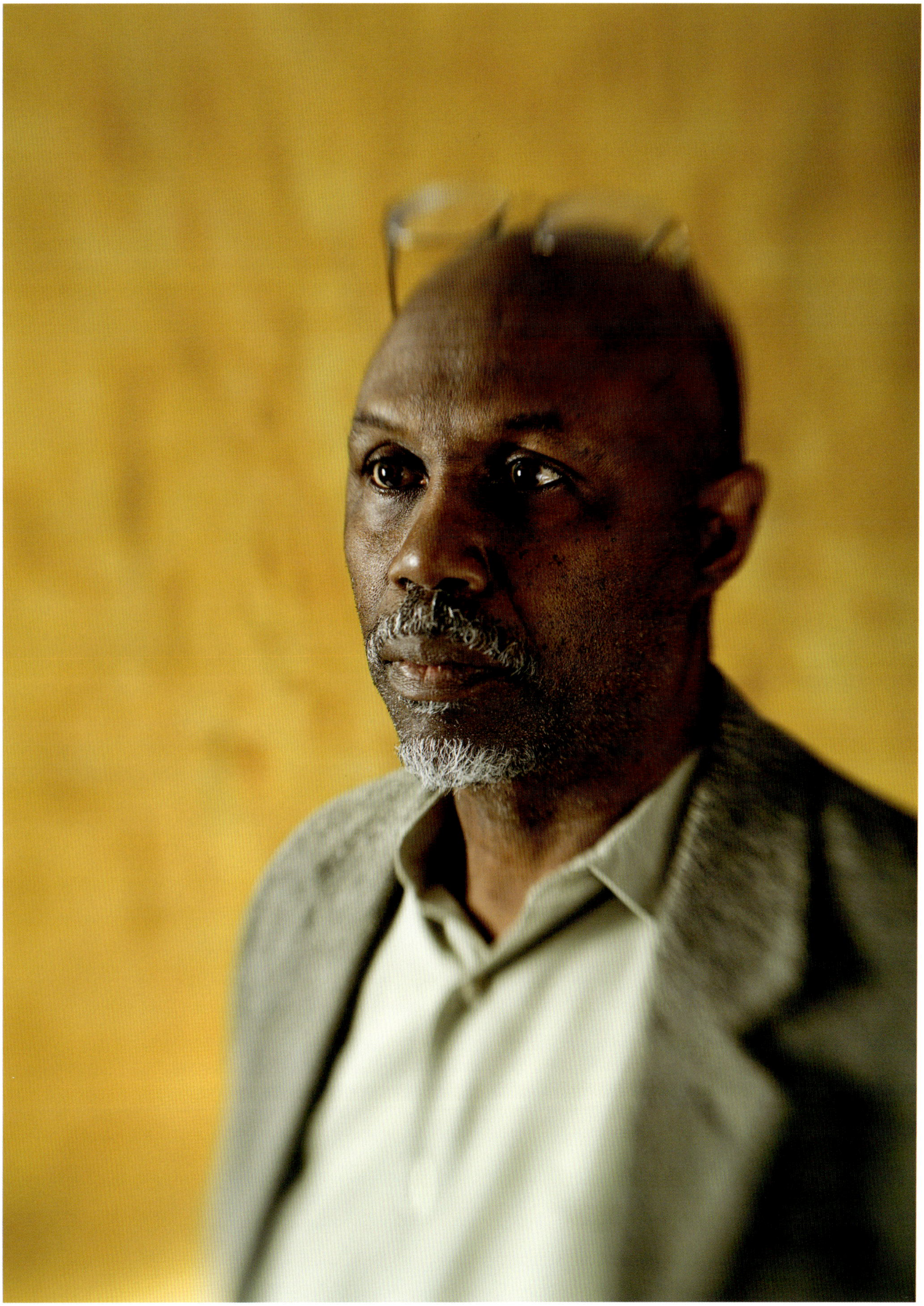

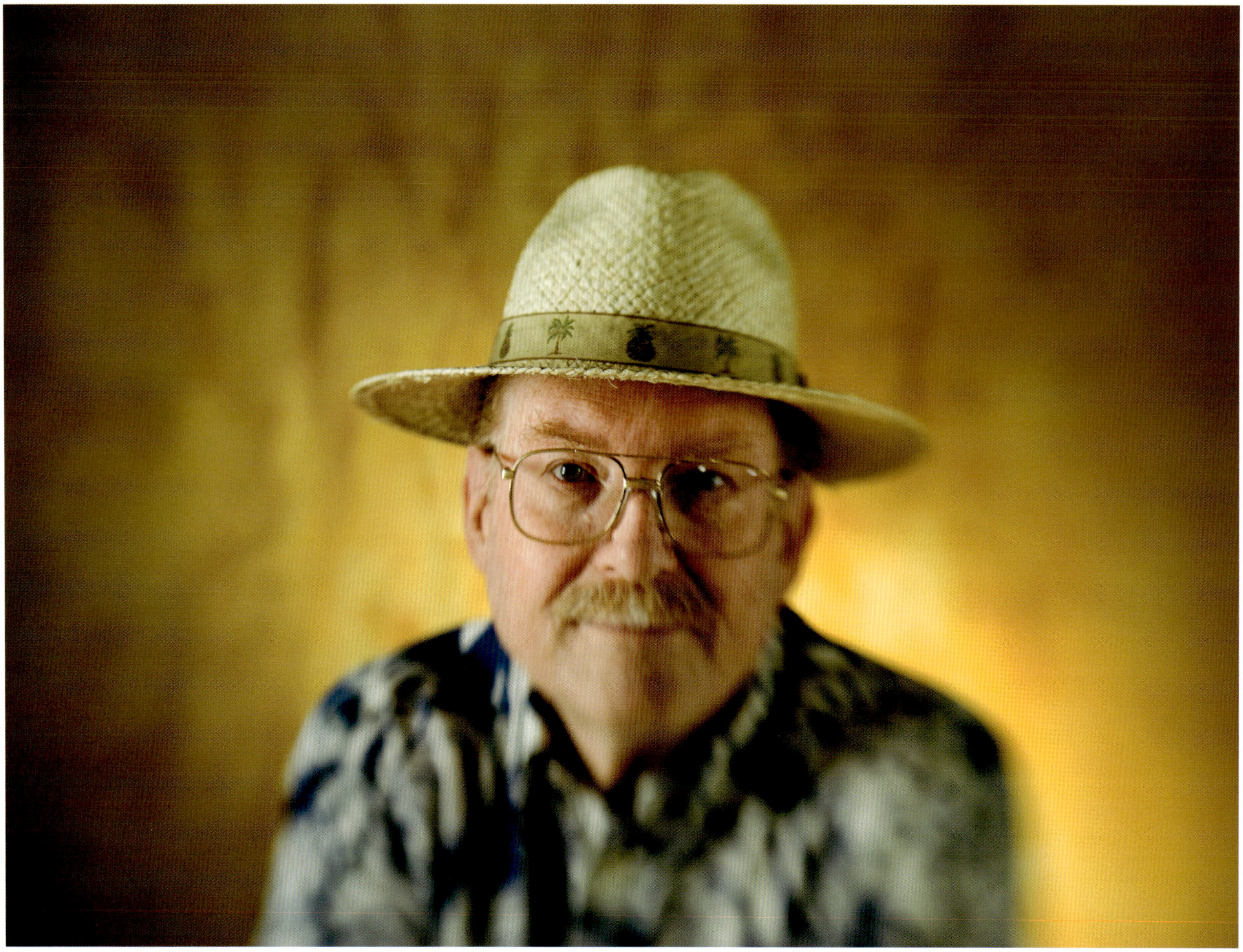

Henry Fagen

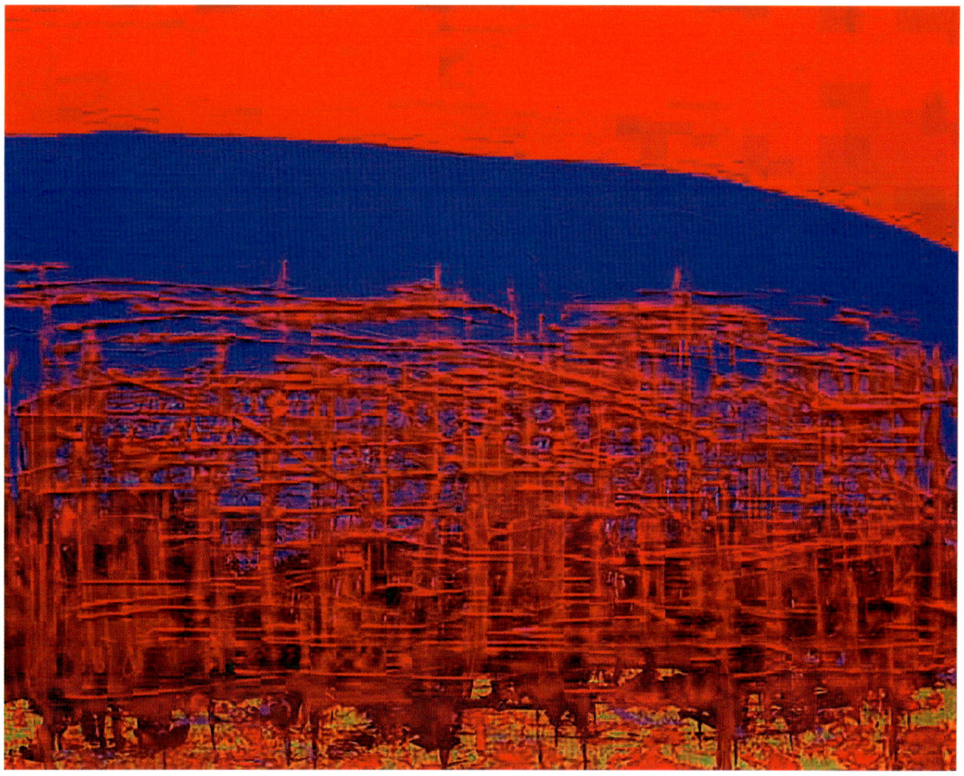

Glances # 113 Barrier Vast

Acrylic on board

16" X 20"

The son of a charter yacht captain, I grew up in Miami from the mid-1940s to the late 1950s, when the city was a hub of sport fishing and cruising. My family traveled up and down the Florida coast and keys, to various Eastern states, and to the Panama Canal Zone.

In grades one through six, I was always drawing images and was often called upon, with a few other kids, to decorate the classroom's back walls with seasonal scenes.

When I was a senior in high school I won the poster design contest for the annual musical stage show. The posters were displayed all over the county—my first public art show. *Ha-Ha!*

I headed off to Emory University for a pre-med program. A faculty spring art exhibit during my freshman year turned my path back to art and to the University of Miami. I had an opportunity to travel for ten weeks in Europe before my senior year; that trip sealed my interest and career in art—the images and ideas still influence me today. I have also lived in Illinois, Arizona, and Texas, and those vistas have influenced my work too.

I am interested in exploring my personal visual memories and those of people I encounter. Another way of looking and perceiving forms is through our memory—sadness, humor, etc.—and these are called mnemonic images, or mind-portraits, mind-scapes. I currently work on "faux-naturalist" landscapes in acrylics, oils, watercolors, and pastels. These landscapes have perceived memory-twists in them, for who can recall the exact image moment of something perceived?

Coming to Spartanburg in 1978 altered my perceptions of the idea of "art community." The uniqueness of the Upstate area offers many visual opportunities for artistic development. The growth and vitality of the arts has been truly exceptional.

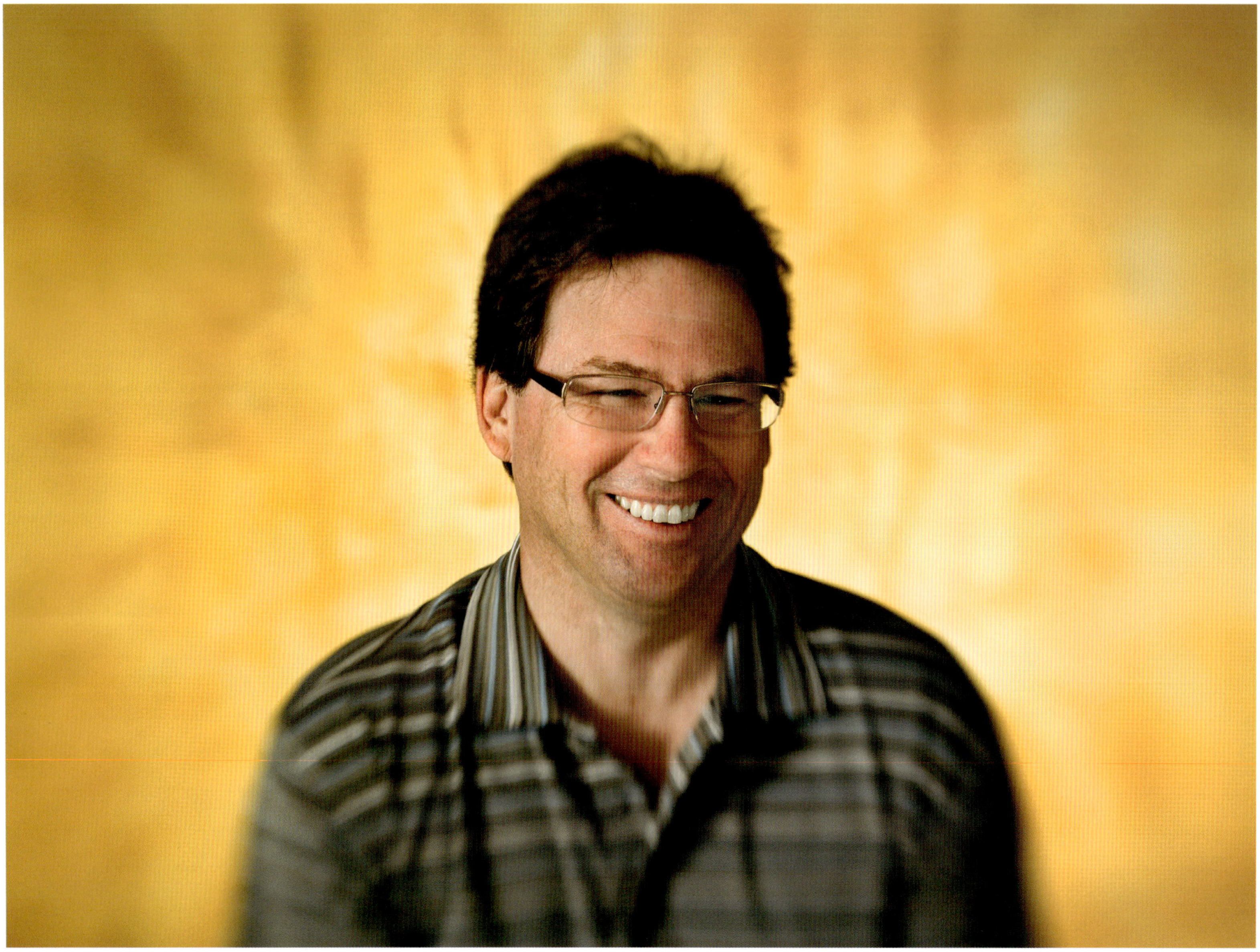

Trey Finney

I grew up in Spartanburg and experienced my first art classes at the Spartanburg Day School. Under the influence of Daingerfield Ashton I was exposed to drawing, printmaking, and ceramics. I graduated from Spartanburg High School and attended the College of Charleston before graduating from Ringling School of Art and Design. After two years of working as an architectural illustrator, I was hired by Walt Disney Feature Animation and spent the next fifteen years as an animator with the Florida studio in Orlando, where I met my wife and painting partner, Christine Lawrence.

While at Disney I contributed to nine animated features and several animated shorts. Some of these credits include *Beauty and the Beast*, *Aladdin*, *The Lion King*, and *Pocahontas*. Disney offered many continuing education classes, including oil painting, which inspired me to pursue a more personal journey, culminating in the decision to leave the animation field and return home. I always wanted to capture the landscapes of the Piedmont and the Lowcountry in oil but never had the skill. Now, after twenty years of professional experience, I feel I can do justice to whatever image inspires me to sit down and paint.

Stacked Rail Fence in Autumn Glow

Oil on board

30" X 40"

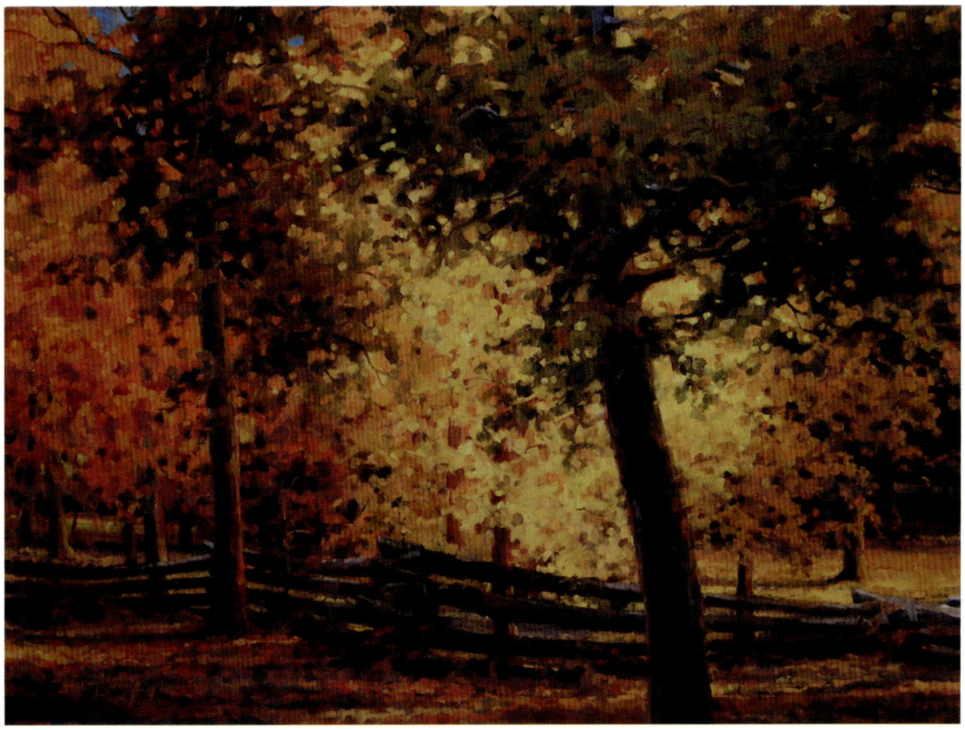

I believe painting is the combination of vision and knowledge. The subject can be copied verbatim or filtered at the artist's discretion. Will it be a copy of reality or an abstraction? Will the abstraction be subtle, violent, or a balance of the two? No matter what the choices, the artist will be influenced by what is in his visual plane at that moment in time or what he has seen and experienced in the past. I believe my paintings reflect that artistic interpretation of vision and knowledge—an impressionistic style with an emphasis on color, drawing, and an underlying abstract design. What I like to call *Natural Impressions*.

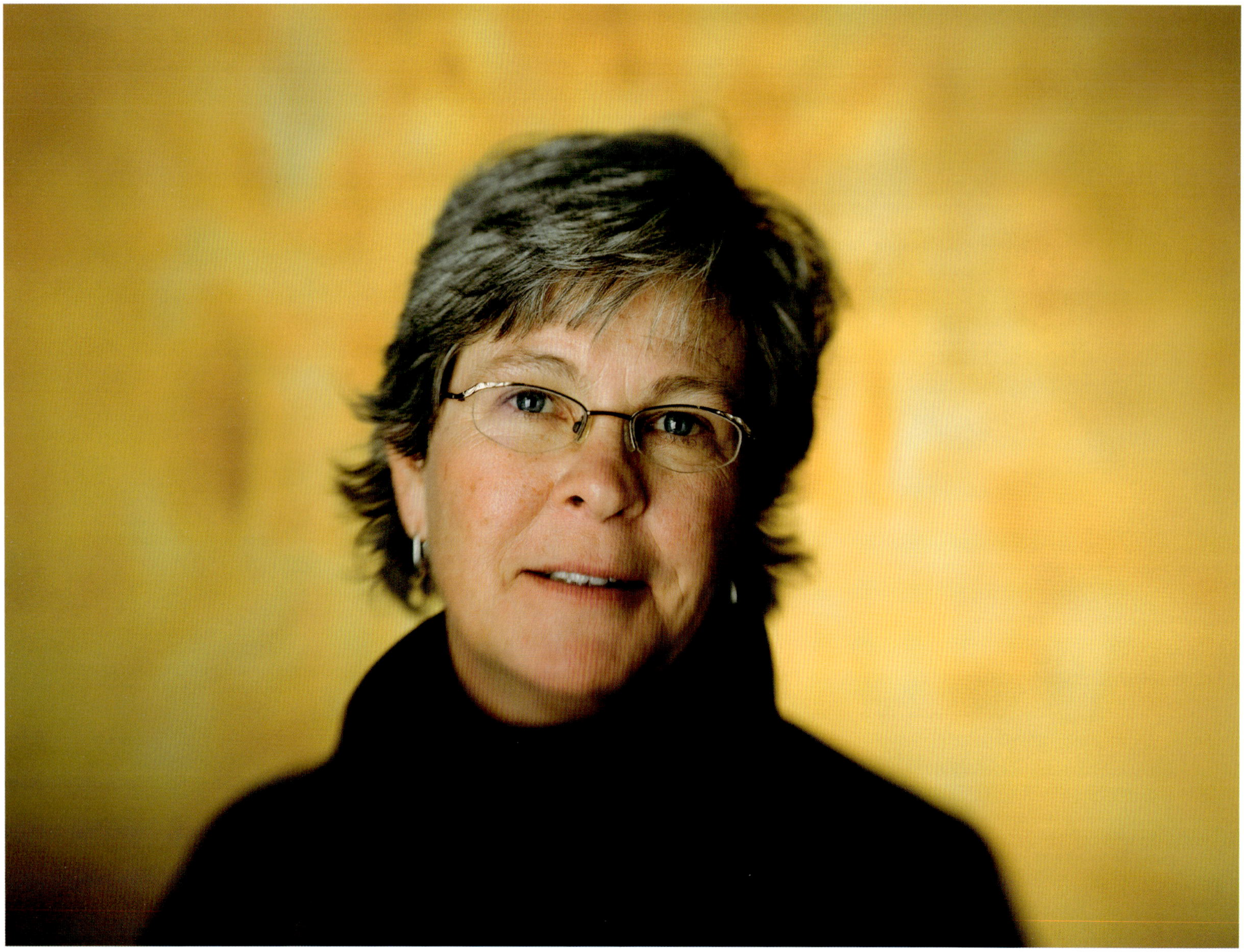

Isabel Forbes

I grew up on South Fairview Extension, three houses down from Irma and August Cook. I remember being mesmerized while gazing through the window of Irma's basement studio while she taught her art students, and wishing I could be in there. My mother would check out master reproductions from the library, like Degas and Manet, to hang in our living room. From my father, I learned how to use a camera and actually printed my own black and white photographs. In Spartanburg's School District 7, my teachers included Betty Bramlett and MacArthur Goodwin. Under Dr. Goodwin's guidance, I applied for and received a scholarship to attend Ringling College of Art and Design in Sarasota, Florida.

The subjects of many of my oil paintings are Spartanburg's urban landscapes, including signage, street lights, telephone poles, old railroad bridges, or even someone eating at a restaurant counter. These paintings are often images that might seem, on the surface, unremarkable, but I find beauty in the most mundane of these settings. I do not consider my paintings primarily as buildings or people, but rather a composition of contrasting elements of light and dark, complementary colors, and negative space. While my oil paintings may be called representational or realistic, my approach is from a more abstract perspective. I also paint coastal scenes, interiors, and figures from my travels. Now that I am back in Spartanburg, I paint in my own basement art studio.

I hope that my artwork expands viewers' perceptions of their surroundings and what they consider beautiful. When my collectors and friends become nostalgic about a piece or tell me how they notice old mill houses or diners they routinely pass by in Spartanburg, I feel like my designs are brought to life and I have succeeded.

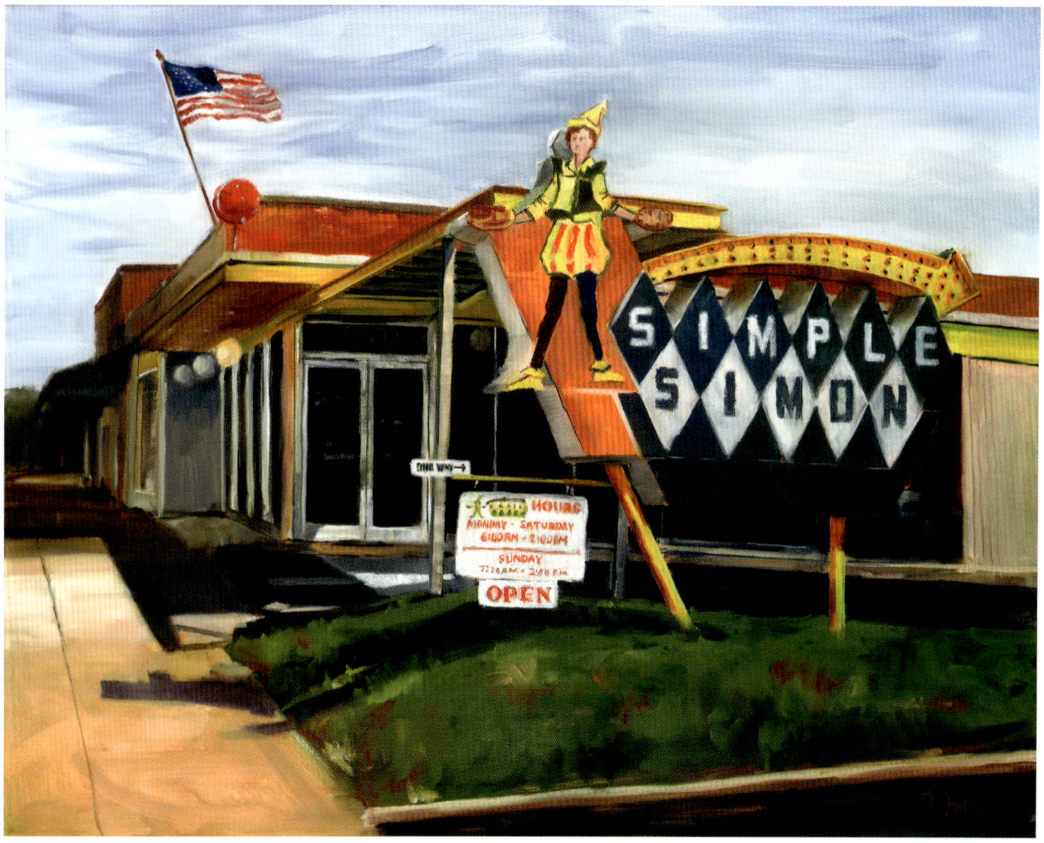

Simple Simon
Oil on canvas
24" X 30"

Carroll Foster

I have to credit my parents as my two greatest influences in art and for how I became an artist. My dad, Arthur, an architect, was always tearing down and redesigning our family home. Taking a mid-century Southern home and applying modern, clean design to every corner of it was a never-ending love for my dad. My mom, Lorelei, filled the house with her eclectic style and imagination. There was always a lot of art, music, and color in our house. My dad gave me my first professional camera, and my mom helped me open my own photography studio here in Spartanburg.

Growing up in Spartanburg, there were many opportunities to learn about art and be engaged in the arts. I took every art class you could take in high school, attended summer art classes at the Art Museum, and had private classes with local artist Carol Augthun. Art has always been a part of my life. It wasn't until faced with college and what to do with my life that I decided to choose photography as a profession. I believe I chose photography because it combined art and the technical aspect of using a camera.

I received my BFA in photography from Savannah College of Art and Design. After completing school in Savannah, I enjoyed the company of artists and photographers working at a fine art studio in Taos, New Mexico. My wife and I relocated to Spartanburg in the late 1990s; it is then that I concentrated my photography in the commercial field. In 2006 I opened Hot Eye Photography, combining the art and commercial aspects of my photography.

The most fulfilling photography for me is photographing people. I see a photo in everyone. Whether it is candid or posed, a face can tell a story. I want my pictures to engage the viewer to ask questions and inspire his or her own imaginations.

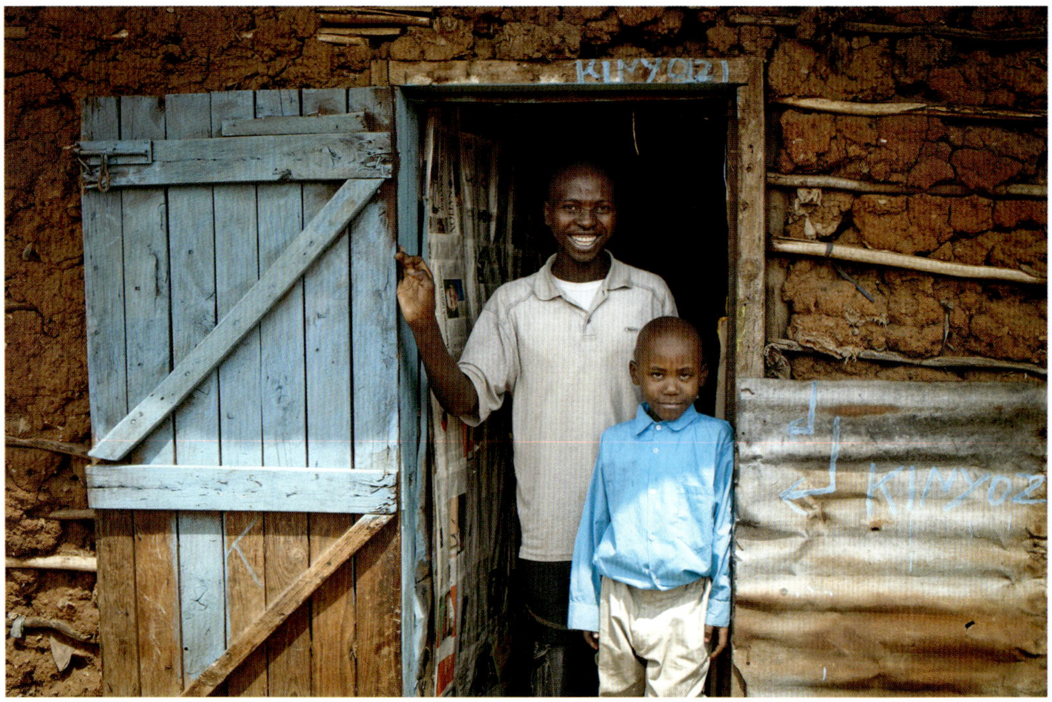

In Blue
Photograph

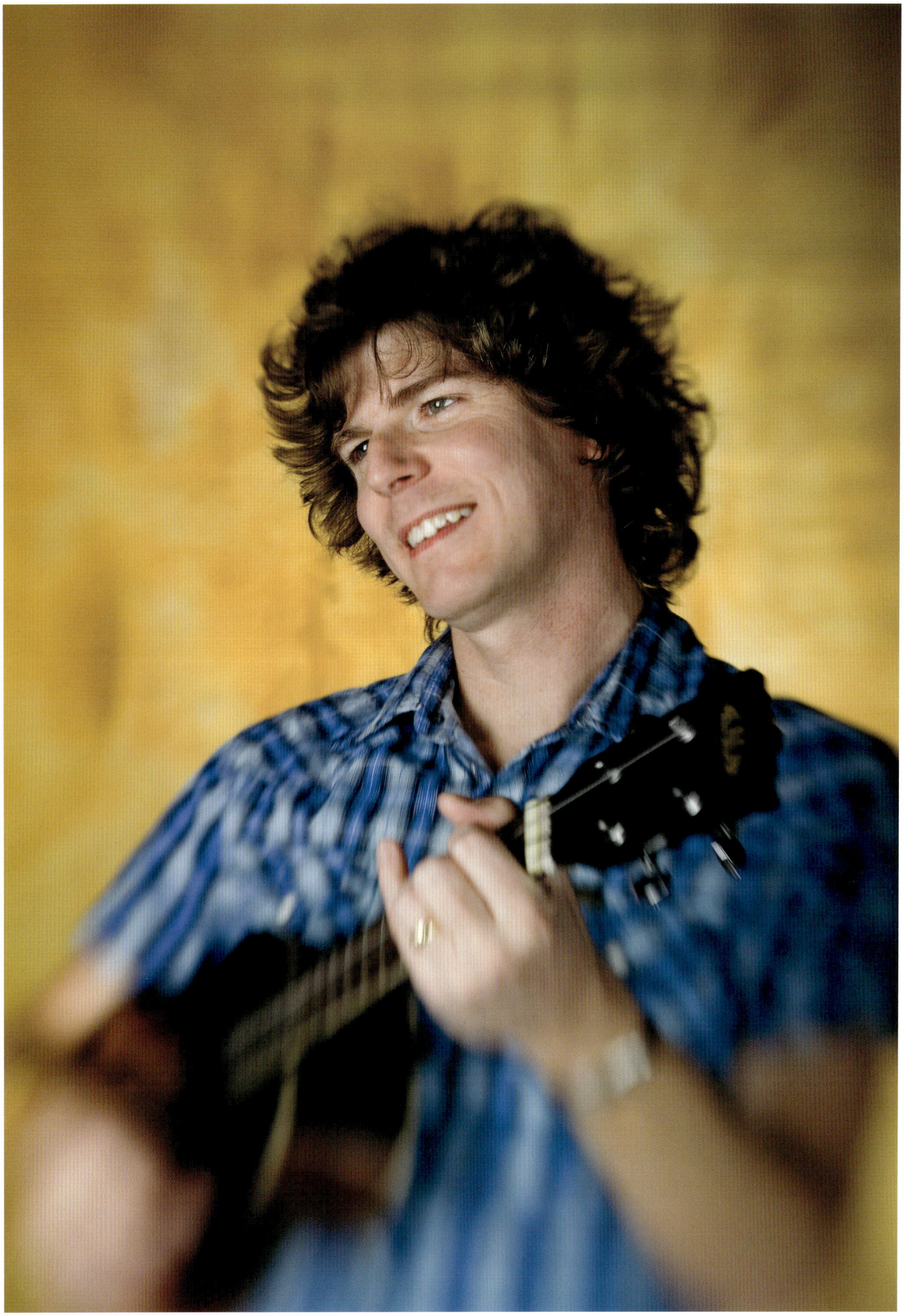

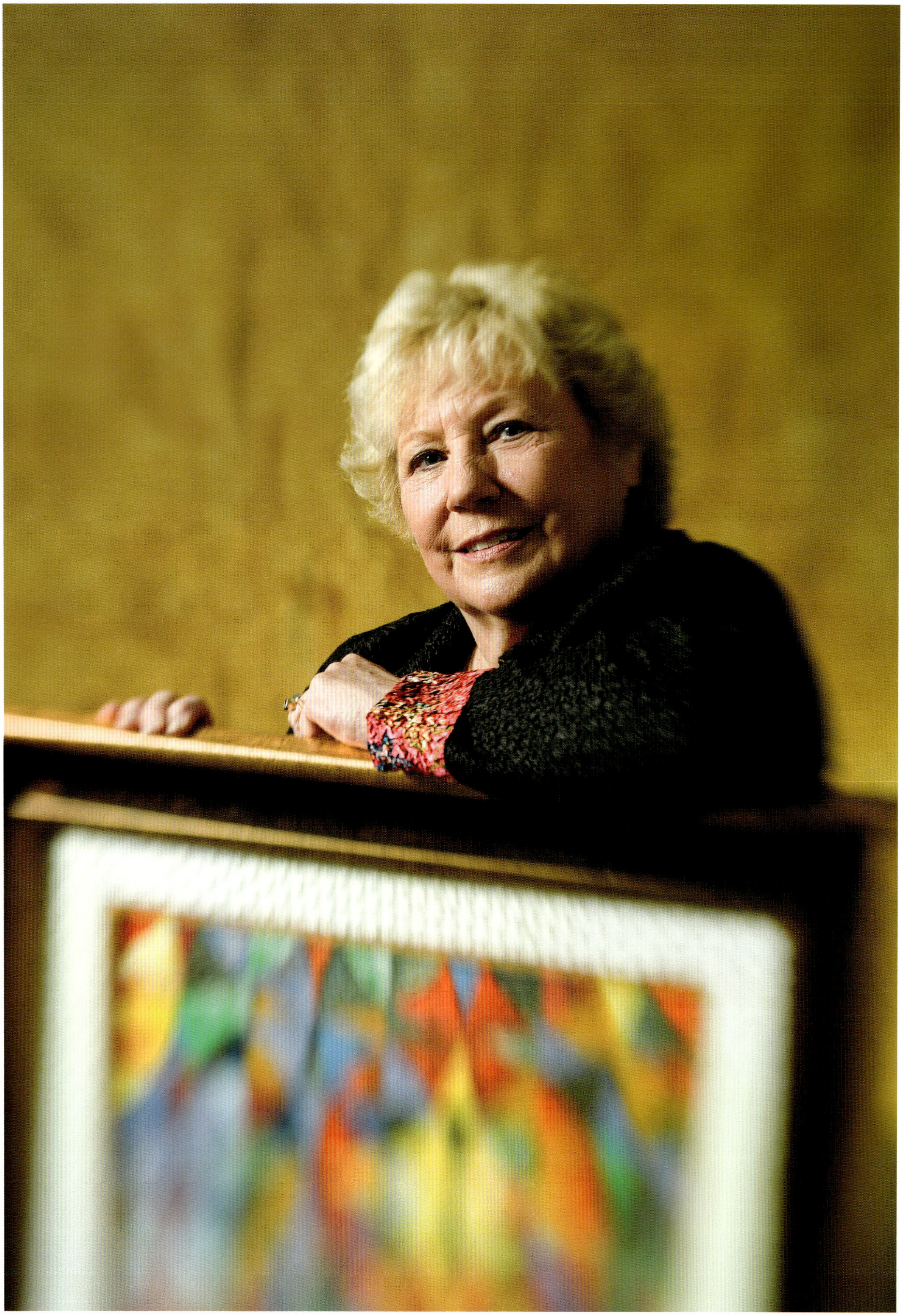

Carol Funke

A papermaker is a true recyclist. I am a paper maker; therefore, I am a finder of "things." I am always on the lookout for different textures, designs, and things to put into my paper. When I find something unique or interesting, I add it to my collection of "things" that someday I may add to the pulp when I am designing a handmade paper piece of artwork. As a child I enjoyed puzzles, and I admired people who would sew beautiful quilts. As an adult I have incorporated these two loves into my artwork.

When I create or find a design I like, I draw it on graph paper. I then color-code this design, using either colored pencils or markers. Step two, the hardest part for me, is to transfer this design onto either watercolor paper or foam core to the actual size of the finished piece of artwork. Step three is the fun part: making the paper. I add ribbon, thread, sparkle, and a multitude of things into the pulp. I also use a variety of textures in the paper to create interest. (I like texture and contrast in my artwork.) Sometimes I use my grandmother's handmade knitted doilies and placemats to create texture in my pulp. After the pulp dries, I then cut the handmade paper into pieces and glue this paper onto the finished design. Each time I finish a piece of handmade paper artwork I am still surprised of the outcome. The final result "comes to life," giving me, its creator, a sense of joy for the part I contributed to its creation.

I also enjoy working with watercolor and pen and ink, often combining these mediums with handmade paper. It still amazes me how one can take a flat piece of paper, draw a few lines, add color and shading, and make this flat sheet of paper into something that someone else can enjoy and relate to. This is an uplifting and satisfying feeling.

Circles and More
Handmade, hand embossed paper
18" X 30"

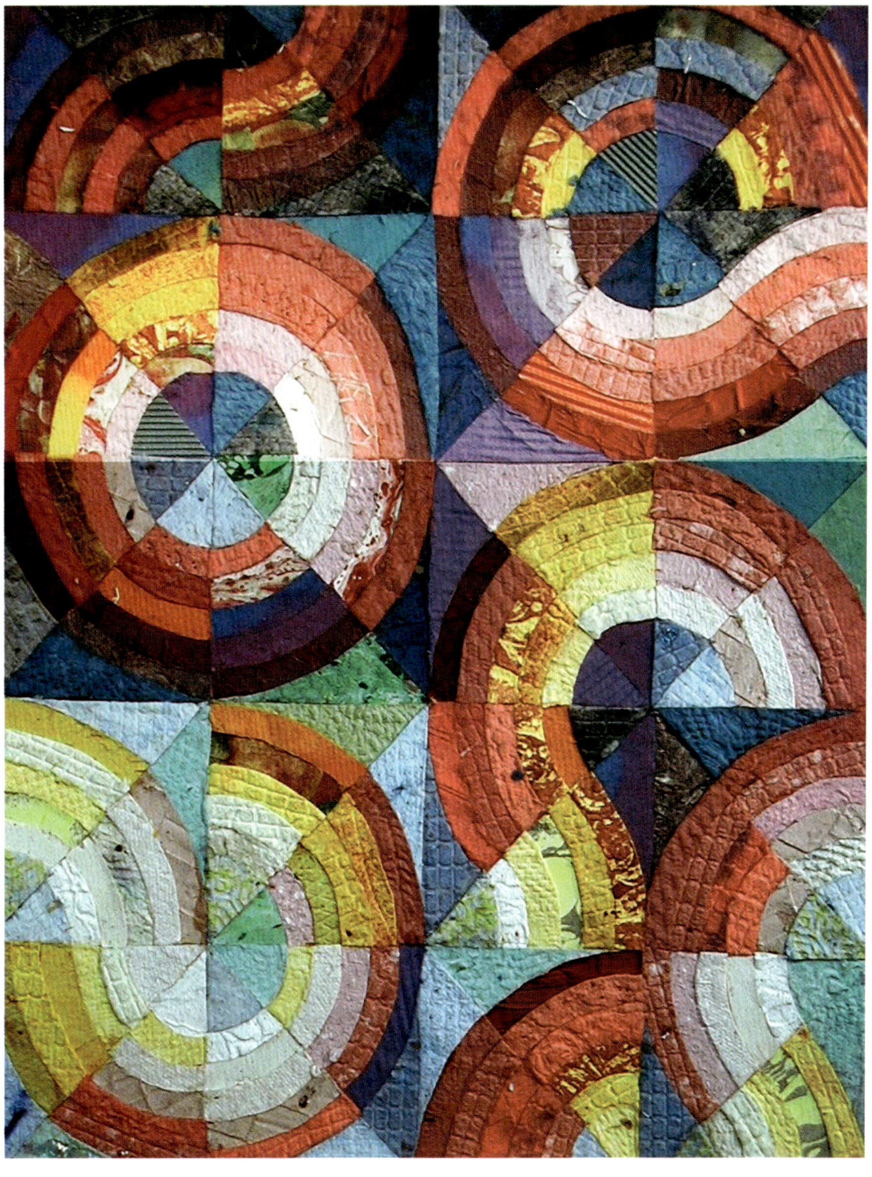

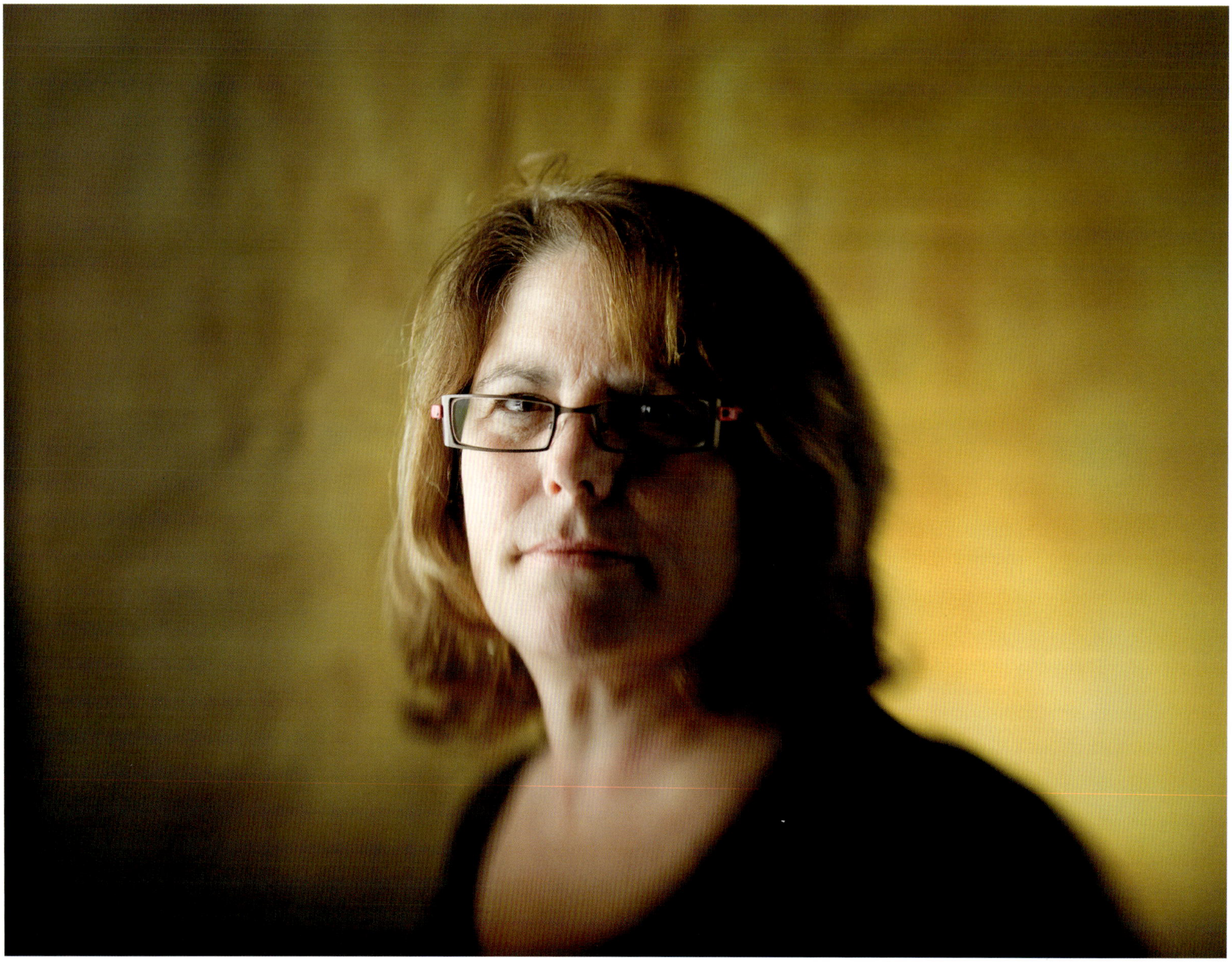

Amy Goldstein-Rice

I am a native of Spartanburg. I received a BA degree from the University of Tennessee at Chattanooga and studied ceramics with a number of established artists at well-known arts and crafts schools: Rising Fawn Pottery Workshop, Penland School of Crafts, and Arrowmont School of Craft.

In 1976 I joined the staff at the Spartanburg Arts Council as their artist-in-residence. During the years with the Arts Council, I conducted adult pottery classes, promoted the visual arts through the visiting arts program in the public schools, and established a pottery studio. Over my thirty-year career, I have won numerous awards for smoke-fired ceramics and whimsical forms. My ceramics have sold both nationally and abroad.

Each one-of-a kind figure is fired to "Cone 04" and is made by a technique of altering wheel-thrown shapes or hand-building the earthenware clay. The sculpting of the clay is done almost entirely by hand, using modest tools. Surface decoration is achieved when textural marks are infused with layering of engobes, slip, and commercial underglaze. Many different brush sizes are used to achieve the varied surface treatments. Each piece is unique and one of a kind.

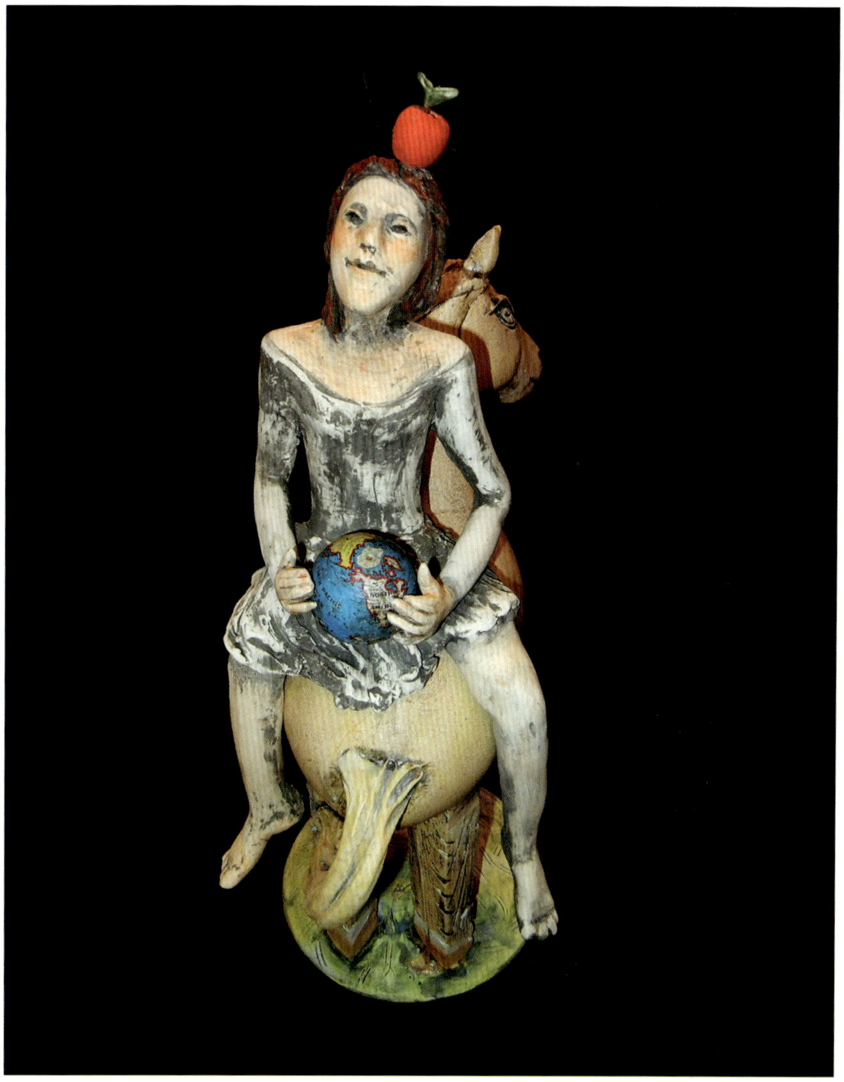

Backwards World

Earthenware clay, wheelthrown & handbuilt forms

12" X 6" X 5"

Behind each one of my sculptural forms is a personal story, which, although it may not be obvious to the viewer, is integral to the personality of the piece. I take a three-dimensional approach to storytelling. However, the textural and sculptural elements that are incorporated into the work encourage viewers to create stories of their own. I often tell people where my ideas come from, but I prefer watching a smile and a nod as the viewer investigates the whole sculpture. Then I tell them the title of the work. The title is my lead line into the story.

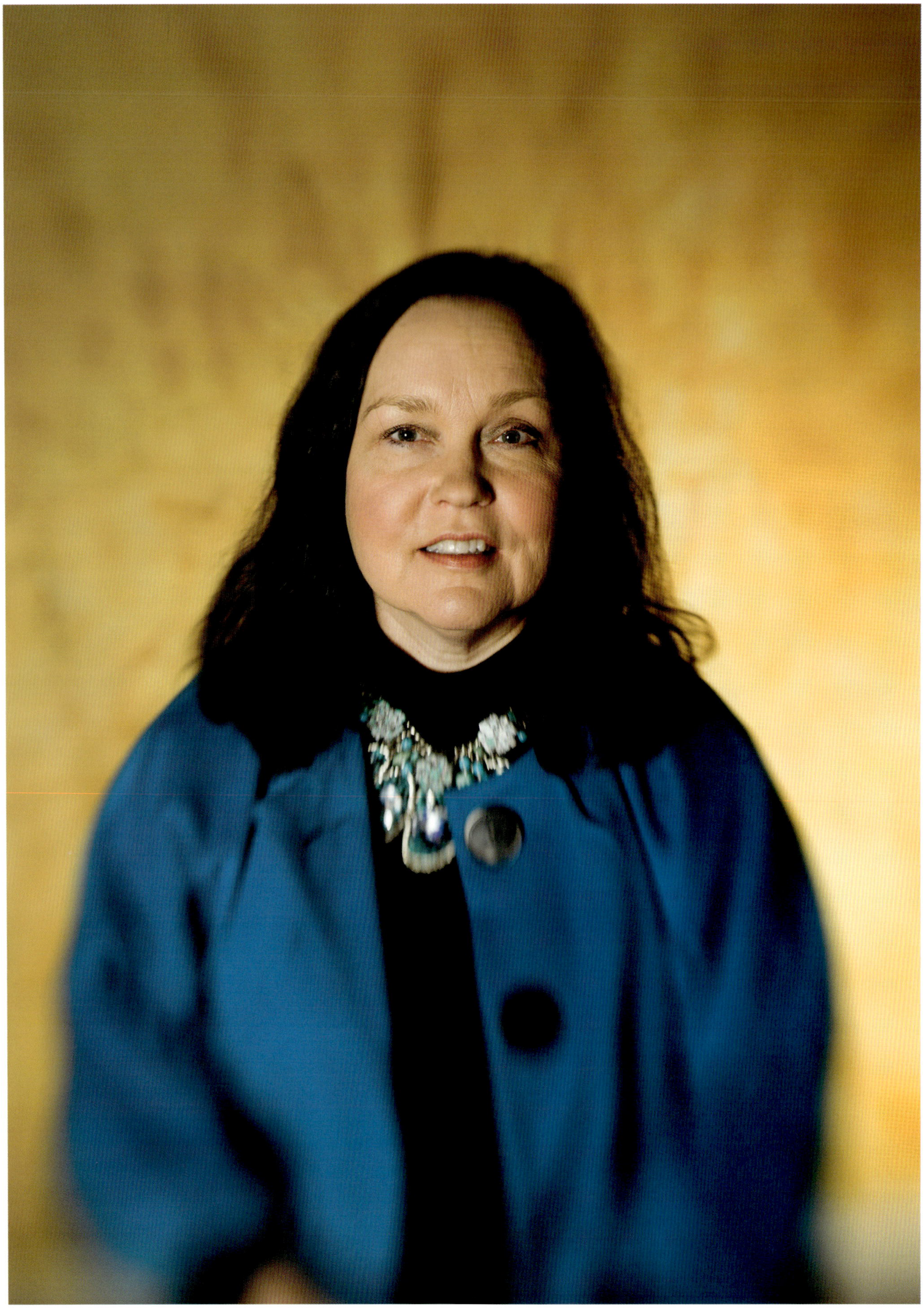

Susanne Floyd Gunter

Family is an important part of my make-up as an artist. From my family and my rural upbringing in Horry County, I developed an intense interest in "the land." Landscape is probably the foundation of my existence as an artist. The people that I know and love are tied to the land through some inexplicable force. The landscape is a part of who they are and who I am.

You can classify my work as the abstract use of landscape and/or figures. The pieces that I keep are dear friends, for they serve as constant reminders that I need to work more. Cowboys continue as a theme today and are from deep in my childhood in the 1960s when a western was on every night of the week. Growing up with Marshall Dillon, Rowdy Yates, Gil Favor, and Ben Cartwright was not a bad thing—the sale of cowboy paintings financed my doctoral studies.

Oil painting is my primary medium, as it is the truest of all for me. Most of my landscapes started as collages or collage/sketch combinations, while the figurative pieces are more likely drawn from repeated sketches from life.

A number of artists, including Toulouse-Lautrec and Honoré Daumier, have influenced my work, and though I knew none of them personally, because I studied their work closely I felt they were "old friends."

I am the most fortunate person in the world to have the family and friends that I have in life, in art, and art education. A number of art educators have urged me and encouraged me throughout my career, most notably Marie Fowler Kurtz, Susan Y. West, David Benson, Jackie Chalfant, Dianne Bagnal, Winston Wingo, Mary Lou Hightower, Linda Neely, Carol Augthun, Doris Turner, Christine Davis, Betty Bramlett, and MacArthur Goodwin. Other influences from higher education included Teresa Prater, David Zacharias, Ann Wenz, Andy Cox, Sara Setzer, and Jane Nodine. Lastly, I must not forget that my students both in the K-12 world and in higher education have had a lasting and continuous impact on my work and, more importantly, my work ethic.

Calico Cowboy
Oil on canvas
30" X 40"

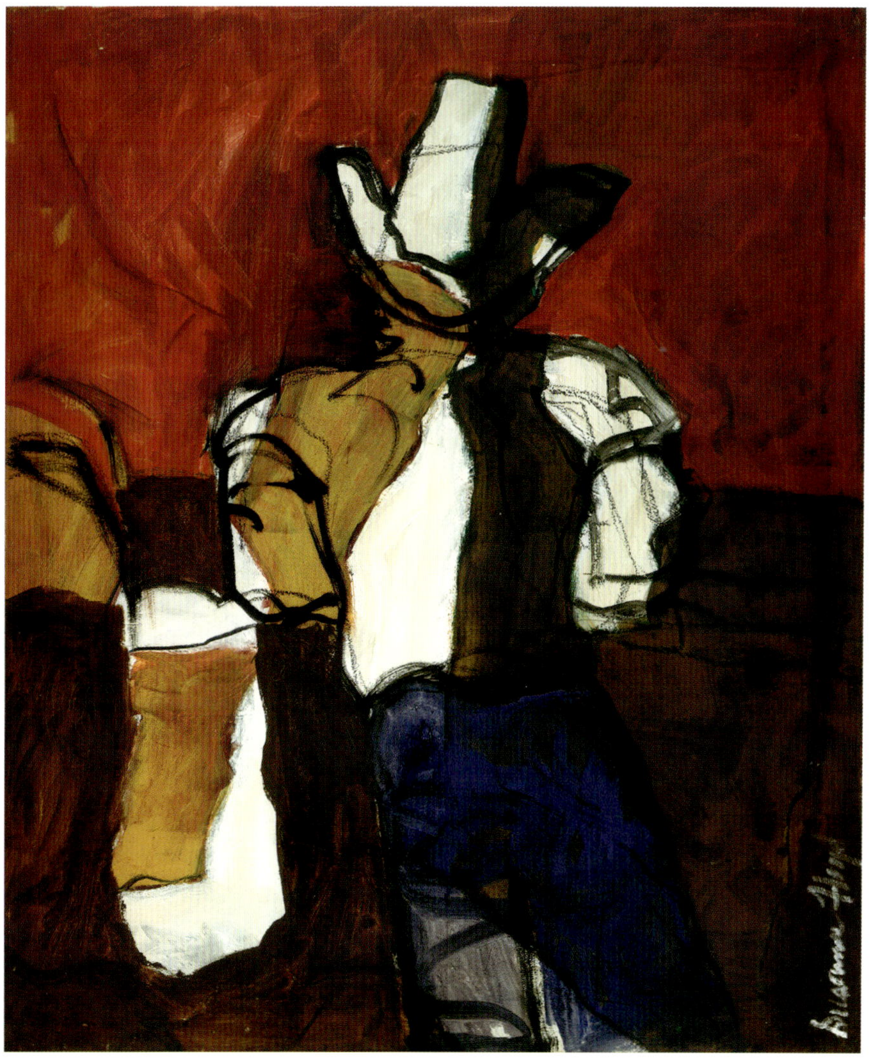

Steven Heeren

I grew up in the flatlands and farmlands of the Illinois prairie. The expansive horizons and skies of the Midwest turned me into a keen observer of nature. Little did I know that observing nature's subtleties would lead to its expression in oil painting. Coming to this passion late, time has created a love of landscape and sky in my life, and I'm drawn to share this with the viewer of my paintings. In my landscapes, I try to present those unexpected moments when nature's light comes together in luminous images. I strive for paintings that speak in a quiet but dramatic way of the beauty that all of us can observe if we look for it.

While I did not study luminism, I painted to please myself and later discovered my work was in the luminist tradition. A great deal of art history has occurred since that style of art was new, and I have been influenced by all of the styles I have encountered. I am drawn to scenes of dramatic lighting that allow me to explore mood and atmosphere with oil paints. In many of my paintings I try to achieve a palpable sense of deep, receding space but also compose a foreground that viewers can feel they could walk into.

My work is an attempt to capture the play of light over the sky and land using a full palette of colors in a subtle manner. I strive to record the images of these transforming moments of our planet. As you observe these moments I want you to hear them tauntingly whisper, "You will never see this again."

Autumn Evening
Oil on canvas
24" X 30"

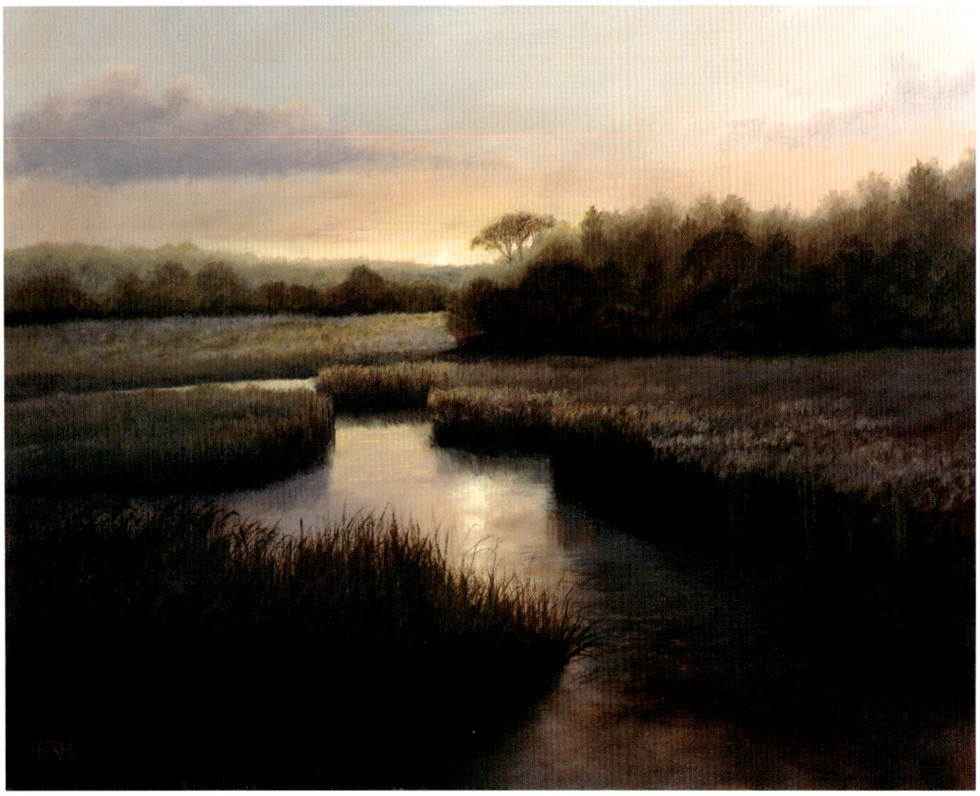

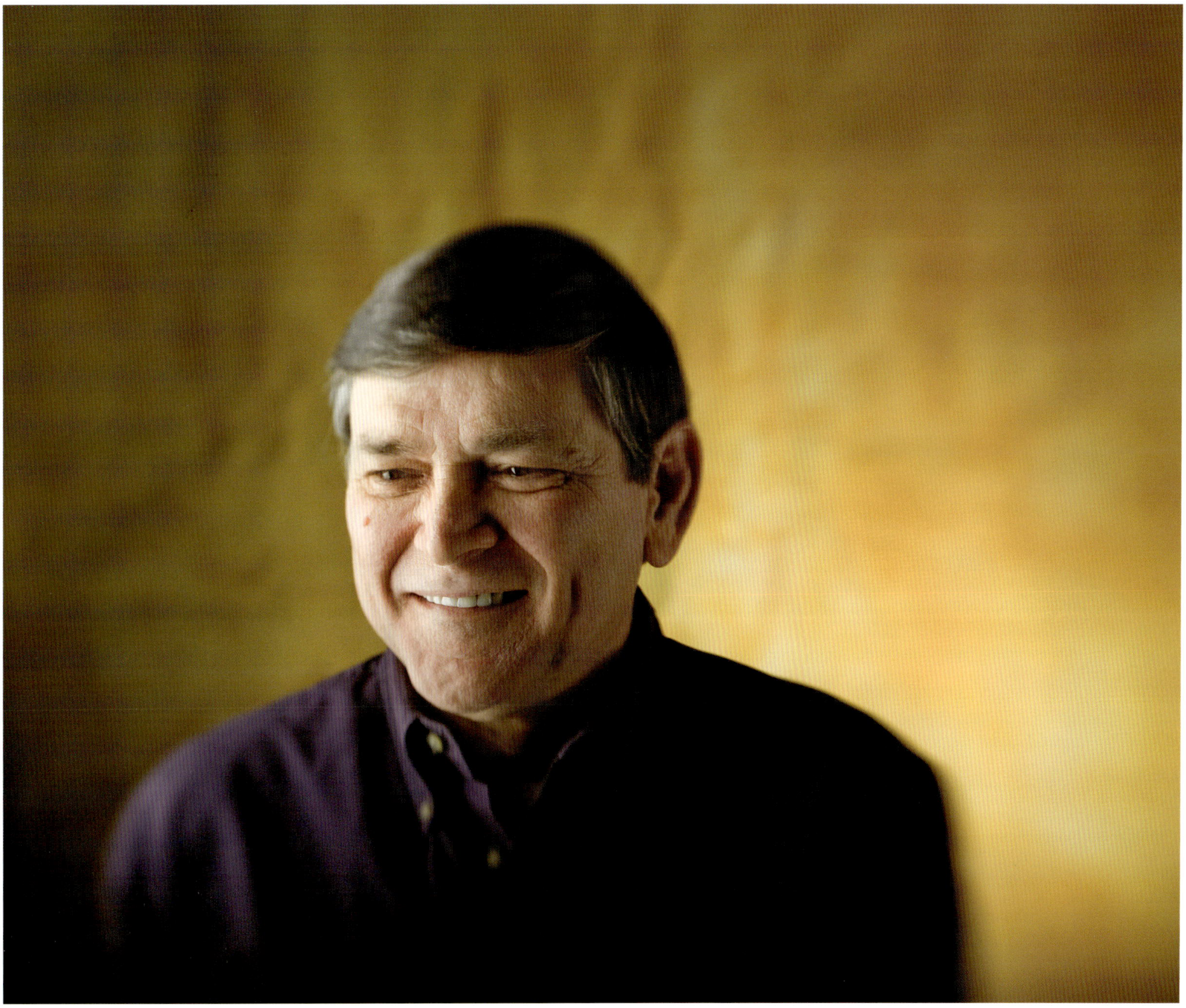

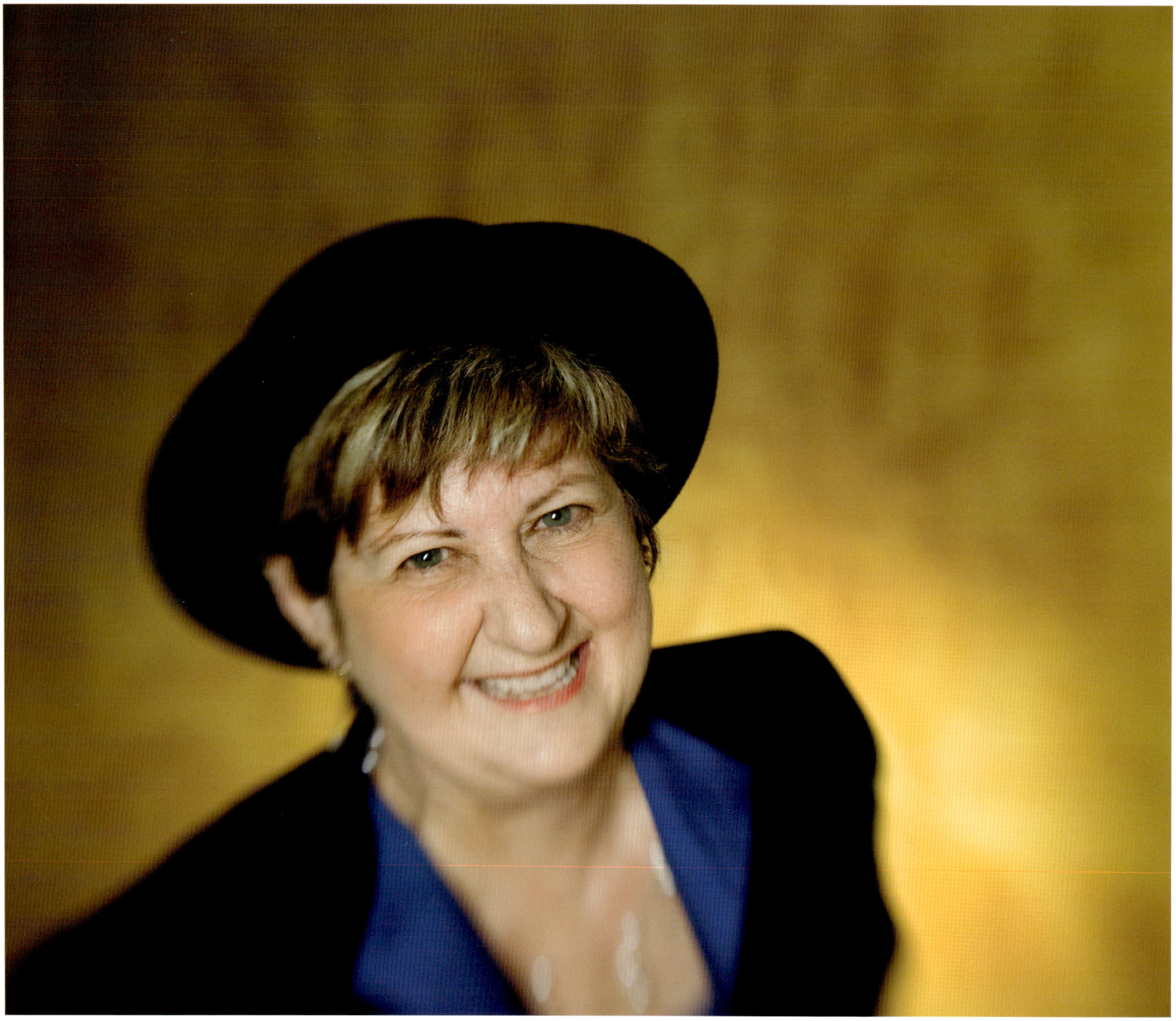

Mary Lou Hightower

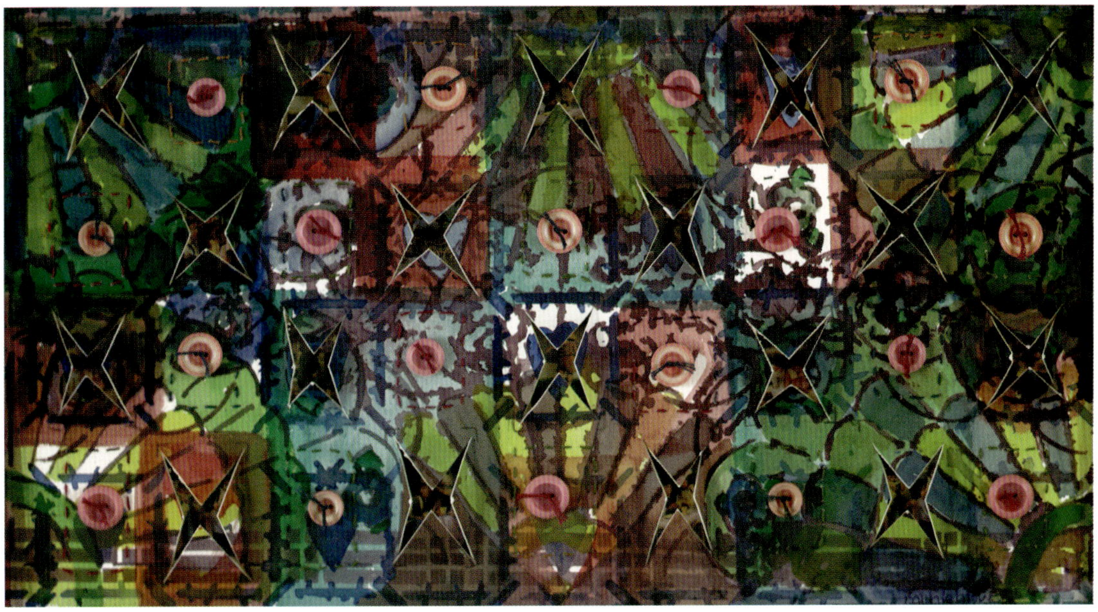

Stain Glass Quilt

9" X 16"

When I was nine years old I spent the summer at my grandparents' farm in West Salem, Ohio. My family lived in Miami, Florida, in a neighborhood far from the rural life that my father, Ralph Swartz, felt I needed to experience. My grandmother, Emma Swartz, was an avid quilter. That summer taught me many lessons about life and gave me a special love for quilts. My grandmother came down with shingles that summer, and I had to spend hours taking care of her and being very quiet. I found her scraps of fabric and began stitching together what she called "patches." These childhood experiences have influenced me to follow my current theme of creating quilts from scraps of paper.

Over the years my artwork has moved from oils to acrylic and now watercolor. The idea of "watercolor patchwork" came from my interest in folk arts and the quilting process. I have coined the word "watercolor patchwork" as a unique process where I have redesigned works through the manipulation of materials, incorporating textural materials to enhance the surface quality. Patchwork is a traditional art form where the pieces of materials are worked into quilts or coverlets. In following this traditional art, "watercolor patchwork" celebrates the legacy of quilts and my love for watercolor media.

This series has continued over the past years in the memory of both my grandmother—and the hundreds of quilts she created over her lifetime—and her son, my father, who was also an artist. My father was always an inspiration to me as an artist. His gentle spirit and courageous fortitude lives on in my work even after his death.

After college, my husband, Bill, and I moved to Spartanburg, where I taught art and served as the art coordinator for the Spartanburg District Six public schools for thirty years. I currently serve as associate professor of art education at USC Upstate and remain a strong advocate for the arts, serving on the Spartanburg District Six School Board for the past ten years.

Katie Adams Hodge

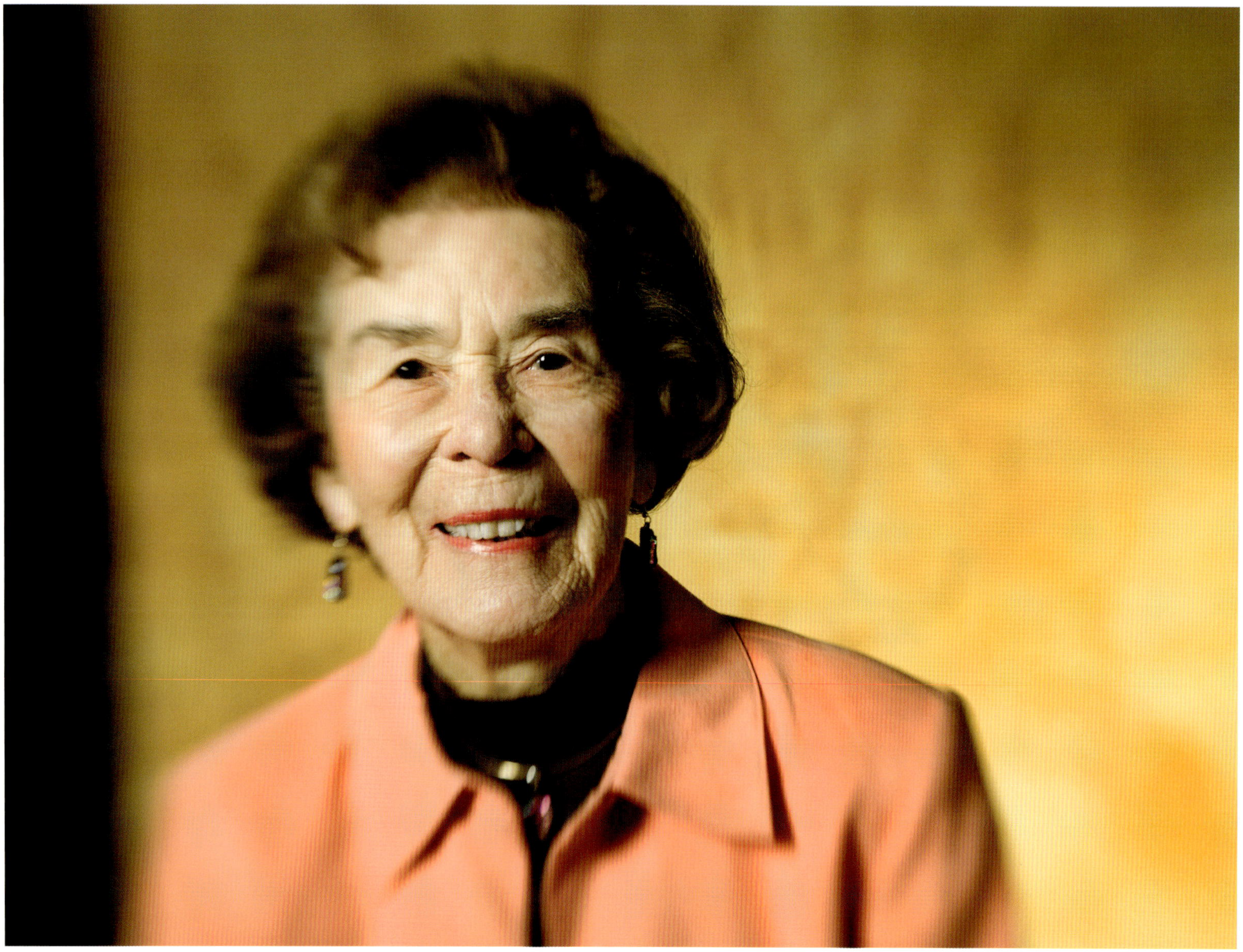

I grew up in Pittsylvania County, Virginia, attended James Madison University, and graduated with a B.S./R.N. degree from Duke University School of Nursing. My earliest interest in art came when my mother took a correspondence course in art and painting. While visiting family and friends in Philadelphia and New York, I spent many days in museums and learned to appreciate and enjoy the works of the Old Masters.

I did not study art until after my children were in school. Art and music appreciation courses at Converse College led me to begin art lessons. I studied pastels with Joan Poppe, watercolor with Marian Janson, Sa Smith, and Carrie Brown, and oils with August Cook after his retirement from Converse. His classes in oil painting gave me much pleasure, sorrow, and frustration. His style, adhering to the classic ideals of realism, influenced me greatly. He always said, "Paint what you see, not what you think you see." My oils are primarily landscapes (including old barns), floral subjects, and still life compositions.

I have always had an innate yearning to create, starting with crewel embroidery in wool on linen, needlepoint, sewing, crochet and knitting, monogramming on linen, and rug hooking (including dyeing and preparing the woven wool and planning my own colors). The South Carolina Governor's Mansion in Columbia owns two of my original designs—crewel-work pillows that depict the flora and fauna ("hers") and the sportsman's activities ("his") of the state. My work has been shown at the Spartanburg Art Museum in a forty-two-painting exhibit, and in a show of fourteen hooked rugs, many of Oriental design. My commitment to art and its healing power led me to establish Spartanburg's Healing Arts program in collaboration with the Arts Partnership of Greater Spartanburg. This program brings the hospitals and care facilities together with art and artists, whose work provides inspiration and comfort to patients, families, and caregivers.

Art serves as a balance to my life. It has been said that "the artist's spirit is the tradition of man. The innate feeling of wanting to live forever comes from the soul."

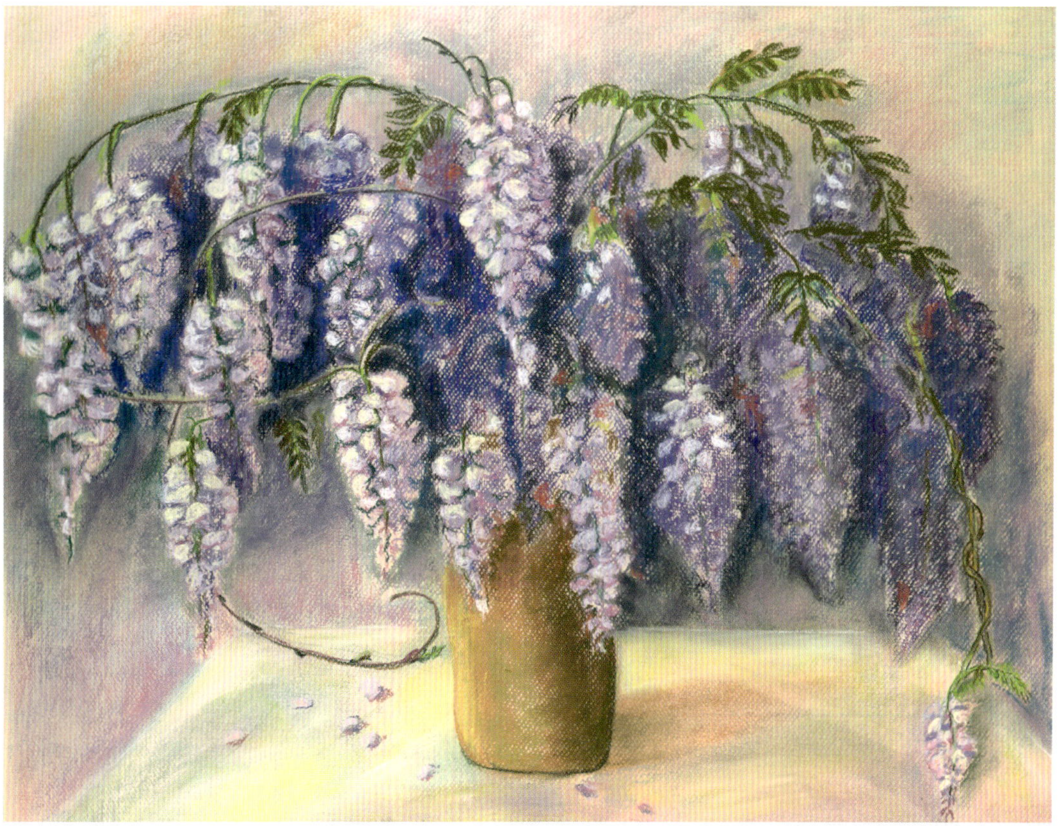

Wisteria
Pastel
20" X 30"

Amy Holbein

I grew up in Raleigh, North Carolina, and have made art all of my life. My family and teachers encouraged me to draw and paint. Art materials were always available, and I remember a constant urge to create. My high school art teacher, Mr. Rankin, really inspired me to take art seriously. He took a group of students to Europe the summer of my senior year and immersed us in art. When I came home from college after a difficult freshman year, struggling with what to do next, he encouraged me to go to art school. He gave the needed push and I graduated from the College of Art and Design at East Carolina University. I majored in textile design and worked as a designer for a few years.

My artistic expression is evolving and changing. A few years ago I learned to paint with oils by painting still lifes, portraits, and figurative work. Recently I started to combine oils with cold wax, which lends itself to an abstract or nonobjective style. No matter what the media or style, I have an ongoing passion for color.

My subject matter comes from the sacramental—that is, where the sacred and ordinary meet. These images can come from dreams, from nature, or photographs. I hope viewers respond to the color in my work. I also hope that my paintings are windows that provide a glimpse of the sacred.

Untitled
Oil on board
8" X 10"

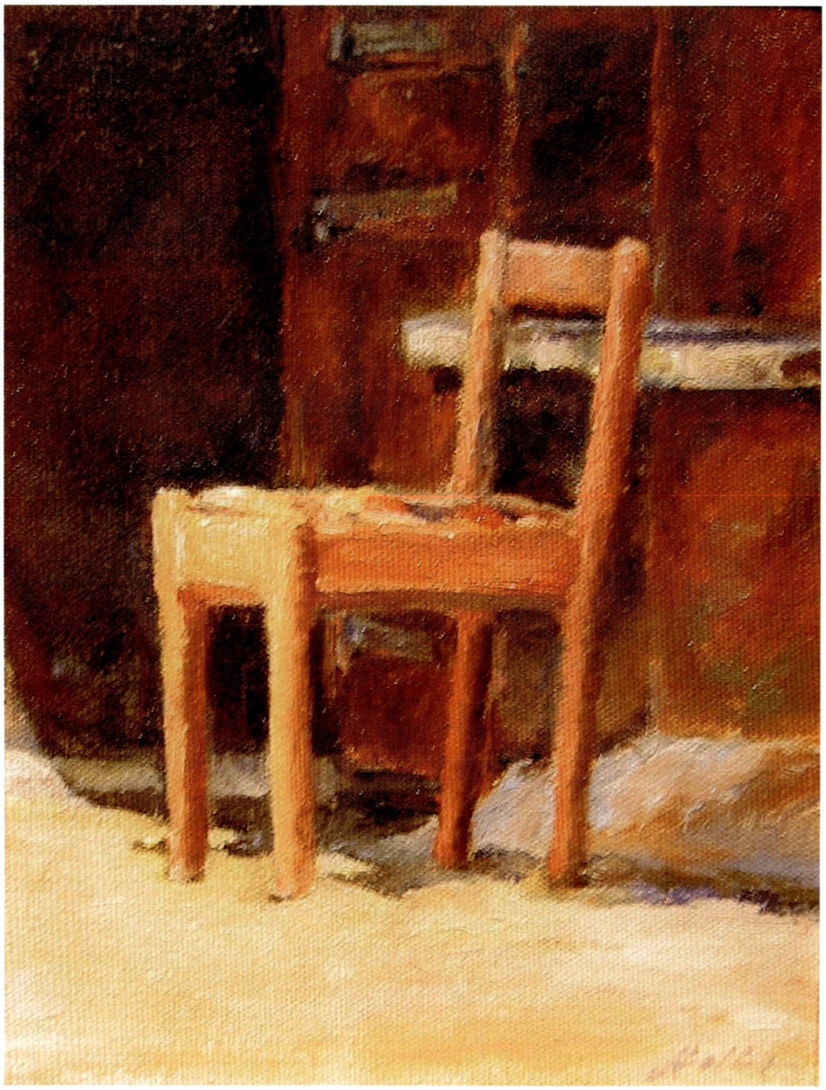

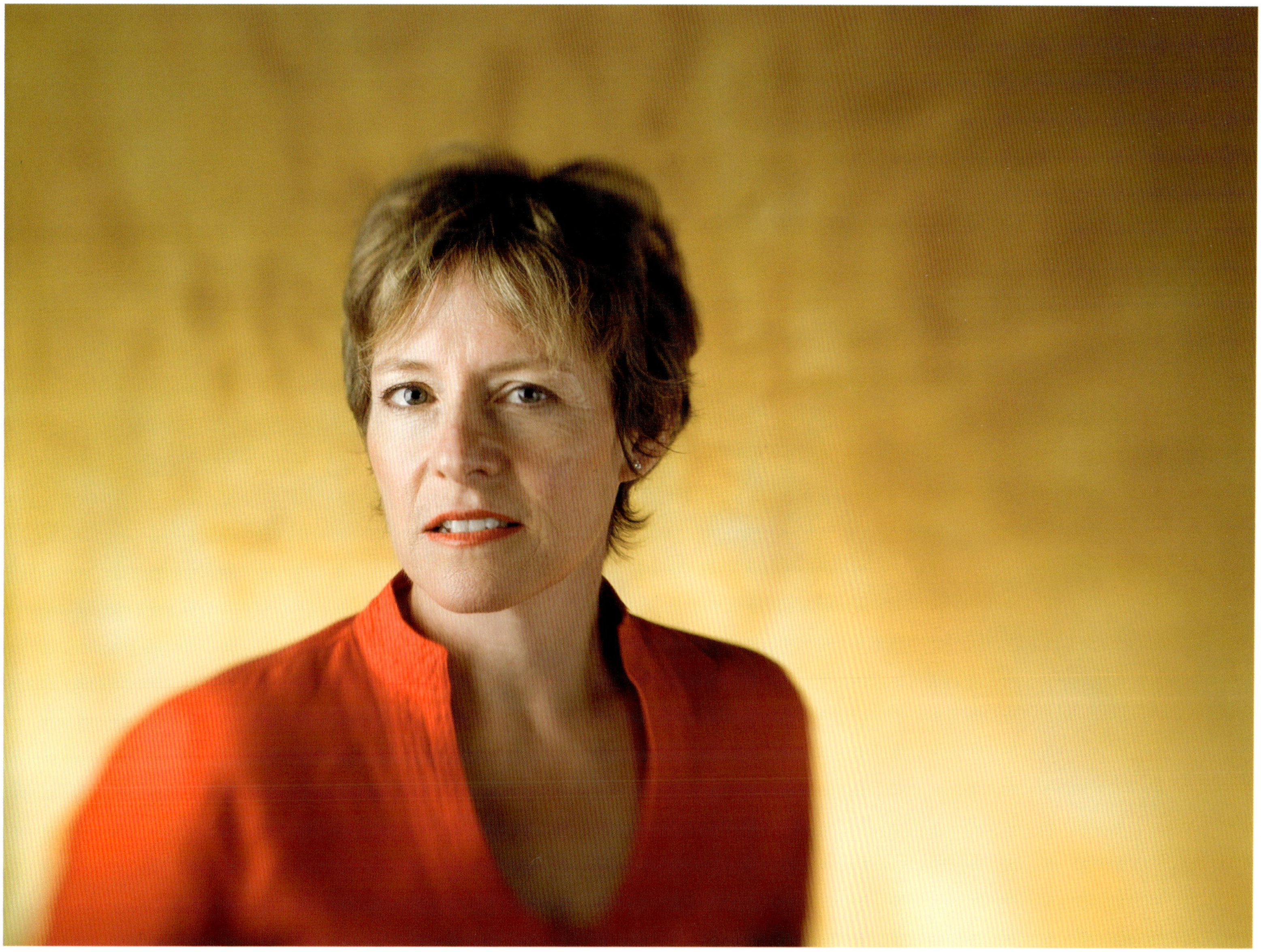

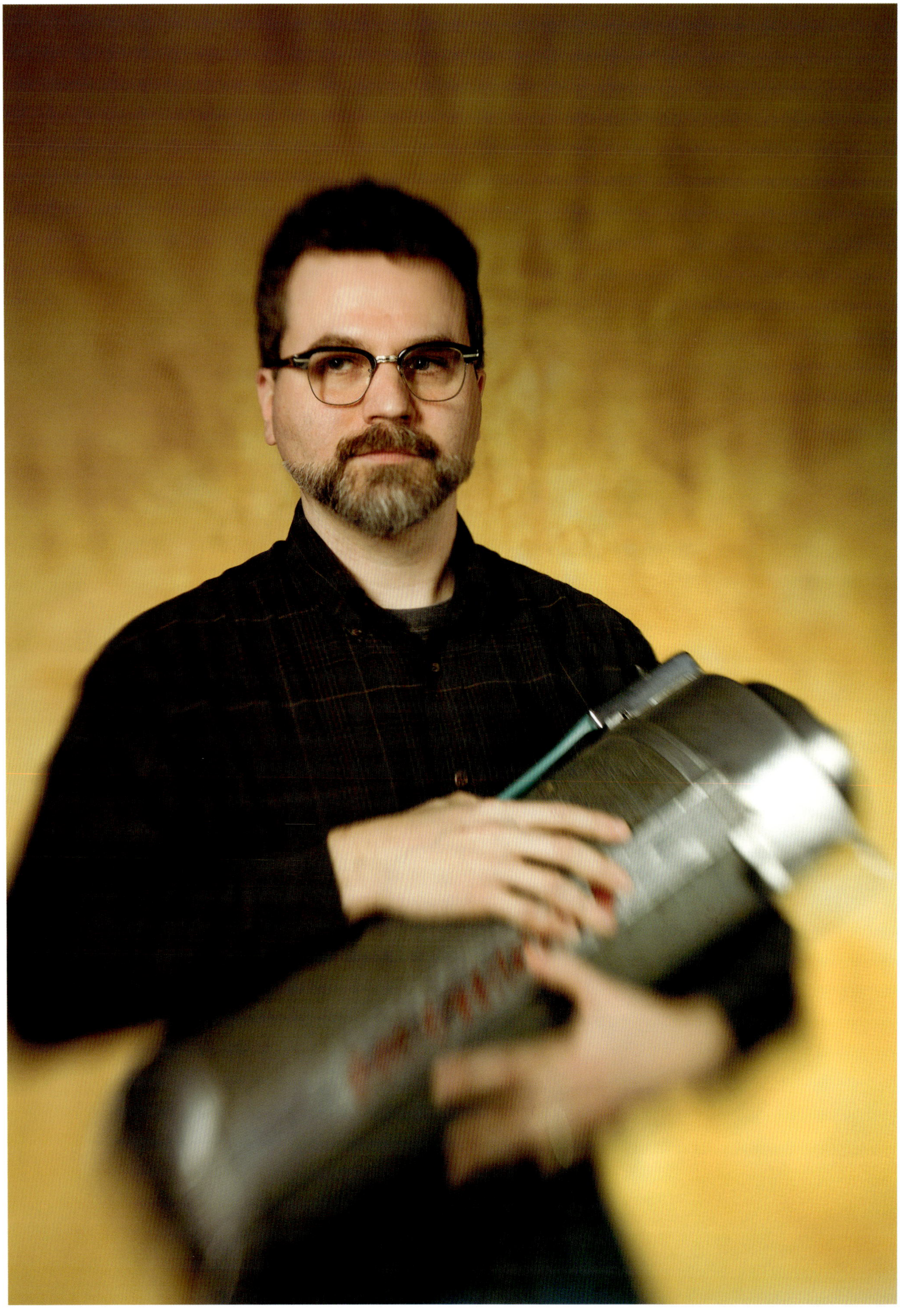

Ashley Holt

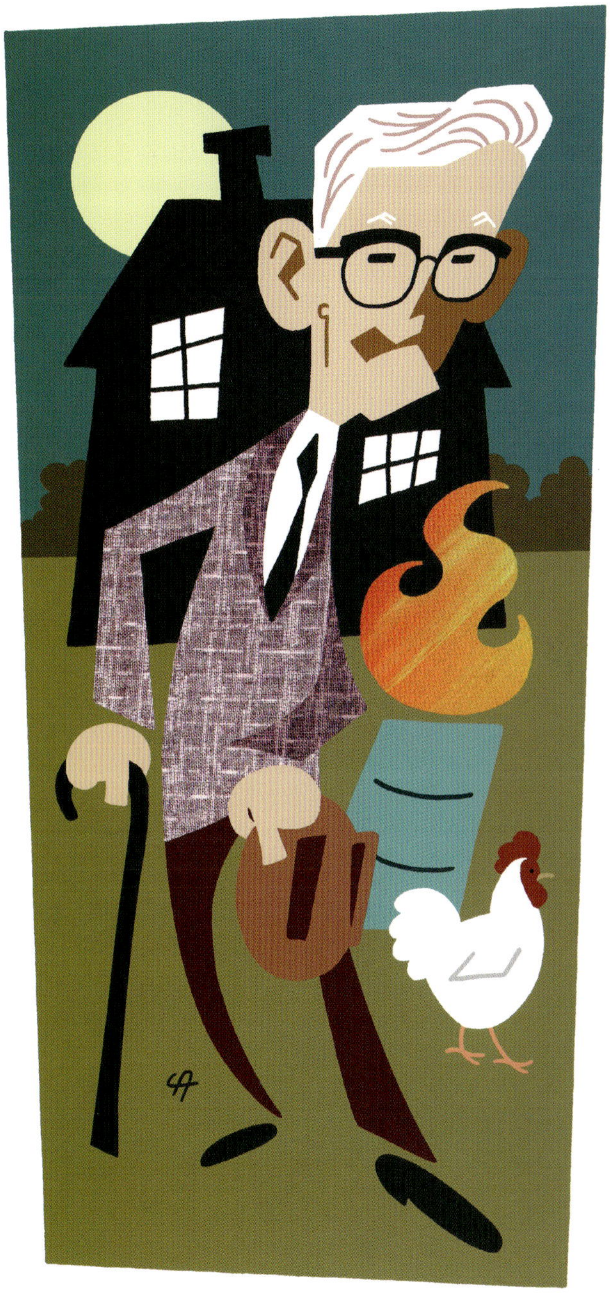

John Easler

Digital Portrait

After twenty-plus years working as a freelance illustrator, with a degree in Illustration from The Art School That Shall Not Be Named (hint: it's in Savannah), I've finally had to admit to myself that I don't have the temperament to be a successful illustrator. I can grit my teeth, up to a point, while the client holds another round of committee meetings to decide whether I should redraw the dog's roller skates or put more jugglers in the background. But eventually, when asked to submit the thirty-seventh round of changes (Cindy in Marketing thought the sunglasses I drew on the muskrat were too "hip hop"), I explode, unleashing curses on the ad campaign or safety poster or 3-D scratch-and-sniff trading cards I've been financially desperate enough to endure.

Perhaps the artistic mentors of my youth are to blame. My older brother, a graphic designer, influenced me to intimidate art directors by being absolutely right about everything at all times. Bill Thompson, illustrator for my hometown paper, the *Charleston Post and Courier*, vindicated my disillusionment with commercial art by reminding me that there was only one true motivation to live the artistic life: nude models. But the late, great Frank Licciardi, modernist painter and intellectual, tried to convince me that life was too short not to seek real joy in personal expression. Remembering Frank's expansive vigor for life and art still irritates me to no end.

So my challenge these days is trying to apply a lifetime of training as an illustrator to subject matter that actually means something to me: portraits of those whom inspire or amuse, subconscious images from my dreams (my subconscious gets a thirty percent cut), and autobiographical renderings of my juvenile delinquency. Plus, for some insane reason, I began producing my finished artwork digitally about ten years ago, a difficult prospect for someone who hates computers.

It is my hope that viewers of my work will connect with the raw honesty of my vision, and that it will inspire them to give me all their money.

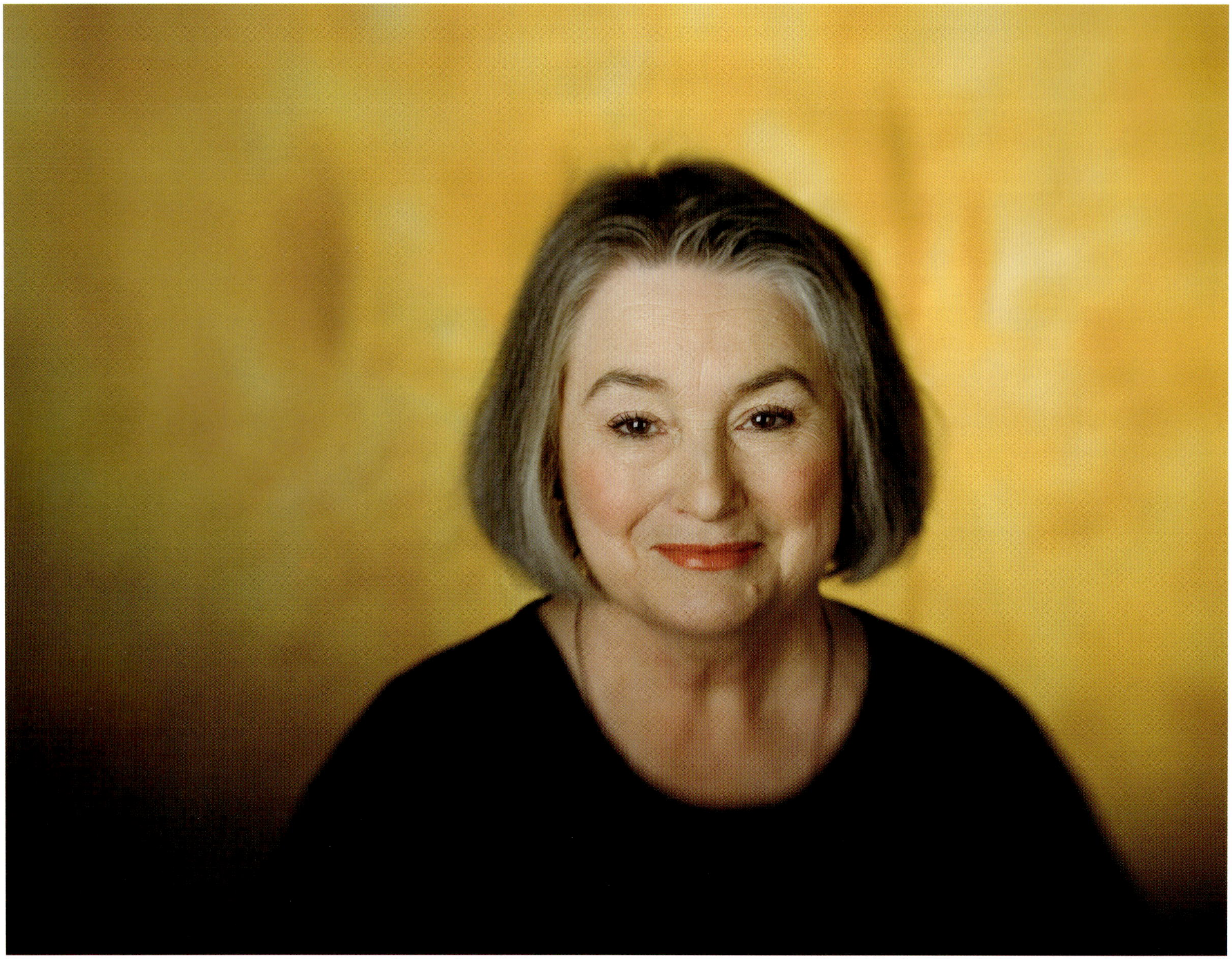

Claire Miller Hopkins

I have been drawing and painting for over thirty years and have served as workshop instructor, juror, and artist-in-residence for the South Carolina Arts Commission. I am a member of the Pastel Society of America and the Pastel Society of the West Coast and have been accorded the "Master Pastelist" designation by each organization.

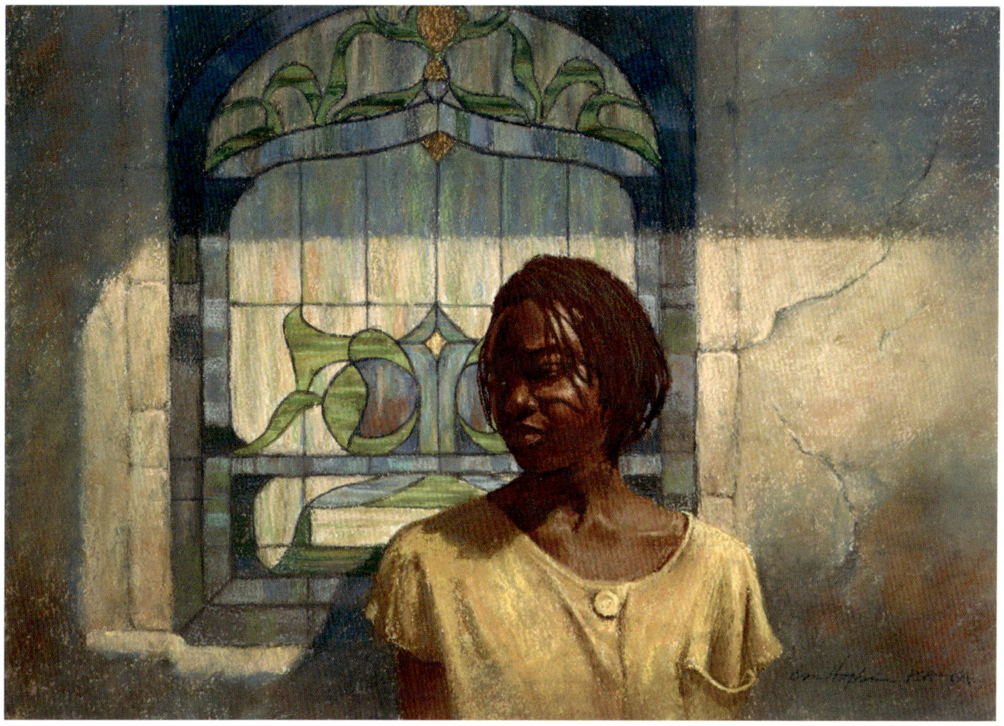

Sanctuary II

Pastel

18" X 24"

As an artist, my inspiration has always been those I'm closely involved with—family, friends, and students—or situations and things that I have an affinity for or a strong emotional response to. Painting allows an avenue of expression that does not impose my feelings on anyone, yet offers them in a way that allows the viewer to respond from his or her own experience. I feel better for having made the statement and gratified when others are drawn to my work. It is a very satisfying way of sharing.

For twenty-five years, most of my paintings have been of people, and the primary medium has been soft pastel. In recent years, I have used watercolor and pastel/watercolor combinations. I recently have begun painting in oils again too. I paint people, landscapes, skies, and still lifes, but the true subjects of my paintings are light and mood. My work has been reproduced in five books and in several magazines.

Linda Hudgins

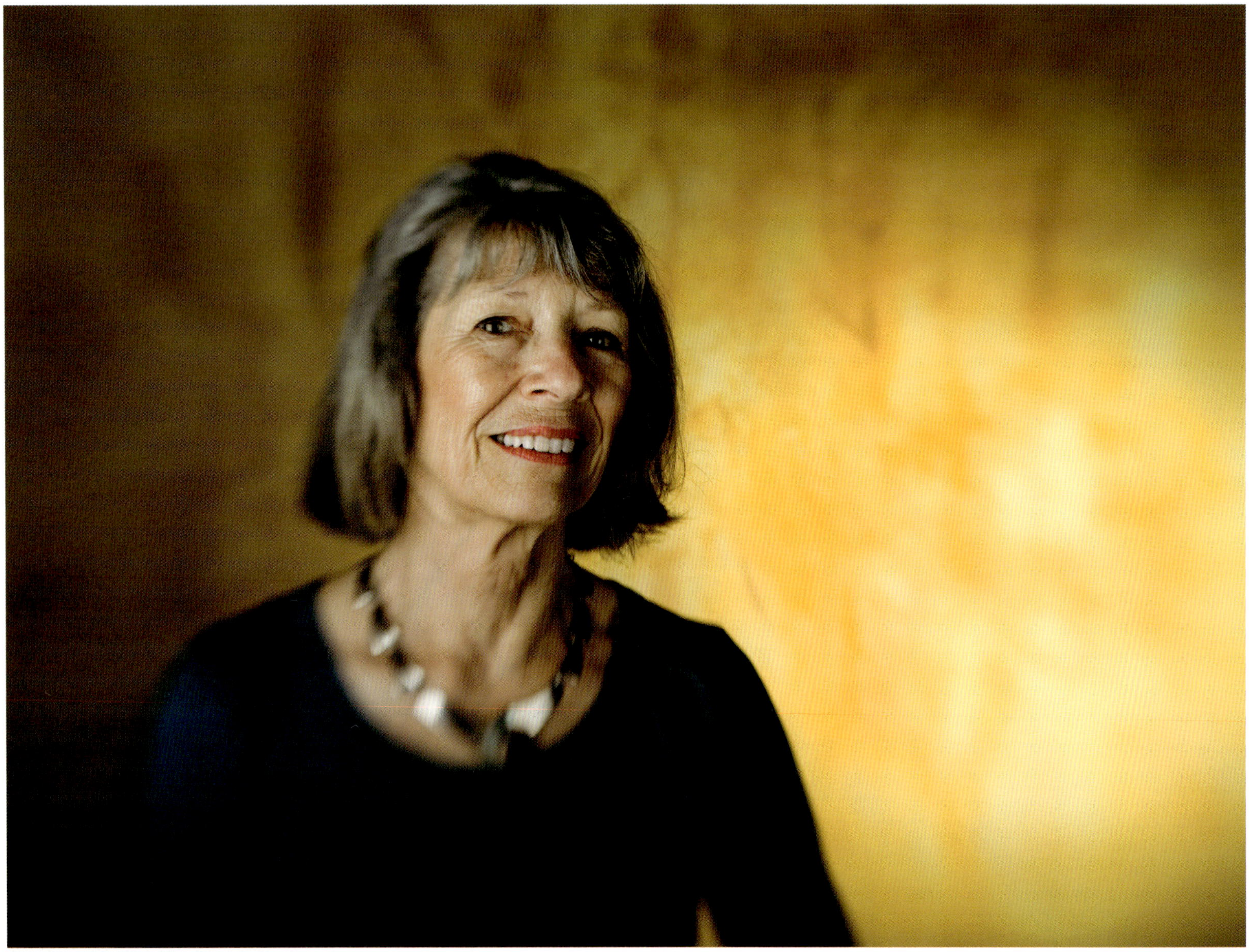

Rural Spartanburg County, with few neighbors and lots of land to roam, encouraged my introverted, sensitive, and creative self, as did the materials for drawing, painting, cutting, sewing, and pasting that were always available. At Roebuck Elementary the teachers recognized that I liked drawing and made me the school artist. An encouraging science teacher allowed me to take a prism home, and I painted my first Impressionist painting looking through it. Neither I nor the teacher knew Impressionism.

I appreciate the attentive care of teachers who encouraged me in art and directed me to Converse College to study art, having no idea what that meant. Soon, I learned the discipline from August Cook. Art history and technique were required learning; Professor Brown's philosophy class provided the pathway to pursue questions that accompany the understanding of art. Studying later at the Rhode Island School of Design challenged me to expand technically and creatively.

Over the years, I loved teaching art at the Spartanburg Day School, in the U.S. Peace Corps, and on my own in China. Wide expansions of thought and feeling awakened the courage of my creative self.

Back in Spartanburg, I discover increased involvement and inclusion of artists of all ages and interests in the arts. Many places to exhibit and a receptive attitude on the part of the Spartanburg community make exhibiting my work an agreeable way to bring my experiences home.

Perhaps, as a sentient being, I am accessing visual records of this expansive, chaotic world and putting them on canvas to share. Is this what happens when I am free of contemplating order that, historically, we have demanded of nature in art? Paintings reflect my perception of natural energy forces of flux and flow in this world. I am excruciatingly content when working with oils and/or acrylics in an open, yet focused, frame of mind and heart. If I am successful, the viewer perceives in my art a connection to the changing and creative nature of existence—and is reminded of his or her own creative nature.

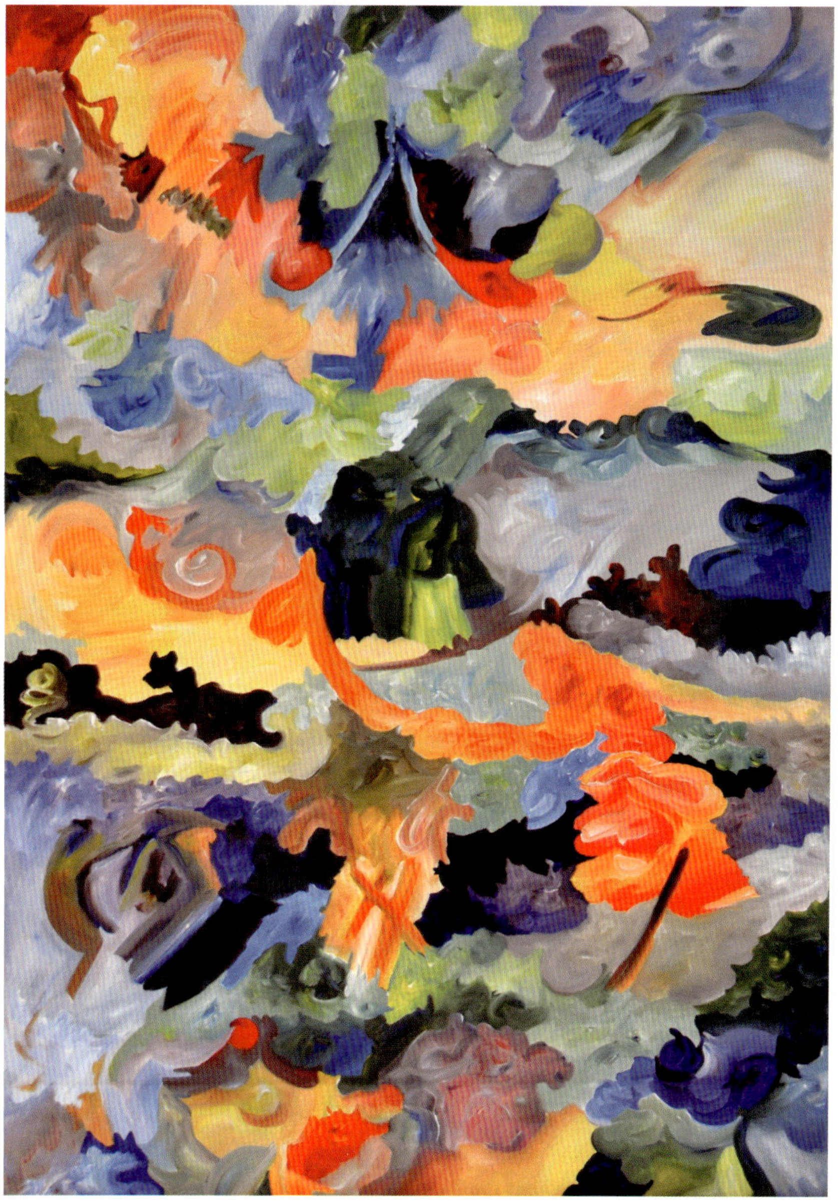

Day by Day II (Detail)
Acrylic on canvas
14' X 43"

I grew up in various states across the country, and much of my artwork, particularly my watercolors, is influenced by living in the Southwest. I spent several years living in Phoenix and San Diego, where I gained much of my training in art and art therapy.

Relocating to Spartanburg to live and teach at Converse College was a big step. One of the positive influences that helped me decide to move to the area was the vibrant creative community, including the new Spartanburg Art Museum, HUB-BUB, Carolina Gallery, and strong arts programs in the schools.

I have always been creatively inclined. An imaginative child, I grew up with music, acting, and art in my family. I struggled at first with structured art courses in college and began working independently, but I eventually returned to take coursework in graphic design and fine art, followed by art therapy. Art has always provided an avenue for self exploration and healing, so discovering art therapy was perfect for me.

Although I began as a sketch artist, I have focused on watercolors for the past ten years. I have thoroughly enjoyed the challenge and success of this media. More recently, I am moving toward found object and assemblage pieces.

The watercolors I show are often inspired by multi-sensory experiences. When I travel—whether to Europe or to nearby mountains or coastline—the experiences involve all the five senses. I attempt to capture the essence of these experiences in my work. For example, sitting on a bench in Old Town, San Diego, one smells the blossoms mixed in with the spicy aroma of authentic Mexican cooking. There is also the scent of sea air, the sound of mariachi music coming from the cafés, and the brightly colored umbrellas that seem to be dancing overhead. How does one capture this in one two-dimensional piece? There is an emotive quality to the experience. Art helps me to internalize and capture the experience and share it with others.

Bazaar del Mundo

Watercolor

14" X 18"

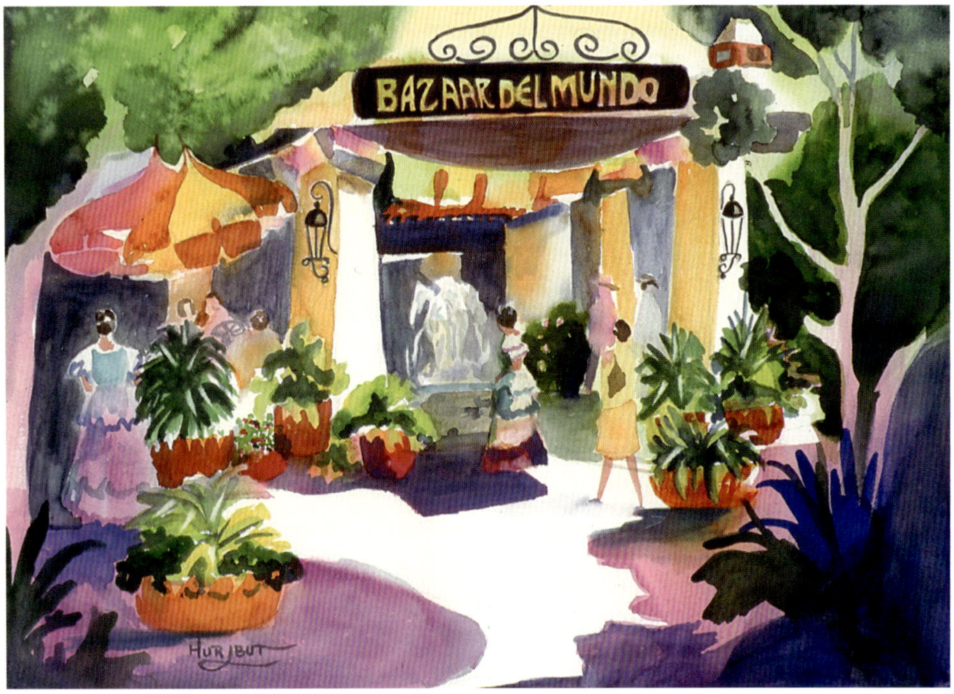

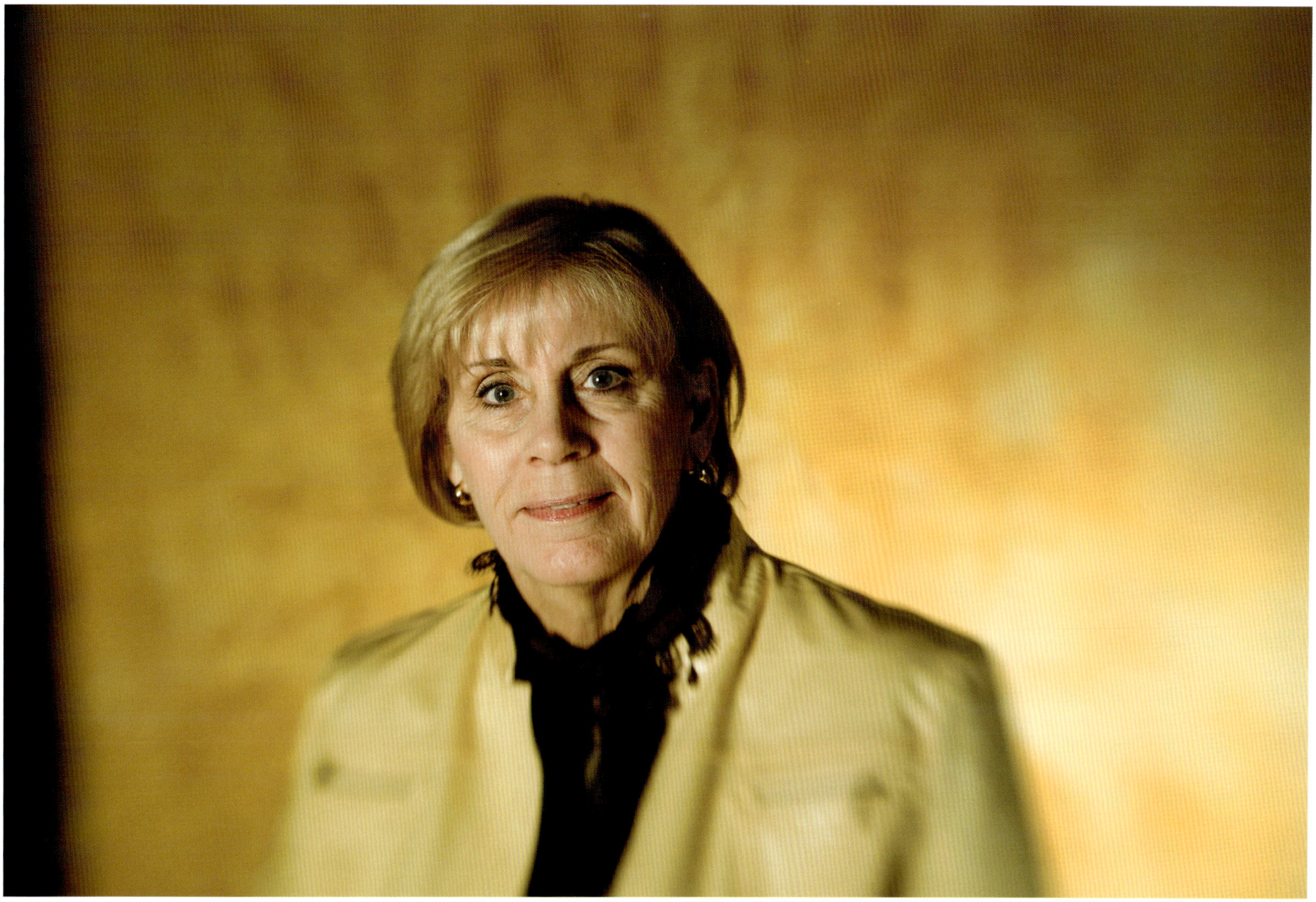

Geri Hurlbut

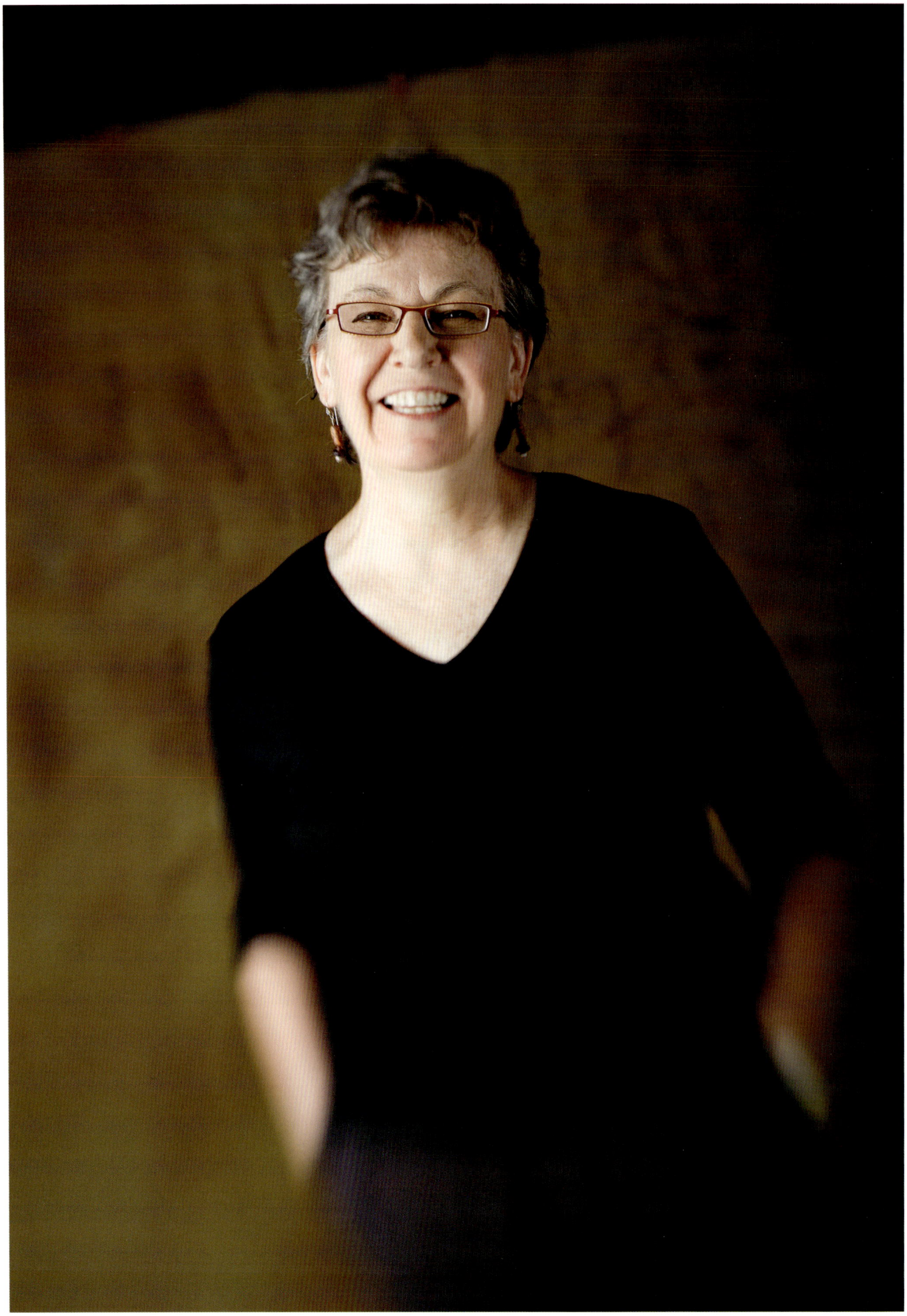

Carol Beth Icard

I was a quiet, introspective child who grew up near Boston in a home with paintings on the wall, music playing, and plenty of books to feed my imagination. But "home arts" were what I was exposed to most, so as a young mother supplementing the family income, I sewed clothes, baked pies, and knitted slippers. Eventually I designed a line of children's gifts that sold all over the country. Basket making followed, and I loved dying the reed into rainbows and finding ways to shape my work in unusual ways, yet I longed for a deeper expression of meaningful creativity.

In my mid-forties I enrolled in the visual arts program at Berkshire Community College, where I joyfully immersed myself in drawing, painting, and art history classes. I felt like a tight bud unfurling in the sunshine of my education. Following graduation I attended a weeklong class in Italy. My heart cracked open; colors flowed out and revealed a new path.

After a number of years, my husband and I decided to move to South Carolina to be closer to our two grown daughters and their families. Moving to Landrum and the supportive artistic environment of this entire region has opened many doors in my artistic journey.

Now I am a quiet, introspective adult. My work incorporates intuition, emotion, and contemplation via color, gesture, line, and form. Each painting can be a road back into the past, winding through the ancient walls of Italy, or forward into the realm of unexpected angels. I play with the paint and the process, trusting and improvising and wrangling, until some mysterious alchemy reveals the finished work.

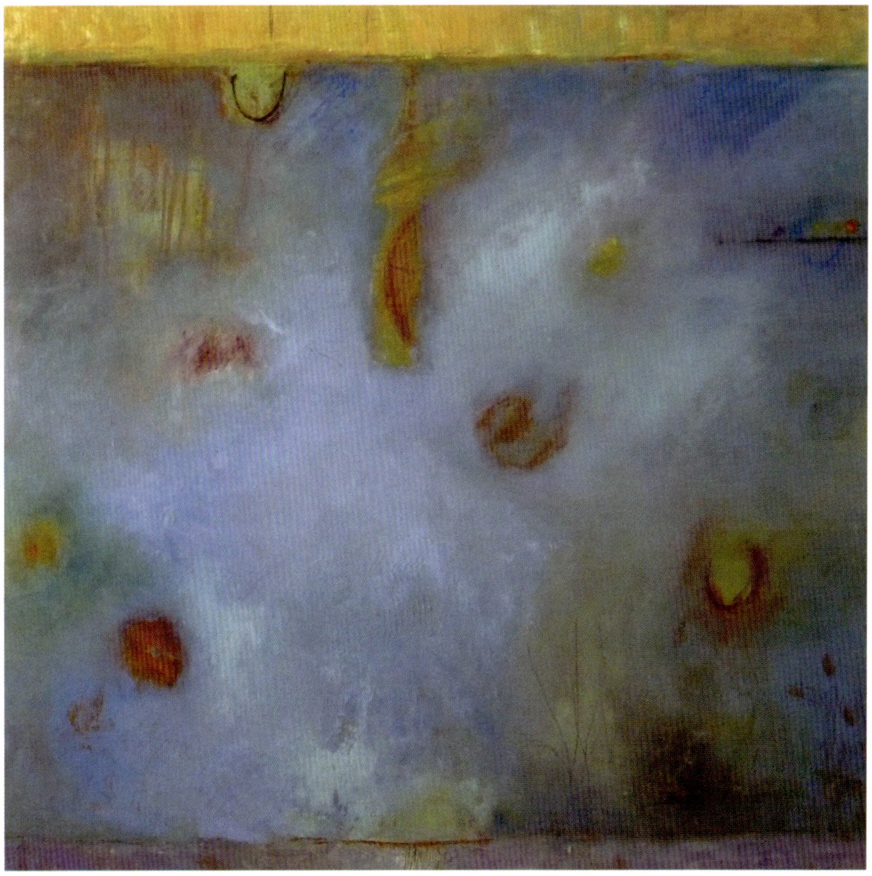

In Between
Oil and cold wax
30" X 30"

Gaffney A. Jarrell

I was born in Augusta, Georgia, and raised in Atlanta. My father is a jazz drummer who has an art gallery and frame shop, and my mother is a television personality and actress on stage. As a child I was exposed to several art forms. When I grew older I realized that for the actor on the stage, once the show has ended, the performance becomes a memory, unless captured on video. Visual art offers something tangible that can be displayed and enjoyed for more than a weekend run of a show.

I am a self-taught artist who utilizes many mediums. I love the combination of acrylics, pastels, charcoal, paper, and earth elements. I enjoy mixing and blending them together, creating depth and dimension. My style is abstract, making my subject matter limitless. It can be what's in my head at the time, my feelings or emotions about any given situation, or an event that moves me. Sometimes it is a piece of art I love.

Lady Di
Acrylic on canvas
48" X 24"

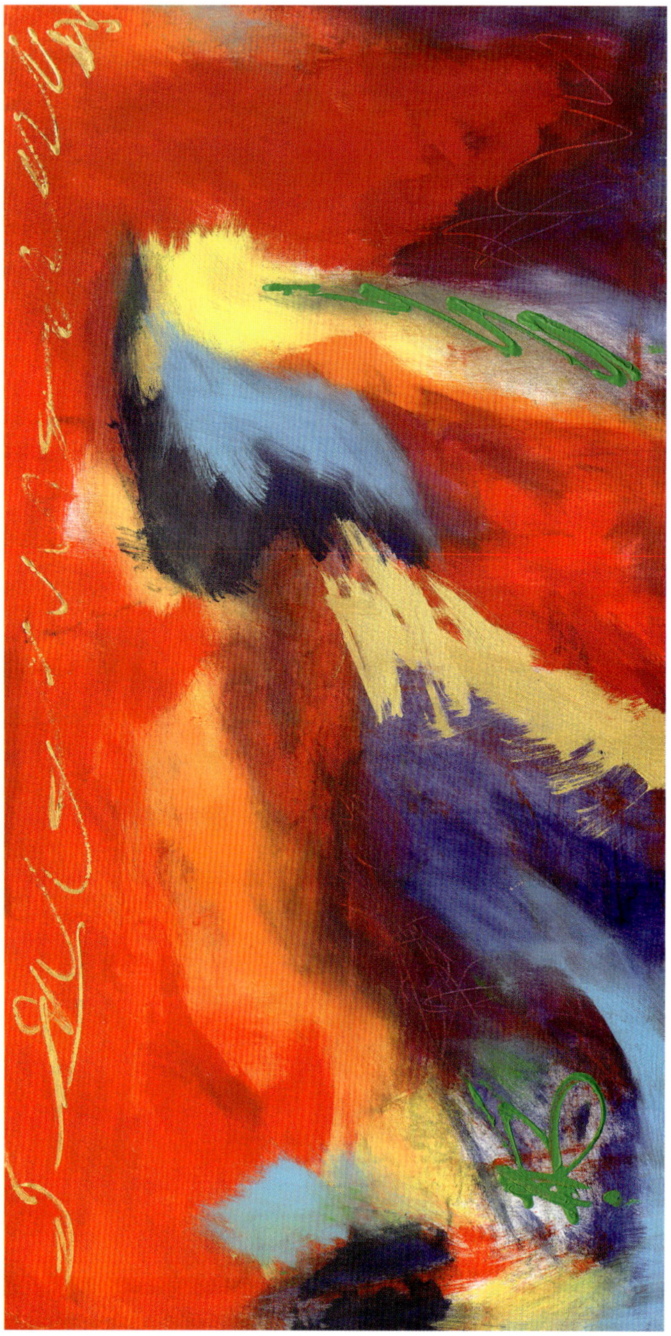

Emotion inspires me—the biggest being love ... okay, okay, anger can creep in, suddenly turning my piece muddy and dark. At times I am touched by someone'sspirit and I enjoy freely expressing it on canvas or wood. I listen to music while I am at play, and that's when the energetic, almost frantic painting occurs. It's easy to be loose and carefree.

Ultimately I hope for an emotion, reaction, or response from my audience. People often see images in my work that were not intended. This draws them in, and then they have to have it. It's a magical process that often leads to a sale! And I enjoy the sale!

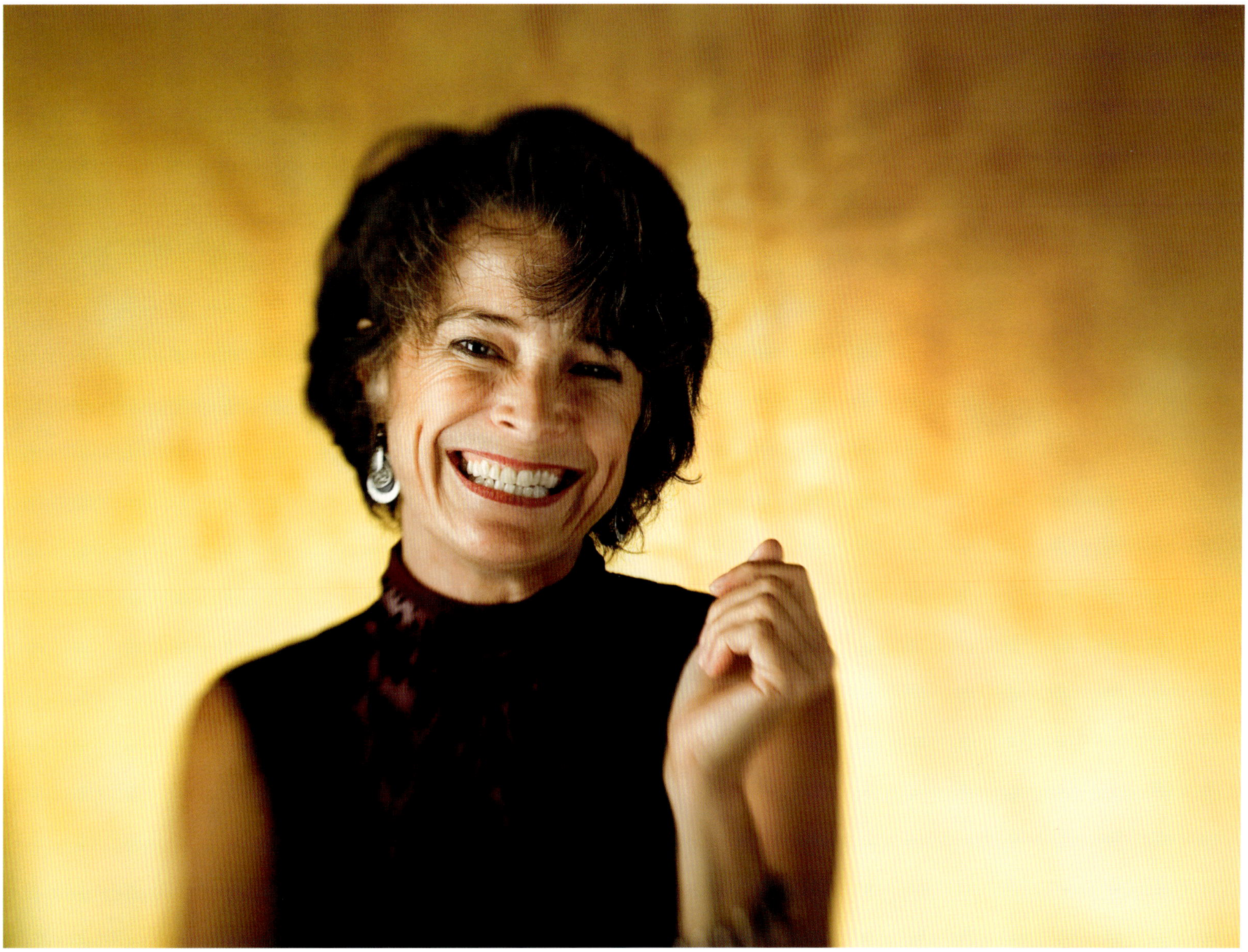

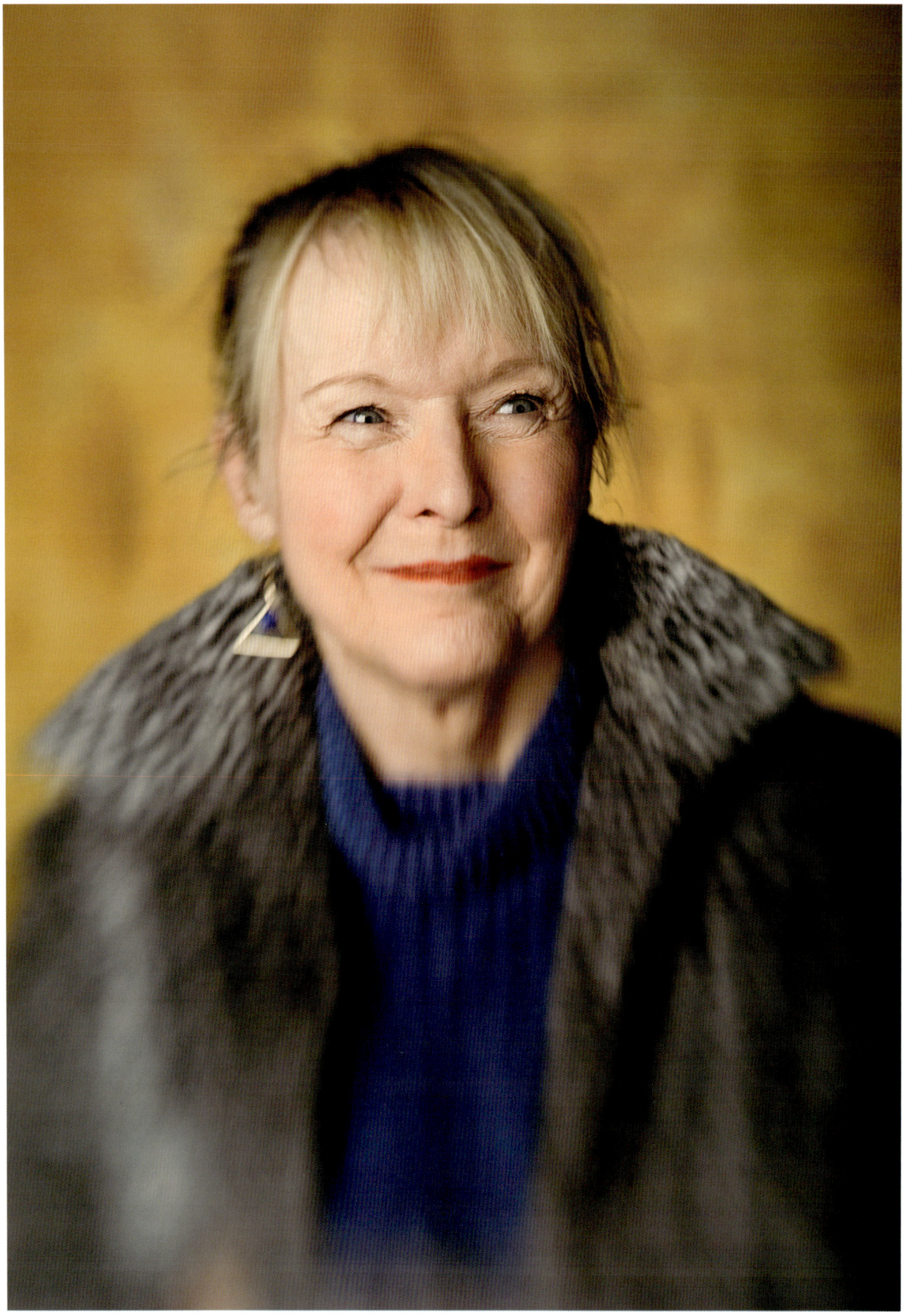

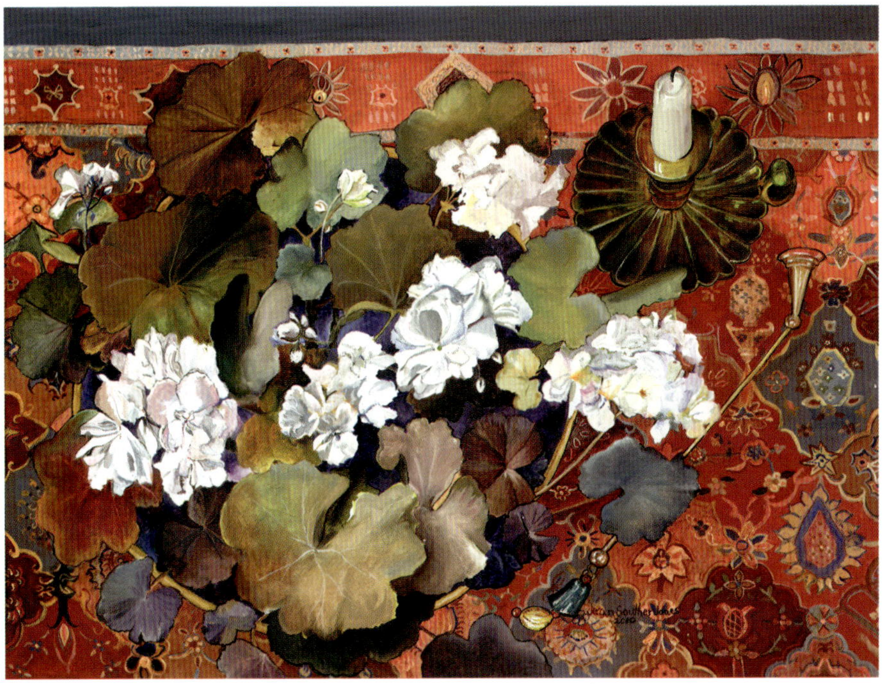

Still Life with White Geraniums

Acrylic on canvas

24" X 30"

Jean Souther Jones

I was born in the Holly Springs community near Campobello and grew up in rural Spartanburg County. Art has been important to me for as long as I can remember. In my childhood I drew constantly, using pencils and crayons. Beauty in nature, color, texture, and pattern were delightful to me as I played with paper dolls. My mother and teachers encouraged me, and I majored in art at Furman University.

My first painting experience was with tempera in an introductory art class. I moved on to oil and later used acrylics in the graduate programs at Furman and the University of South Carolina. I was introduced to china painting while living in Texas. Back in South Carolina, I started watercolor painting. Now I am enjoying alternating between watercolor and acrylics.

My painting style is representational with an emphasis on color. I paint flowers, peach-related themes, and people from my rural home community.

The art atmosphere in Spartanburg enriches the soul of an artist. Our school art program has inspired multiple young people to continue in art-related jobs and activities in adulthood. While teaching art in Spartanburg County School District 7, I was awarded Southeastern Elementary Art Teacher of the Year and later National Elementary Art Teacher of the Year. The advanced educational opportunities for the arts and the support of the community for art-related venues enrich our community with cultural as well as economic opportunities. While on the board of the South Carolina Arts Commission, I emphasized the importance of the arts in all of South Carolina.

I hope my work is perceived as an expression of love and beauty of South Carolina and my Spartanburg County roots.

Jill Jones

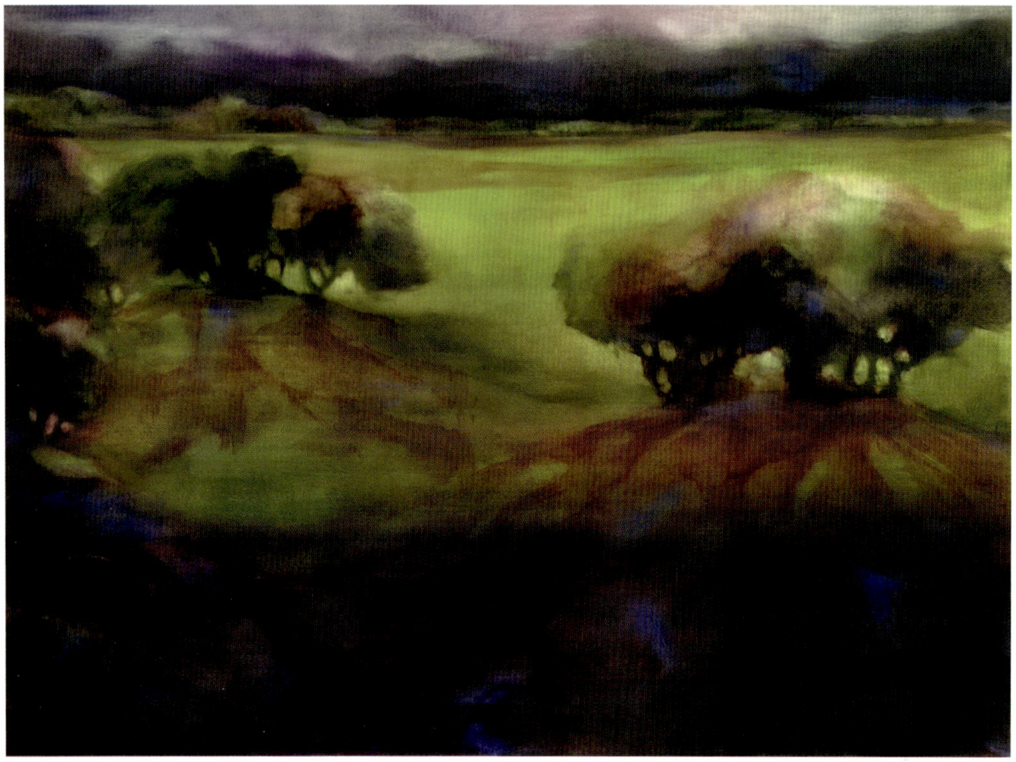

Sacred Spaces
Oil on canvas
20" X 30"

The first question I'm asked about my landscape paintings is usually, "Is this a real place?" My answer is, "Yes. Sort of, anyway."

While I paint exclusively from my imagination, the imagery is fueled from memories of growing up in the once-bucolic farmland outside of the little town of Chesnee. Long days on horseback spent exploring my surroundings led to my catalog of subject matter: fields overtaken by kudzu, forgotten peach orchards, yellow skies with roiling gray-green clouds, seemingly endless seas of soybeans.

As an artist I am more interested in mood than in detail, in conveying how a place "feels" rather than how it looks. Because of this my painted memories are less sentimental than they are dark and dreamlike. I err on the side of simplicity, believing—like Francis Bacon—that the job of the artist is always to deepen the mystery. Too much information and the mystery is spoiled.

It's why I paint from memory. Without the crutch of photographs to guide me, extraneous details fade away. What remains are shape and shadow, mood and feeling—the expression of an inner landscape that can be far more interesting than the real world.

I completed my BFA in studio art from Converse College in 2002, coming on the heels of a fifteen-year career as a newspaper reporter. The similarities between my two careers are great: I once painted pictures with words. Now I use brushes.

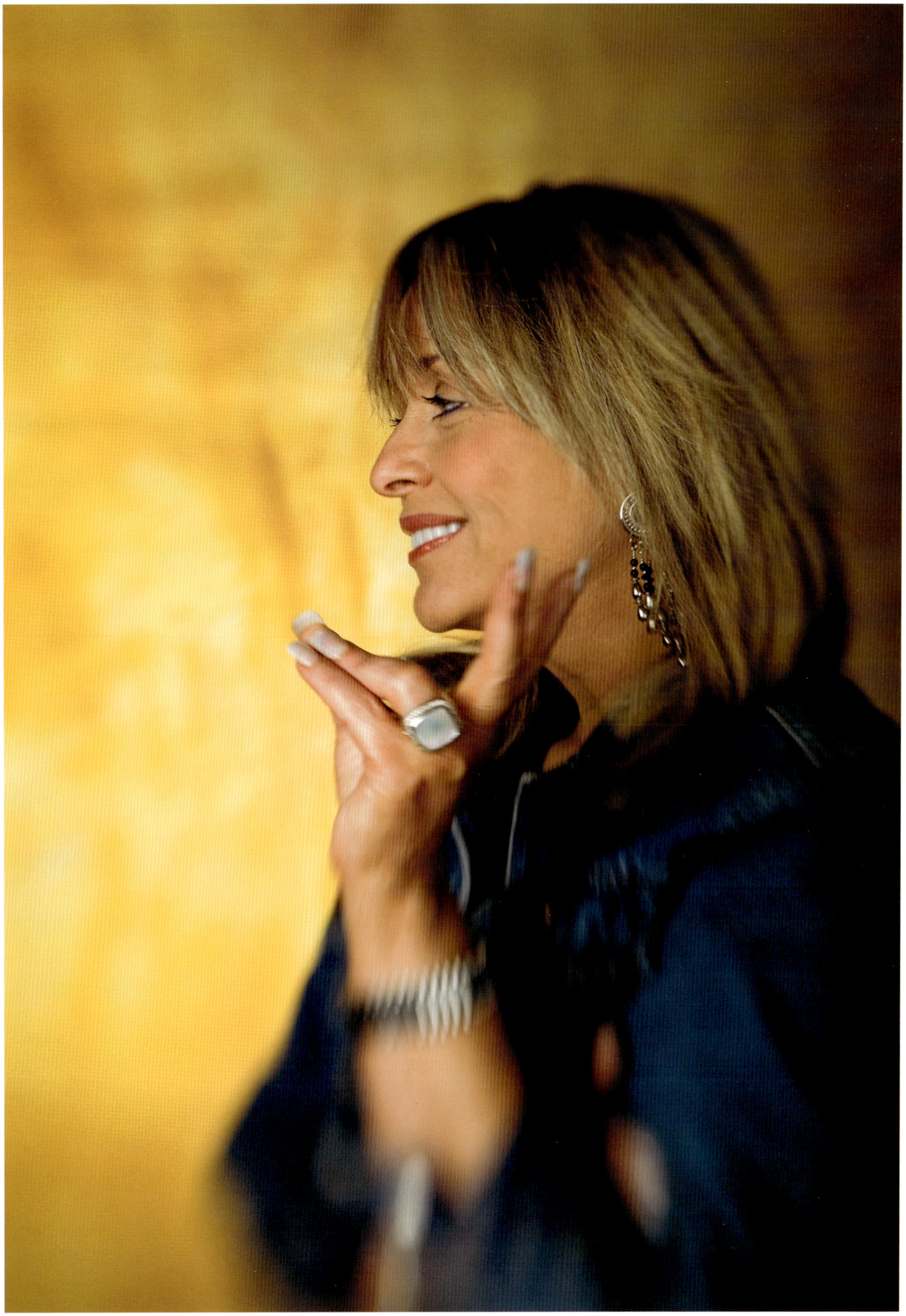

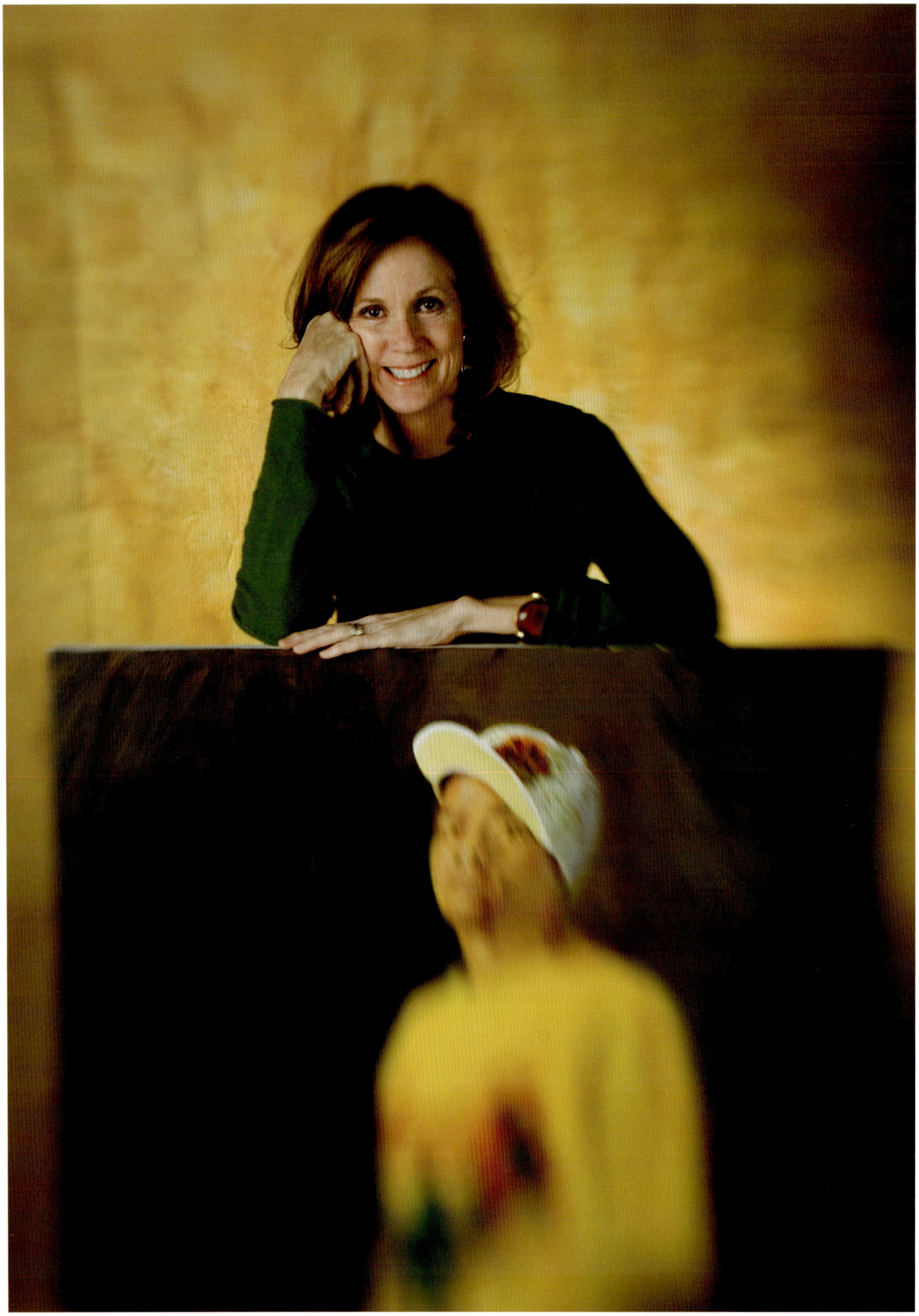

Dorothy Chapman Josey

Just as I find it hard to articulate my spiritual beliefs, it is nearly impossible to communicate why I paint and what the process means to me. I know beyond the shadow of a doubt that when I start my day with prayer my day goes better, just as I know that when I paint I am a nicer person to be around. Somehow that long line at Wal-Mart is tolerable if I've been in the studio that day.

I am from the "let-it-rip-tater-chip" school of art. I rarely do preliminary drawings. I dive right in and start painting. I am not afraid of changing a painting. If there is a part of a painting that seems just perfect, I try not to get too fond of it because if it needs to be moved or removed for the greater good or finished painting, I figure I can paint it even better the next time. Any given piece may go through many changes. This is why my preferred medium is oil paint. It is so forgiving, unlike watercolor or acrylics.

A painting may take me one sitting or fifty-one sittings. I never know. I struggle and go through a lot of fear to get a piece the way I want it. I believe that it is the struggle and the changes that give my work its soul.

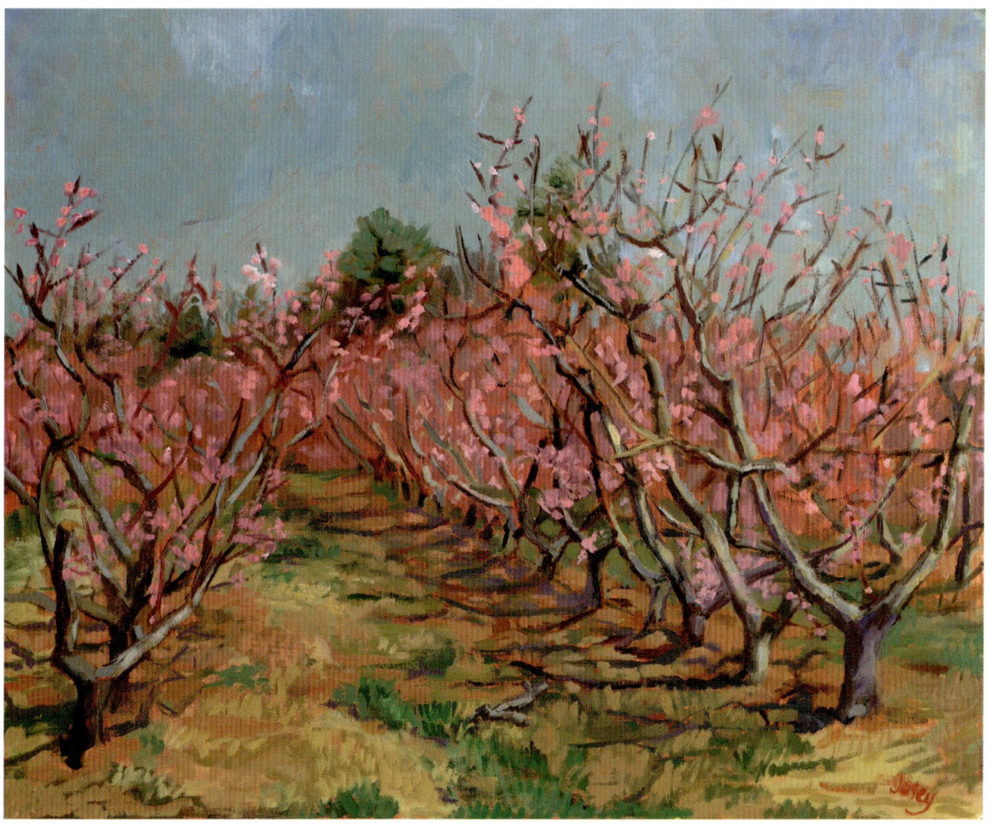

Peach Orchard

Oil on canvas

20" X 24"

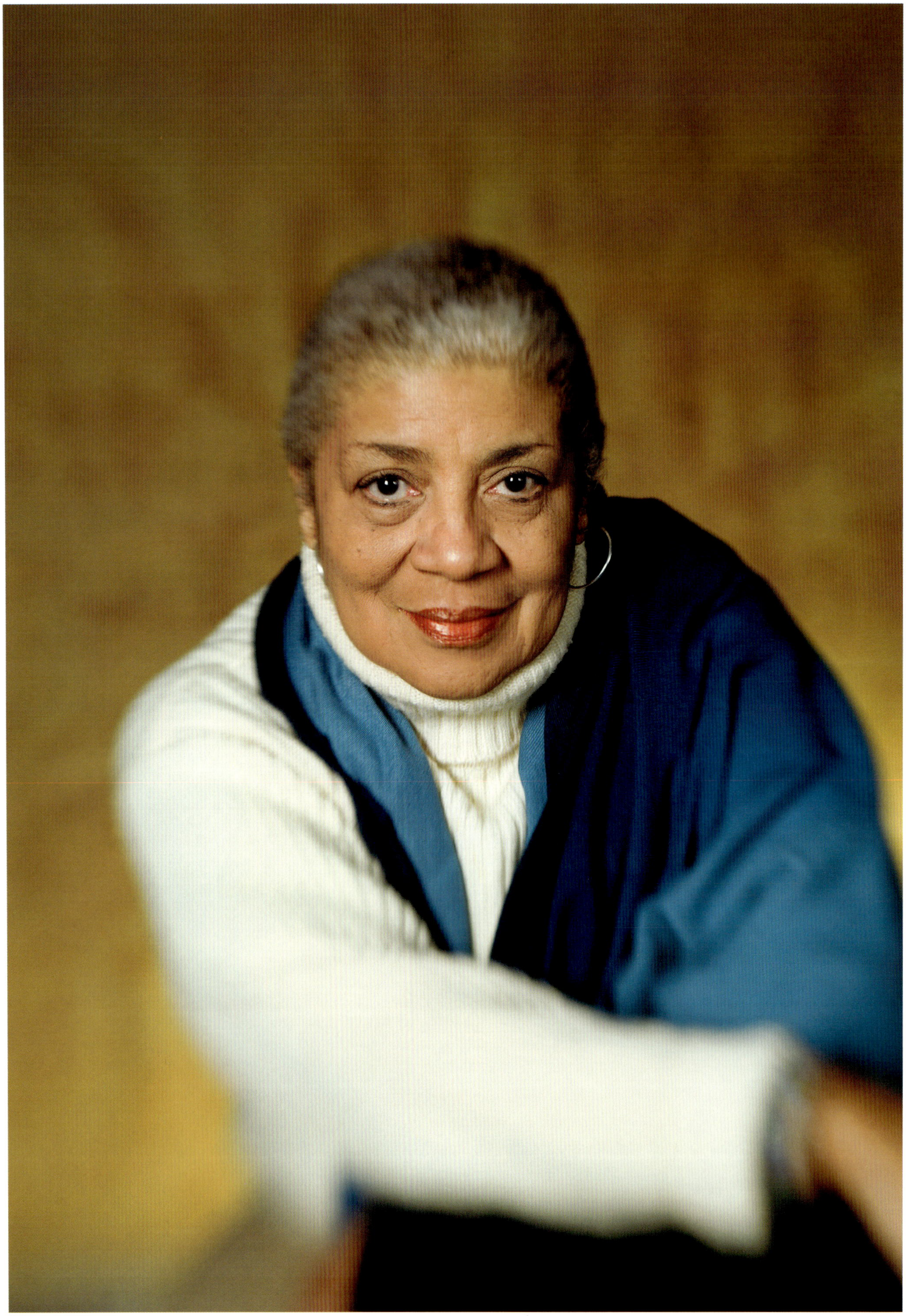

Pat Kabore

My art is my inner voice. It is the visual expression of all my extraordinary experiences as an African-American woman and artist. I was greatly impacted by the art I saw when I lived in West Africa. My artist signature is *Pag A*, a Mossi word meaning "women." I want my art to build bridges and connections between cultures and people. Much of my art is woman-focused, telling and sharing their stories.

I am an award-winning printmaker and mixed media artist. My work has been exhibited nationally in fine art museums and galleries. My work has been included in the Washington Printmakers Fine Art Print Calendars and in the following collections: Georgetown University, Longwood University, the Detroit Branch of the American Civil Liberties Union, the Federal Reserve, the Library of Congress, the National Museum of Fine Art, the Women's Museum, the Phell Collection, the Smithsonian, and the University of Miami.

As much as I love making and creating new artworks, I also have a great love for sharing my talents in the art of printmaking with others, particularly young people, seniors, and disabled persons. I have participated in art events all over the country, including the Paducah Arts Alliance in Kentucky, a one-month artist residency where I worked on community interactive printmaking program and had a showcase exhibition at the end of the residency. For three years I was artist in residence for the Boys & Girls Clubs in Spartanburg. I did printmaking demonstrations for ten years at the Jubilee Historic Celebration in Columbia, South Carolina. I was also a visiting artist at Yorktown High School in Yorktown, Virginia, for a year.

As an artist I want to connect both visually and spiritually with the viewer. If this connection happens then I have done my job.

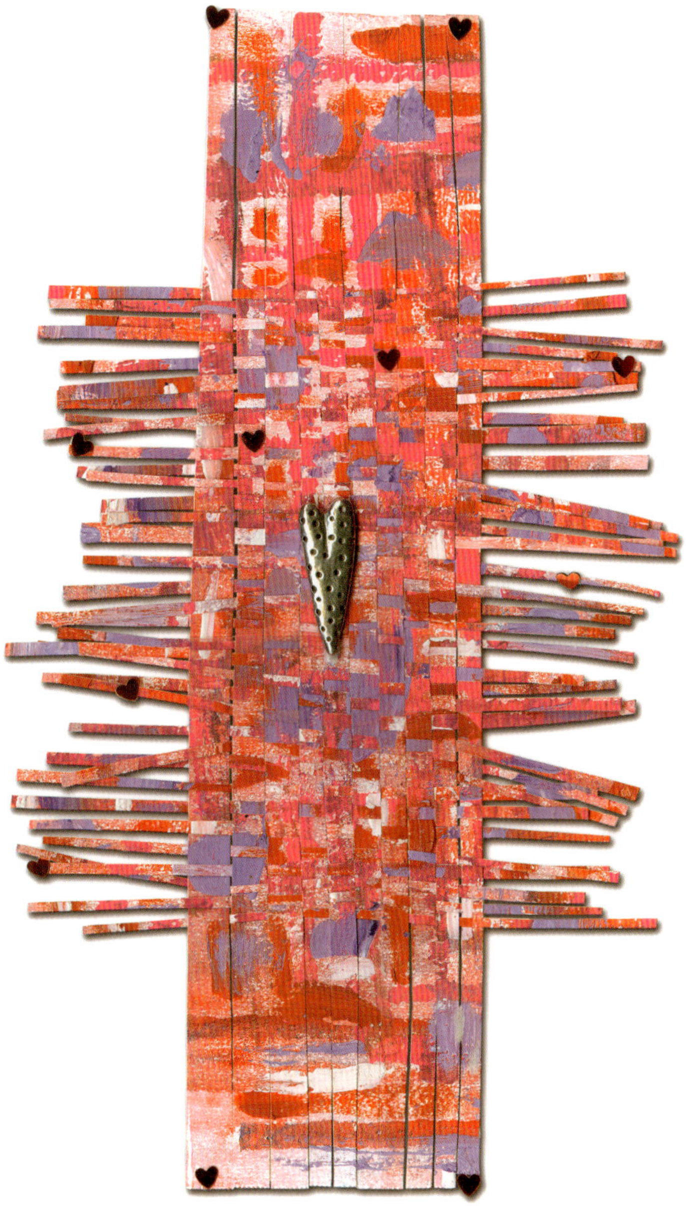

Thin Love Aint No Love At All
Mixed Media
10" X 14"

I lived all my life in rural Ireland until 2008. During a couple of business-related trips to South Carolina in 2007, I was completely taken aback by the tight-knit artist community and the warm and friendly people of Spartanburg. The art walks, the galleries, and the varied opportunities available to artists of all mediums was staggering to me. Ireland is sparsely populated, so you simply do not get a community or body of artists in numbers like that in the Irish countryside.

I have never studied art. Everything that I have learned has been through trial and error. I have always loved the idea of "the story" and the idea of telling a story on a canvas, whether it is with one or multiple pictures. My preferred media has always been oil, but I occasionally use pencil or graphite for detailed studies.

I studied industrial design for three years, from 1989 to 1991, but the introduction of computer-aided design took away a lot of the free-hand element. I took the emphasis on detail with me from those years and incorporated it into my oil paintings.

My style is representational, with an emphasis on detail. The subject matter varies throughout the year. It can be something as simple as my son eating ice cream or my daughter picking flowers—ordinary, everyday little moments that will put a smile on your face, that will bring all those childhood memories flooding back. I'm from a farming background, and the natural countryside settings of farm life have also been a great source of inspiration. I was inspired from a young age by both John Constable, a self-taught English landscape artist, and Dutch artist Jan Vermeer. When looking at my work I like the viewer to pause and to question: *What has happened? What is happening? What is about to happen?* I want the viewer to get involved in the story.

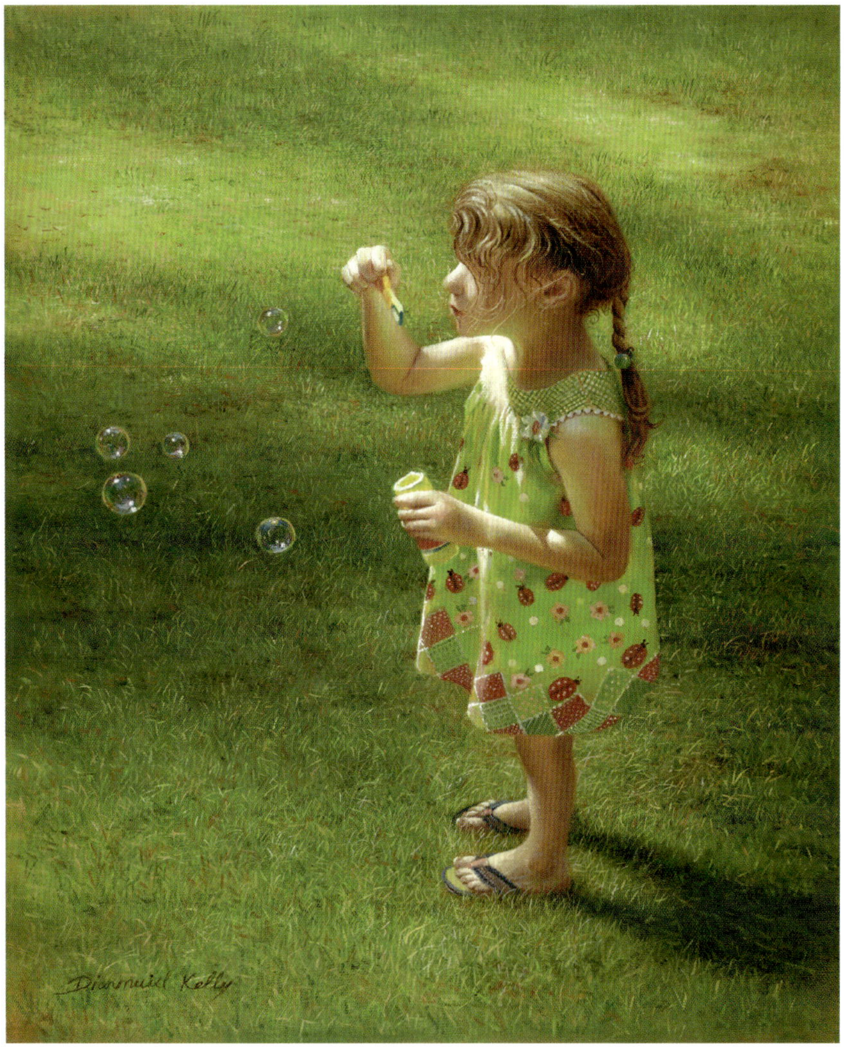

Bubbles and Daydreams
Oil on canvas
18" X 14"

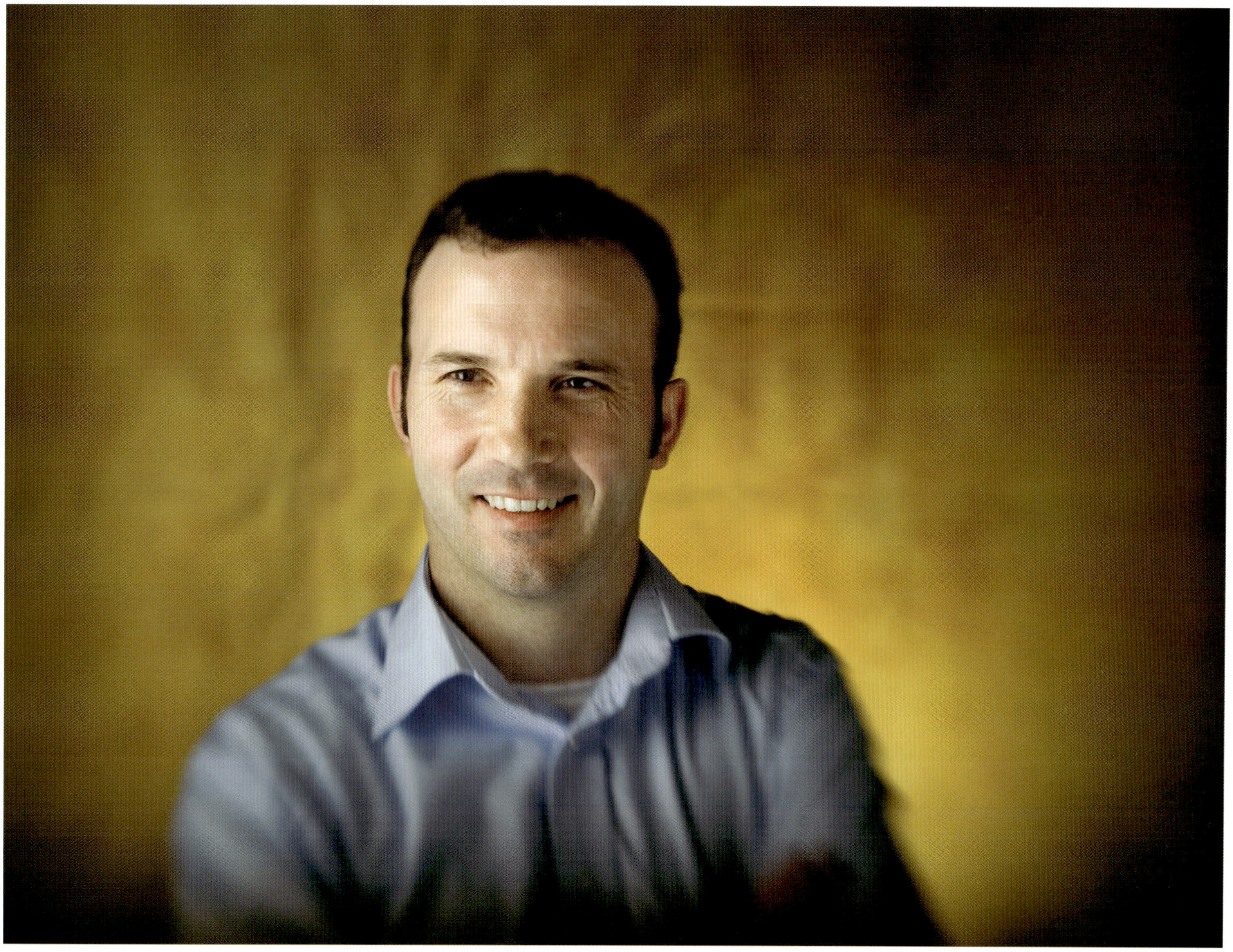

Diarmuid Kelly

As a young child I sat beside my mother in New York City and watched her draw, totally spellbound by her artistic ease and by the charm and perfection of her vignettes. Desiring to emulate the confidence, balance, and beauty of her art, I began to practice drawing. This led to an interest in painting, which became my hobby and continued for many years until, I believe, I was providentially led into a career as a full-time portrait artist in Spartanburg. Many of the gracious people here are enthusiastic about having portraits painted by local artists.

As I work on a portrait I pray for God's help, and I ask Him to bring a sense of life to my canvas. I am delighted and inspired by the personality and characteristics of each subject as presented through the formations of light and shadows on a person's face, the glint of intelligence or mischievousness in an eye, the hint of a smile, a thoughtful expression or subtle gesture. It's a great joy to express these qualities with oil paints on canvas, or with watercolors on paper.

I have grown to love and appreciate the Spartanburg community as I have been privileged to paint many of those they esteem and hold dear. It has been tremendously rewarding to create works of art that are treasured as tributes to the lives of the individuals and families they portray.

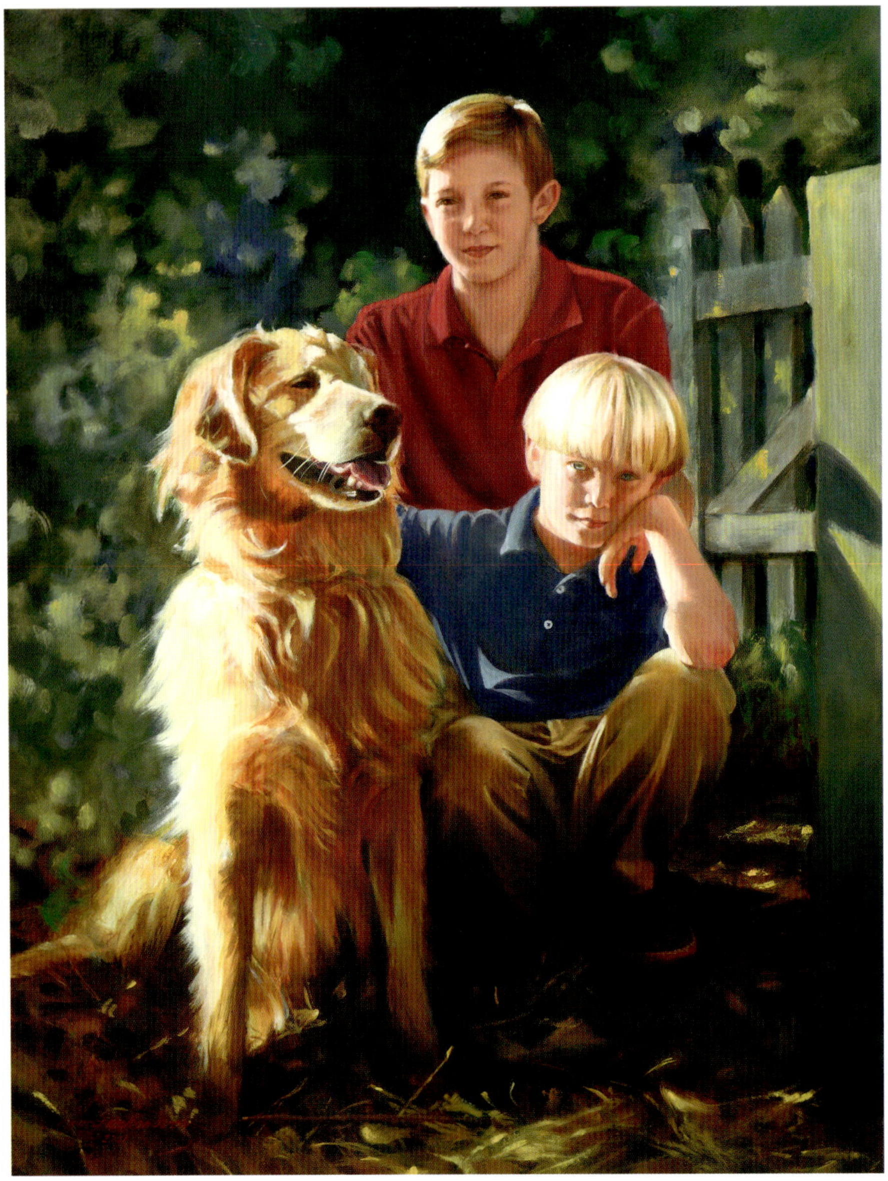

Portrait

Oil on canvas

30" X 40"

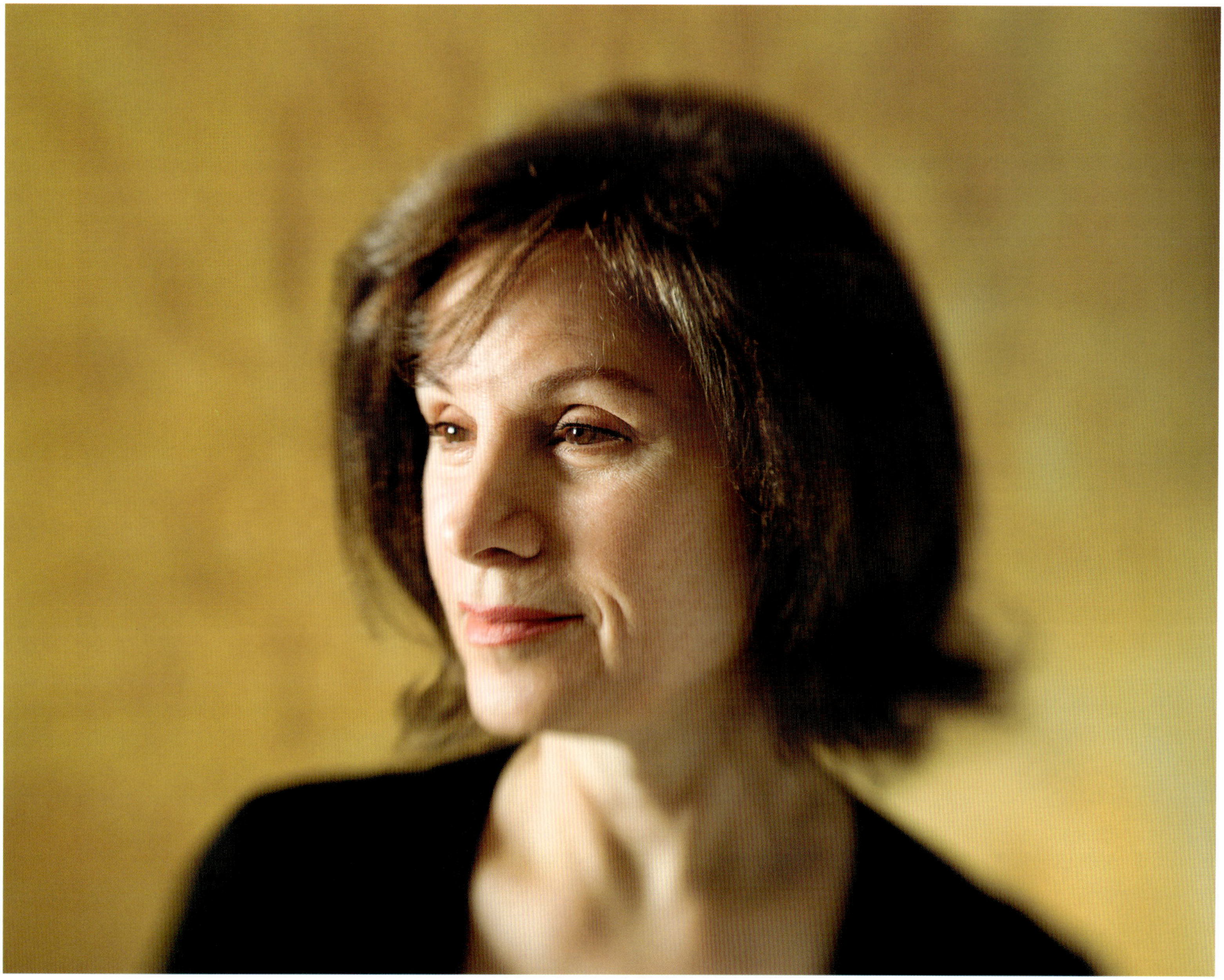

Nancy Kochenower

Eula La Croix

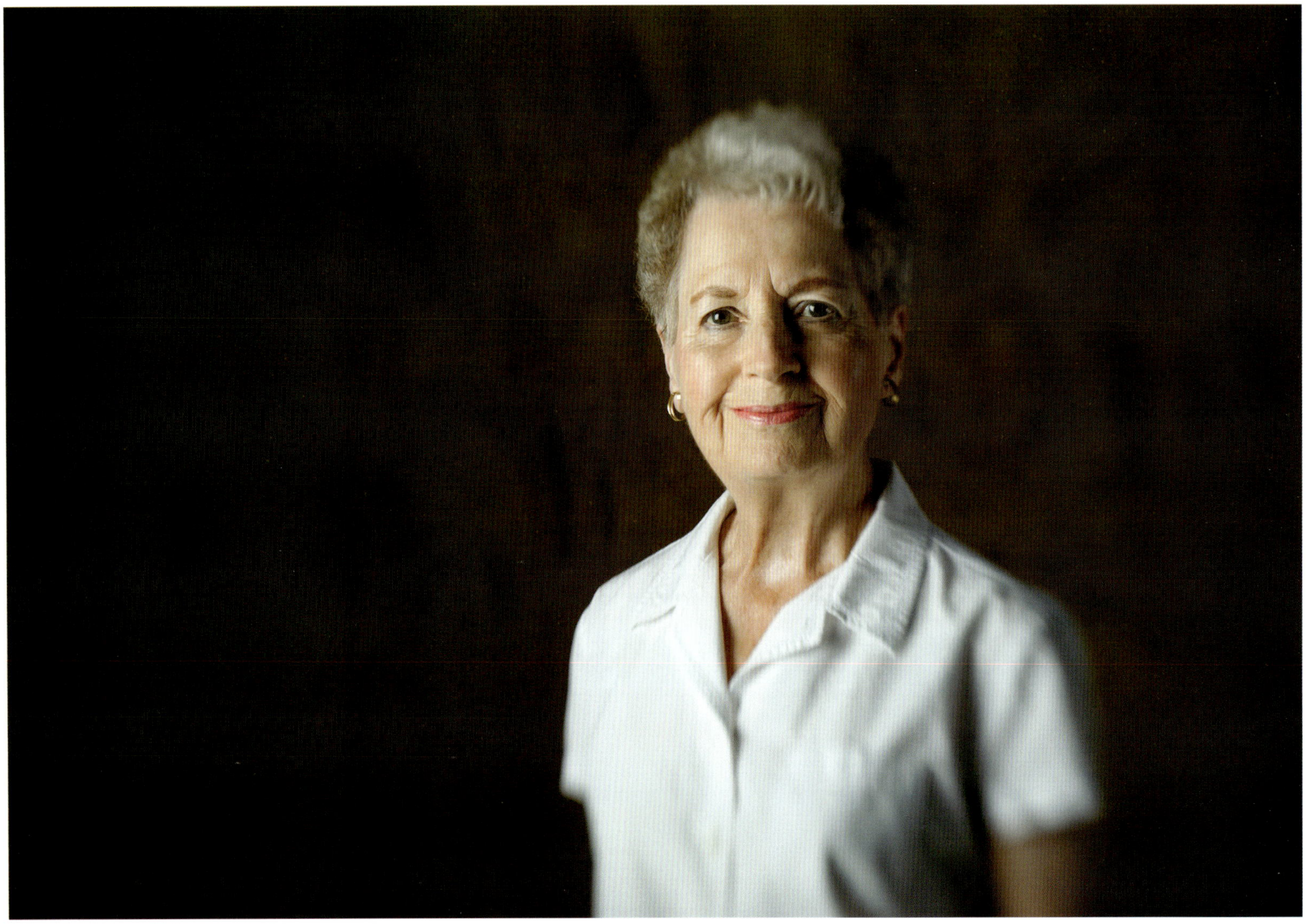

I grew up in the bluegrass area of Kentucky in a family of three girls who all became professional artists. Although I'm mainly self-taught I studied at the Art Academy of Cincinnati for a brief time and had some college classes prior to that. When I was ten years old my teacher entered a piece of my work—a very complicated drawing of Mother Goose characters—in the local county fair art contest. Upon looking at my work the judges claimed that "no ten-year-old can draw that well—it must be traced," and so no ribbon was placed on my work.

My first commissions came in high school when I was asked to paint small watercolor portraits of the grandmother of a fellow student. Many other portrait commissions were to follow; portrait clients have often told me their children's portraits are their greatest treasures and would be the first things they would rescue from their burning house after their children were safe.

My works reflect my love of the natural world. Although I've been a signature member of the Pastel Society of America since 1976 and worked exclusively in pastels for many years, I have recently returned to working in oils as well. I have always been interested in rural landscapes—I am inspired by the manner in which the play of sunlight and shadow alters not only color, shape, and volume but also the emotional quality of a scene. Many of my works are water scenes with reflections, representing something hidden, beautiful, and mysterious. I love the effects of late afternoon light and the intense colors offered by the setting sun. Although I work in a representational style, I have been characterized as "abstract," which in essence is true of all effective works of art.

I have experienced a fun and exciting adventure in art since coming to the Spartanburg area. My hope is that my work turns the mundane subject into something extraordinary for the viewer. If so, I will have succeeded as an artist.

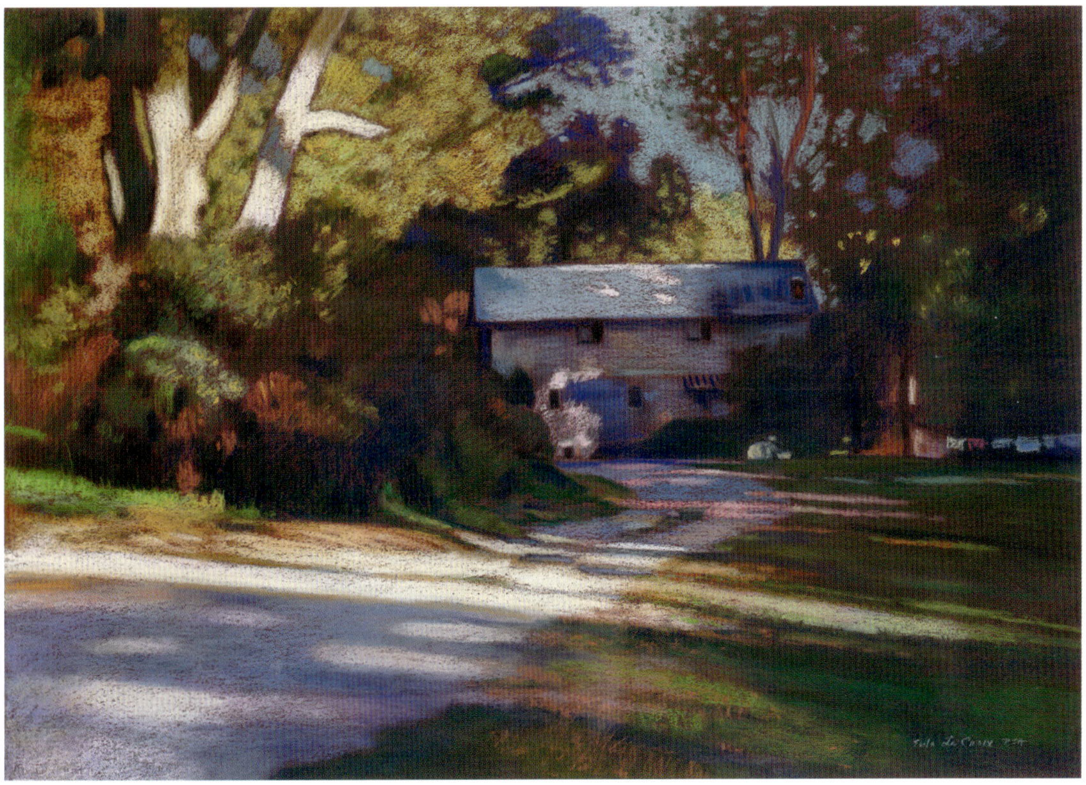

Wash Day

Pastel on canson paper

15.5" X 21.5"

Christine Lawrence

I am a coal miner's granddaughter. I grew up in southwestern Pennsylvania in an area reminiscent of Spartanburg. We lived at the foothills of the Allegheny Mountains. Trains were just as integral to the industries and the community there as they were here. My family encouraged my earliest interests in art. My father was my first art teacher, and my artistic passions were further fueled when I attended the Pennsylvania Governor's School for the Arts while in high school.

I left Pennsylvania when I received an artistic scholarship to attend the Ringling School of Art and Design in Sarasota. Upon graduation I was selected for an internship with Walt Disney Feature Animation Florida in Orlando. I left art school one week early to start what I thought would be a wonderful six-week program—fifteen years later, after having worked on eight features (such as *The Lion King*, *Beauty and the Beast*, *Mulan*, *Lilo & Stitch*, and *Brother Bear*) and several shorts, I left Disney. But not before I met and married my husband, Spartanburg native Trey Finney.

Leaving commercial art to pursue fine art was the fulfillment of a dream both Trey and I shared. While I cherished my time at Disney with all the multi-talented artists I worked with and the friendships I made there, I was ready to make the leap and see if this dream would take flight. Given this community's rich cultural history and its embrace of the arts, I am happy to call Spartanburg home.

For me, being an artist means being a fact-finder, an explorer, an observer, and forever a student of the world around me. Sometimes I have a strong vision for something and just go for it! Other times I work up to it. My primary medium of choice is oils, and my work is representational. My subject matter varies from florals to landscapes, still lifes to interiors, figures to travel scenes. Art is my passion! I hope the viewer senses that.

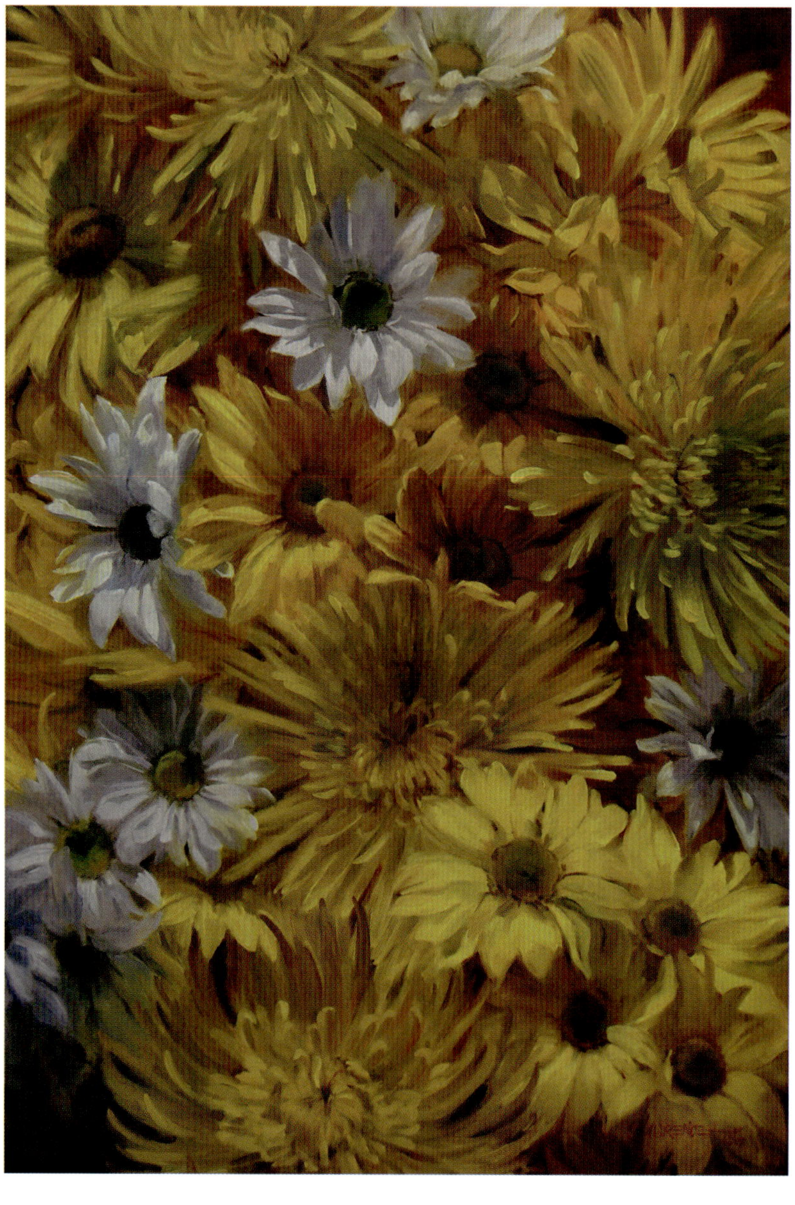

Eternal Sunshine
Oil on panel
24" X 36"

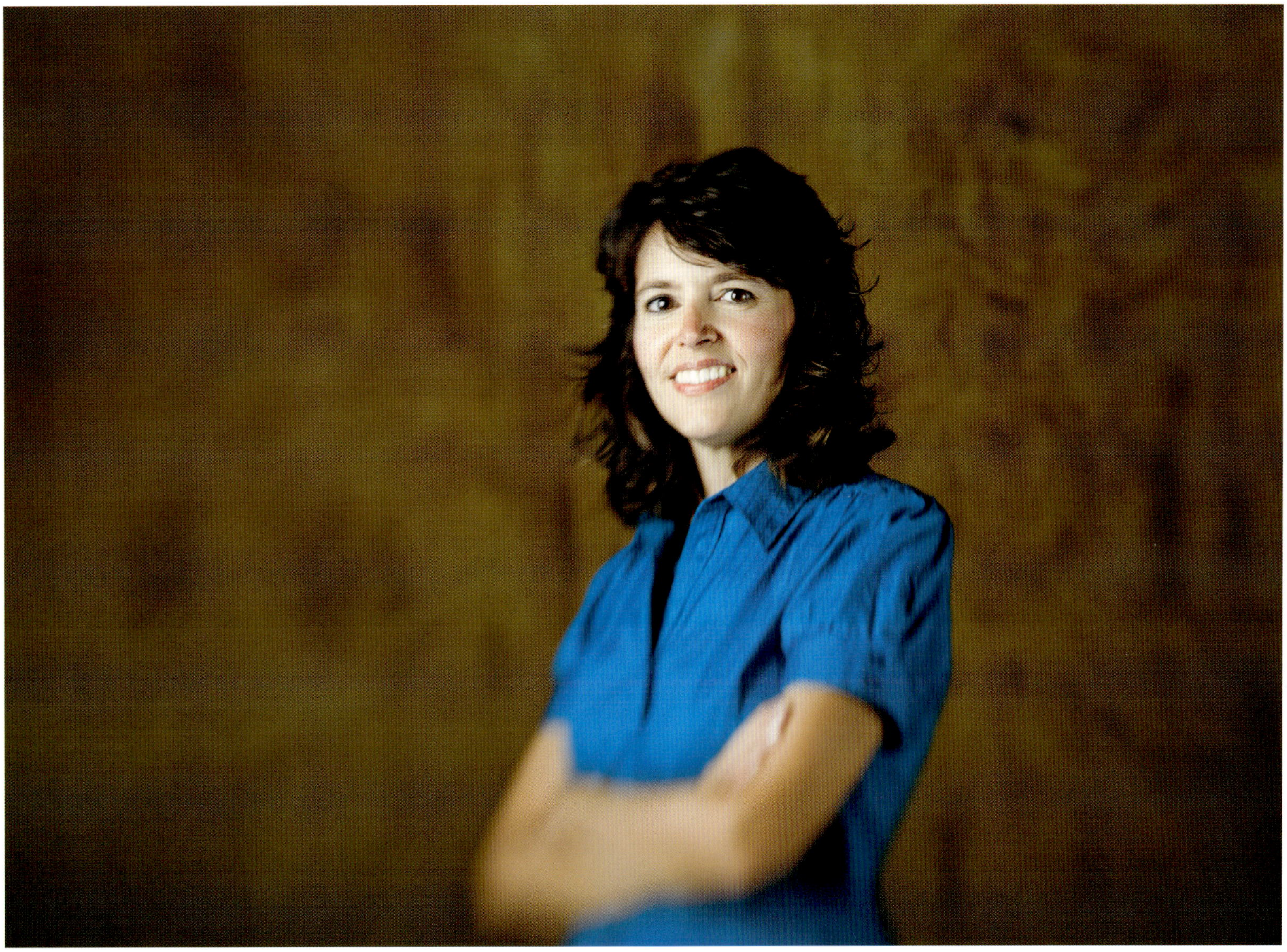

Cats and dogs, birds and fish, wind and water: these are the things that awaken the creative muse in me. I live in the woods and above a creek, so nature is a prominent aspect of my life and my artwork. My sculptures of clay and metal are an extension of my environment and of my past, which culminate in my desire to create something that can be treasured for its beauty, its craftsmanship, and its meaning.

My father and my grandmother influenced me to become an artist. There were no idle hands in my family; everyone worked, and then worked some more for pleasure. My father was a mechanic, woodworker, handyman, and "Sunday Painter." My earliest memories are of following him around in his workshop. My grandmother raised flowers to sell to the public and made beautiful wool hooked rugs in her spare time. I was right there beside her when she planned her design, when she formulated her color scheme, when she dyed her yarns, and when she hooked her rugs. My father and grandmmother each had me as a shadow. I learned many things from them—to make things with my hands, to appreciate the beauty of nature, and to recognize the craft of a thing made well.

Leaving my hometown of Lincolnton, North Carolina, I moved to Gaffney, South Carolina, for my first teaching job. This was a good move for me; through the different aspects of the art community in the Spartanburg and Gaffney area, I've been encouraged to pursue my artistic interests. The Spartanburg Artists Guild, the Spartanburg Art Museum, and Southern Exposure—the local art collective I have been a member of for many years—have given me many opportunities to show my work and to participate in the artistic community.

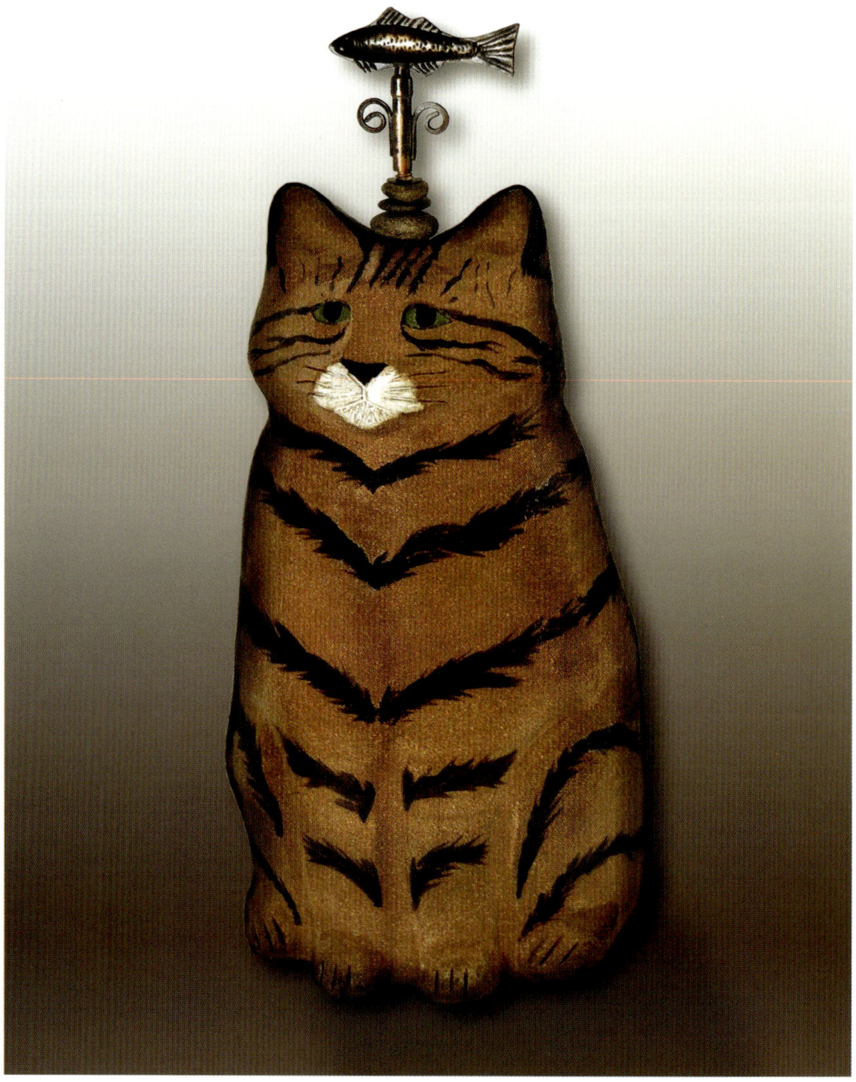

Cat Dreams at the River

Stoneware clay, copper and river rock

20" X 9" X 9"

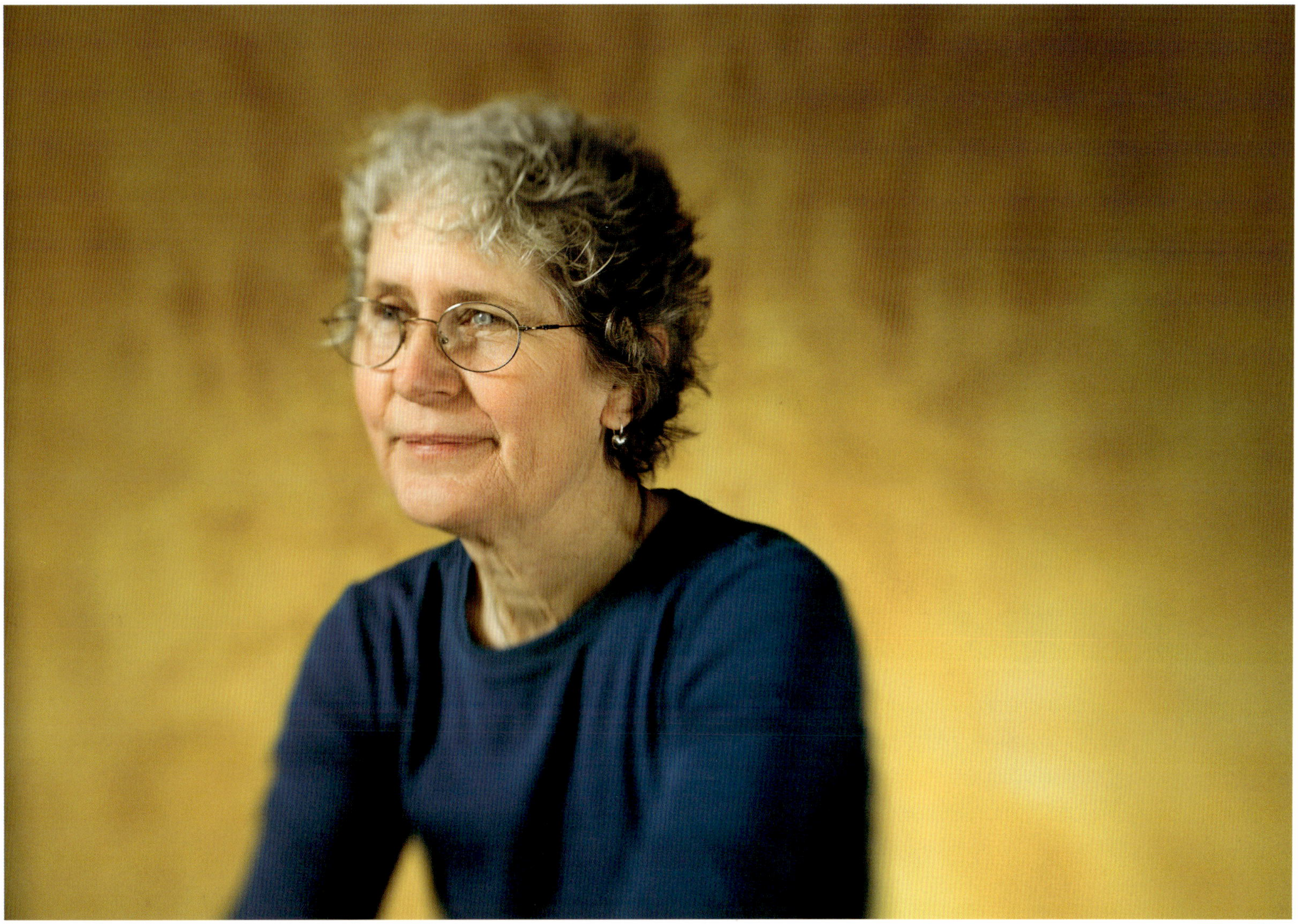

Cynthia Link

Robert LoGrippo

I was born in 1947, which makes me old now. I grew up in the Bronx, New York, and attended New York City schools, which at the time were very good. I was always drawing something in school, and teachers began to notice I had some art talent. They of course told my mom. I was encouraged to try out for the High School of Music and Art (now called LaGuardia High School) and somehow got in. I guess this is when I started to get serious about art.

When I graduated I went to the School of Visual Arts in New York City and for the first time actually enjoyed going to school. Encouraged by great teachers, such as Marshall Arisman, Bob Shore, and Burne Hogarth, art began to become my driving force. At Visual Arts I discovered two artists, Hieronymus Bosch ("The Garden of Earthly Delights") and Pieter Bruegel, and they influenced my style of artwork for at least ten years.

In art school I majored in illustration, thinking that was the way to make an actual living in art. I did become an illustrator and was one for more than forty years. I found there were some art directors who felt my artwork matched their projects—enough to make a living. So I was satisfied to paint and get paid for it.

I work in acrylics and always have because I don't like the smell of oils. Most people call my style primitive or naïve. That's funny to me because when I start a painting, I always see it as realistic, but it always seems to become a poorly painted—or should I say an artistically naïve—painting.

The most important thing for me is to be able to escape and find myself in this sometimes strange world I am creating on canvas. This world is like a stage setting, with actors, special effects, fun, and even drama, all there for the viewer. I hope sometimes the viewer sees and experiences it.

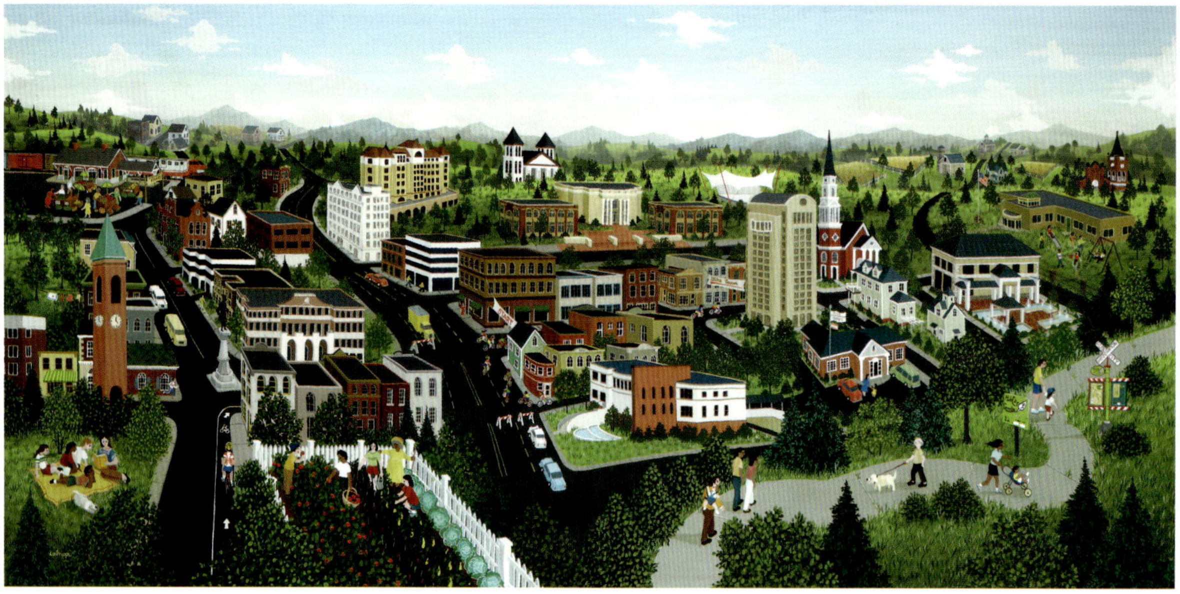

Spartanburg
Acrylic on board
12" X 30"

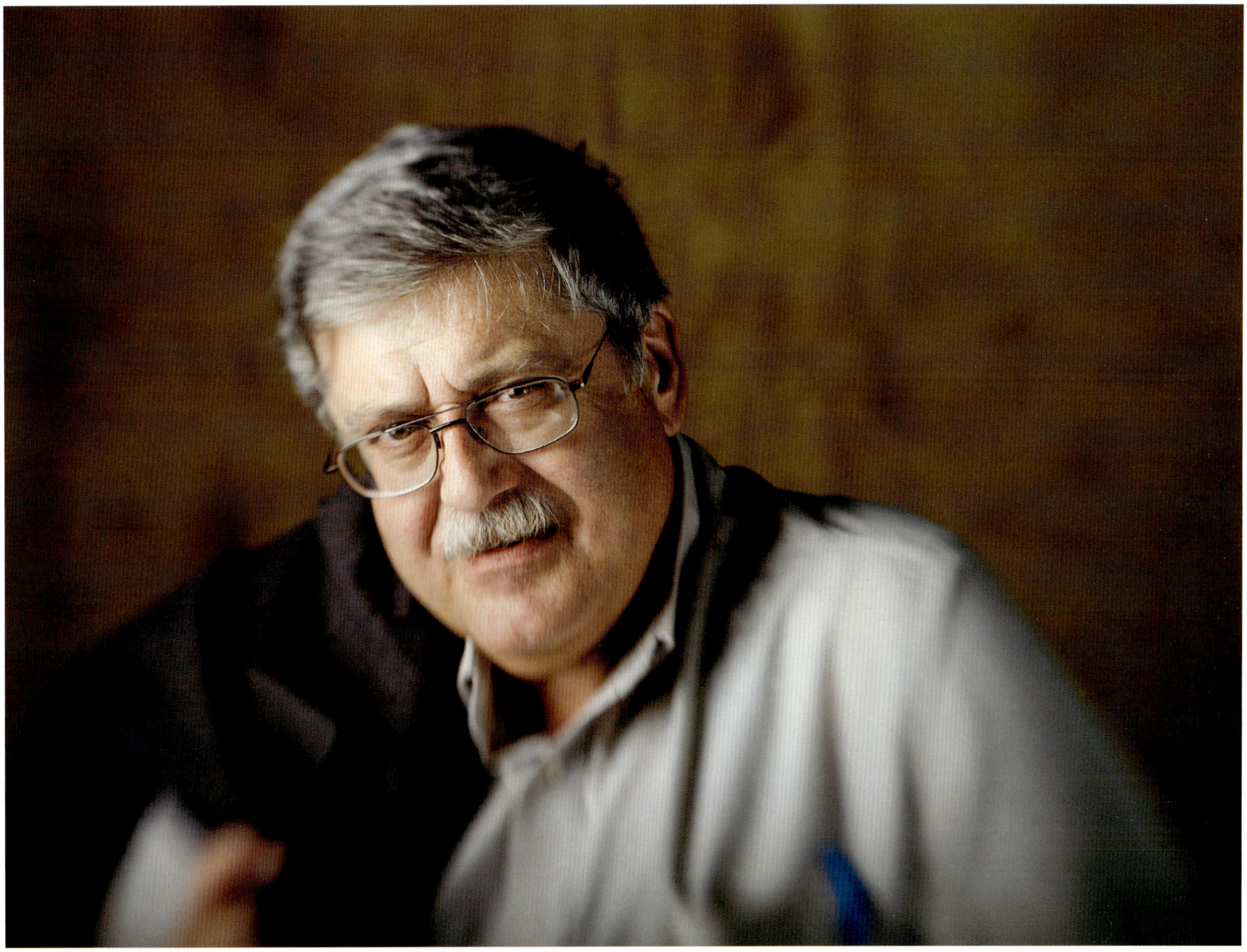

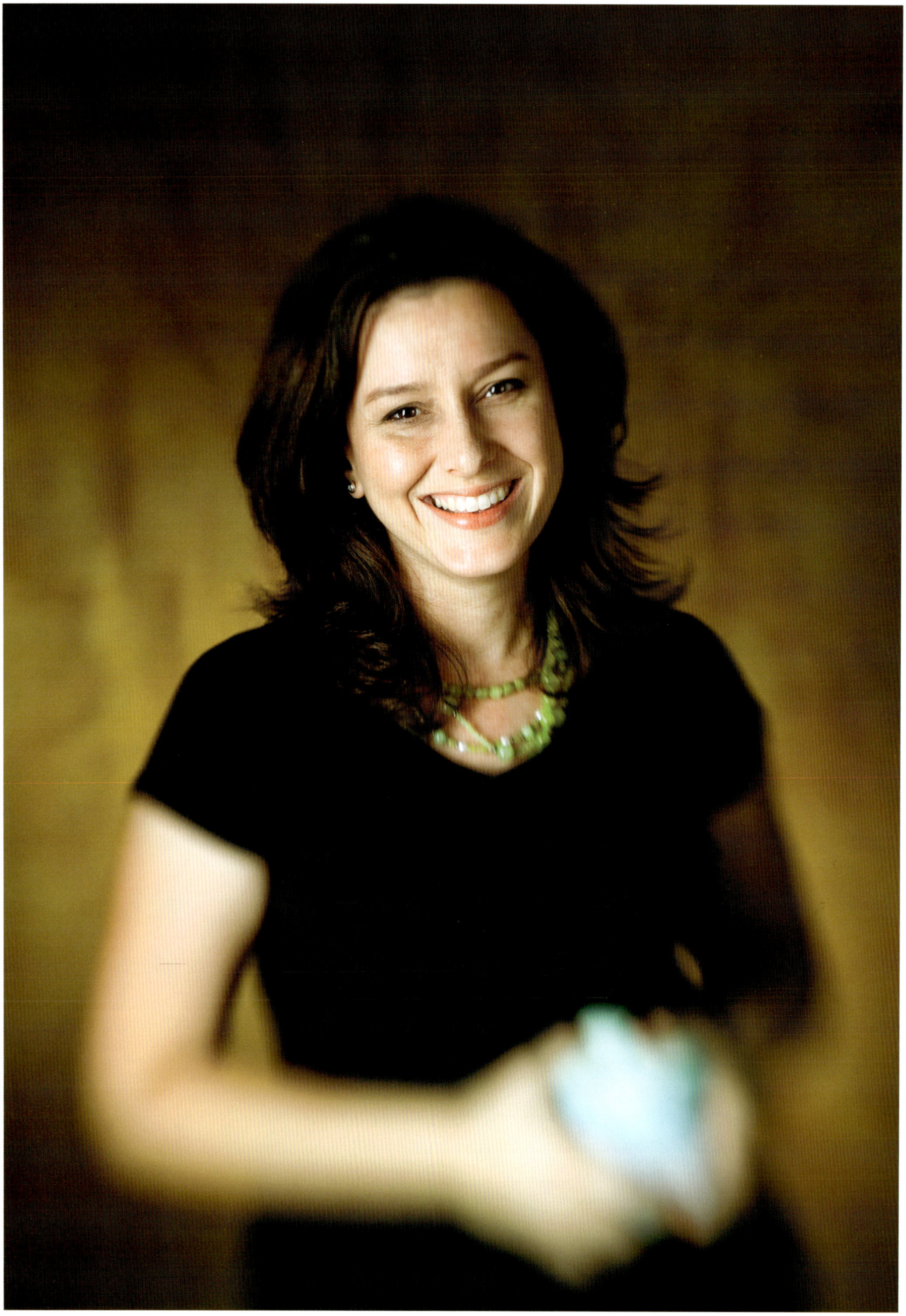

Alicia Mack

I grew up in Gainesville, Florida, where being close to the University of Florida offered me a wonderful, multi-cultural, and dynamic experience. My earliest interest in art came from my parents, who are both makers; they instilled my love to create. When I was in high school, I had a fabulous art teacher who introduced me to clay. She also assisted me in shooting slides to apply for a scholarship to college, which I was awarded.

I attended college at the University of Florida, where I received a BFA in ceramics, and followed with an MFA in ceramics from the University of Miami. When my husband and I decided to move to the Carolinas, I was excited to become part of a strong craft culture. When we moved to Spartanburg, I quickly became part of a close-knit and supportive art community. I have met many friends and teachers who share the same love of clay.

I am inspired by soft forms, pillows, textiles, succulent plants, and by the sweet, fat-bellied birds that live in Spartanburg. I make forms that reference softness, even though clay is hardened in its fired state. I want the viewer to want to touch my pieces, bring them into their homes, or place on their dinner tables to be used by their families.

We now have a family here, and we bring our daughter to the monthly Art Walk and gallery openings in town. I hope to inspire her to become a maker, and to appreciate those who do.

Blue Birdie pillow box set
Handbuilt porcelain wall piece
12" X 12"

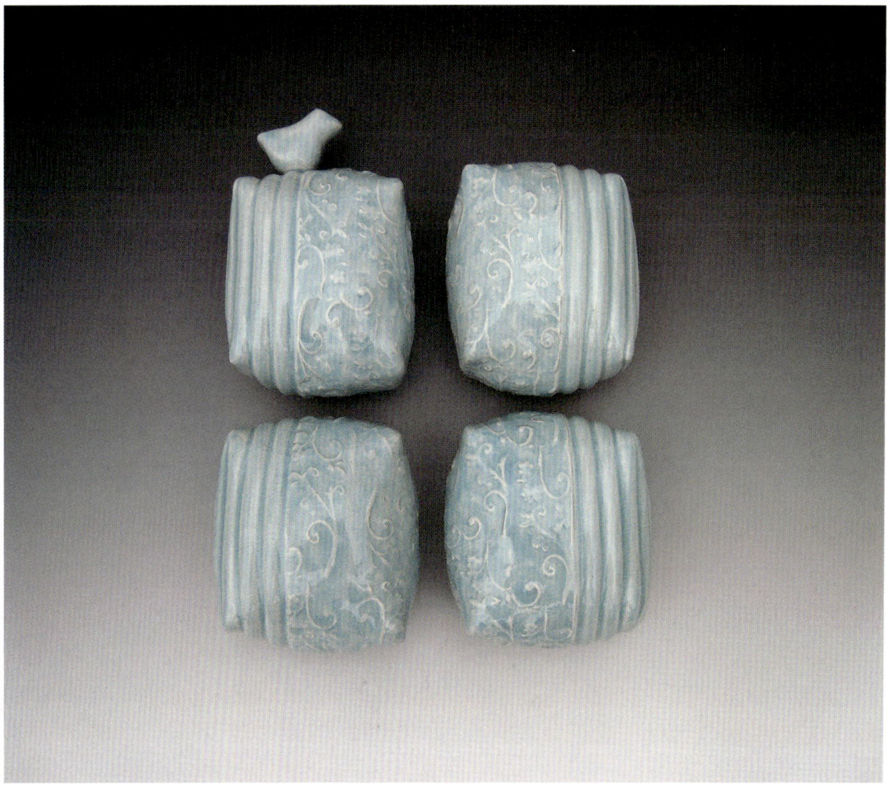

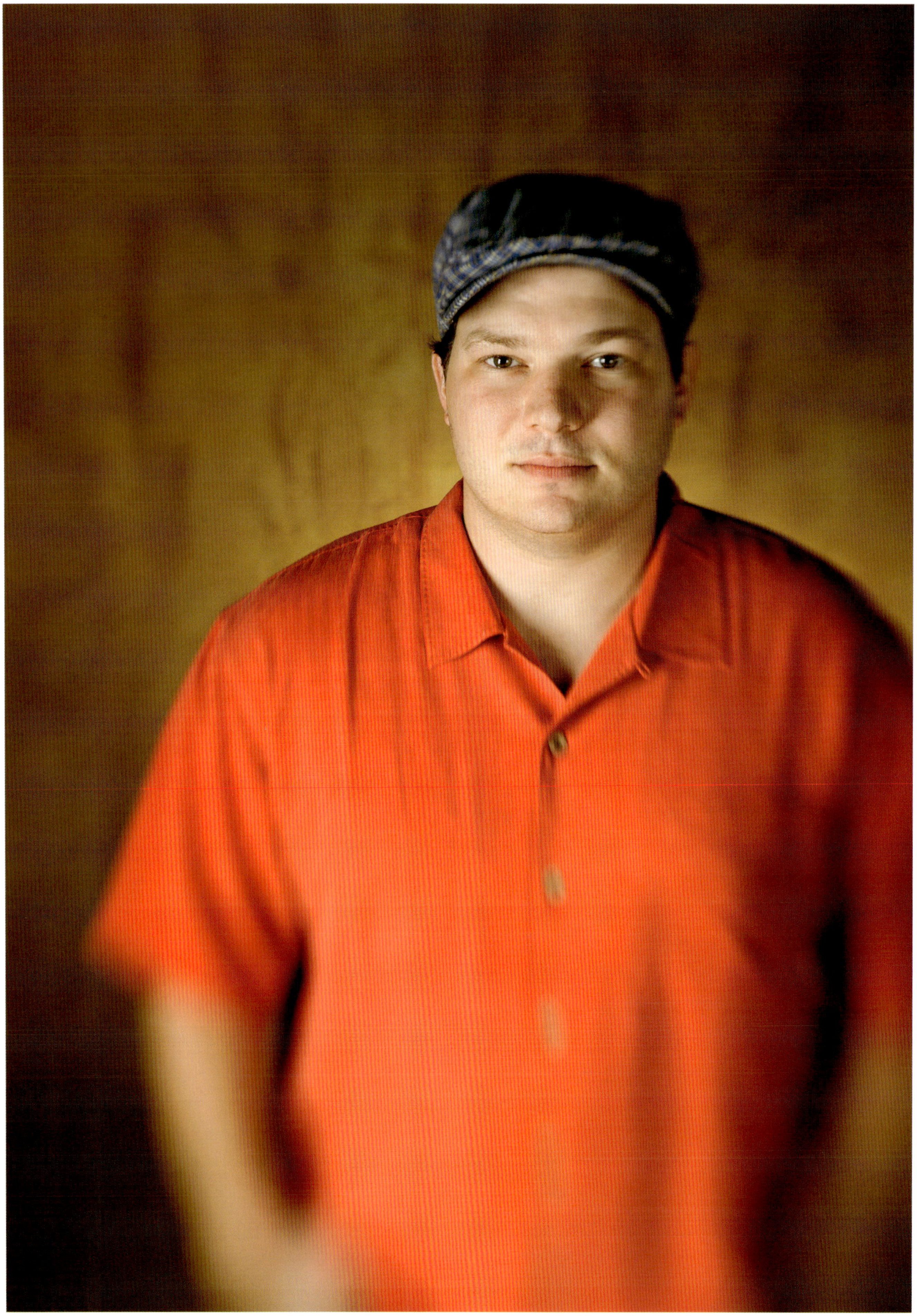

Richard Mack

I don't have any one place I technically call home. I was born in New York City and have lived half of my life in a number of towns and cities throughout the Eastern Seaboard. I have also lived in various places in Europe, Asia, and Australia. I'm very thankful for all of the opportunities I have received in life and believe my work is a reflection of my nomadic lifestyle.

My life with art began at an early age, visiting museums on my travels. My mother was the first person to teach me art. We would spend afternoons drawing, coloring, and painting together.

I received my BA in liberal studies from St. Edward's University in Austin, Texas, and took a job as a graphic designer for a satellite company. After five years I wanted more art in my life and enrolled at the University of Miami, where I received an MFA in graphic design and multimedia. If not for these three years in graduate school I would not be an artist now. There, I truly learned to analyze my process and to experiment. I became interested in mediums and materials that were unfamiliar to me. I used glass, metal, plexiglass, video, software, collage, and type in my work. Process and experimentation became my art. Even now, I am still researching, experimenting, and creating work in ways unfamiliar to me.

If I had to categorize my current work I would have to say it is mixed media. I incorporate different materials and textures with various mediums to create graphic panels. The subjects of my work span from social interactions with the people I meet to the abstract shapes that exist in negative space. My work changes with every new adventure and art process I learn. The future for my art is clear in one way—it will evolve. I hope that when people view my work they see the subject, the objects, and the compositional treatment in a whole new way, and that they too take an adventure onto unfamiliar ground.

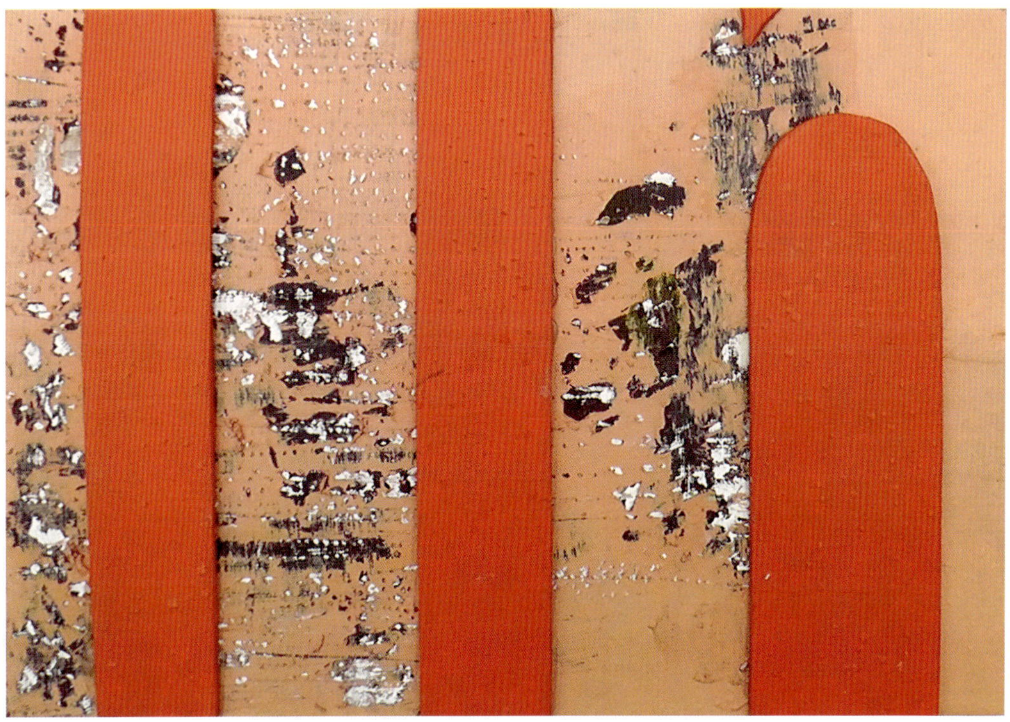

In Between #1

Mixed Media

15" X 10"

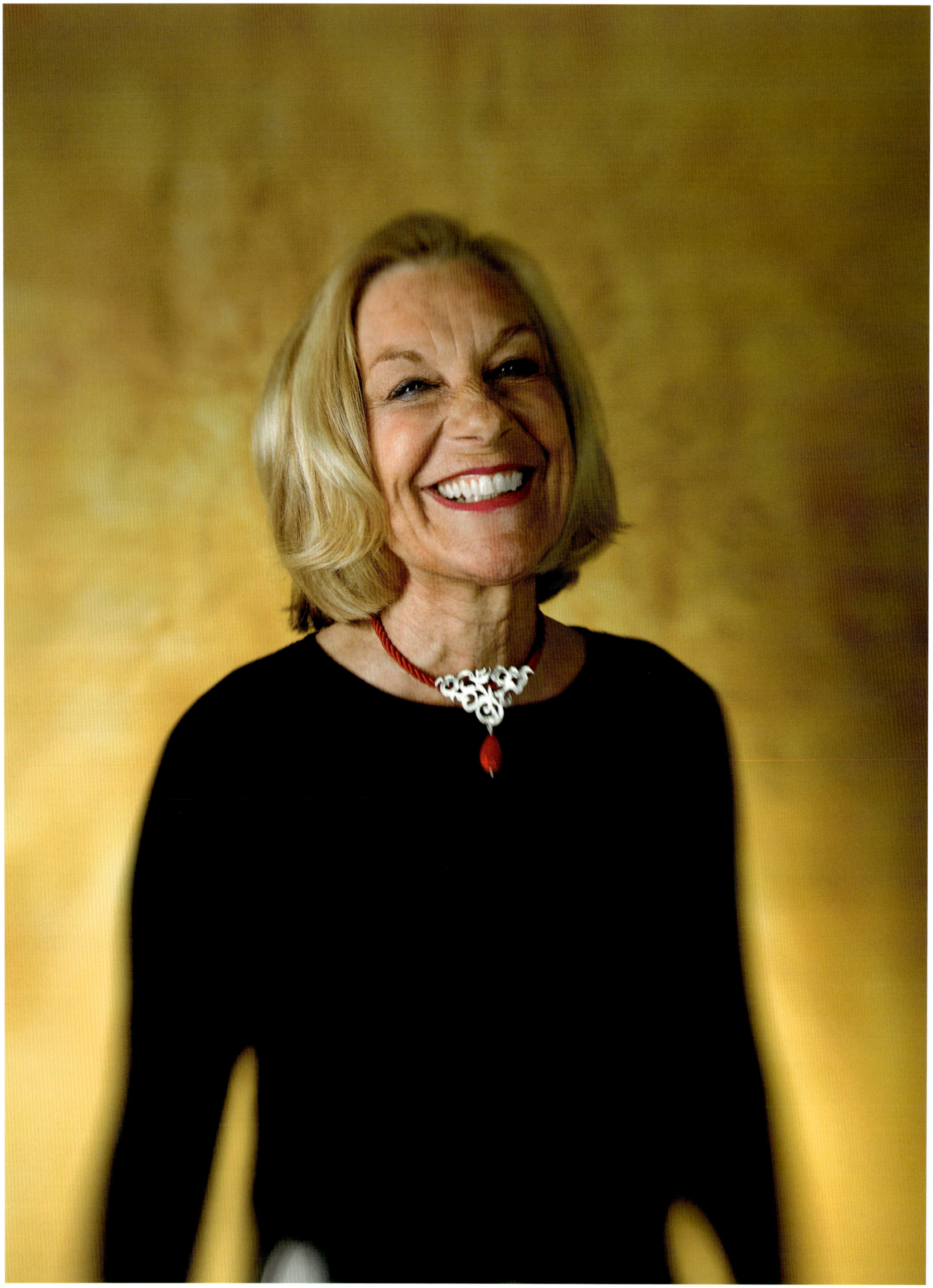

Marie-Christine Maitre de Tarragon

Born in France at the family historical estate, I was exposed from a very young age to antiquities, art, and the best museums in Europe. After formal education in French boarding school, I traveled the world and have lived in the United States most of my adult life. I have had the privilege of working with many great sculptors in France and in the States—especially in the American West—who were generous in sharing their knowledge.

I love to draw and paint, but my central work is sculpture, mainly in bronze. Giving life to a blank canvas or a piece of clay is a challenge. It is also an ambition to leave a legacy. Challenging the viewer to see and not look, awakening emotions and dreams, has become a passion for me.

Being able to exercise the intellectual and aesthetic freedom intrinsic to the role of art and to use it as a tool to express a feeling and start a connection—maybe a conversation with my surroundings—is the key to knowledge. It is up to us to unlock our spirituality.

I have always had an admiration for Alexander the Great, and through my horses I convey the human quest for glory and legacy in history, specifically with "Bucephalus" and "The Red Canyon" I and II. Other bronzes simply express grace and natural beauty in its state of innocence.

In my bas-relief I love the possibility to tell a story as it was done in ancient time, the subject in direct correlation with his surroundings and his past through architectural details. I also love the South, its natural and diverse beauty of nature, its attachment to the past, and its history and traditions.

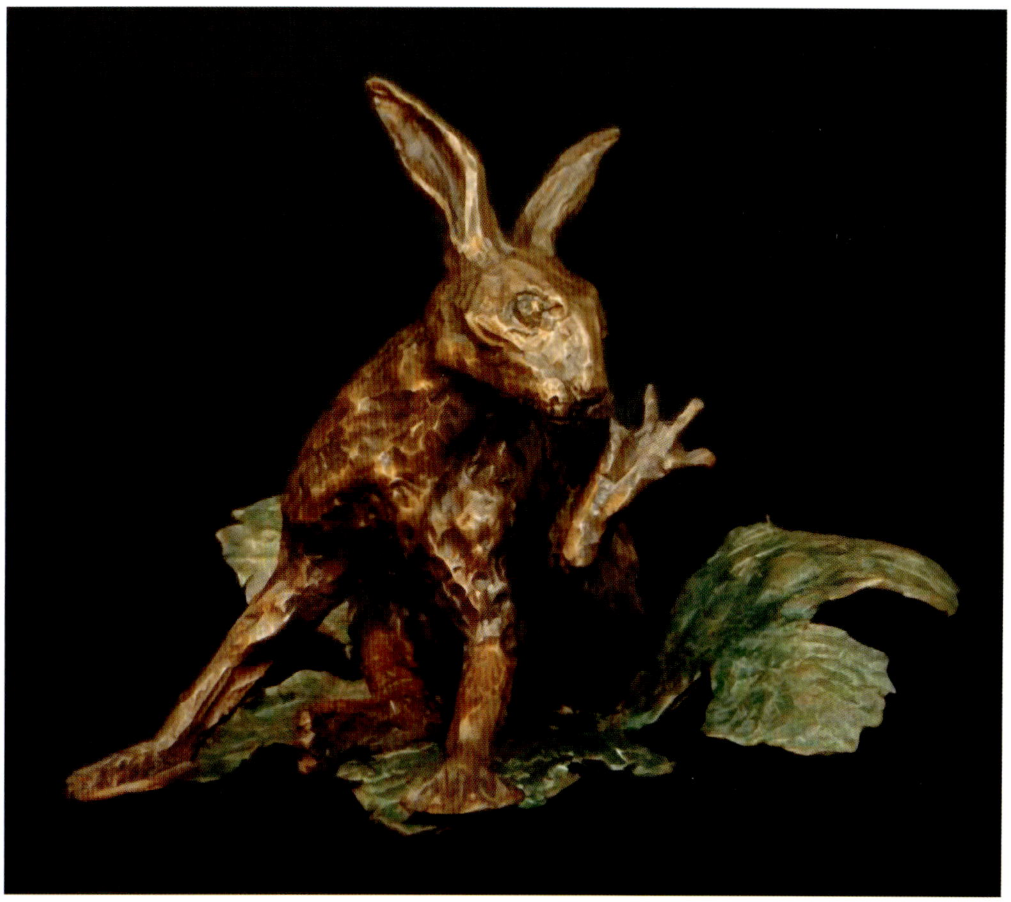

L'Innocence

Bronze

12" X 12" X 10"

Larry Mauldin

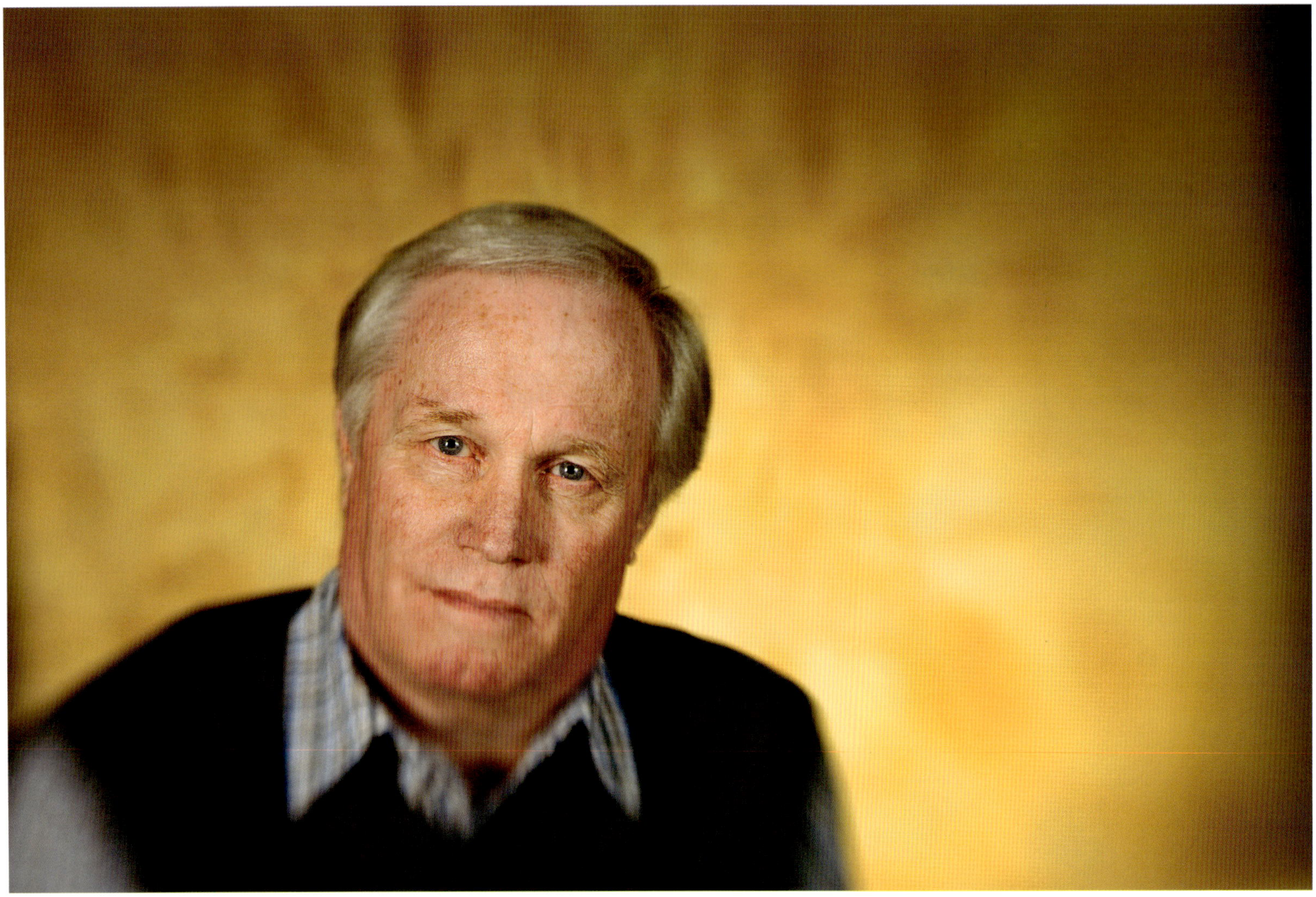

I have been a professional artist in Spartanburg for more than thirty years. I am self-taught and have proven that hard work pays off. I have been featured in *Watercolor Magic* and a watercolor instruction book by Nita Leaman, the revised edition of *Exploring Color*. I have served as president of the Artists' Guild of Spartanburg and the South Carolina Watermedia Society and am a patron member of the American Watercolor Society. I teach airbrush and watercolor workshops across North and South Carolina, including at the Spartanburg Art Museum Art School.

My work in black and white stems from a simple understanding of art. I concentrate on lights and darks in my work, whether with a light source or with color. Black and white is the best method of doing this. Color for me can complicate the feeling or mood. Black and white sets the tone from the very beginning of my work. In the past I found myself getting so involved with the color of a palette of a painting that I would lose what I was trying do in the piece. I was constantly concerned with what colors dictated a warm or cool painting, and whether the colors would mix or complement each other. I solved all these complex problems by using a black and white pallet. I use just a touch of color somewhere in the painting to remind me that it is a painting. For me, a black and white world is less complicated and easier to see and understand.

My works are found in domestic and international collections worldwide. I currently have several limited edition prints and posters on the market. I have won numerous awards in regional and national shows and have also served as a juror for various art shows.

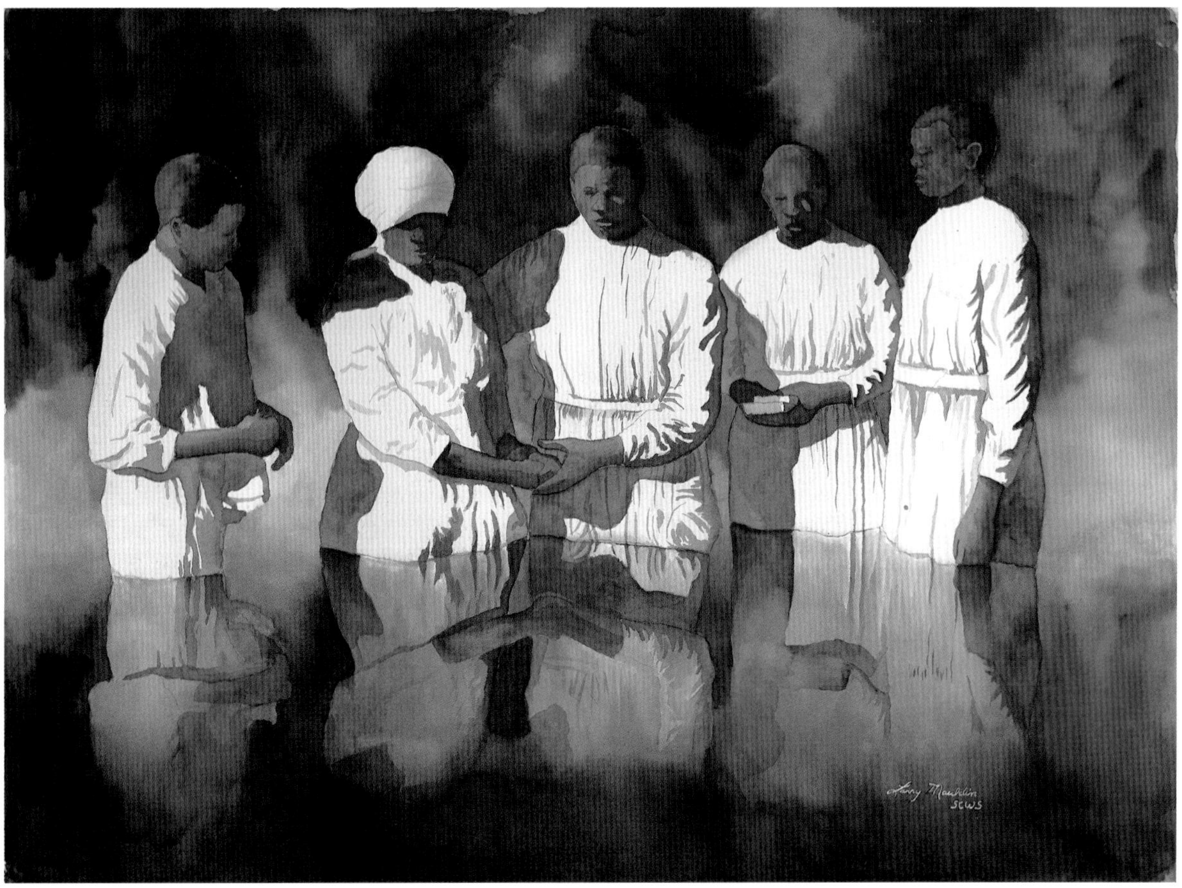

The Cleansing

Watercolor

22" X 30"

David McPherson

I spent thirteen of my first eighteen years in Spartanburg. When I went through school, I never connected with art, but I always remained interested in the history of art. I went to school at Davidson College. My freshman adviser there happened to be Herb Jackson, the head of the visual arts department. Since Davidson was a "liberal arts school," I was required to take a class related to art. I took the class and produced some horrible work, but somehow I connected to the visual creative process. I worked hard because I felt "unqualified" and because I loved the mysterious act of creation.

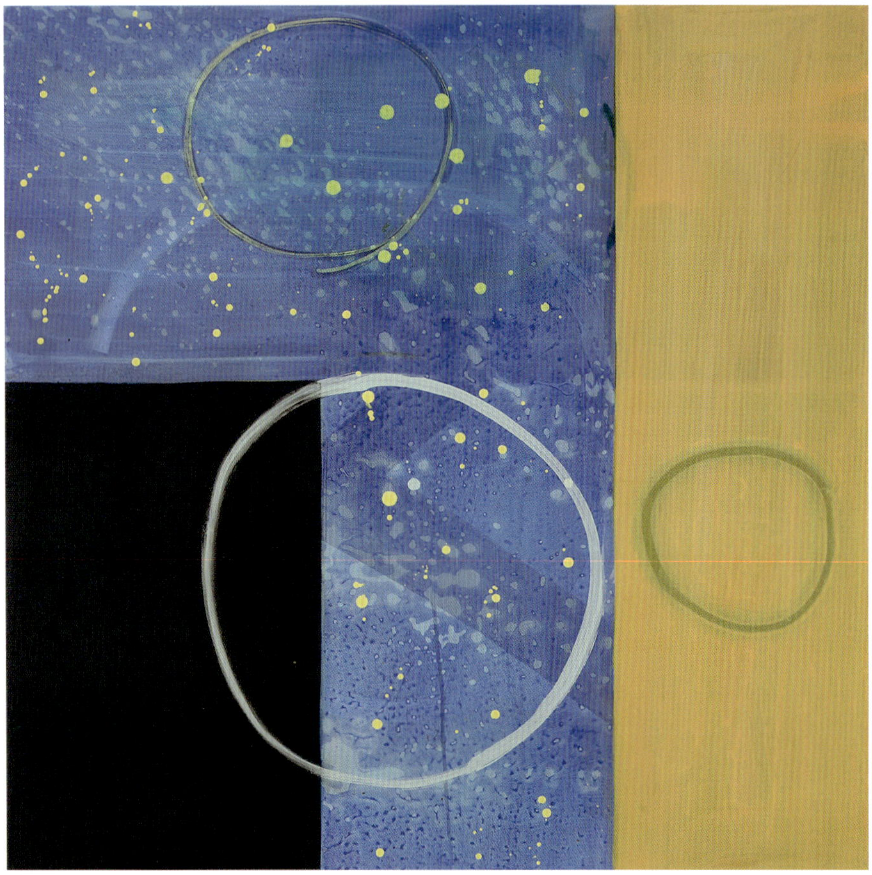

Blue Light
Oil on canvas
32" X 32"

I spent two years working in a book warehouse in Huntersville, North Carolina, and painting in a rented mini-warehouse storage facility. I went to Arizona State University for my Master of Fine Arts degree. My work since that time has been abstract, colorful acrylic paintings and collages. In addition, I make smaller abstract oil pastel drawings. I have taught at the university and high school level for twelve years. When I returned to Spartanburg I was impressed by the artistic community here. There was strong diversity, and I felt the quality of much of the work was very high. In particular, I have seen great support for the arts through HUB-BUB and the Artists Guild of Spartanburg. There are many opportunities for showing your work in Spartanburg.

I sold my work for ten years through galleries. My biggest influence has been Herb Jackson, as well as Milton Avery, Willem De Kooning, Stuart Davis, Franz Kline, and Richard Diebenkorn. My most recent gallery representation was with the Victoria Boyce Galleries in Scottsdale, Arizona, and the Center of the Earth Gallery in Charlotte.

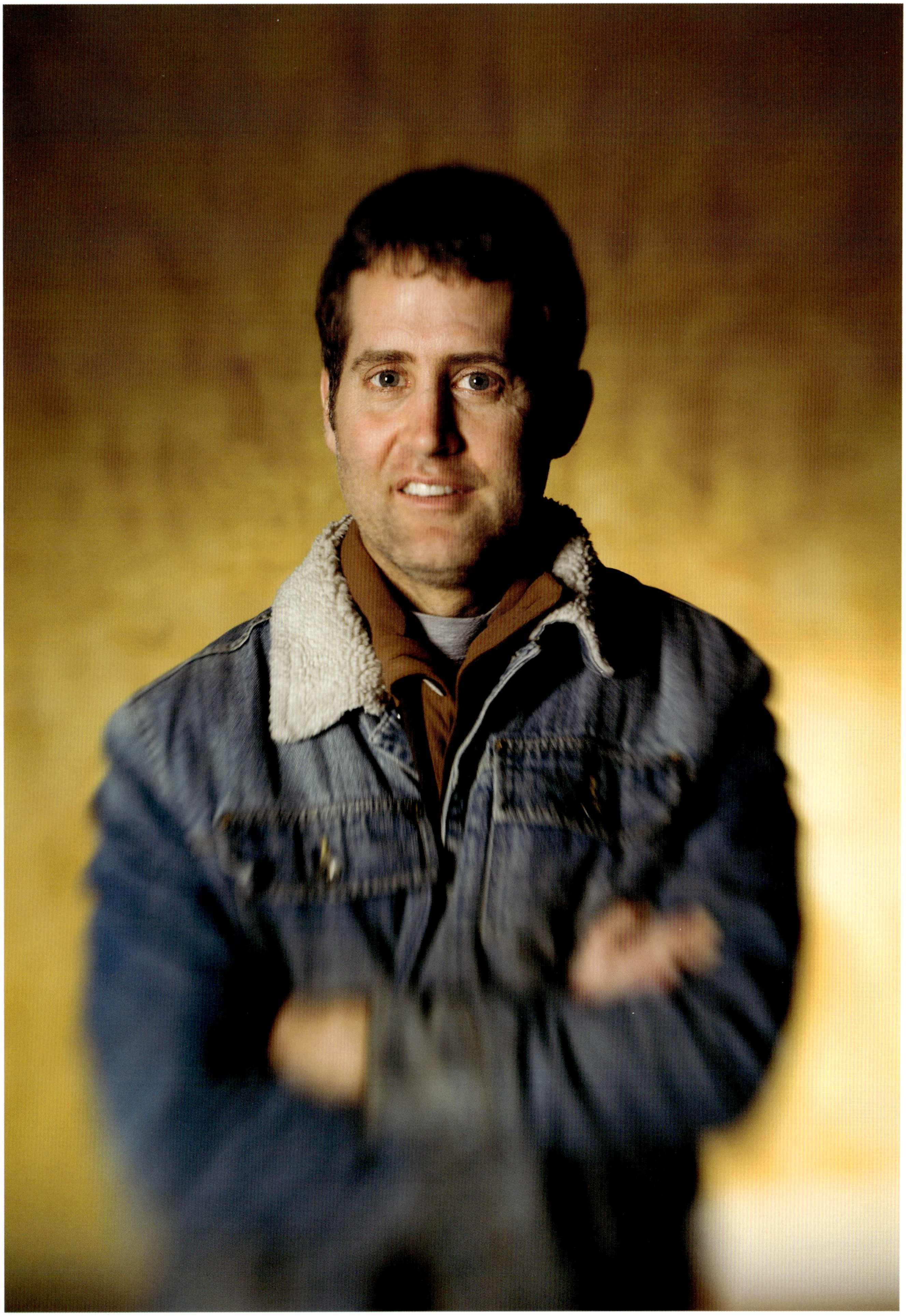

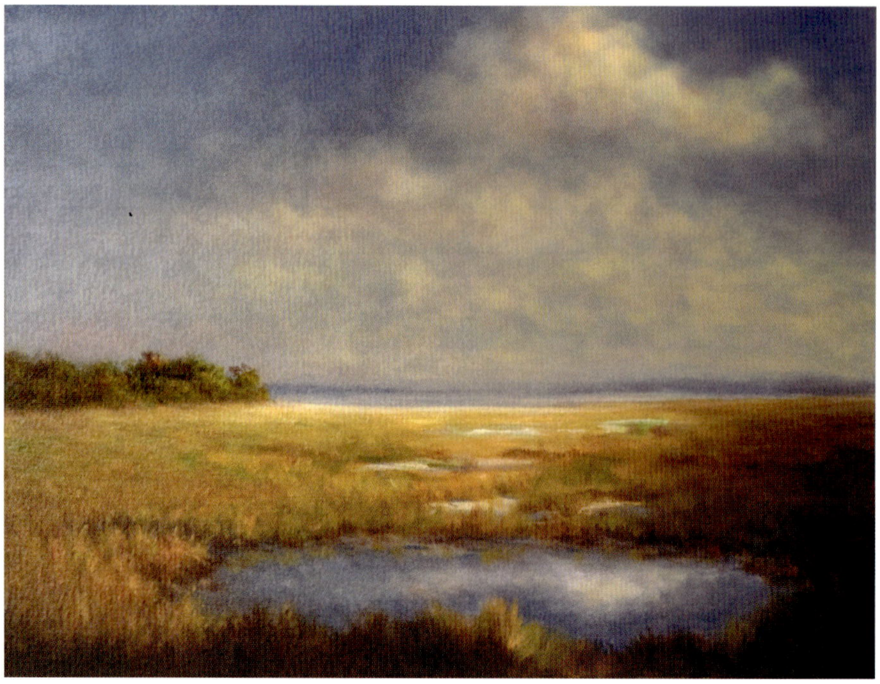

Sunlight Over the Marsh

Oil on canvas

24" X 30"

After a twenty-six year hiatus, I returned to my favorite pastime, painting. I find great pleasure in painting and feel rewarded when I successfully capture my interpretation of a scene onto canvas.

I received most of my training back in the 1970s when I was president of the Society of Creative Arts in Newtown, Connecticut. As president of the art group, I studied privately with many of the professional artists who were members. During this time I became familiar with the art elements and principles that I apply to my paintings today. I am primarily a self-taught artist who believes you can learn from doing and by observing the shape and colors of objects you are trying to capture.

Originally from Connecticut, my wife Eileen and I moved to Hendersonville, North Carolina, in 2001. After spending a few cold winters in the mountains, Eileen and I decided to move to Spartanburg to enjoy the warmer weather.

I find great reward in painting and in capturing the mood and beauty in a scene or still life painting. I consider myself an acute observer of shape and color, composing oils that reflect the many colors of nature. Since an early age I have appreciated the beauty of our landscapes and how they evoke an emotional response. My best works are created when that emotional response is expressed freely. This can be seen best in my use of the pallet knife and brush strokes to define color, space, and form.

To strengthen my use of color, I have painted with and learned from many well-known artists in Connecticut, North Carolina, and South Carolina. I am grateful for their help. I am also thankful for the ability given to me by prior generations. I use this gift each day to create my art, and I appreciate the unexpected results I often see in my paintings.

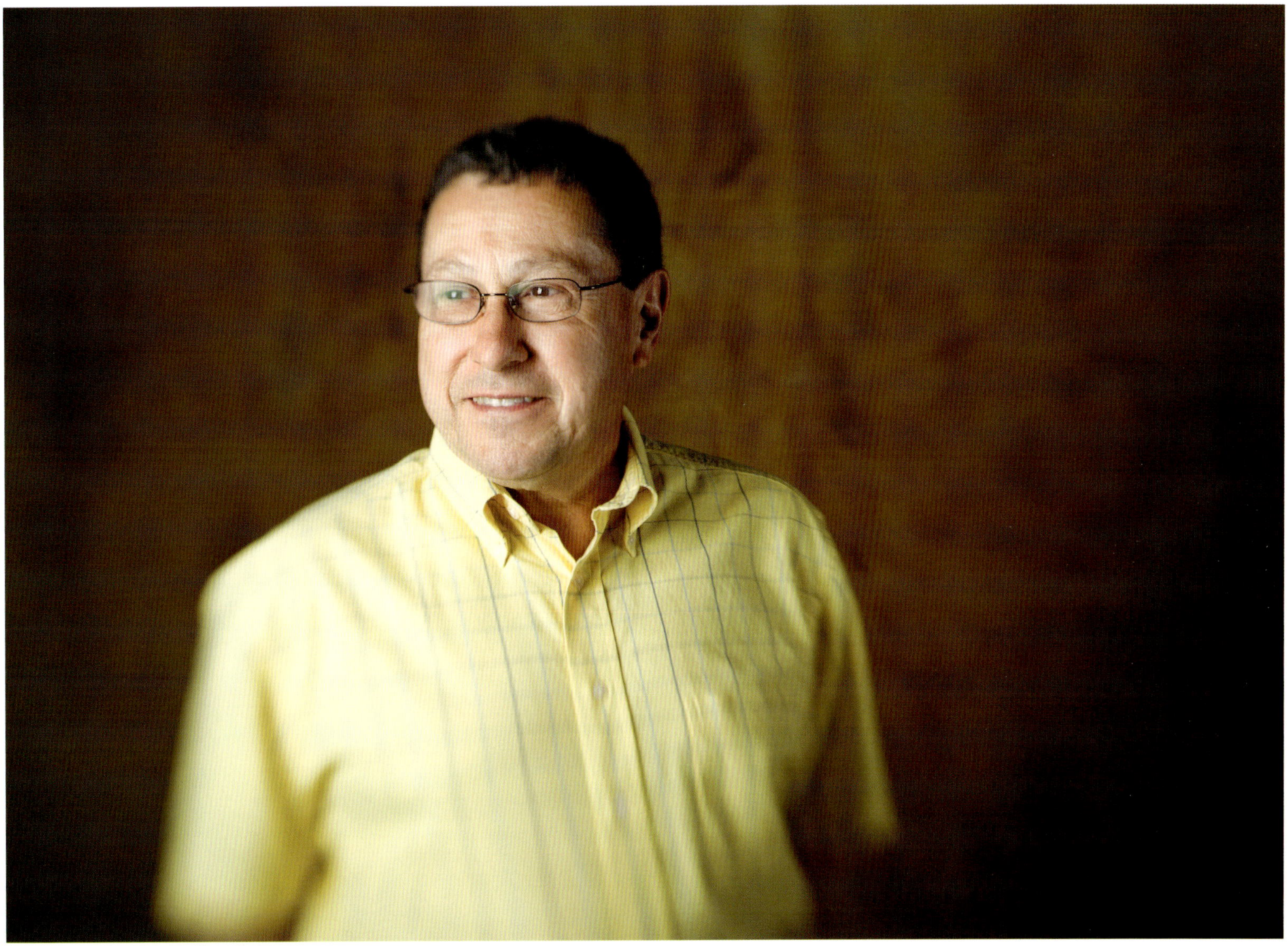

Guido Migiano

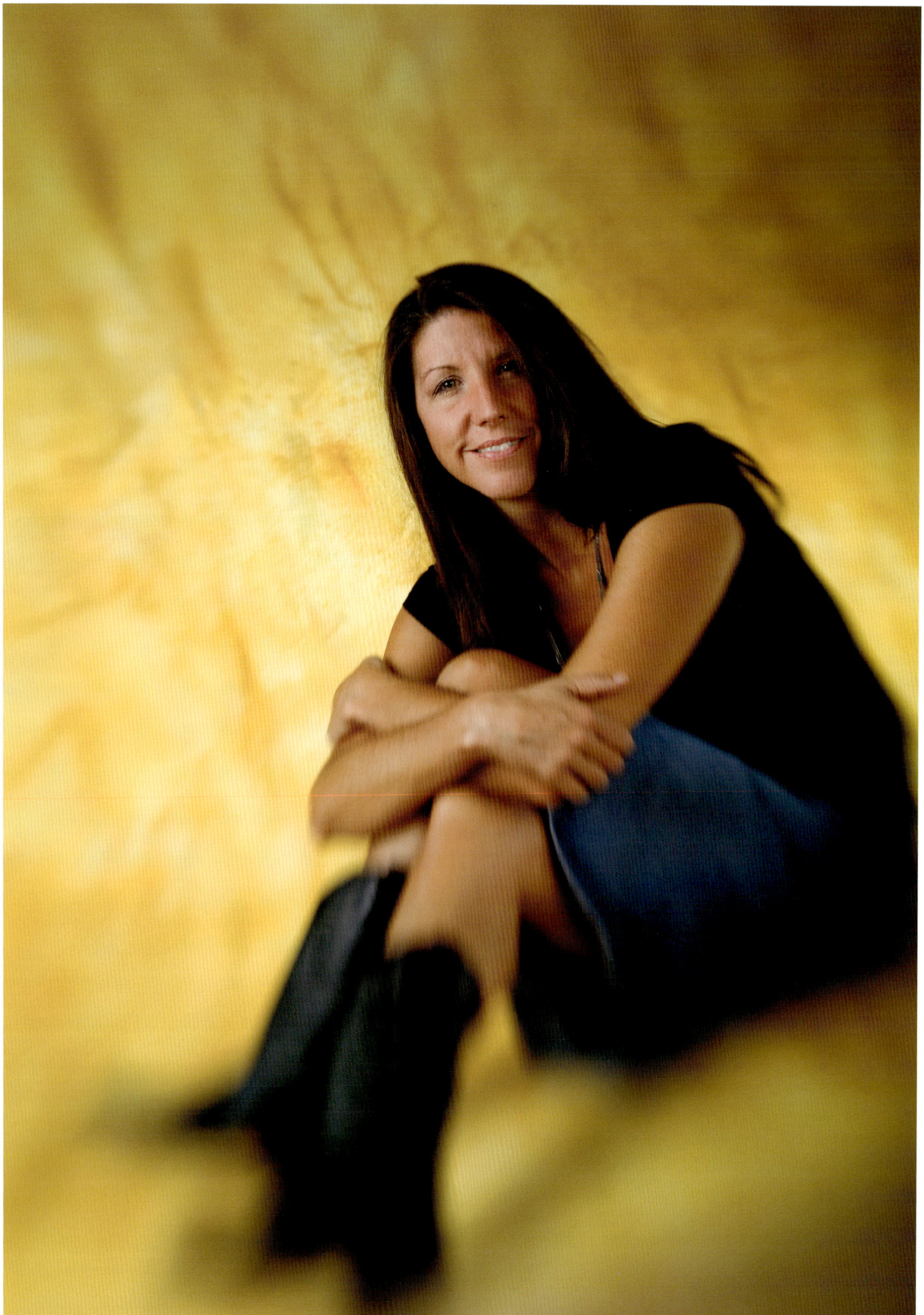

Suzanne "Sam" Kasparek Mitchell

I grew up in Oregon surrounded by textbook "beautiful" landscapes. Of course I took it for granted, for that is the disposition of most children. Respect for the environment is not a new or passing fad to any Oregonian I have ever met ... you are just born with it. But reflecting back, I just let it pass by, mostly unnoticed.

In 1987 I came to understand a more southern landscape. I moved to New Orleans for my undergraduate degree at Loyola University. Here, my visions became much more cement-oriented. Cement that oozed life. Every crack was filled with lush, green weeds, for it is a city six feet below sea level. As a dutiful art student, I studied, painted, and delighted in pottery. However, the water won in New Orleans during the devastation of Katrina, and there was an unimaginable change of landscape—one I never captured on canvas.

So only having memories of these places within the time periods I called them home, I feel an urgency to depict where I am now. I've lived in Spartanburg since 1993 and have embraced the beauty of my not-so-native land. I now paint where I live, where I travel, and what I experience. The literal land or cityscape is transformed into an almost abstract yet recognizable form that is lush with painterly strokes and texture.

What we pass every day is so diverse. I intend my paintings to present the anxious feeling of motion, be it blurred or frozen, to leave the viewer guessing where or what it is. However, my ultimate goal is to relate to the viewer that we are stewards to the land and that it is the land that enhances us all, even if the view is just for a speck of time.

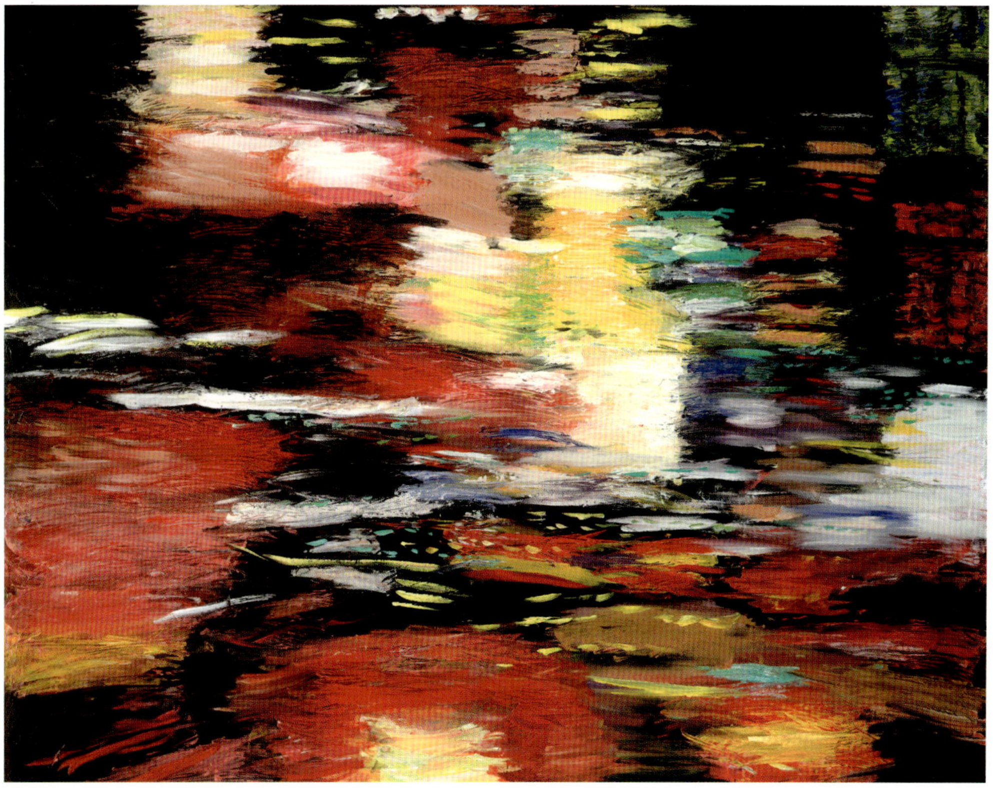

The Rush
Acrylic on canvas
48" X 60"

Kristofer M. Neely

A Baptist minister's son, I grew up doodling on offering envelopes in the back pews of local churches. During the workweek, I was always interested in the industrial objects around the lumberyards, railroads, oil companies, and textile firms that surrounded our family home on Union Road. That is where I developed an eye for collecting and repurposing scrap materials.

As an undergraduate at Wofford College, Professor A.K. McMillan refunded my materials fee in the only studio art course the college offered. She said I was only using the materials left in the trash by my classmates and it did not seem right to collect two fees for the same supplies. Reusing materials allows me to embrace experimentation as an essential part of my artistic practice. I am guided by intuition as I work, whether I am painting with discarded bicycle parts or finding niches in an urban landscape where a painting can be hidden. The MFA I earned at Goddard College in Vermont did not teach me how to paint; it taught me to understand why I paint.

I am haunted by images. They are never in short supply for me, and I have few inhibitions in releasing a piece into the world or into the hands of others. I am interested in visionary artists, ephemera, and ideas that infiltrate the established order with unexpected humor and hope. The specific meaning I am making in a piece determines the appropriate tools and materials I need to employ. I consider my time in the studio to be a manual act of contemplative prayer. The only work I like more than painting is teaching.

I enjoy my share of travels and residencies, but my best work begins when I rinse Spartanburg red clay off of found wood and start to paint.

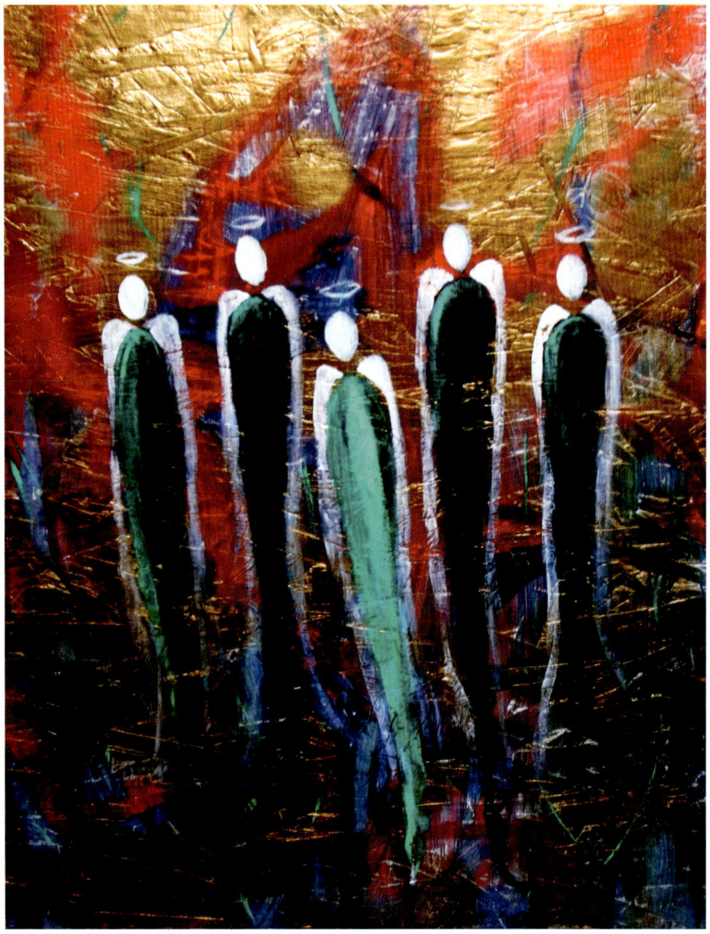

Five Guardians
Acrylic on found wood
36" X 48"

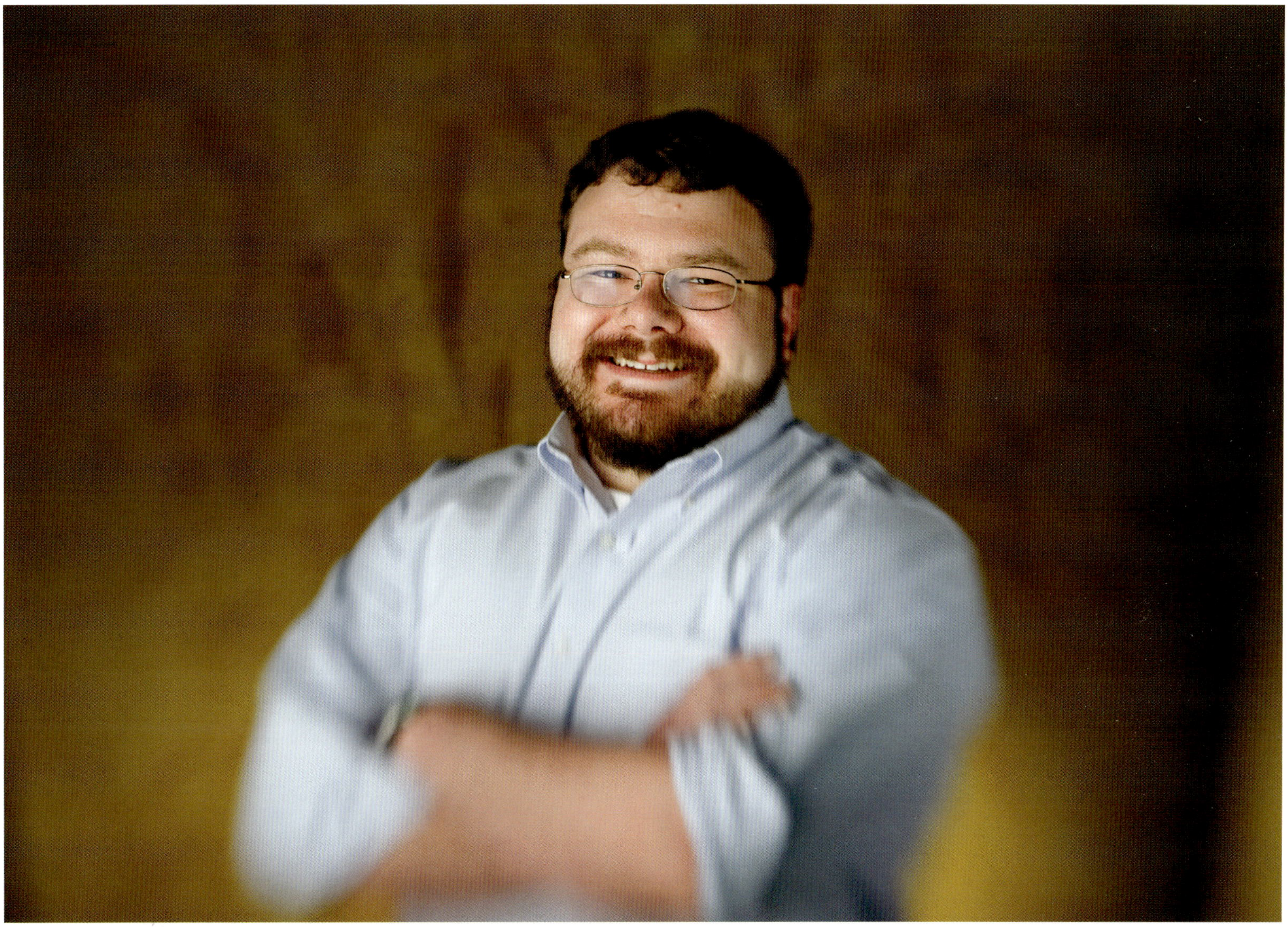

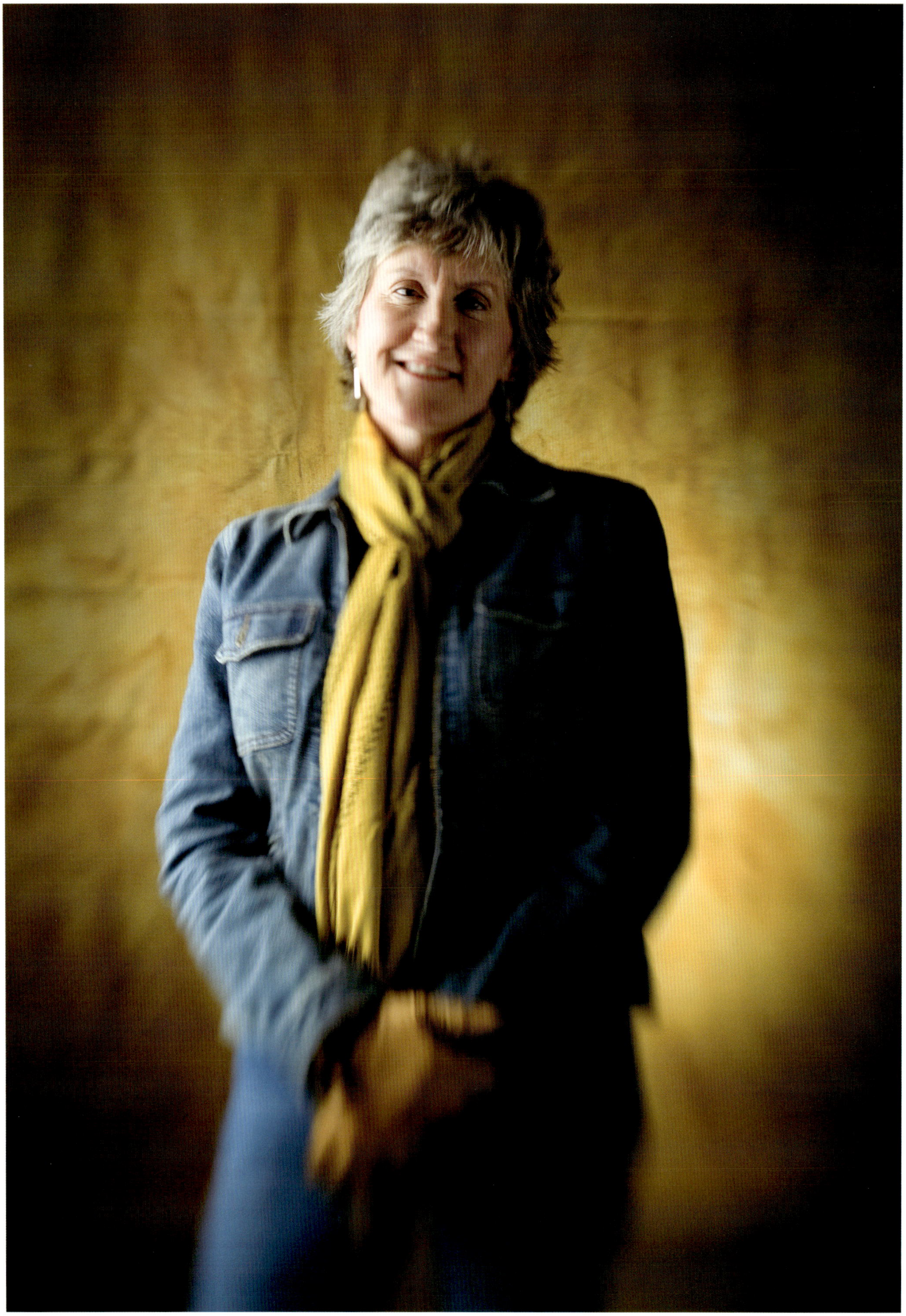

Jane Allen Nodine

I was born in Spartanburg, but I am an amalgamation of worlds beyond. As a child I wanted to be an artist and actively involved in working with my hands. My father was a residential builder with drafting tables, t-squares, pencils, and blueprints, so those were things I saw as everyday tools. My maternal grandmother was very creative; she had a "green thumb," fished, enjoyed wing shooting and textile crafts, and taught levels K-12 in her career. My mother recognized my early interest in art and enrolled me in private lessons at Spartanburg High School when I was in the first grade. The class was taught by Spartanburg artist Betty Jane Bramlett, who had graduated from college and returned to Spartanburg to teach art in District Seven. That was 1960, and she taught us sand casting, melted crayon painting, and enameling on copper. Those were complex processes that were bold experiences for young artists and highly influential in my career development.

My work is strongly related to memory and experience, often the trace or vestige of some past thing or event. In the studio I typically have a dozen or more works in progress, and each informs the next as it moves toward completion. I rely on sketchbook/journals that I have kept for years, and I find their significance important for developing ideas and maintaining a record of where I have been. My influences include nature, advertising, popular culture, history, and, by all means, living and working in the South.

I hold an MFA degree from the University of South Carolina in Columbia, and I am currently professor of art and director of the Curtis R. Harley Art Gallery at the University of South Carolina Upstate in Spartanburg. Prior to joining the University I operated Jane Nodine Hardwear, a jewelry design and manufacturing company that specialized in fashion and art jewelry. My work has taken many forms over the years, including drawing, painting, installation, and photography, and many of my works have been exhibited throughout the United States.

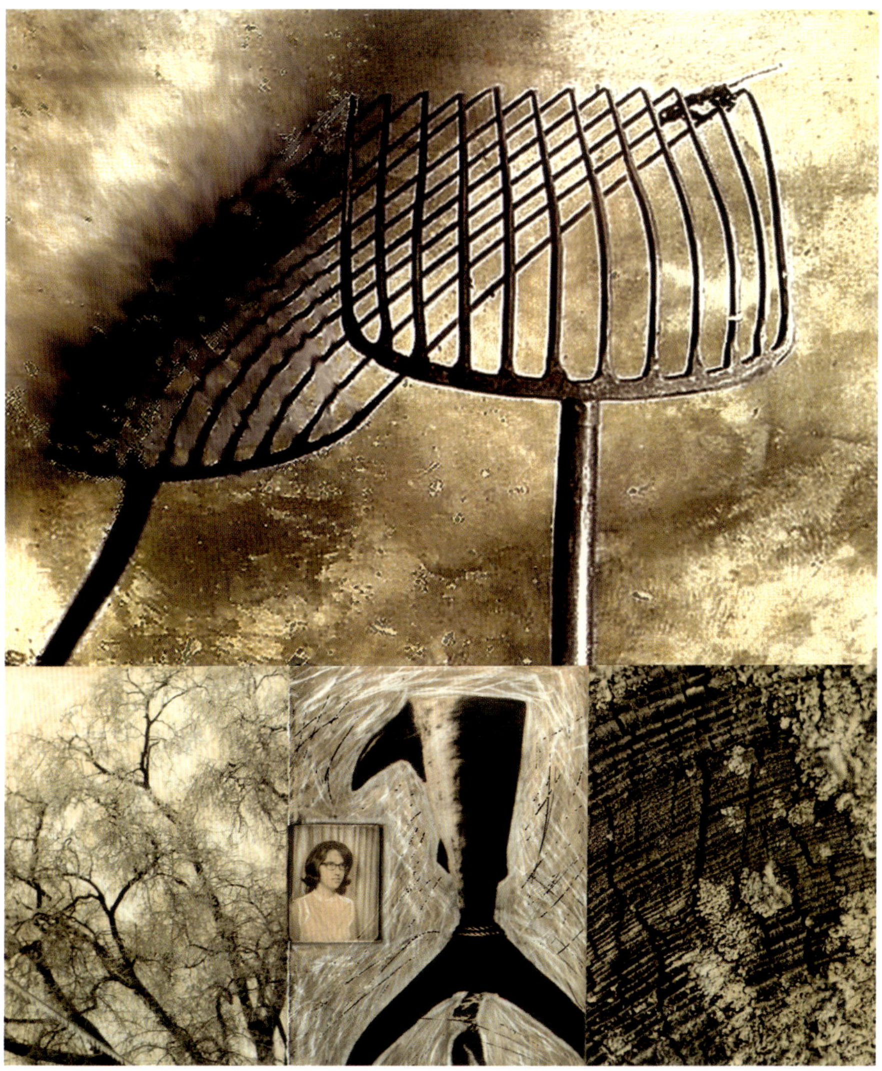

"conjunct suspension"

Digital and film photography, graphite with other media

36" X 30"

Nancy O'Dell-Keim

As a child in the small town of Union, South Carolina, I spent a great deal of time riding my bike along the slow-paced streets. While riding one hot summer day, I came across an "art mobile" stationed at a local park. This amazing vehicle—a cross between a trailer and an ice cream truck—offered free pottery lessons to any bored kid that happened to ride by. Every day for a week or more, the vehicle returned, and so did I! The artist on site talked to me about my art and suggested programs such as the Governor's School for the Arts, which I attended years later. At the time, I didn't understand that this "art mobile" was part of a rural outreach program funded by the South Carolina Arts Commission. I just understood that this artist took the time to look at my work. His encouragement had a profound impact.

This type of encouragement, mentoring, and cyclical energy is at the heart of the Spartanburg visual arts community, which I first experienced as a student at Converse College. I quickly understood that my teachers lived their lives by example, dedicating themselves to their art, to their students, and to the community. As an artist now living in Spartanburg, I am inspired by the passion, commitment, and goodwill among artists.

At times I paint for the pure fun or rush of applying paint and color onto a surface, and at other times it's about such elements as conception, movement, metaphor, and light. For example, my painting *Growth* is influenced by small still life objects that sit on my studio windowsill—twigs, a snake's skin, a moth's wing, and rocks. In abstract form, these objects symbolize new beginnings, growth, and change.

Much of my work speaks primarily of hope, faith, and survival. It speaks of the courage to embrace, to create, to move forward, and to take flight without giving in to fear and uncertainty and without losing one's faith when confronted by a harsh and unpredictable world.

Growth III
Oil on canvas
36" X 48"

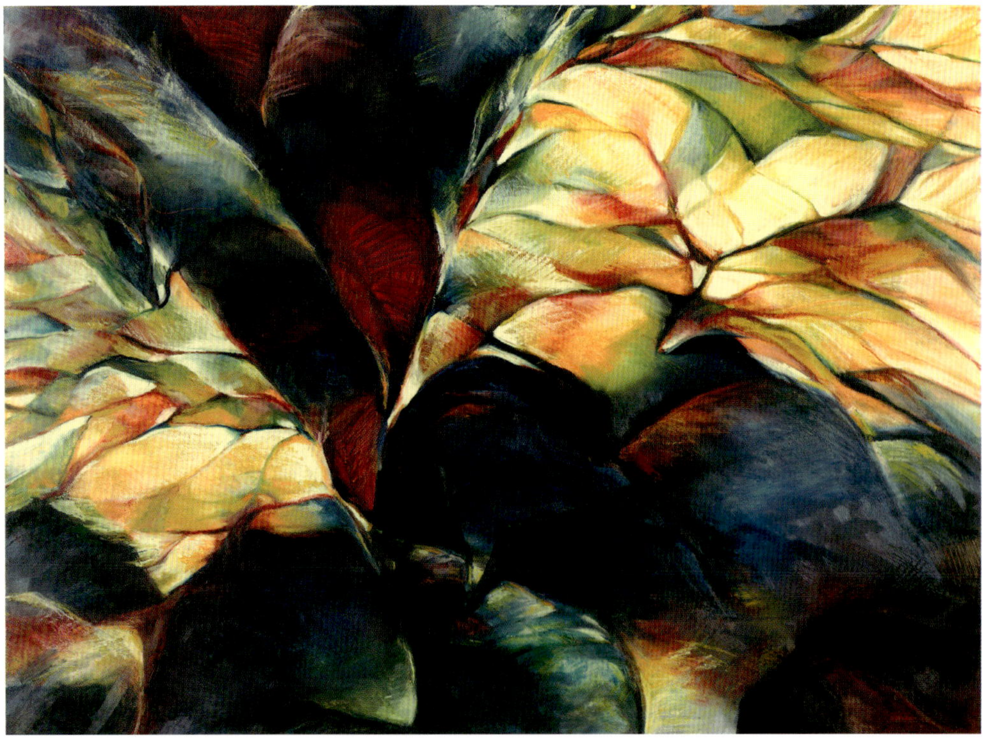

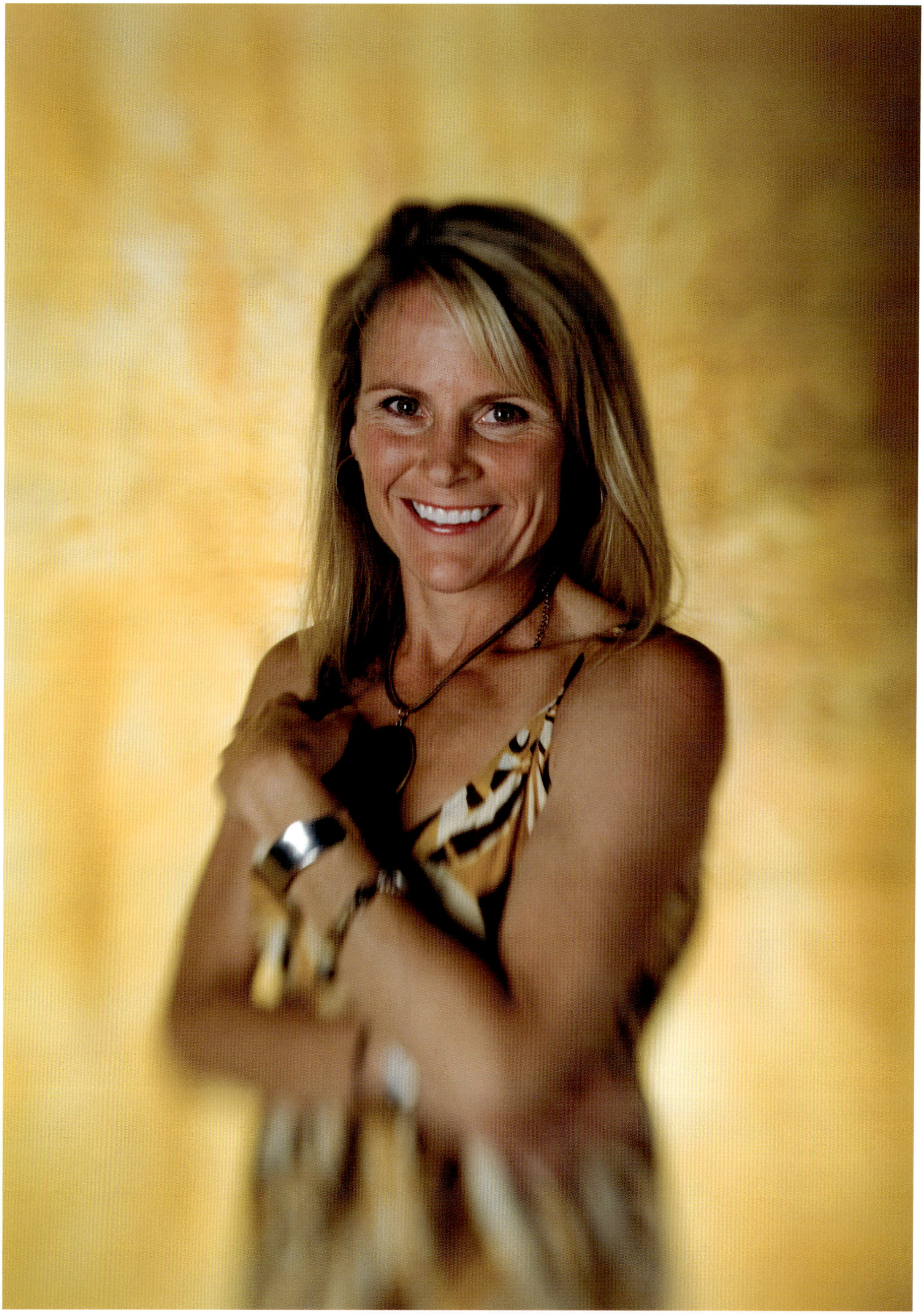

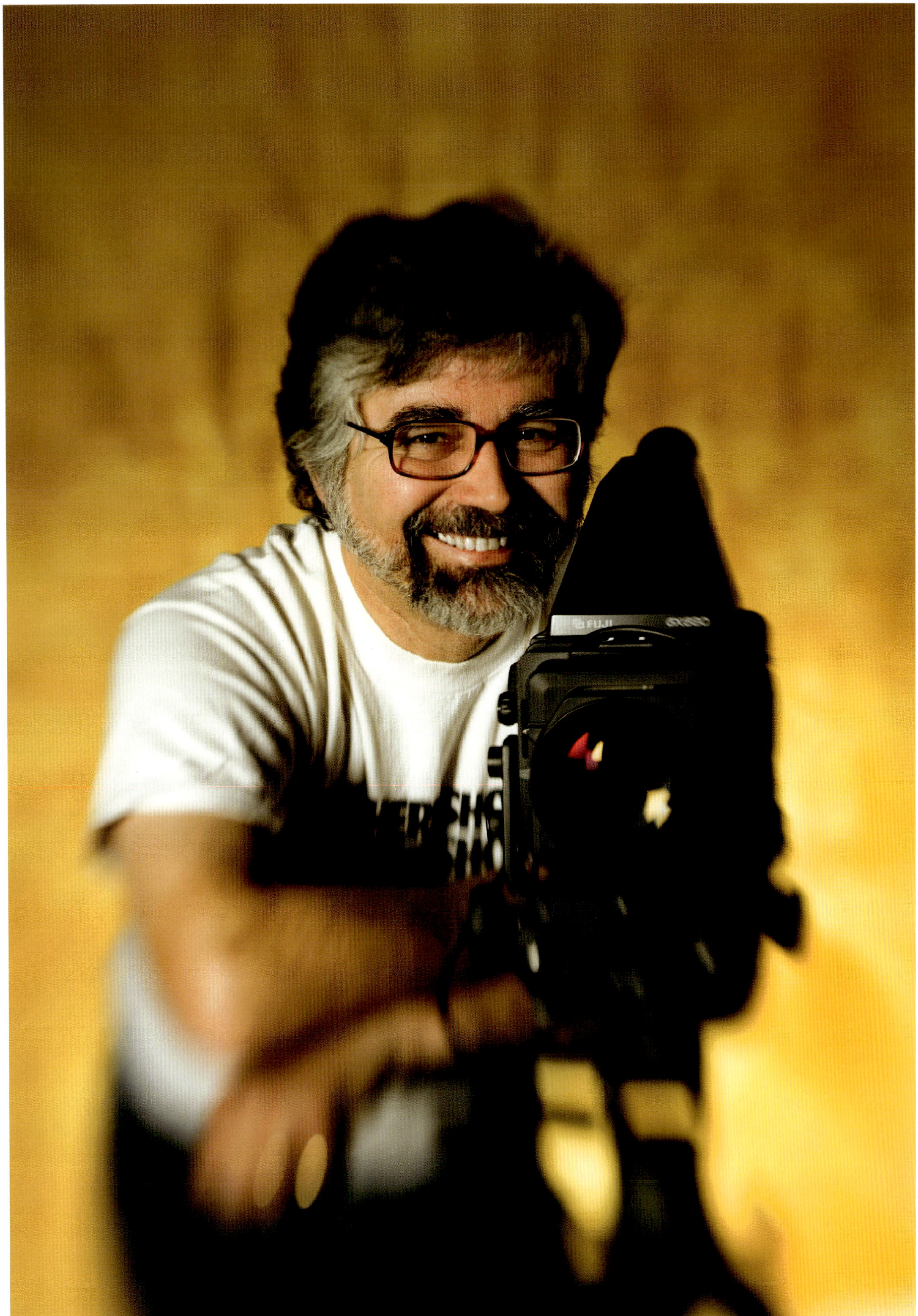
FUJI

Mark Olencki

Growing up in the early 1950s in metropolitan Newark, New Jersey, did not prepare me visually for the path my life would take. Neither did my elementary and middle school years in the suburban tri-city area of South Plainfield. My high school experience in South Carolina hinted at the fact I had a "knack" for visual communication; routinely I was taken out of class to work on design projects and bulletin boards for West Florence High, and I even painted the school mascot in the center of the newly constructed gym. I was first introduced to photography my senior year. I continued my informal design training at Wofford and Converse colleges, working on annuals, newspapers, posters, and t-shirts.

I graduated magna cum laude from Wofford in 1975 with a BA in studio art with a concentration on printmaking, becoming one of Wofford's first and only studio art majors. In the thirty-plus years since, I have worked as a freelance photographer and commercial artist. All this time, experience has been my teacher.

Because of commercial success, my personal photography always has been an intimate visual conversation with myself—how I see, interpret, and make sense of the world. But being a commercial success has never been a goal. To be able to freeze a unique split-second in the human experience and tell a story is enough for me. My body of work is always evolving and encompasses all subjects.

Using the cliché "a picture is worth a thousand words," visual statements for me are unnecessary, and they mean I have failed as a photographer. I am guided by the wisdom of others. Here are a few from my notebook:

"If a day goes by without my doing something related to photography, it's as though I've neglected something essential to my existence, as though I had forgotten to wake up." (Richard Avedon)

"There are no rules for good photographs, there are only good photographs." (Ansel Adams)

"There is no off switch to genius." (David Letterman)

"Twenty-four hours, maybe sixty good years, it's really not that long a stay." (Jimmy Buffett)

Lawson's Fork

Photograph

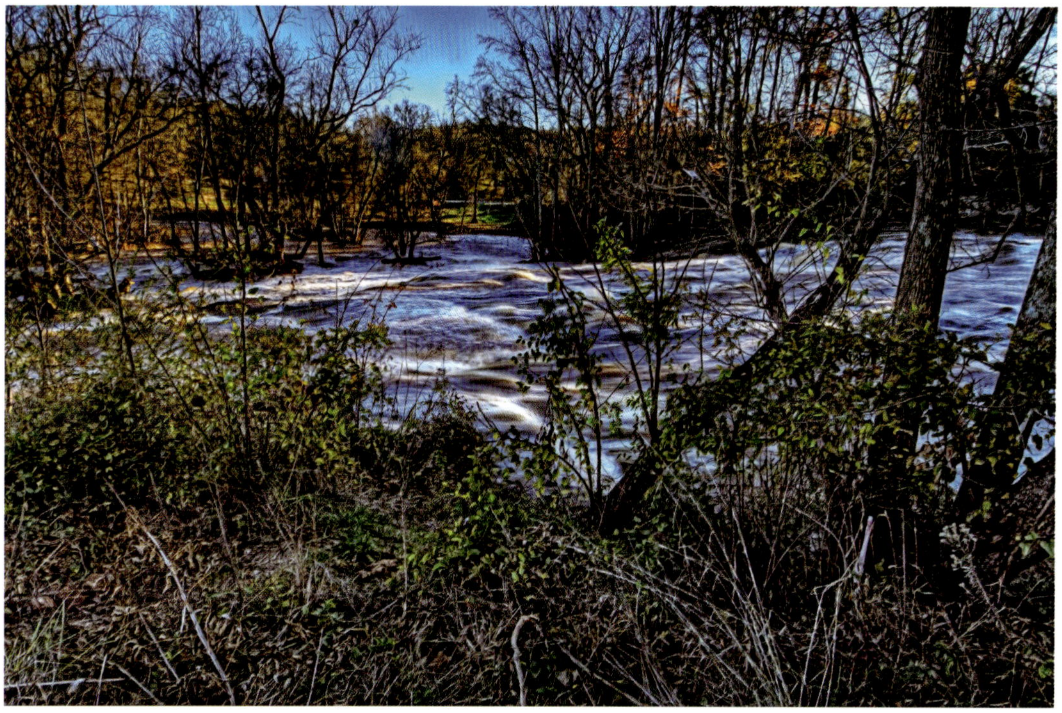

Ralph Pàquin

As an art student, I read Jean Tinguely's New Realist's Manifesto. To this day, machines, science information, sound/music, and, most of all, what it is to be human propel my art making. Out of all this, sculpture and drawing have become my broad genres of choice to communicate.

Observation and technical ability are essential for me, but I am more in sync with the medium when I am operating in the "serendipitous mode"—it is then that I move through the physical world into a more imaginary and illusory one.

Early on, my need for creating sculptural forms came out of a developed obsession with the human body and nature. My artwork has been called anthropomorphic. New York art critic Donald Kuspit said, "Pàquin's figures are a contradiction in terms: ceramic monuments in the grand manner ... he has given the noble nude a modern existential twist: rich, sensual, muscular substance on the outside, they are nothing on the inside."

Prior to making this series of figurative sculpture, I worked collaboratively with Ann Stoddard. We were both interested in creating our own landscapes and story lines via large-scale environments/installations, and these evolved and unfolded like "mouse trap" games—cause-and-effect events that had sound, movement, and lighting.

With the dismantling of visual arts grants and awards from the National Endowment for the Arts, we dismantled as an arts team. I "install" less frequently now. I continue to draw, and since moving to Spartanburg in 1992 have returned to object making. For the past four years, I have been working on the idea of "reduced and related genetic forms." Currently, these forms are being fabricated into sculptures using modern casting methods, processes, and materials. These new erotic sculptures will evoke a sense of humor, innocence, birth, gender, and beauty. My key sources of visual and conceptual inspiration are modern-day genetics and other "super" organic exotic forms.

Genes and Chromos
Acrylic, plastic film
8' X 16'

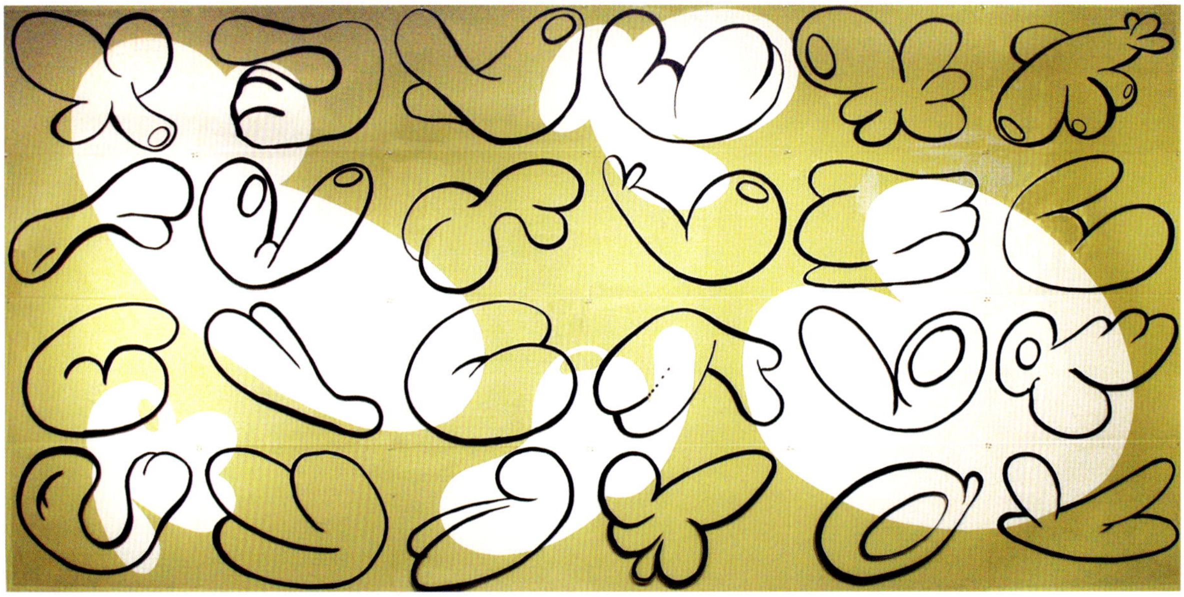

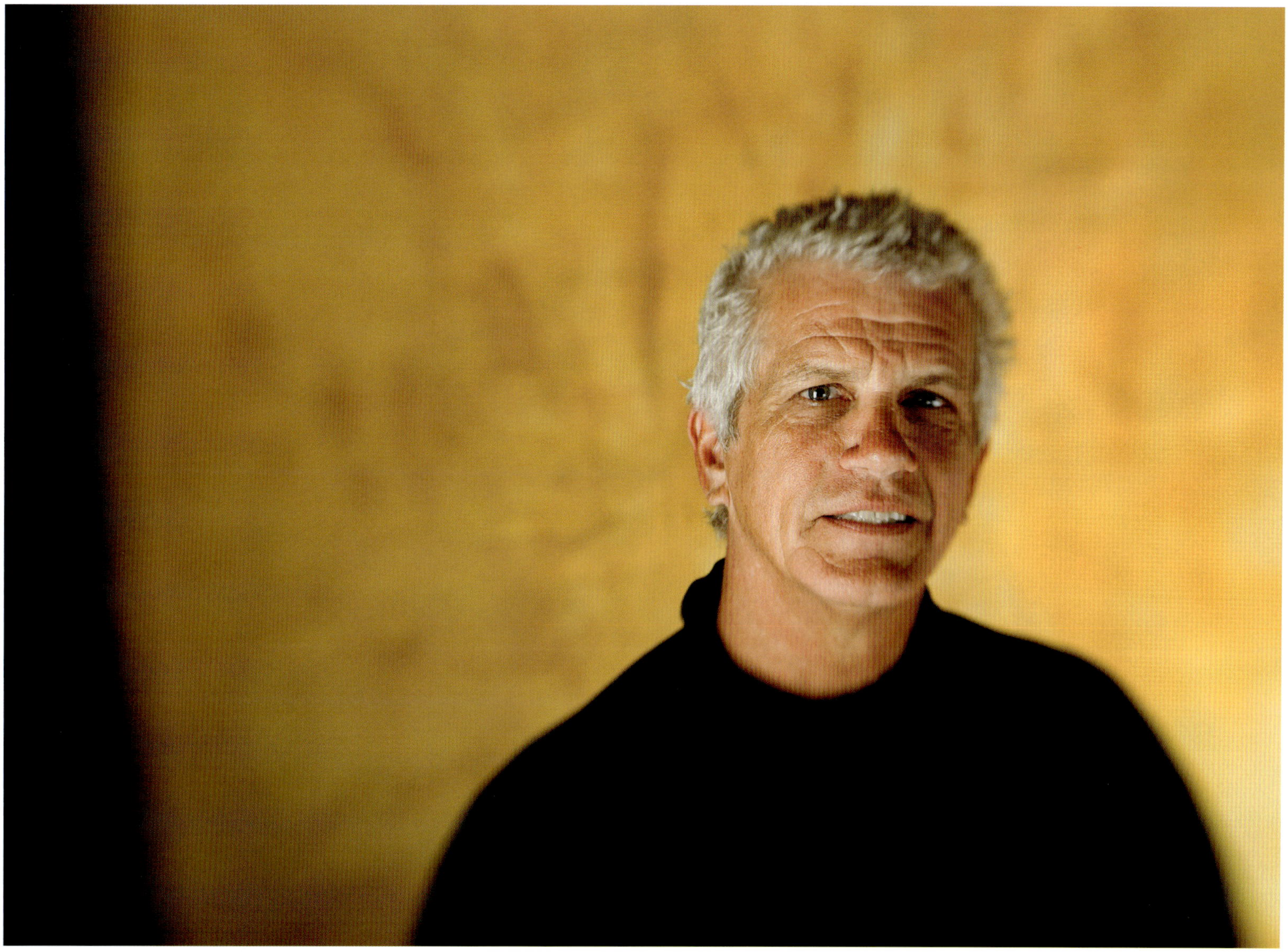

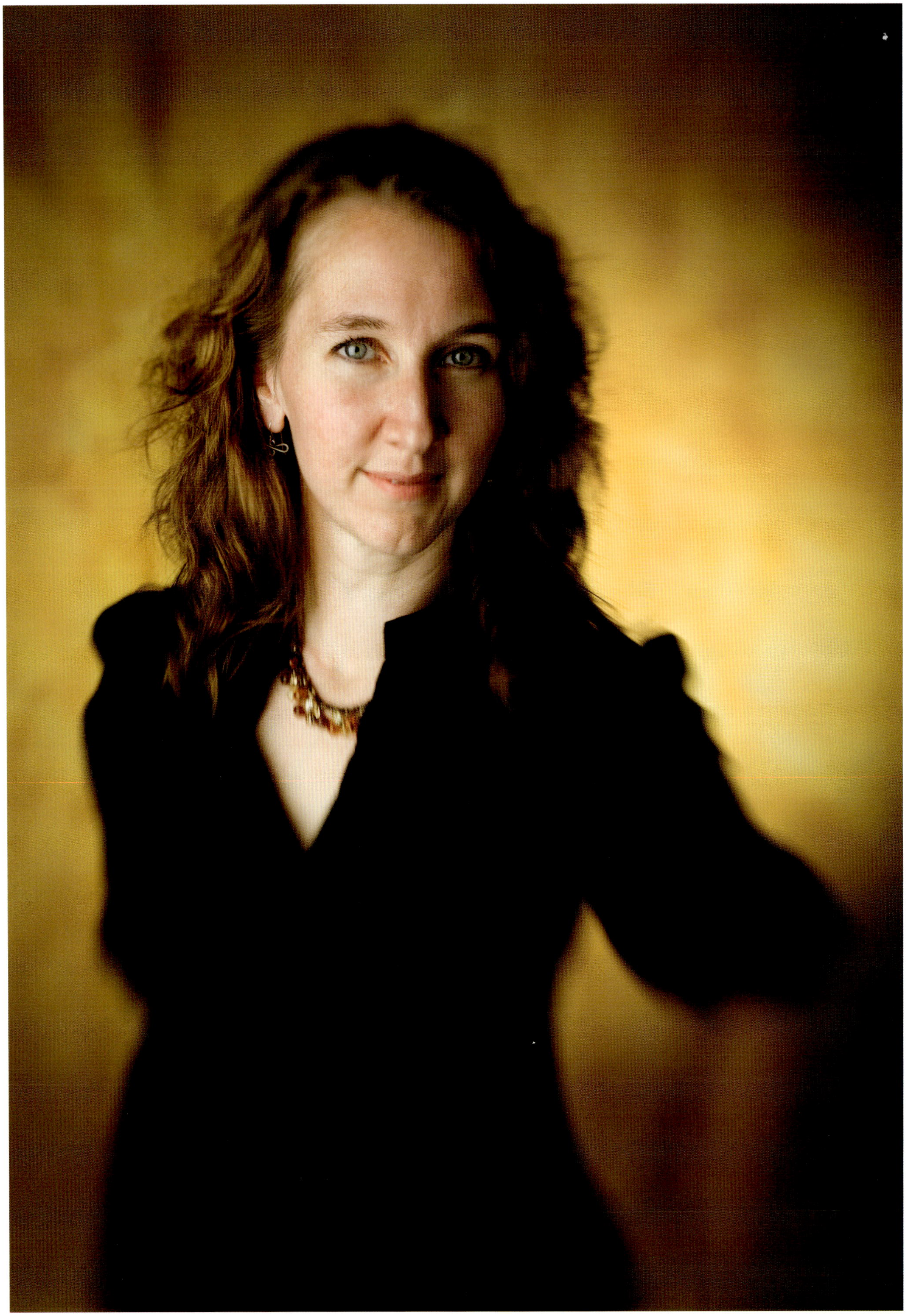

Melissa Pittman

Growing up in Spartanburg, I grew accustomed to living and finding refuge in the outdoors and my imagination. I was blessed and cursed to have been born to wildly creative people, my father a gifted writer and my mother an artist, not to mention many colorful characters in my family. In addition to my creative parents I have art in my genes as the great-granddaughter of American illustrator Maxfield Parrish. If I am not creating art, I am either thinking or dreaming about it. I constantly recognize art or beauty in random objects, scenes, or people around me. I am continually inspired by people. Spartanburg's cultural richness lies in its people who foster my creative process through the exchange of ideas and experiences. I benefit from these on a daily basis.

Noted painter Phillip Guston said, "When you're in the studio painting, there are a lot of people in there with you—your teachers, friends, painters from history, critics. One by one, if you're really painting, they walk out. And if you're really painting YOU walk out." I recently read this quote and it perfectly captured why I paint or what I aspire to when I paint. I seek that sumptuous communion with creation, a universal hum that resonates when I create, when there is a perfect stillness that cannot be found any other way for me. I also find this when I make music—everything, absolutely everything falls away.

My work is an intuitive process of mixed media layers, a dialogue between myself and the surface. Each mark is dependent upon and a response to the one before it. I strive to create depth through texture and richness through layers of color.

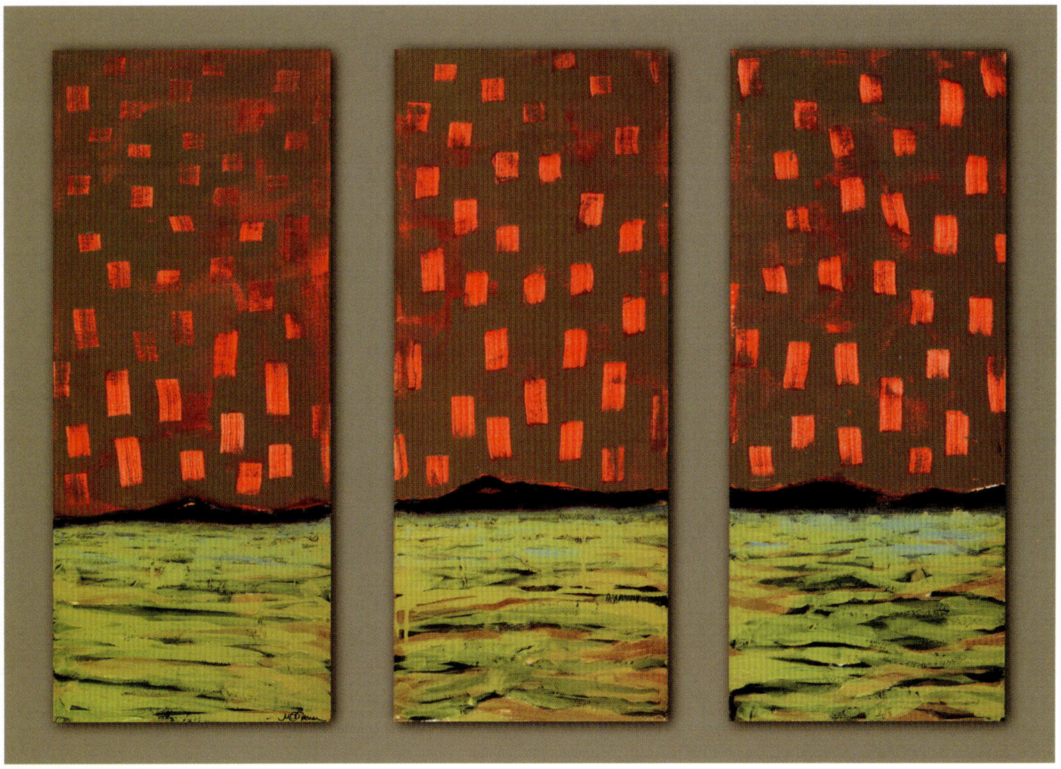

The Great Divide
Mixed Media
24" X 36" triptych

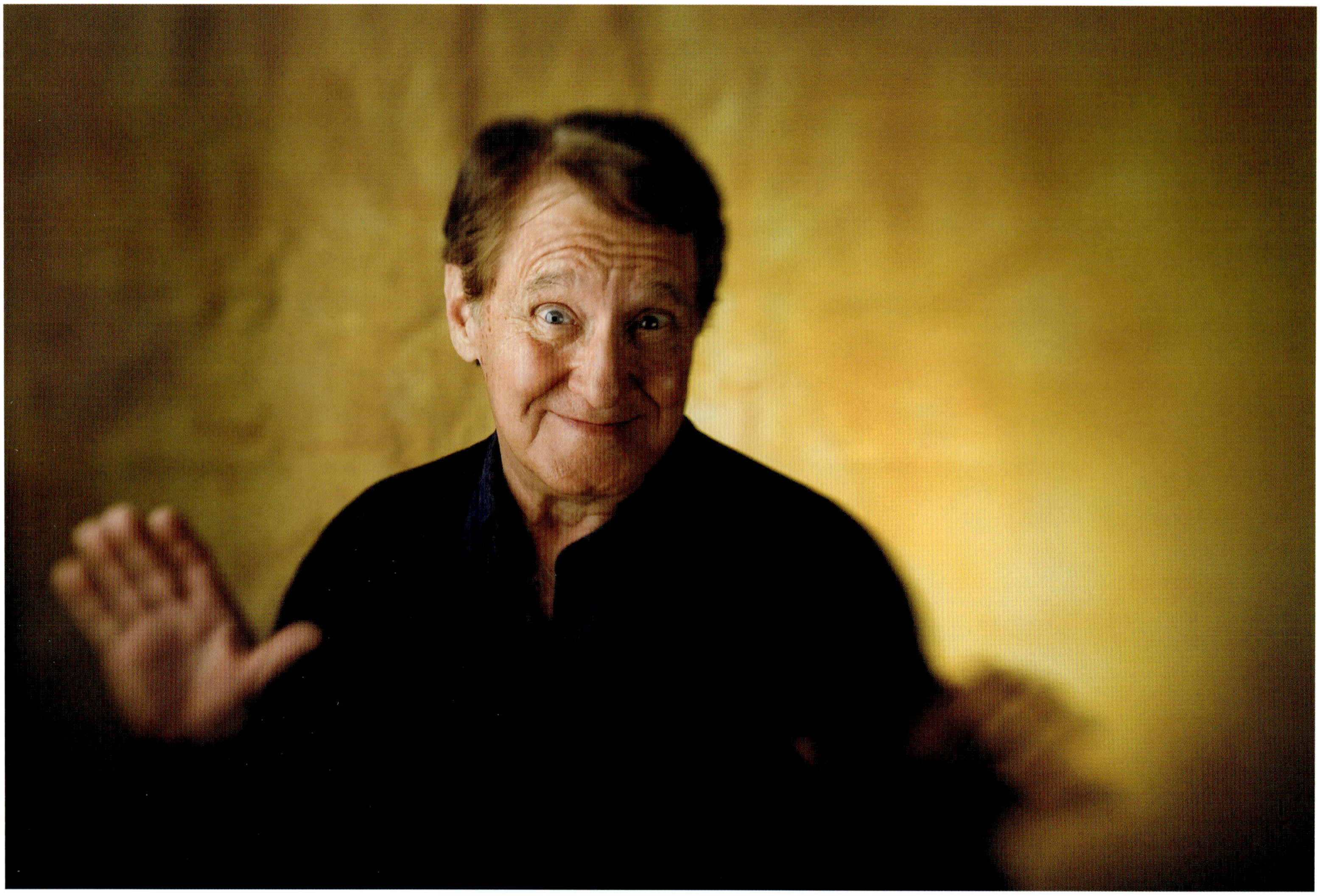

Gary Poole

I began drawing when I was five or six years old. A "how to draw" book written by the creator of Popeye got me started drawing cartoons, and I continued all through school instead of paying attention in math class (even now my fingers are my abacus). My first published cartoons were for *The Indian Post*, my high school newspaper. I also illustrated the headings for various columns and the covers for our high school annual with realistic pen and ink sketches. I have had cartoons published in books, magazines, and newspapers throughout my life. I later branched out into drawing and sketching whatever interested me.

I moved to New York City when I was seventeen. The museums in the city allowed me to study works from the great artists of the world. I was influenced by Miro, Chagall, Matisse, Picasso, Klee, and others. Those artists gave me the freedom to go wherever my imagination took me—be it abstract, impressionism, dada, or "pop."'

I am self-taught, so the learning process is continuous and exciting. I prefer to work in mixed media and to use whatever it takes to get the desired result. My subject matter is borne out of looking at the world with a comic eye. I hope those who view my works will walk away with a smile on their lips, a sense of well-being, and, perhaps, a little more lighthearted view of life.

The visual arts community here is an amazing concentration of fine artists who are profoundly talented, equal to those found in any gallery in the world. No wonder someone has dubbed it … spARTanburg.

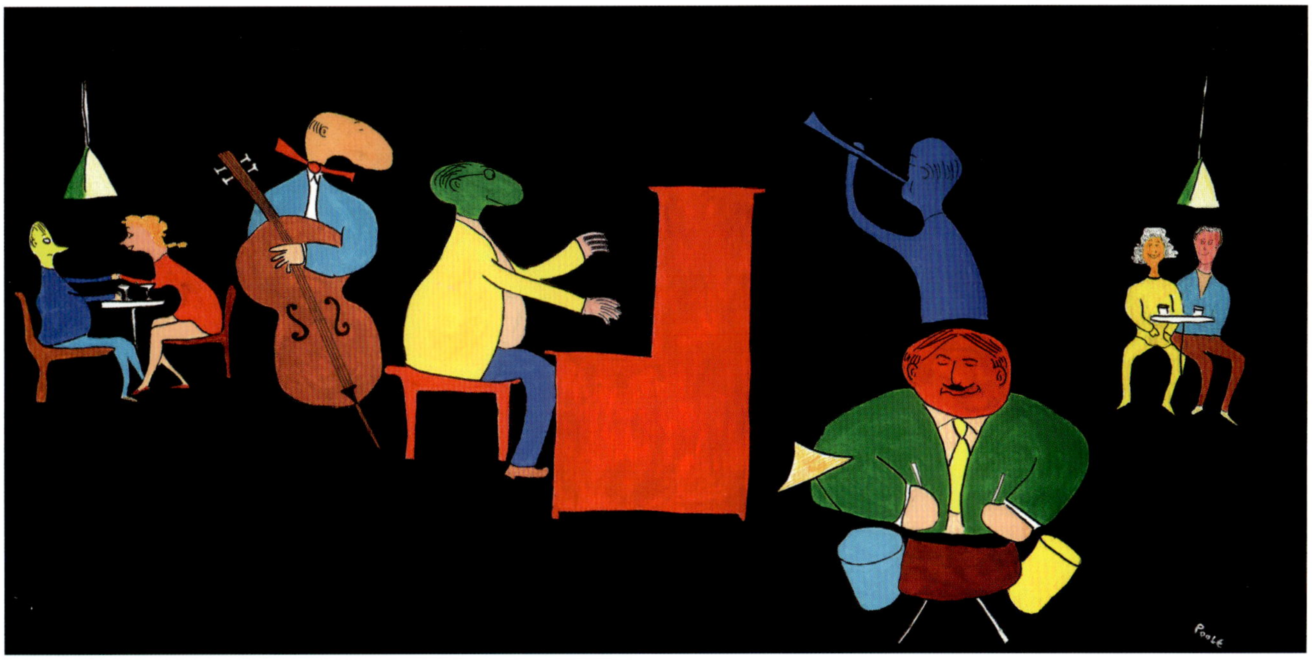

Let's Jazz It Up

Acrylic on canvas

24" X 48"

My art grows from those things that I cherish most and the experiences that have shaped my life. It was in the rural countryside outside of Knoxville, Tennessee, that I found my first passions: riding horses, reading fantasy, drawing, and exploring the outside world. Drawing came naturally to me. Supportive parents and an insightful art teacher guided me toward the career that was to mark my life.

Though I have three professional degrees in painting and drawing, it is the external experiences that have shaped my art. Sixteen years as a single parent influenced the strong narrative figurative direction that my art took. My work in community organizations as a VISTA volunteer shaped my belief in justice and social responsibility. My love of the outdoors and gardening developed within me a sense of environmentalism that provides text and concepts for many of my books and paintings.

I am an artist who loves to continue to learn and experience new media. I came to Spartanburg as an oil painter, yet over the years I have created series of charcoal drawings, artists books, alternative and digital photography, and encaustic wax paintings. The thread that holds the work together is the use of the human figure and my distinctive style.

Blue Dress

Encaustic

9" X 12"

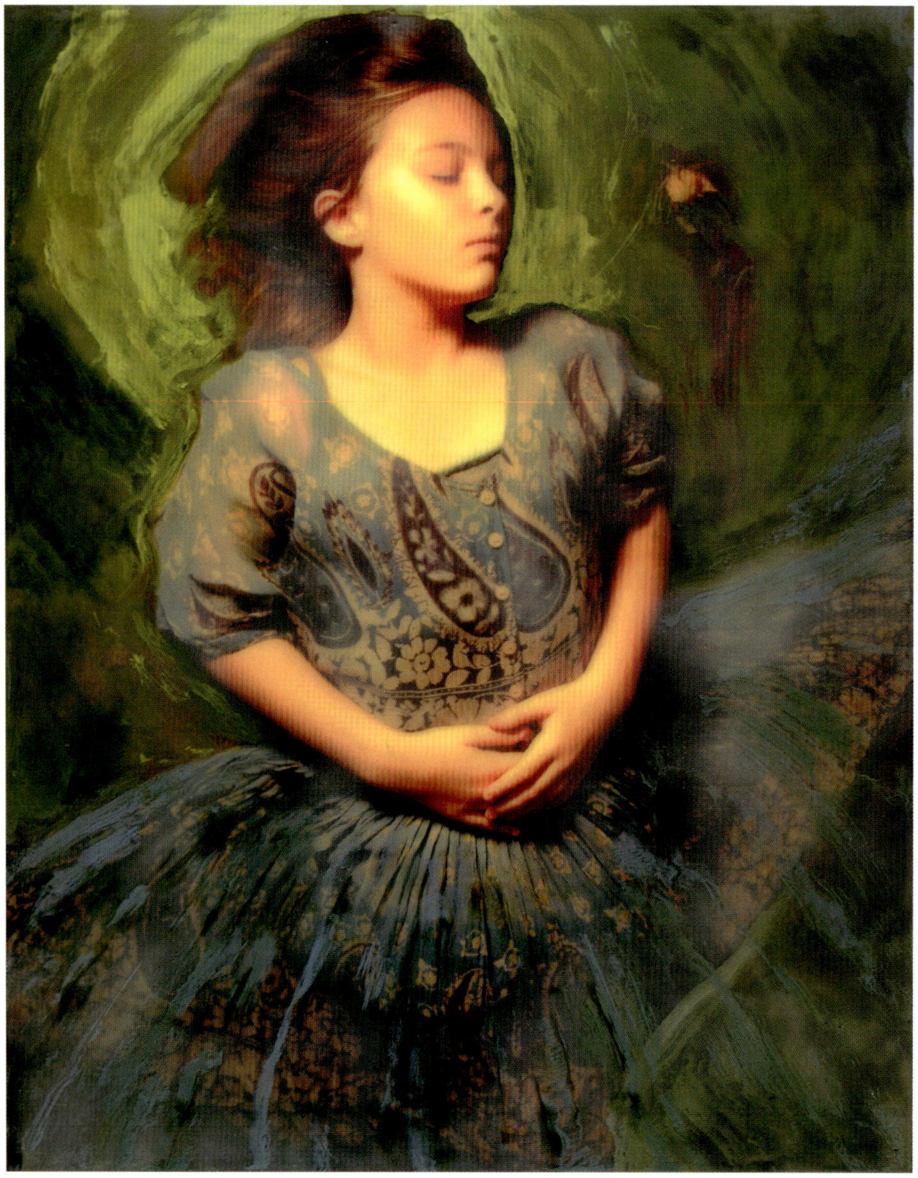

I strive to engage the viewer with seductive figures, distorted reality, and dark undertones. Working with the figure as subject matter, references to mythology, archetypes, contemporary social issues, and human relationships are intertwined among the images. Using textures and a variety of techniques, I love the way layered images and materials create work that evokes both aesthetic appeal and mystery. I am interested in having the viewer both startled and awed.

Within the Spartanburg artists community I have been both a leader and participant. It continues to provide the support that I need, a community in which to share, critique, and compete. As a founding member of the West Main Artists Cooperative I feel we have given to the community an alternative artistic environment in which artists can gather and create.

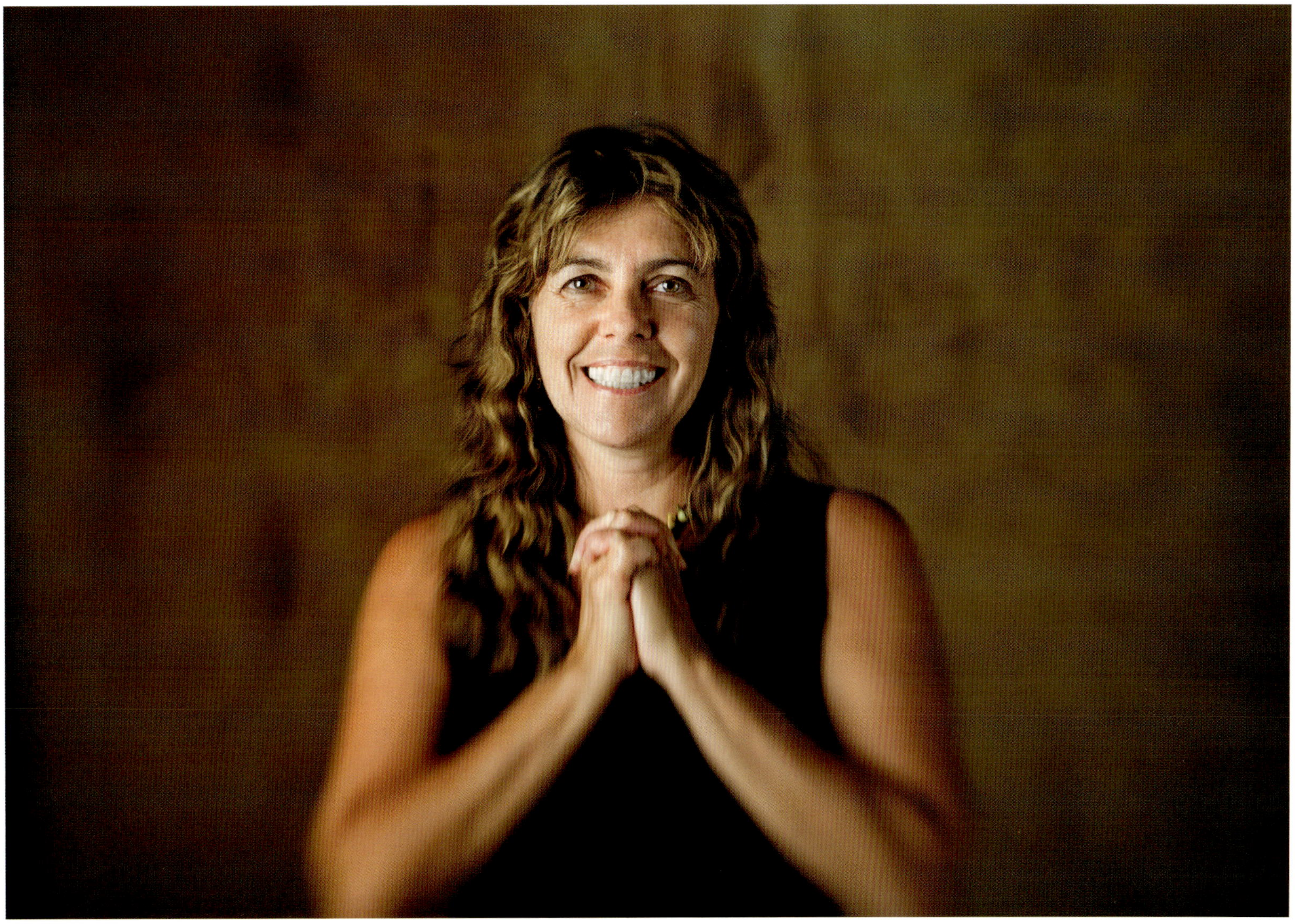

Teresa Prater

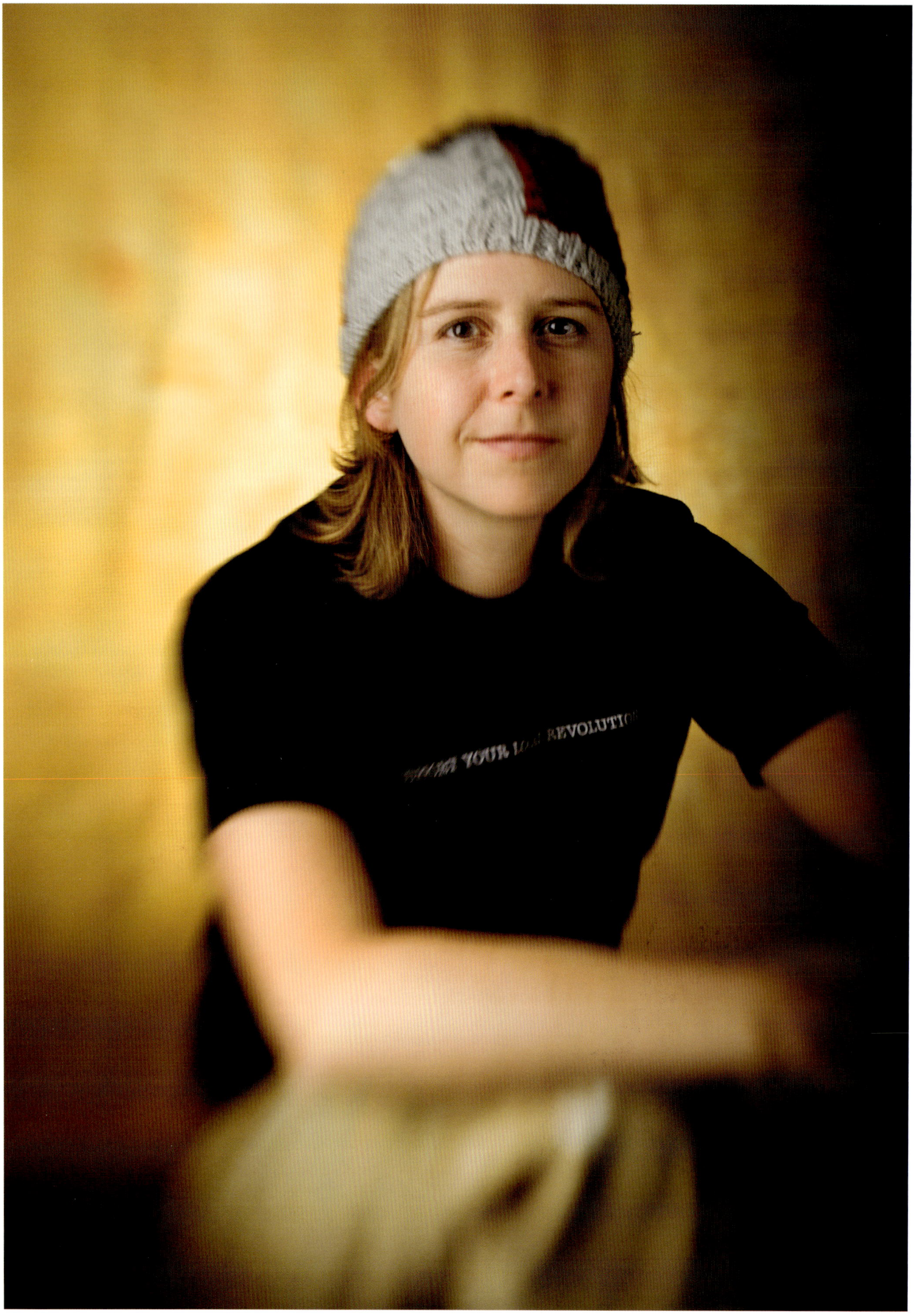

Alix Refshauge

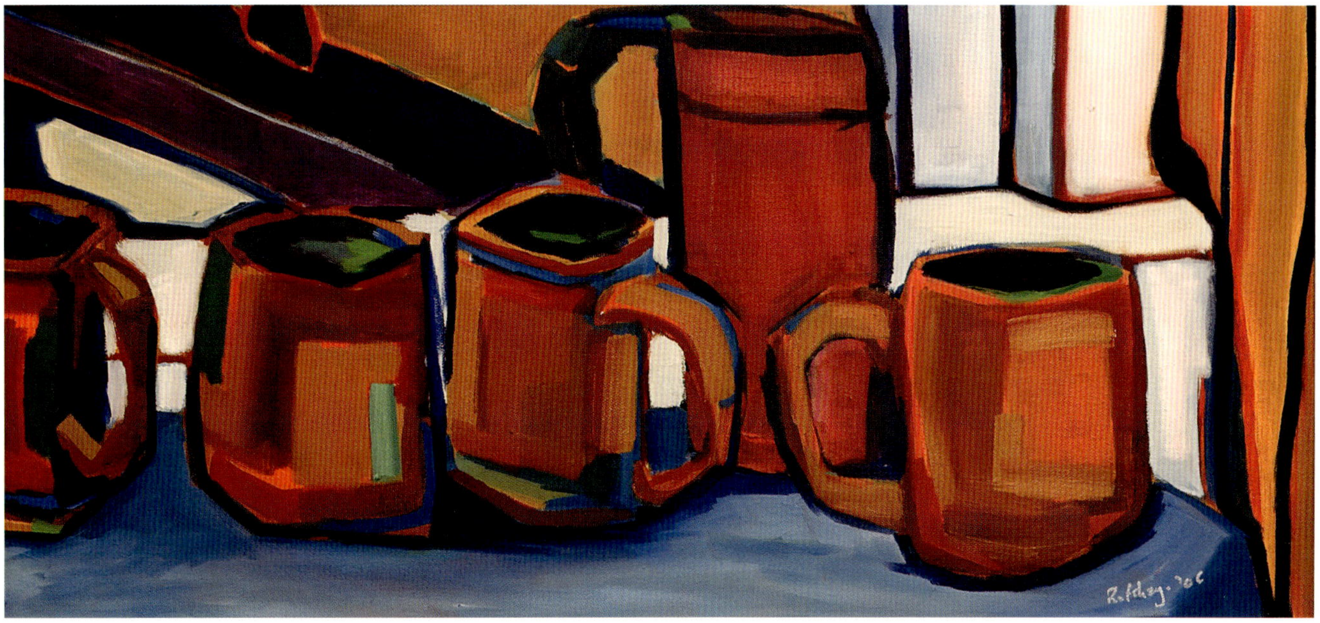

Coffee Cups
Oil on canvas
12" X 30"

I grew up on Connecticut Avenue about a block away from my grandmother, Jean Blackford. She loved the arts and was a big supporter of the local Arts Council. I have many memories of going with her to the old Arts Center on Spring Street and of being in her house, which was full of art books and catalogues.

Growing up, I was a competitive tennis player, and in the 9th grade, an elbow injury took me off the tennis courts for the better part of the year. I began taking watercolor classes after school. While I had always loved making art, these classes made it something I wanted to pursue. In 1996, I went to Furman University to be an art major. During the summer of 1999, I traveled to Cortona, Italy; there painting became my true focus. Inspired by the vivid landscape and the culture, I switched from acrylic to oil and began making work that would drive the style and motivation of my work for the next twelve years.

Since graduating from college, I have traveled the world and lived in various places. My paintings are colorful representations of these adventures. Bold colors and intentional brushstrokes aim to capture the energy and emotion associated with these experiences. The work is reflective and energetic and fun. I hope that when people view my work it makes them feel good.

From 2007-2011, I worked as the director of the artist-in-residence program at HUB-BUB, a grassroots movement that has taken Spartanburg by storm and influenced residency programs across the country that want to build community through the arts. At HUB-BUB, I learned what a supportive community for the arts can and should be. It's powerful stuff!

I grew up south of Spartanburg in a small community named Roebuck. This was during the 50's and 60's, and everyone knew each other and the family from which you came. Some of my earliest memories are of my mother sewing and my father building houses. It is from them that I received my greatest art lesson. As I saw them creating with cloth and wood, I too wanted to make something. They allowed me to use their scraps, and it wasn't long before my room became my art gallery.

During the time that I attended schools in the Roebuck area and later at Dorman High, there were no art classes. I relied on the Spartanburg County Library for my art education, and my parents supplied the materials for me to make "art." I always knew that I wanted to study art, so when I went to Winthrop College I declared art as my major. After college I taught art in public schools in Spartanburg and Charleston Counties.

Today, I am a mixed-media artist. I work in a studio located once again in the Roebuck area. Most of my recent works are sculptural. These works represent the things I think about and my reaction to the physical world around me. Nature and especially trees are a primary focus. The works are constructed from different materials and usually contain lots of detail. I like for the viewer to be drawn to the work first by the overall form and then by the detail within.

If asked why I make art, I can only reply that not to do it is not me.

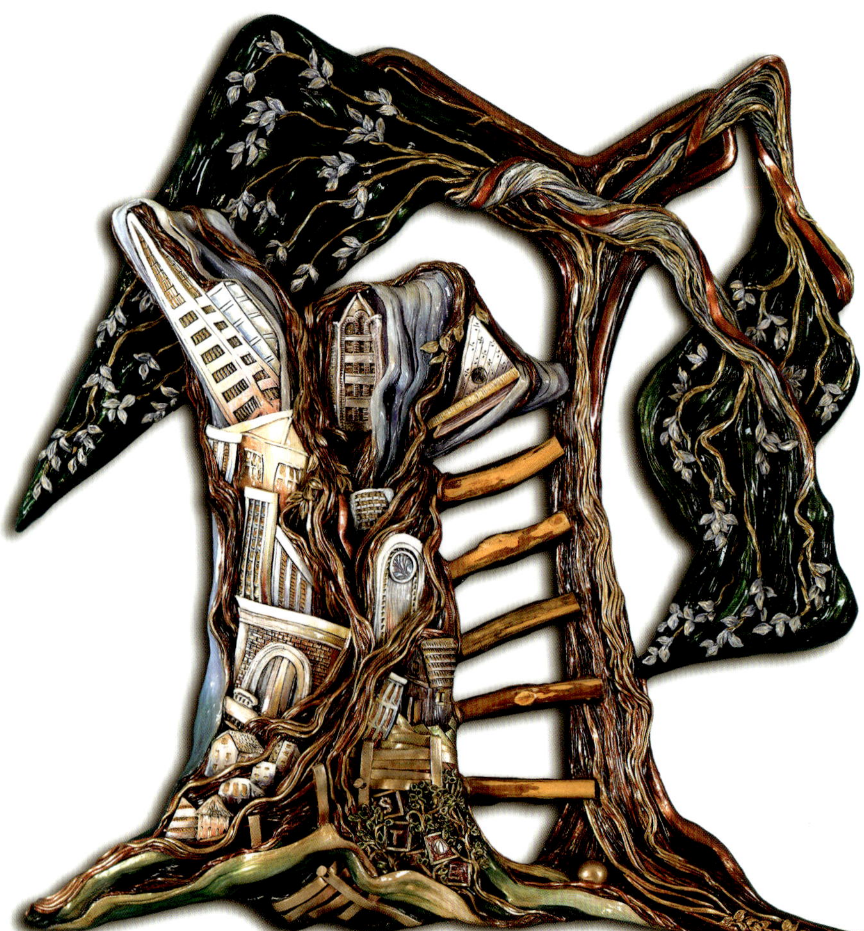

A Little Boy's Dream, A Man's Reality

Mixed media

21" X 22"

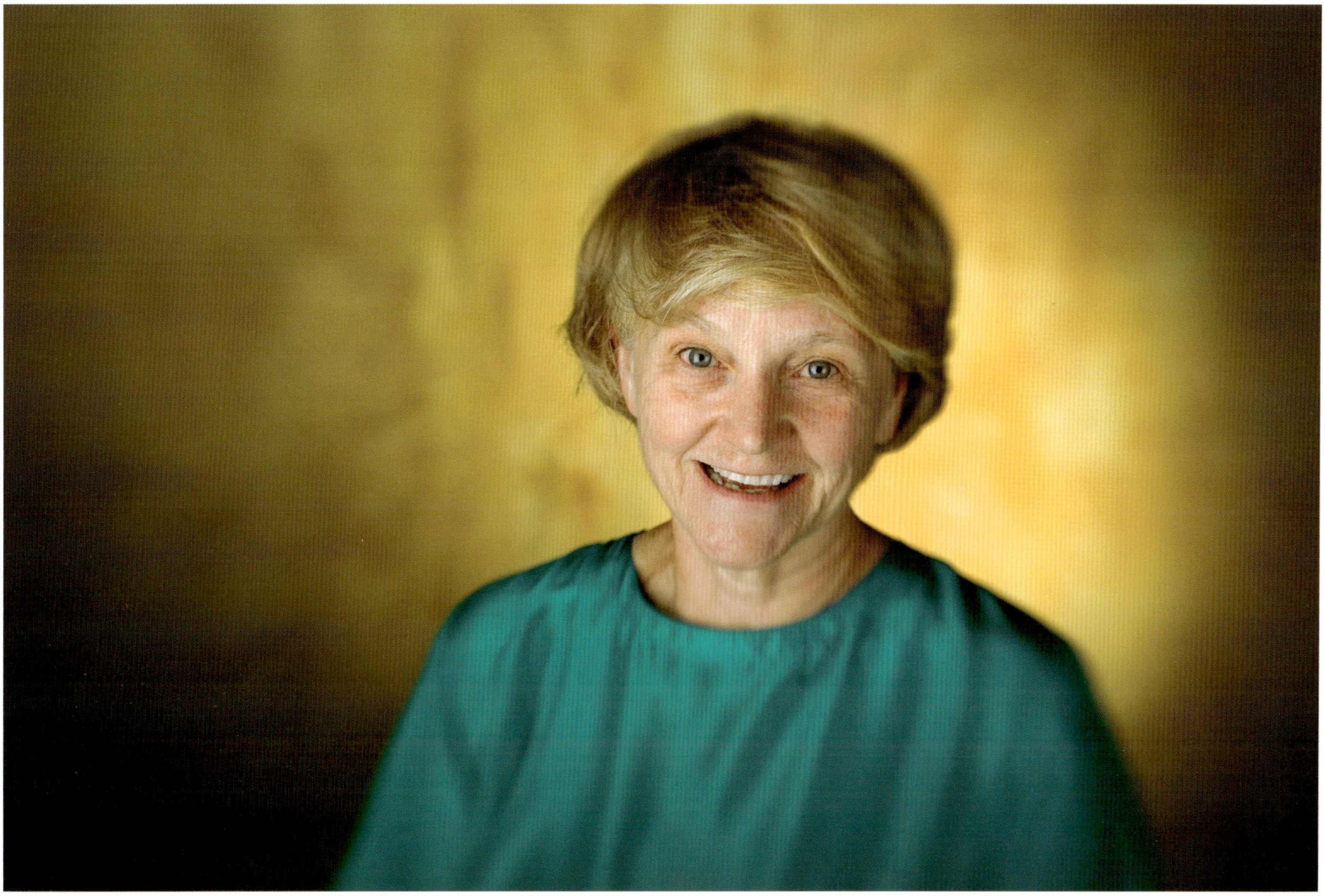

Beth Bullman Regula

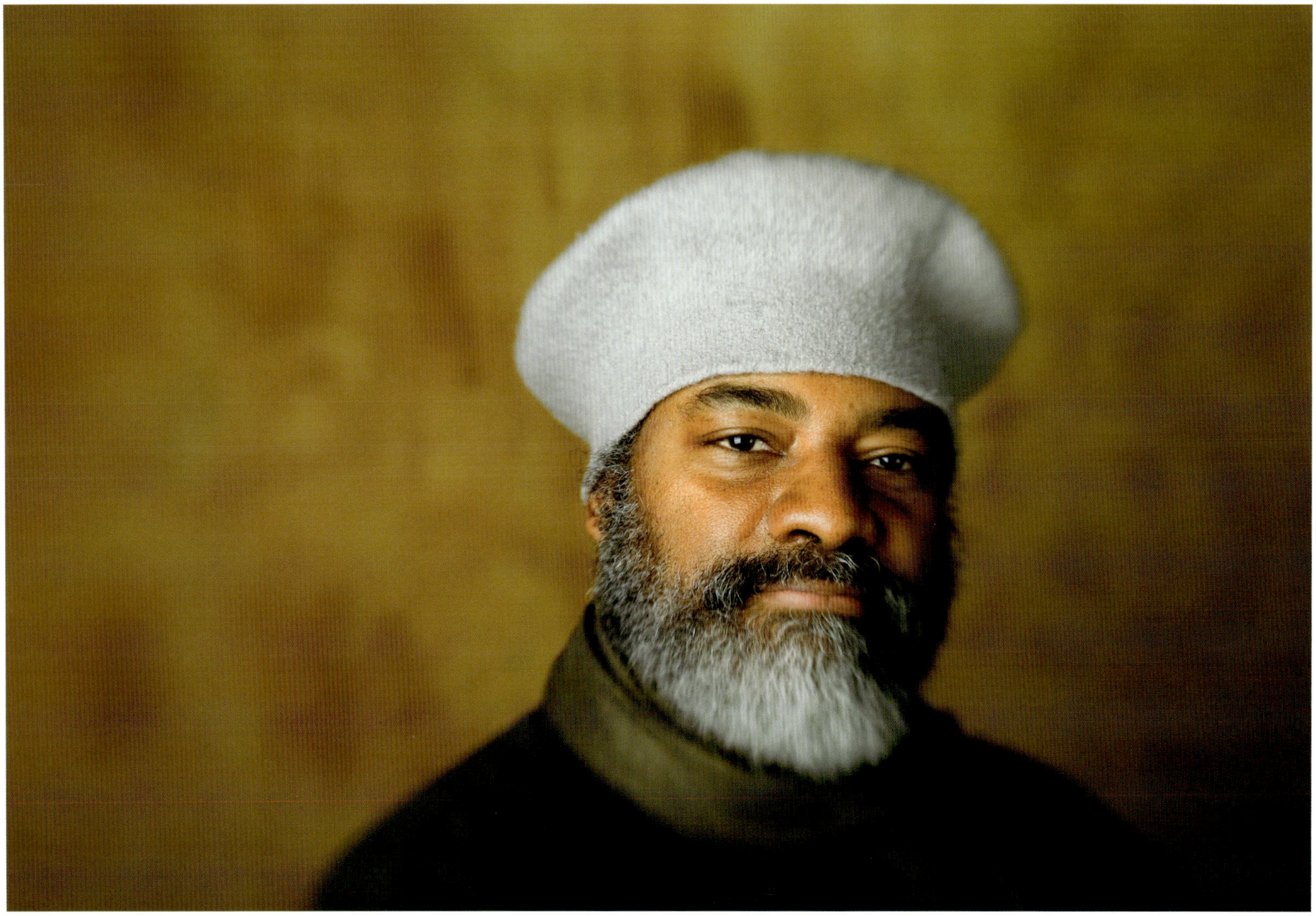

Dwight Rose

Growing up in the town of Port Antonio on the island of Jamaica had a profound influence on who I am today. My earliest interest in art came from my father, who supported our family as an illustrator and commercial artist and later as a fine artist. After graduating from the Ringling College of Art and Design, I have maintained an on-going scholarly approach and exposure to other accomplished artists. Teaching art to adults allows me to constantly reflect on what I've learned as I gain new insight.

My paintings start with a color idea, and then evolve into compositions in which color remains the primary subject. To me, art is a synthesis of personal feelings, the subject or colors that inspire, and the materials and techniques available. My paintings are an exploration of these collective tools. Serenity and simplicity are my primary goals. My duty is to convey the beauty of the moment and add focus to the essence of that beauty.

My works are based on the principles of good graphics, which comprise the use of line, the modeling of light, and experimentation with color. The line provides the foundation for the subject. Through experimentation with color shifts I can create contrasts. I observe the transient nature of light and other elements that qualify a landscape, structure, or still life. I am interested in large areas and intimate spaces, incorporating the entourage of people and objects and surface textures defined by pattern formations.

I use wet on wet watercolor washes, which usually set the style for my paintings. My work depicts depth through contrast, which in turn gives the paintings weight and substance.

Working toward a style that combines traditional painting techniques with inherent personal characteristics is the impetus behind my current body of work. Experiences, from my travels and exposure to world cultures, are the root of my work. Perhaps this accounts for why I seek out subjects that sometimes resist change and/or embrace it. Despite the diametric of this process, my paintings inherently become snapshots referencing a moment or significant passage of time.

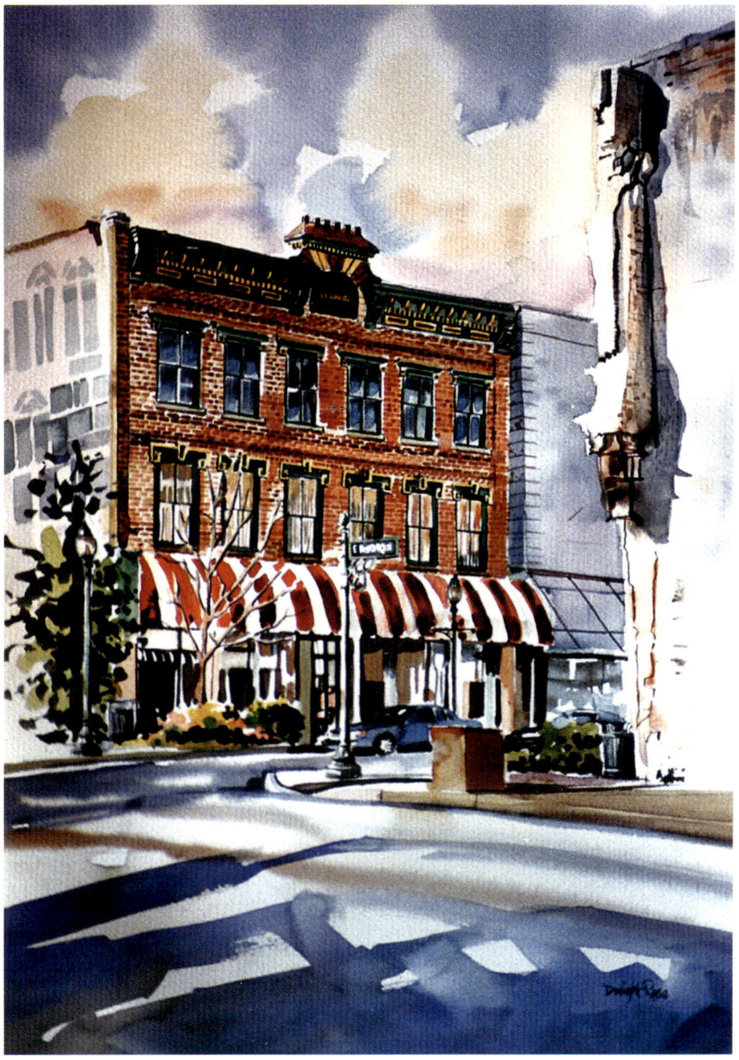

Greensboro, NC
Watercolor
15" X 22"

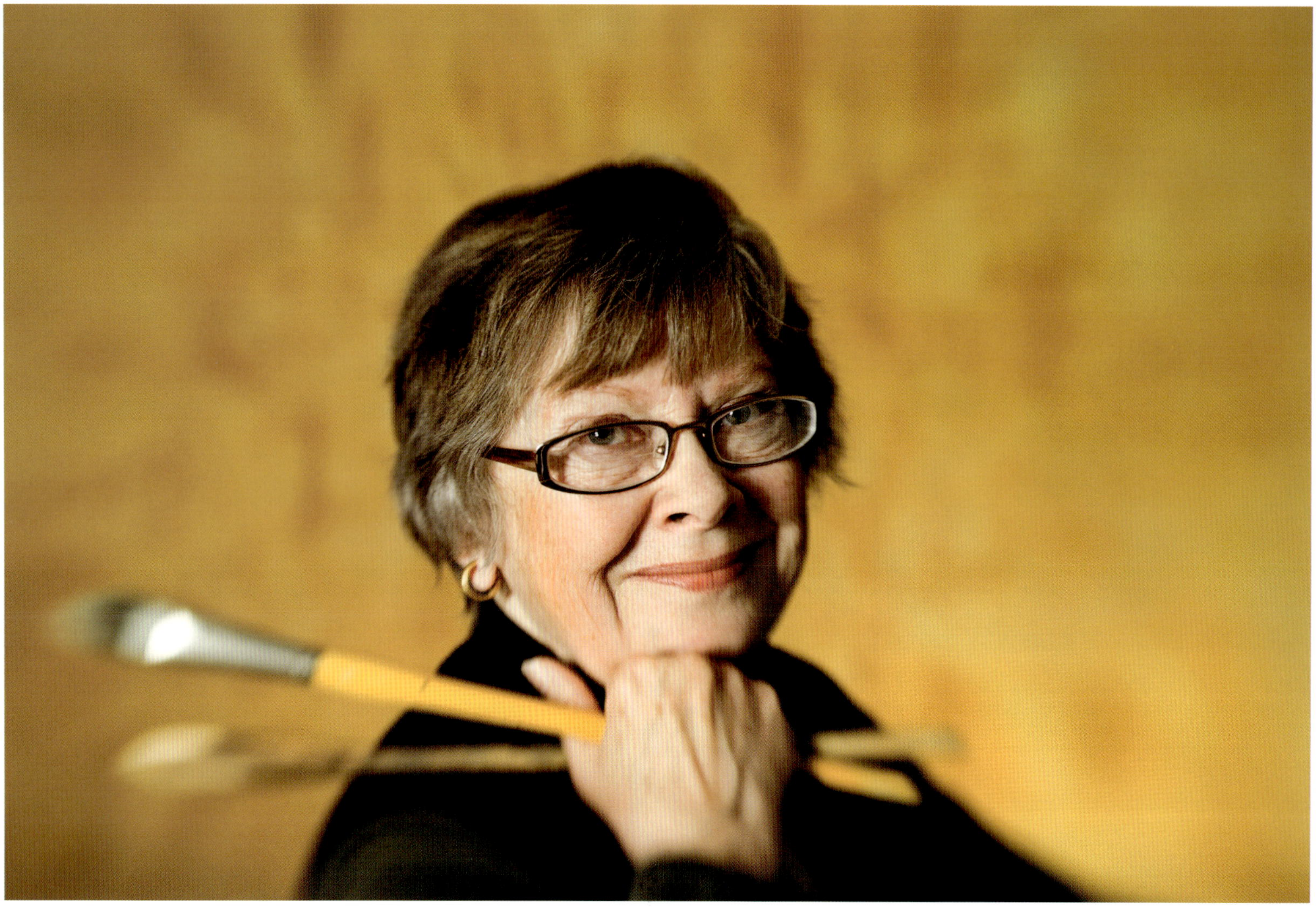

Sara Dame Setzer

I grew up in a small town of 4,000 people in western Kentucky, the daughter of an English teacher and a building contractor. Despite my school system's not offering art, I always drew—perhaps the result of being an only child. I believe I headed into art because a young music teacher who coordinated elaborate, end-of-year, song-and-dance productions asked me to do the sets for those musicals. I attended Murray State College, where I majored in art. To offset such an impractical degree, I also majored in English, perhaps as impractical.

After receiving my MFA in art I took a position at predominately black Virginia State College, a positive, formative influence in my life. I taught at Limestone College in Gaffney for thirty years and feel so fortunate to have had wonderful students, some of whom have influenced more students than I as teachers in Spartanburg and other South Carolina schools.

I think of myself as a painter, but for the past five years I've done hand-printed monoprints almost exclusively. However, I do plan to get back to painting in the future. My subjects are taken from life, from experiences that are meaningful or things I've seen that are touching or demand my attention. They are not realistic, but they are representational—you might say somewhat abstract—often with an emphasis on line and texture. I hope the viewer finds my images provocative or at least aesthetically pleasing!

Subjects for my paintings are most often taken from my life—my daughter's rescue of a baby blue jay, a neglected playground, my late husband's garden, my studios, our house and cats. Lately the subjects for my monoprints are a single, repeated, more realistic image—toothbrushes, paintbrushes, "crape murdered" trees.
What should people take from my work? Primarily visual, aesthetic enjoyment, perhaps laced with a bit of laughter or a smile of understanding and recognition.

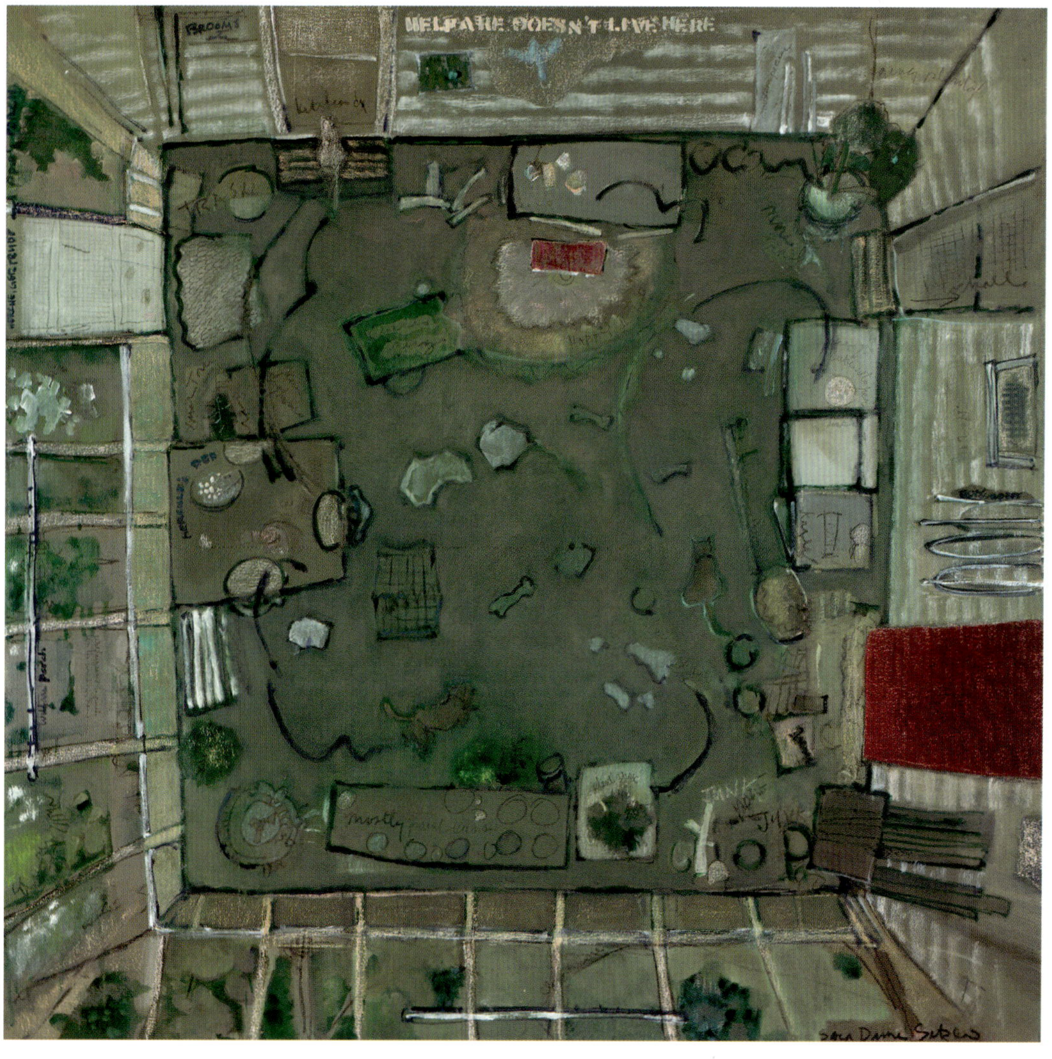

Welfare Doesn't Live Here Anymore

Oil-mixed media

41" X 41"

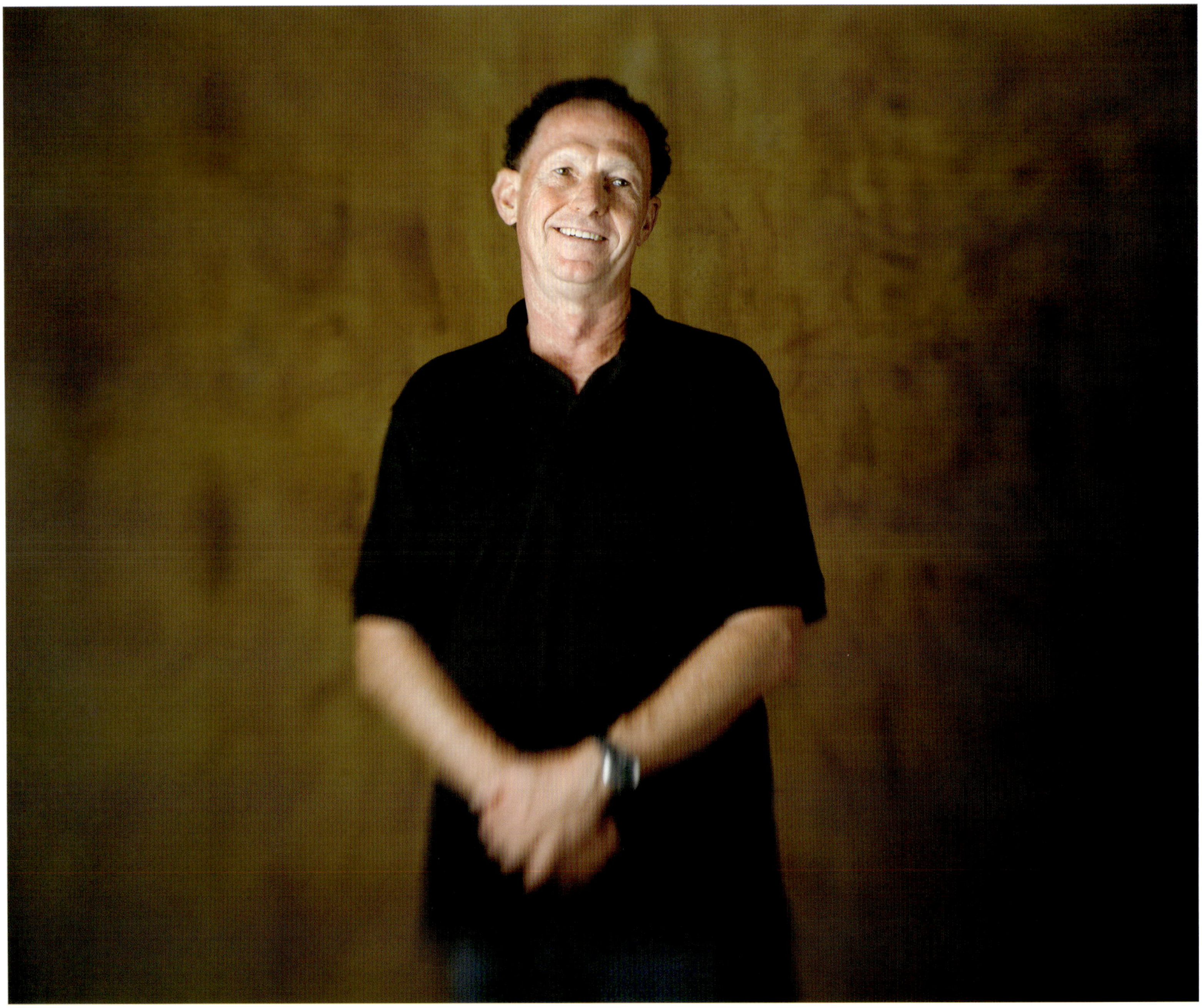

Howard Solomon

Passion, not for art, but for a beautiful woman brought me to Spartanburg. My search for happiness with a partner of like-mindedness, skills, and individuality led me to the love I was seeking. Spartanburg turned out to be a gem of its own. Spartanburg's community of artists and intellectuals welcomed me with open arms; however, I noticed something was missing, and the West Main Artists Cooperative was created to fill a shortfall in this artistic community. WMAC is a non-profit, all-inclusive arts center dedicated to providing affordable studio/exhibition spaces and a close-knit community of peers for artists in and around Spartanburg.

It is our human pursuit to know, define, and create that fosters our worlds. Advancing through Modernity, Enlightenment, Romanticism, and Modernism/Post Modernism, we have learned to adapt and redefine our art and ourselves. Art for me should transcend the individual ego and express a universal message/emotion. The non-restricted artist works to express this universality. My art contains representational, abstractive, and non-objective characteristics, sometimes individually depicted and sometimes intermingled. These fundamental characteristics change in proportion with each specific work of art. Often, I am seeking a pattern that depicts the transition from one style or characteristic to another. These characteristics frequently are displayed in multiple images of the same subject or theme. In developing my work I use whatever means or media I think will most appropriately convey my concept, and I am always seeking new ways of expression.

The Folly of False Sacrifice

Photograph

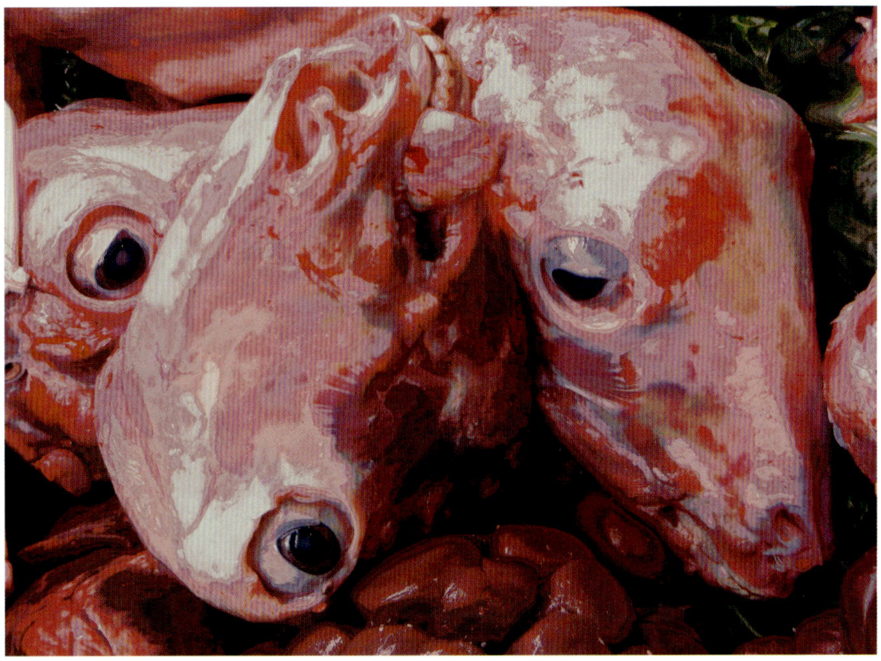

My artworks depict some of my thoughts on various aspects of the worlds we create as individuals and communities. To achieve this, I explore as many perspectives on reality as possible. Given the premise that mass globalization and the rapidly changing technological advances of the day both overshadow the individual and have failed to answer our most fundamental questions, it is easy to see that individuals are still searching for answers to many of philosophy's fundamental issues. It is this search for answers that drives my work: a search for art that has significant form, meaning, and value.

Sylvia Spears

I grew up in Rock Hill, South Carolina, and lived there until soon after I graduated from college. I have always been interested in drawing and painting, even though I had no art classes of any kind until I was a senior in high school. Even with a lack of exposure to artistic experiences, I knew from the time I was in junior high school that I wanted to major in art in college. I attended Winthrop College and was under the tutelage of Dr. Edmund Lewandowski, chairman of the art department, who encouraged and challenged me and became my mentor.

I am a painter working in the medium of oil. I find that painting with oils is a satisfying and sensory experience—from the textures of the paint, to the smells, to the way paint feels being applied to the canvas. I work in a loose representational style with bold strokes of color. In my paintings I strive to explore the relationship between color and form and to show the energy this relationship can bring to a painting. I try to instill a sense of the life that emanates from the subject, even if it is an inanimate object. My subject matter can vary from street or coastal scenes to very close-up floral depictions, but I am mainly drawn to painting figures in my work. These figures are usually shown in motion, whether dancing, jumping, or walking.

I want to engage the viewer, to draw the viewer into my paintings through the use of color or perspective. It is my wish that the viewer will experience in my work a sense of the stirrings of life, whether quiet or robust.

I feel so fortunate to be a part of the Spartanburg visual arts community. It is rich and alive and brimming with talented and diverse artists. Working in the midst of such a creative pool inspires me to stretch and grow in my own work.

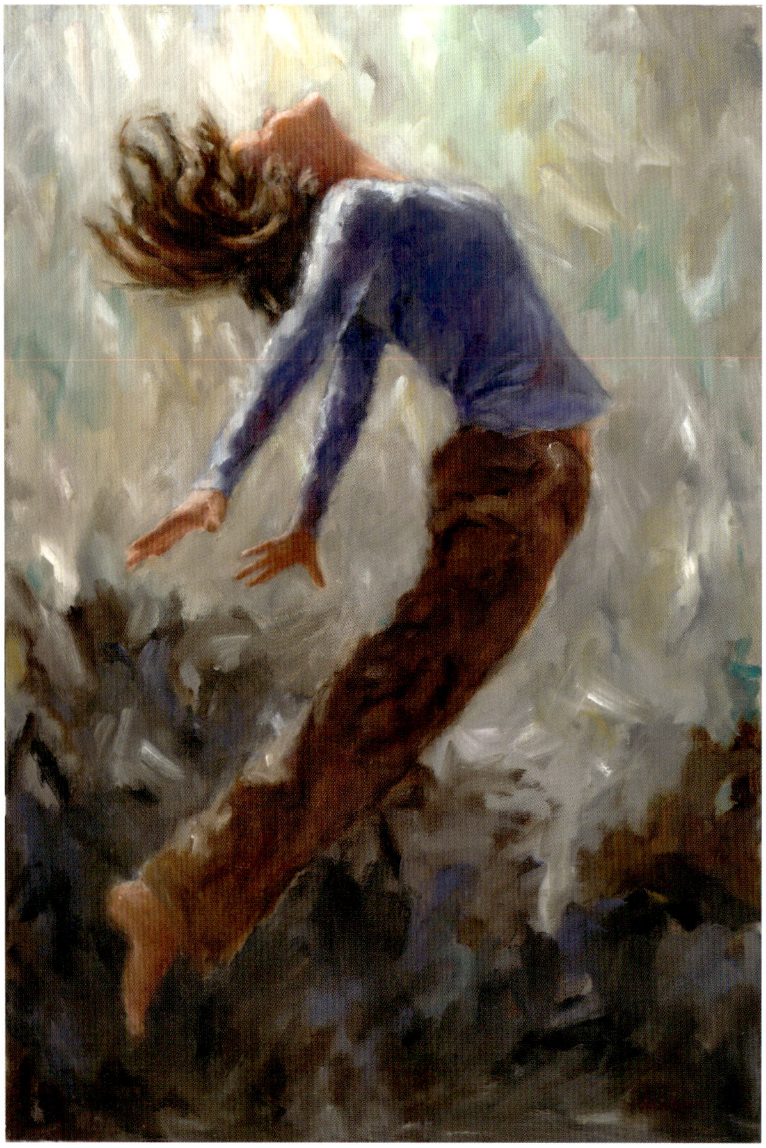

Exuberance
Oil on canvas
24" X 36"

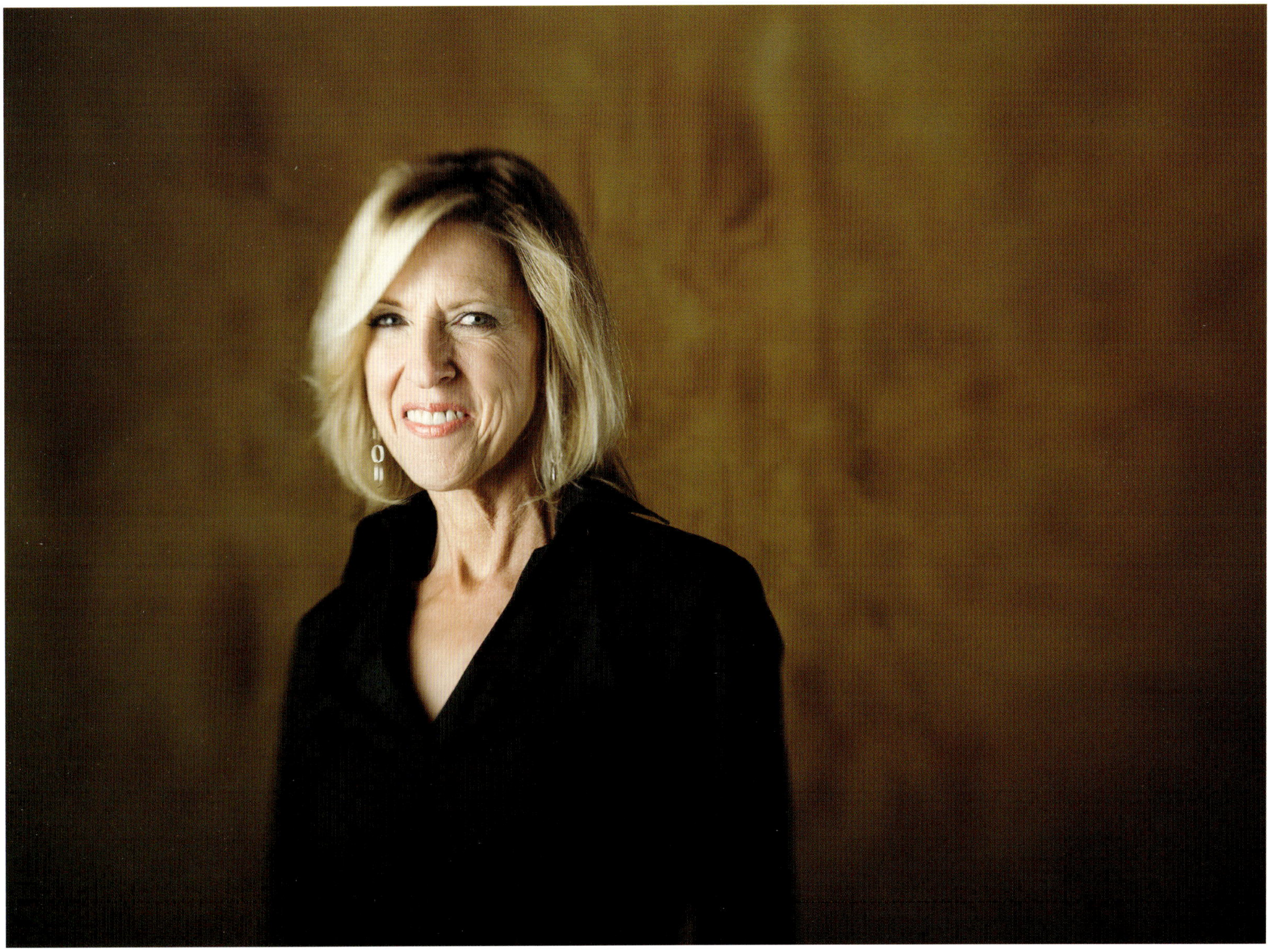

Keith Spencer

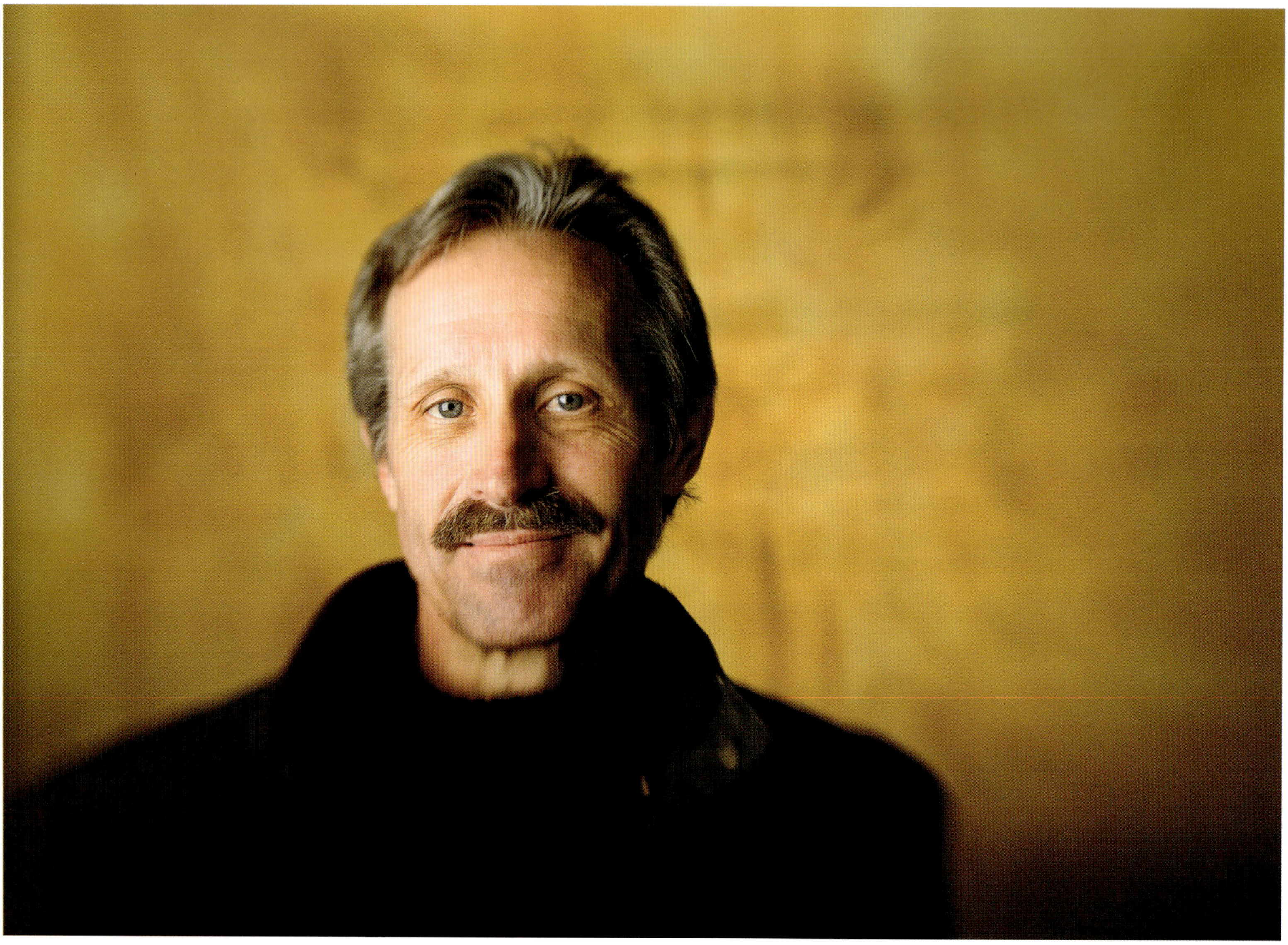

I grew up in Louisville, Kentucky, in a creative household, and I began to draw at an early age. My dad was an amateur photographer and set up a darkroom for my brothers and me to use. Taking pictures on family trips out West may have been when I really became aware that I wanted to be an artist. I found myself in a constant state of "looking for the picture" and knowing that the opportunity may be there only for an instant.

Why one thing catches my eye and another doesn't has always interested me. Usually, I see something in the world around me, such as a person with character in his face or some aspect of a landscape, and I just need to paint it. It's kind of like love—it either happens or it doesn't. After years of not knowing quite what to do with these urges I decided to honor my intuition and do art seriously.

I have found that working from life is where I tend to be free and experimental. Whether painting people, horses, or living landscapes, the key for me is that it is alive. I love to work very fast but very focused. Something tends to come through in the work that is very natural and real. I work mostly in oils and acrylics now, and I tend to work directly on the canvas rather than from sketches.

I moved to the Upstate in 1992 to work as a creative graphic artist for the soccer company Umbro and was a regular at a Landrum life drawing group hosted by Richard Conn throughout the 90s. I began painting full time in 2000 and am currently represented by six galleries in five states.

Managing a cattle/horse farm for eleven years has given me practical work experience and a deeper connection to nature and animals. I enjoy solitude and the inspiration of being surrounded by nature. Living in this beautiful area with my family and being a part of a wonderful creative community is a dream come true for me.

Shadow play
Oil on panel
24" X 20"

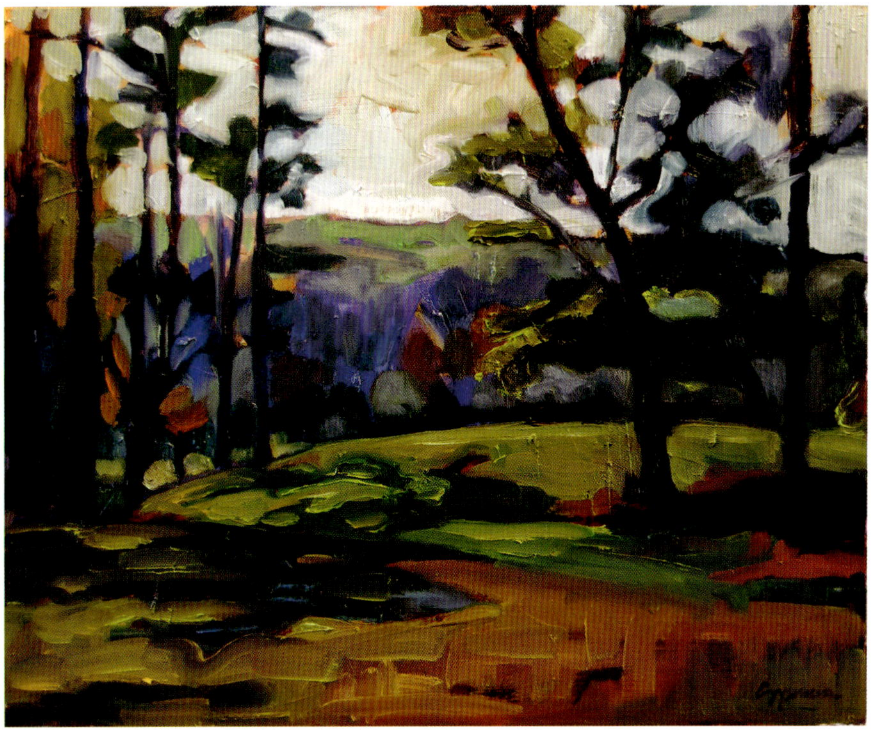

Ann Stoddard

I learned to observe early on.

When I was just one, my grandmother gave me a rag doll that could only be looked at and not played with. At age two, I cut squares out of the doll's hat, shirt, and skirt, and these became my toys. This foreshadowed my interest in fabric and overlapping multiple colors. I was asthmatic, and so I spent a great deal of time indoors, making paper dolls and folded paper furniture. My condition stimulated my interest in bringing nature indoors and incorporating its elements into my work. The poems and murals that my mother painted on the walls in our house inspired me and influenced my use of sewing, manipulated and cut canvases, installations, and poetry. I also was influenced by my father's role as mayor of Spartanburg; his sense of community informed my artwork in later years, especially my sculpture, which always seems to need "a message."

Our home was filled with original paintings, portraits of relatives, still lifes, landscapes, and china closets filled with collectibles. These influenced my later interest in curatorial work and collaboration—the idea of bringing together disparate components into the same room. My enjoyment of the collaborative process grew from the time I spent drawing with my five siblings on large sheets of butcher paper.

I attended Converse College for two years and received a BFA from the University of South Carolina. I received an MFA from Cranbrook Academy of Art, where I explored printmaking, sculpture, and architecture.

Since graduate school I have lived in the Detroit area, New York City, southeastern Massachusetts, and now South Carolina, balancing studio time and teaching on the college level. For ten years I did collaborative installation performance projects with my husband, artist Ralph Pàquin. I returned to painting when we moved to South Carolina to work and to raise a family.

I have exhibited my artwork throughout the United States as well as internationally. My artwork is included in both private and public collections.

What I hope that the viewer perceives from my artwork is *inspiration*.

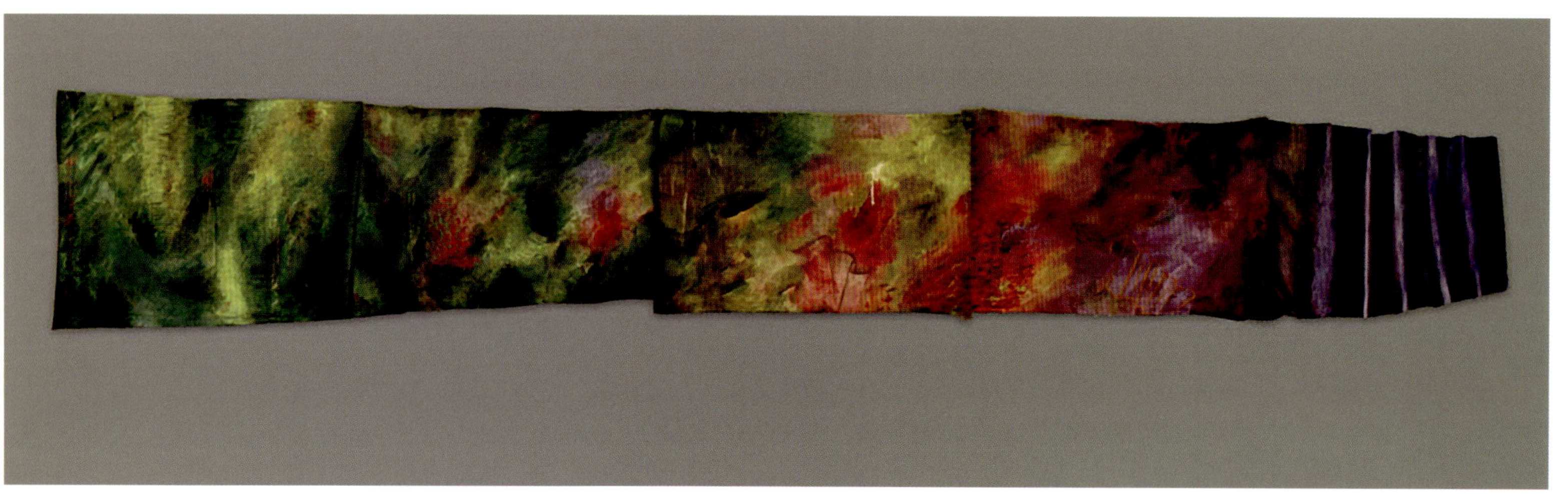

Phenomena
Oil on canvas
26" X 132"

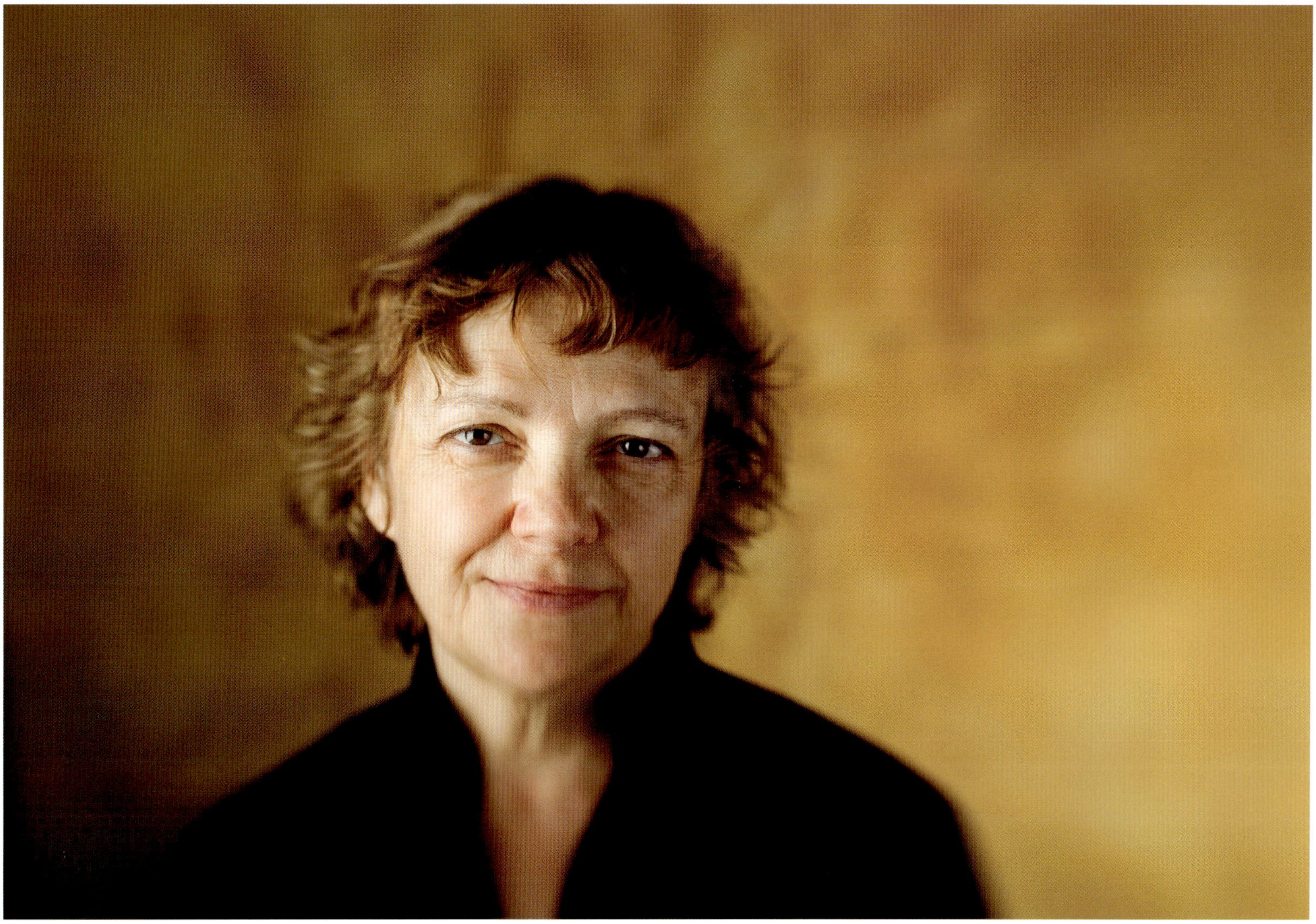

Mary Ellen Suitt

I am a native of South Carolina. I received formal training at Stratford College and the Ringling School of Art and Design, with postgraduate work at Converse College and the University of Arizona. I spent thirty-one years as a cartographer with the U.S. Soil Conservation Service, composing and drawing maps of various countries for the Army and the Air Force. I have traveled all over the world and studied with well-known artists from across the United States.

I use both opaque and transparent paints on painted paper—I never like painting on white paper—in an array of bold acrylic colors, and I exercise my techniques and expression in a variety of forms. My blue people make my art unique and easy to identify. (Blue people are universal. The color removes any identification.) One of my paintings is featured in Mary Todd Beam's book *Celebrate Your Creative Self*. My work has won awards across the United States and can be seen in galleries across Upstate South Carolina.

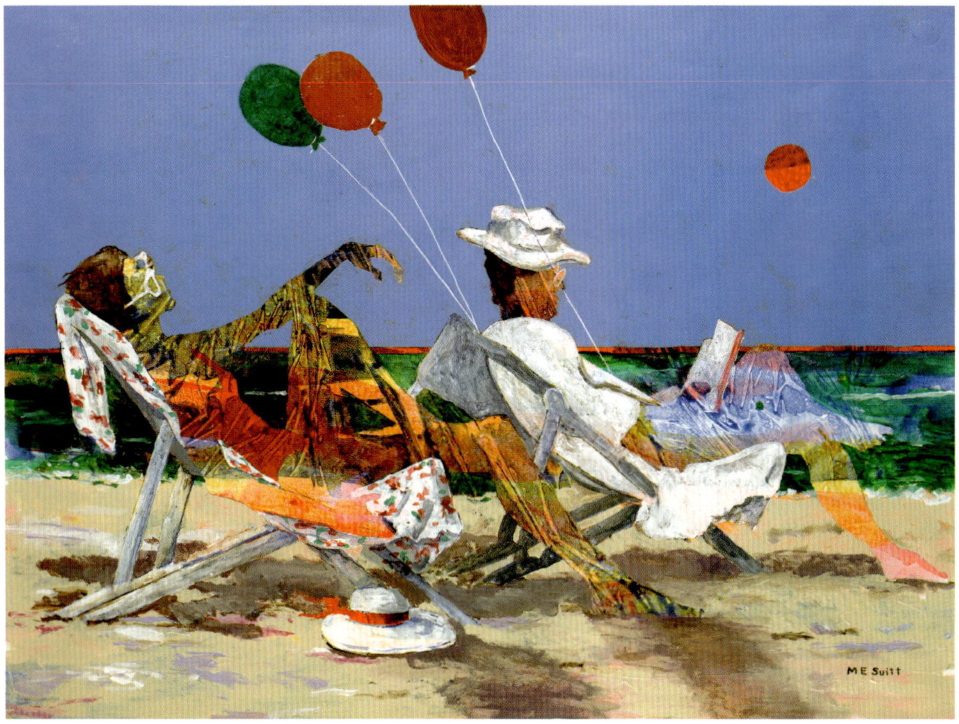

Beach Balloons

Mixed media

22" X 30"

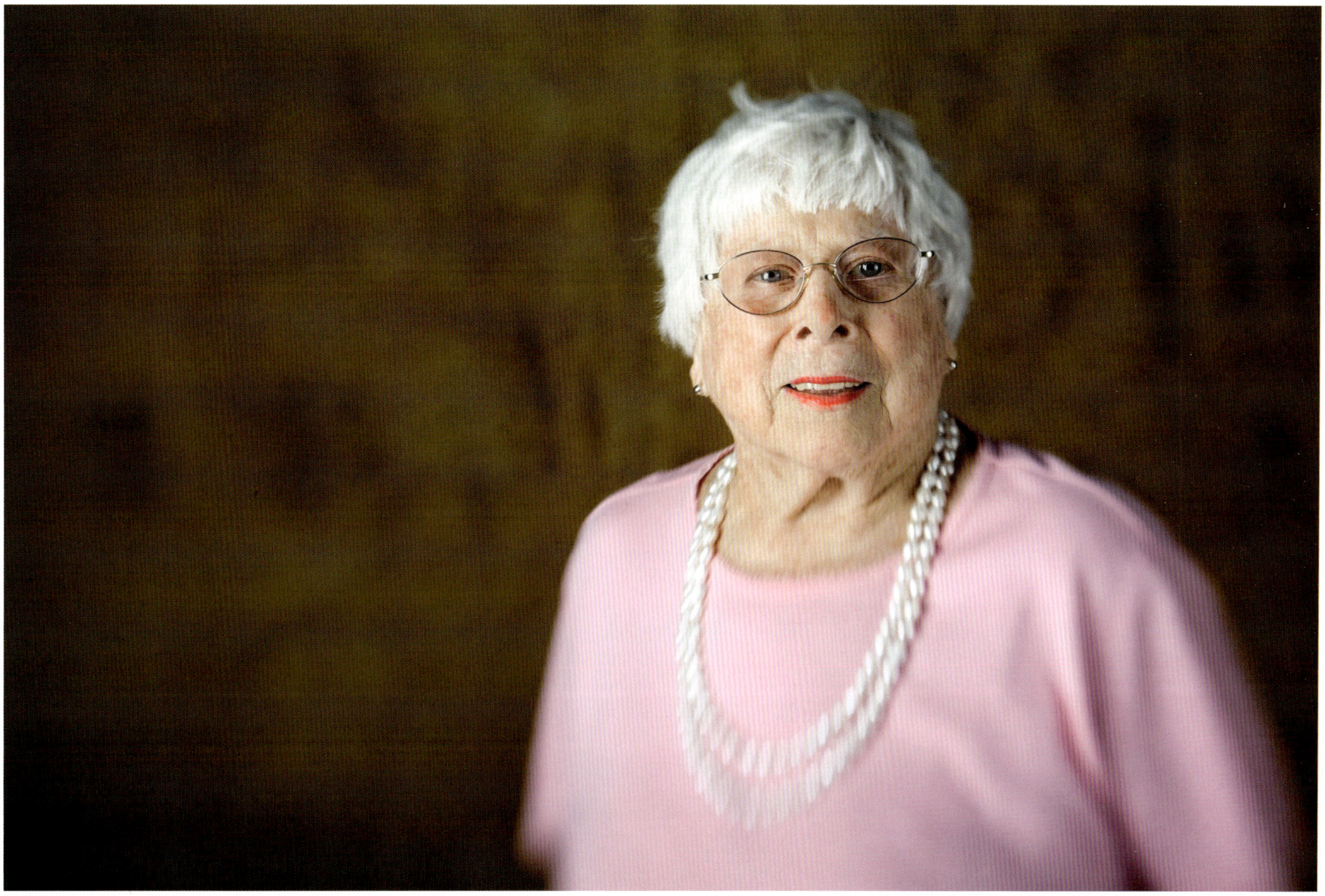

I was born in Spartanburg in 1948 and grew up in Spartan Mills. Many Saturdays were spent swimming and fishing in the lakes at Cleveland Park and wandering through the water pipes that ran underground all over Spartanburg. It was my usual practice to get up on Saturday morning, deliver papers, and meet buddies for a quick snack at the Goody Shop or Baber-Rhyne Drugstore, while on the way to the movie theater downtown.

I've been producing art since I attended Cleveland Junior High School. At Spartanburg High School I won several awards and knew immediately I was involved in something bigger than I was. While in the Navy during the Vietnam War, I was one of the ship's cruise book illustrators. Even during times of war, I felt the need to communicate through my drawings.

The artwork that first put me on the map in Spartanburg was my pointillism drawings using permanent colored markers. The large drawings, consisting of millions of small dots of color, drew a lot of attention at shows and local fairs and won many awards. My subject matter was hometown memories—Cleveland Park, Spartan Mills, and scenes of the historic neighborhood where I now live, Hampton Heights. The homes there remind me of a slower, Victorian past. Details of moldings, cornices, balconies, and wrap-around porches find themselves within my drawings, photographs, and designs.

Recently more of my work includes my own photography. Some photos were taken while using a camera attached to my telescope. Using Photoshop, photos and drawings are manipulated, diffused, distorted, twirled, or embossed until the desired effect is accomplished.

Recently I have begun a new role as an art teacher. The private studio in my historic home has been the perfect backdrop to drawing and painting classes for many aspiring artists. I have found it enjoyable working with all ages and sharing what I love to do best, creating original pieces of artwork that will last a lifetime.

Falling Leaves and Raindrops
Pentel colored pen
17.75" X 24.5"

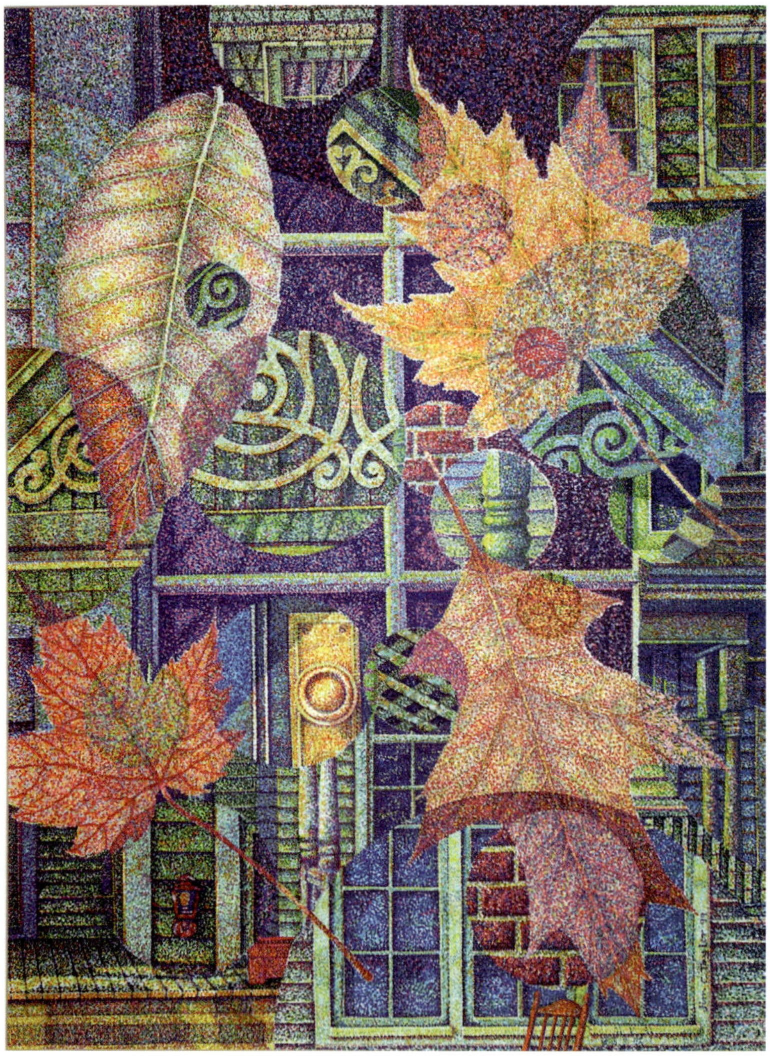

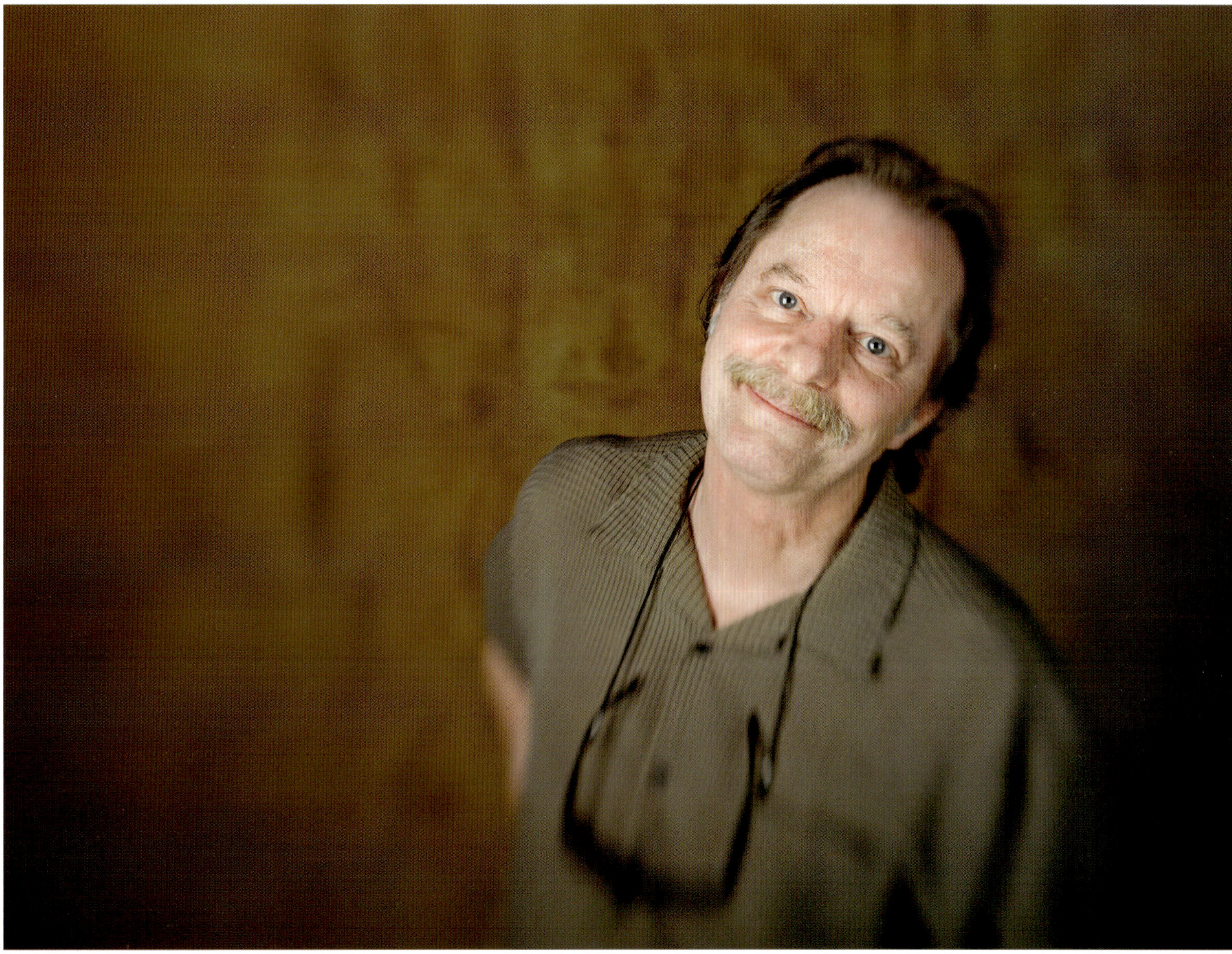

Jim Taylor

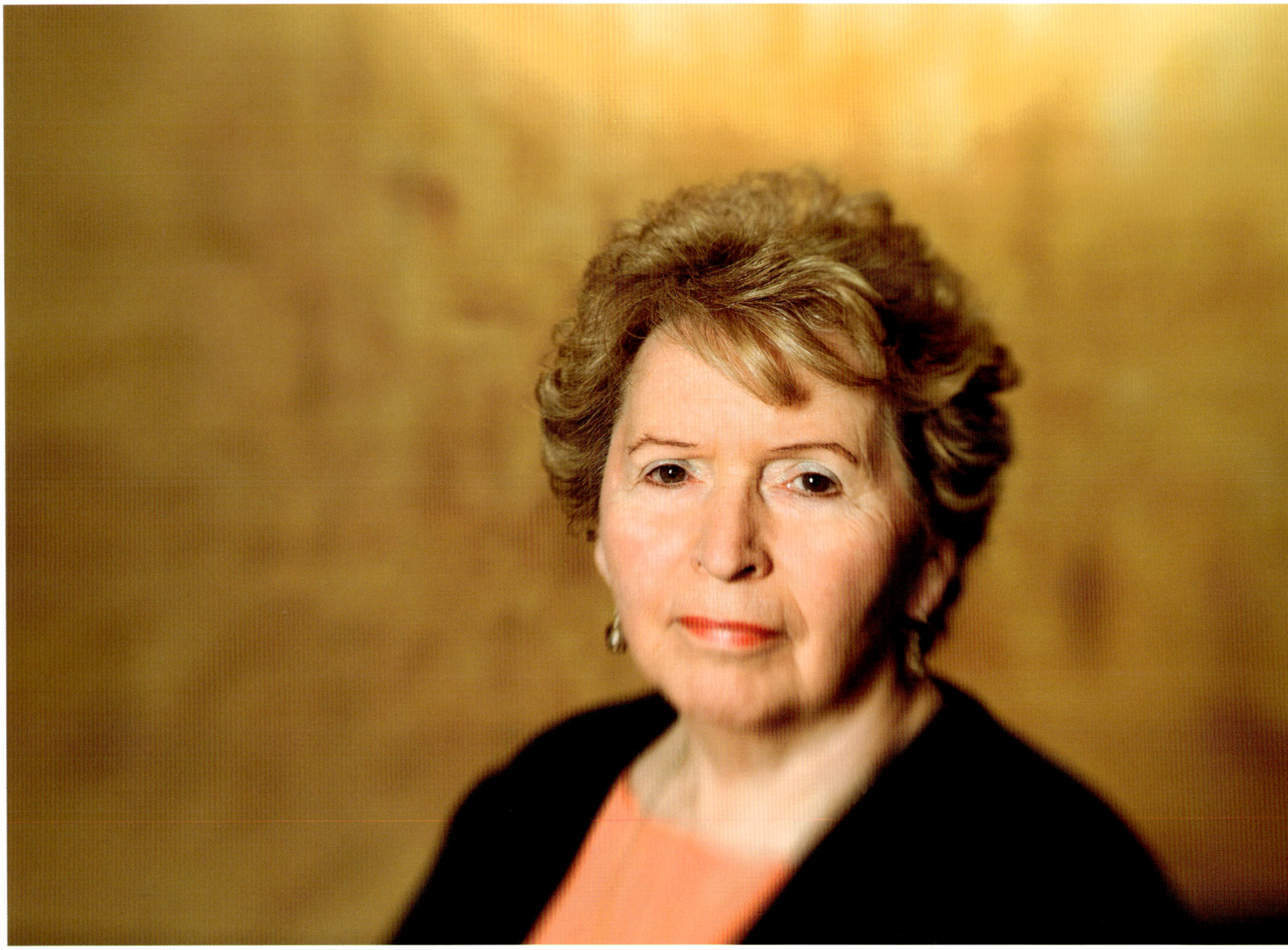

Carole Knudson Tinsley

I grew up on a livestock and grain farm near Springfield, Illinois, where my father and brother found many Native American Indian arrowheads while tilling the soil. The culture and history of the Native Americans—especially their architectural structures—have intrigued and inspired me.

I entered an ink sketch in the first Sangamon County Fair when I was ten and won first place. As a child I liked drawing pictures to go with a story I had read. When I went to college the professor wanted us to draw and paint like Picasso, and I became very discouraged, as I had never even heard of him and didn't understand what he was doing. I changed majors from art to elementary education and later taught third grade, but always had a good art lesson for the children.

As my husband and I moved around the country, I longed to create. I took as many art classes as I could handle, but in some ways I taught myself. Teaching art in the public schools or privately to students applying for the Governor's School in Greenville really strengthened my own innovative ideas as I urged them to think "outside the box."

I work in aqua-media, using acrylic and collage. I work abstractly, but primarily non-objectively. My subject matter comes from landforms, ancient dwellings, or just interesting shapes. I want to express in color, line, and form the temperature, mood, rhythm, time of day, and sounds of a place. I try to create a composition that pulls viewers into the picture and keeps them there, using their imagination. I hope they come away from it with questions and enjoyment or even an "ah-hah!"

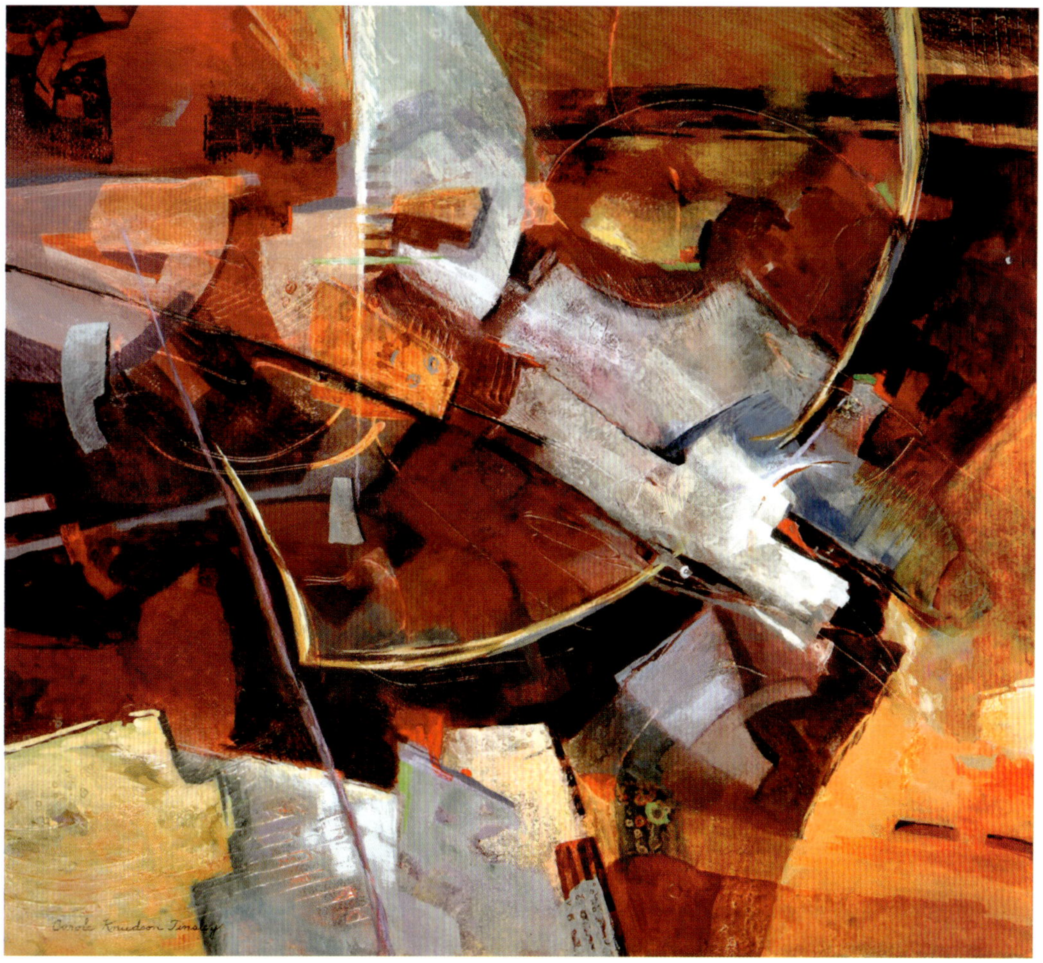

Evening Flight
Acrylic on paper
30" X 30"

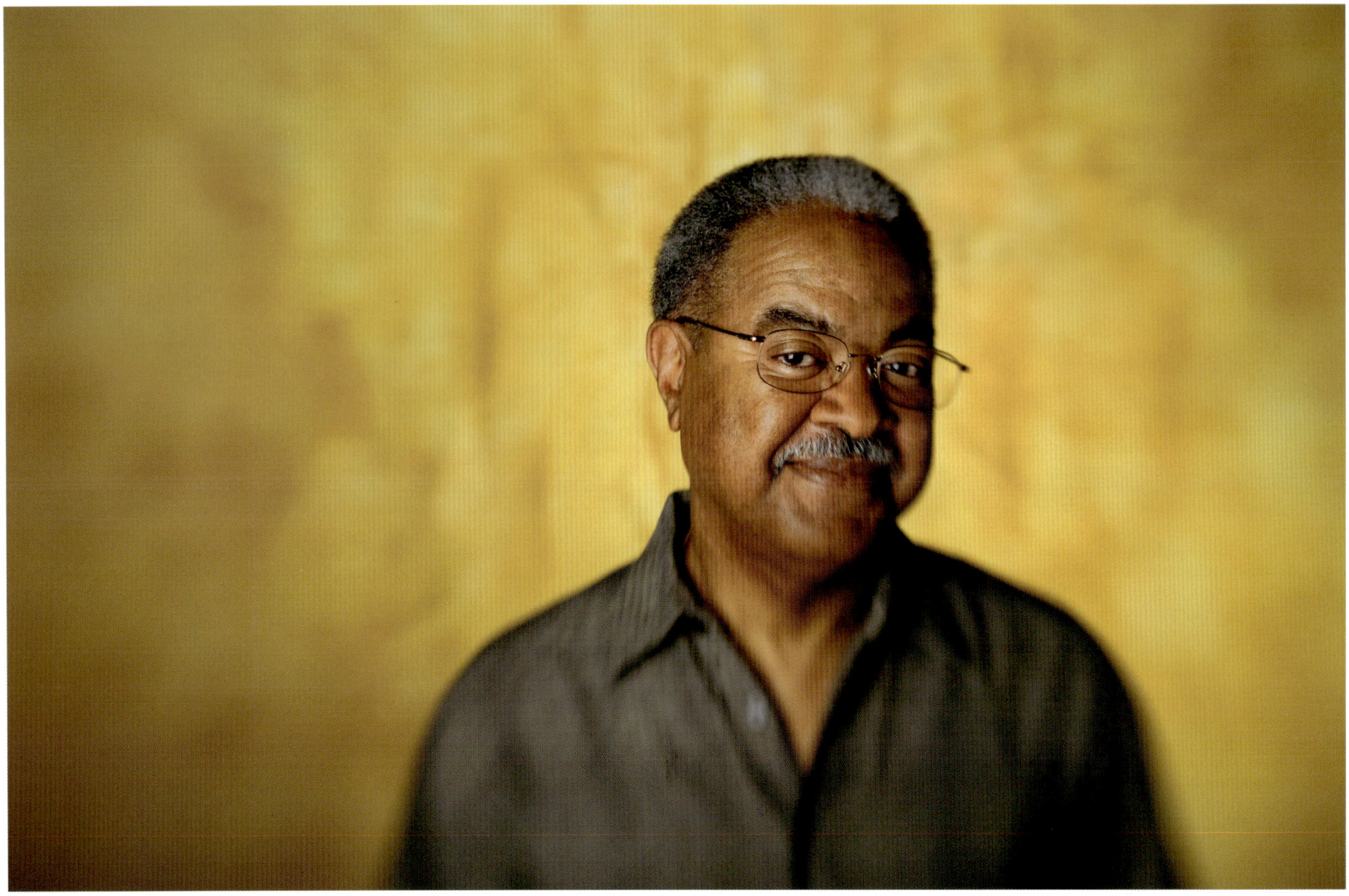

Thomas A. Tucker

I am a printmaker, photographer, and art educator born in Spartanburg County. While at Carver Senior High School I was fortunate enough to be taught by two great art educators, Raymond Floyd and MacArthur Goodwin. They encouraged me to become an artist and art educator.

After graduating from Carver, I received a bachelor's degree in art education from Berea College in Kentucky and a master's degree in art education from the University of South Carolina. I have also engaged in additional studies in art at Converse College and Furman University. I find the Spartanburg arts community to be culturally diverse, well trained, educated, and its members enthusiastic supporters of the arts. The visual arts community is driven by the freshness of new ideas and competition, while supporting each other's craft.

Although I favor photography and printmaking, I also sometimes use the mediums of painting, watercolor, and sculpture. My artistic style is realistic, and my subject matter is mostly people and buildings.

I am inspired to create because art ushers in novelty. Art is a universal form that embraces humankind. Artists are problem solvers and merchants of new ideas. I hope my work will engage the viewer long enough for each one to appreciate the technical qualities of my work, my story, and my point of view in space and time.

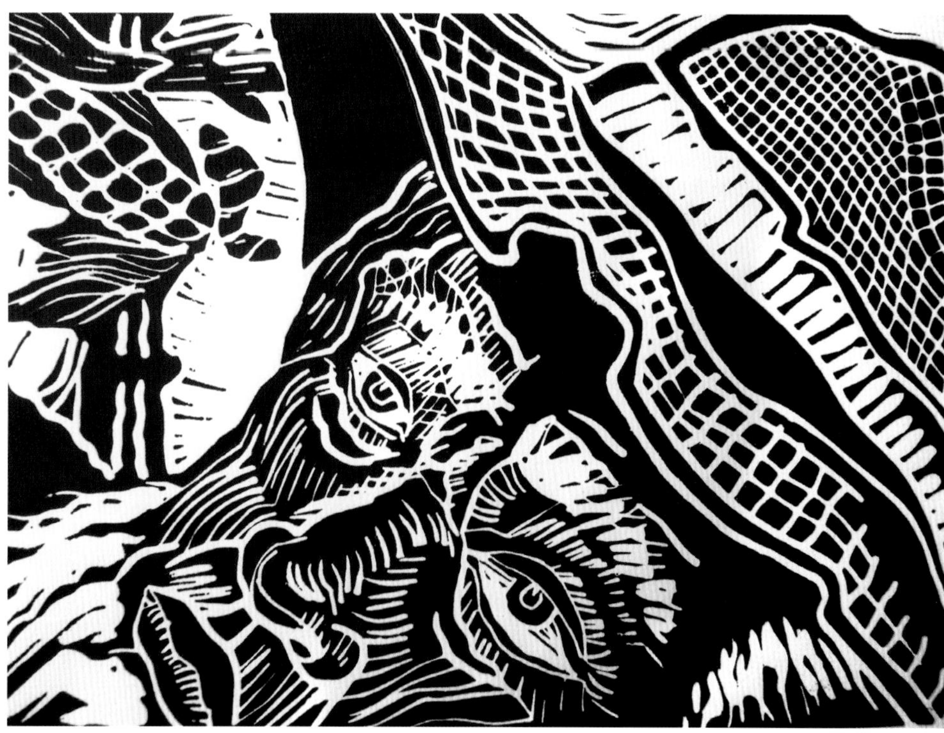

The Farmer and the Worm

Lino-cut

8" X 6"

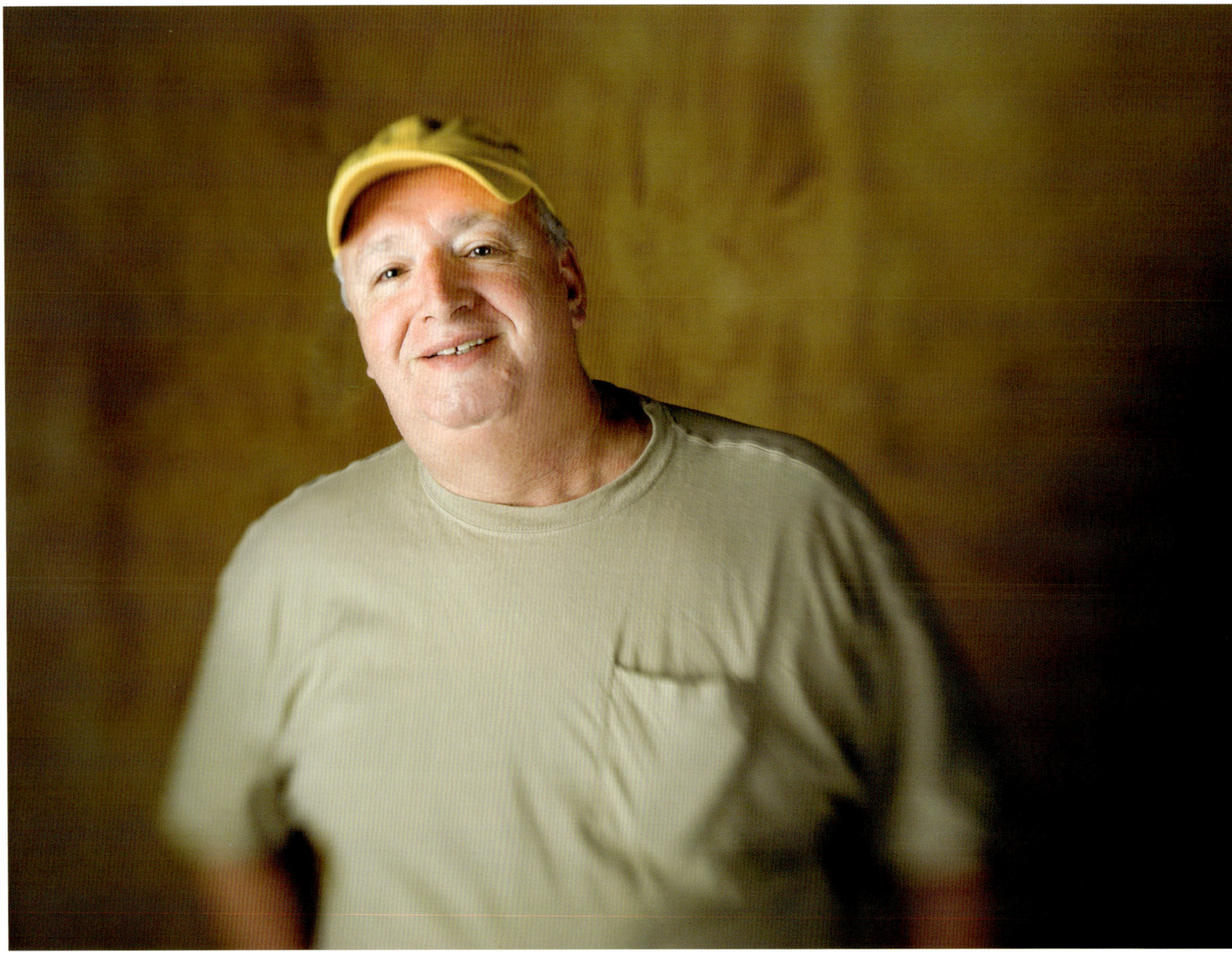

Mike Turnage

Many old buildings and landmarks in the Upstate are disappearing, and part of my artist's mission is to save them on canvas. At the same time, I believe I owe something back to the place that gave me the beginnings of an excellent art education. I'm also dedicated to the local legacy of my forebears—especially my father, an artist who never got to develop his own gift but encouraged me to do it for him, and my grandfather, who settled here almost accidentally, when a train conductor told him, "This is where your money runs out."

I began taking art classes at age ten in 1961. The drawing classes were in a building where the Chapman Cultural Center is now.

I have completed thousands of paintings. Many of them were lost in a fire at my studio a few years back. About a dozen have been reproduced as limited-edition prints in custom sizes. They include the children's train at Cleveland Park and the pavilion and diving tower at Rainbow Lake. Some works I complete in days. Others take years. I typically work on numerous paintings simultaneously. A constant passion has been collecting photographs and photocopies that show "old" Spartanburg. From time to time, some of the subjects emerge in full color.

I also enjoy working on location, where passersby often pause and observe. While painting the Cleveland Park train, I especially enjoyed talking with children. The children were really interested in what I was doing, and they asked very intelligent questions. Occasionally I experiment with other media. Metalwork has been a recent fascination. As for the future, I hope to develop a larger national audience. I will continue to paint Spartanburg area scenes, but I'll depict them in such a way that they'll be meaningful to people in different parts of the country.

Rainbow Lake

Acrylic on canvas

44" X 64"

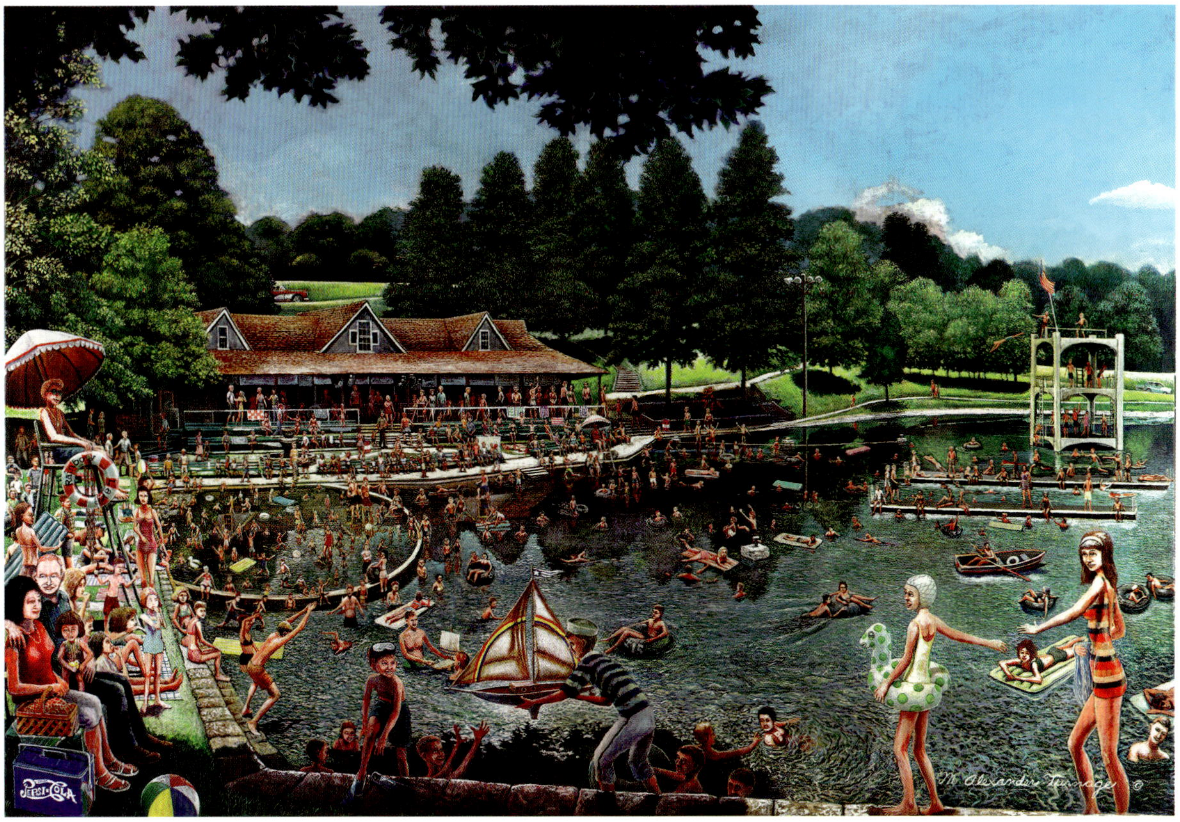

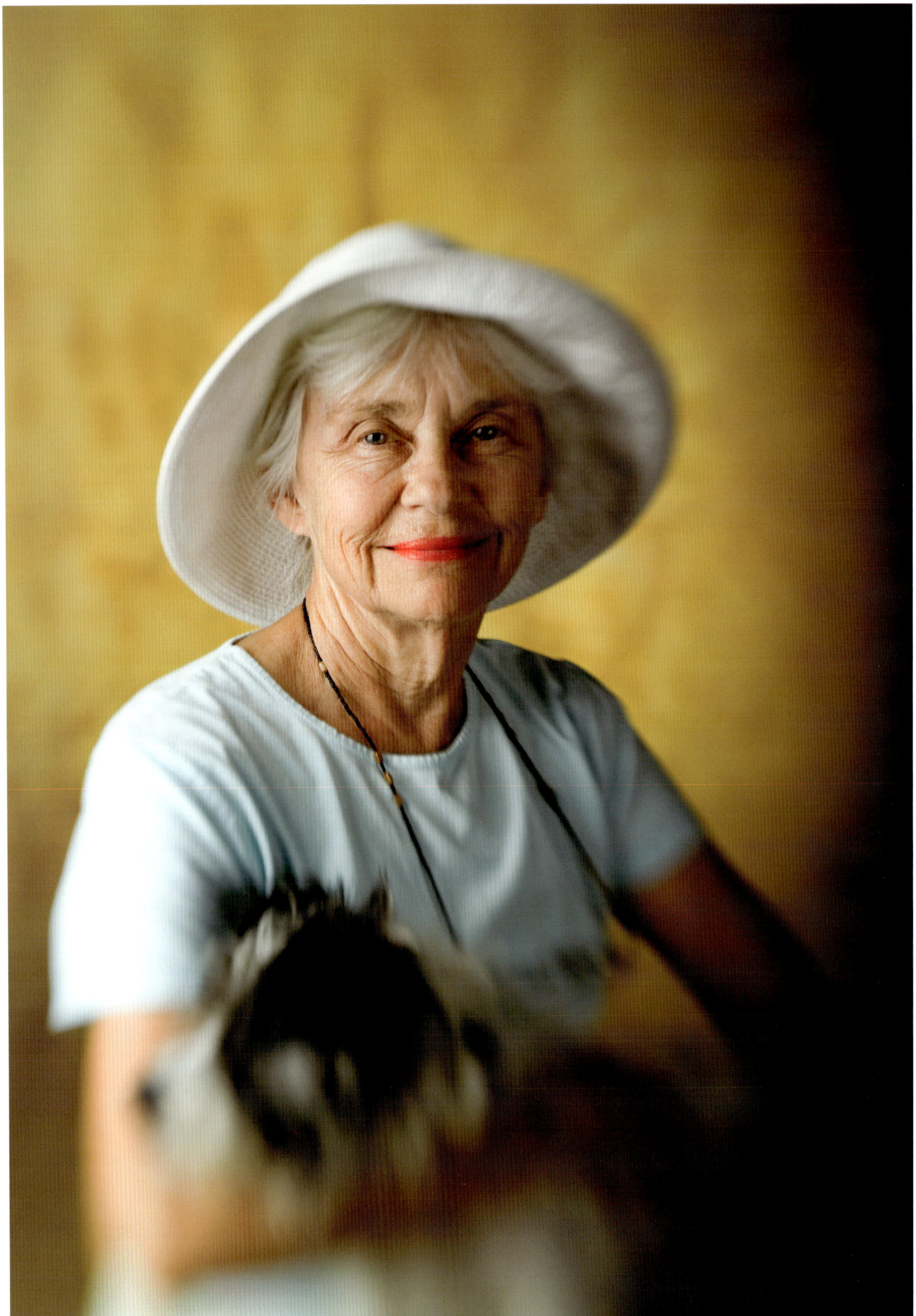

Doris Turner

"I can do it and I will do it," I suppose has been my mode of operation. My mother didn't know whether it was a compliment or criticism when my teacher at Pine Street School called me "a most deliberate child." Later, "Miss D" in junior high and Miss Sue Cook at Spartanburg High led me to believe that I could make art. My interior design studies were housed in the University of Georgia's art department, where we had "Art in the Dark," which encouraged students to find their own way. I think you have to be brave to do art … and tenacious.

I fell into teaching art after my children were in school, and there I found my niche in life. I learned the most about art by establishing a professional artist gallery in Roanoke, Virginia, at North Cross School. For years I came back to Spartanburg to enter the Springmaid Juried Art Exhibitions and the Piedmont Interstate Fair art contests. Eventually I moved back, where my education continued as I worked with the many wonderful artists exhibiting in Cannons Elementary School Art Gallery. I am inspired by viewing art exhibits and feel there is much opportunity to do this in the area with Spartanburg Art Museum, our colleges, and galleries. The Artist Guild of Spartanburg and my art group, Southern Exposure, remain very supportive of me as an artist and keep me working for our shows.

A painting class with Scott Belville of Converse College set me on the course of acrylic on canvas painting. I like to do people and places, with a bright color pallet and ratty brushes to keep the art from being tight. I hope the viewer becomes excited by my color—usually transparent, which is mostly mixed on the canvas—and enjoys my perspective of life. Other media suits me fine too. I am very creative mainly because I can't follow directions, don't remember how it was done before, and don't want to do anything like anybody else.

Maybe the teacher at Pine Street said I was obstinate too.

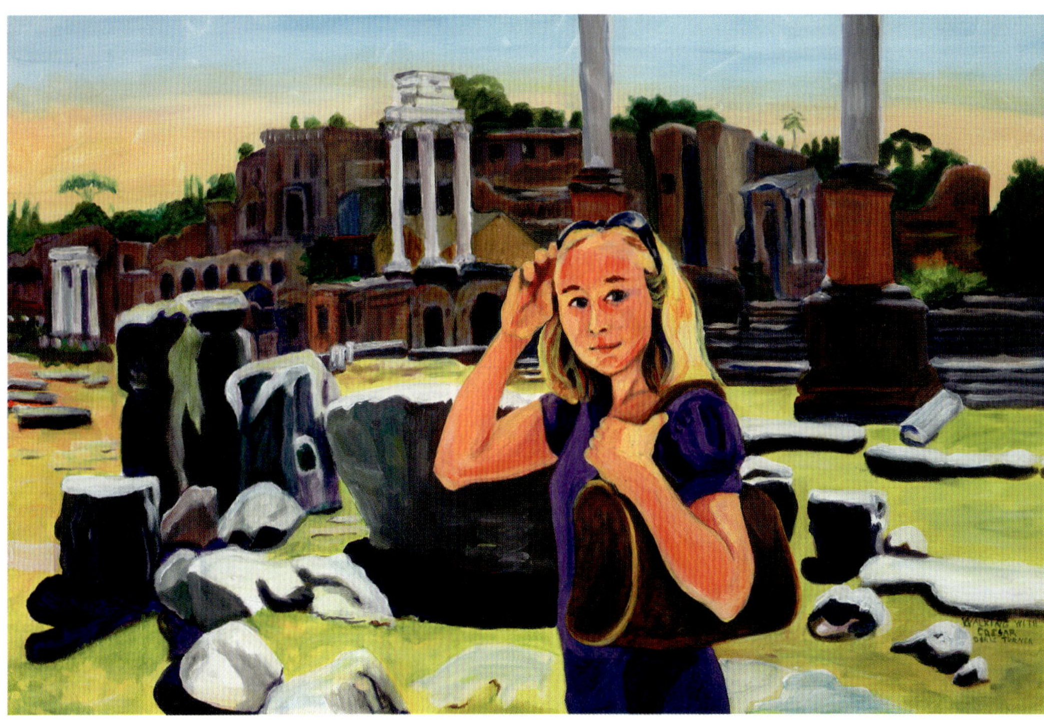

Walking With Caesar
Acrylic on canvas
24" X 36"

Garry Turpin

I was born in the Smoky Mountains of North Carolina and have spent the greater portion of my life in the Carolinas. I received a BFA in studio arts at Mars Hill College. I enjoy capturing man-interacting-with-his-environment and painting nature. I love the atmospheric challenges of painting the mountains.

I love painting rivers and streams. Painting water is always challenging, whether a mountain stream or the rolling surf at the beach. I enjoy capturing moments in time and adding my interpretation of the event, creating a painting that is unique yet representative of the situation I viewed. Another subject that I love to address is people interacting with people. Painting a scene that involves multiple subjects interacting provides the viewer with an image that he or she can interpret. I use the rich, variable colors of oil paint to capture my feelings and the presence of my subject.

I find a sense of community in Spartanburg's art scene. It's most apparent on Art Walk Thursdays. Spartanburg's citizens love the arts. The grand opening of the West Main Artists Co-Op in 2010 made that clear. More than one thousand guests visited the center that night. Artists from all walks of life showed their work and interacted with both patrons and visiting artists. Young artists talked with older artists, and there were discussions of future events. Opportunities in the fine arts are ripe for the pickin'—classes, artist residencies, juried shows, and wonderful monthly exhibitions. This interwoven community includes the self-taught to the professional, the independent non-profit groups to the art departments at major colleges and universities.

I hope for two things with my work: that viewers are taken by the painting to an experience that they enjoy and that they also realize that I, the artist, found pleasure in creating it.

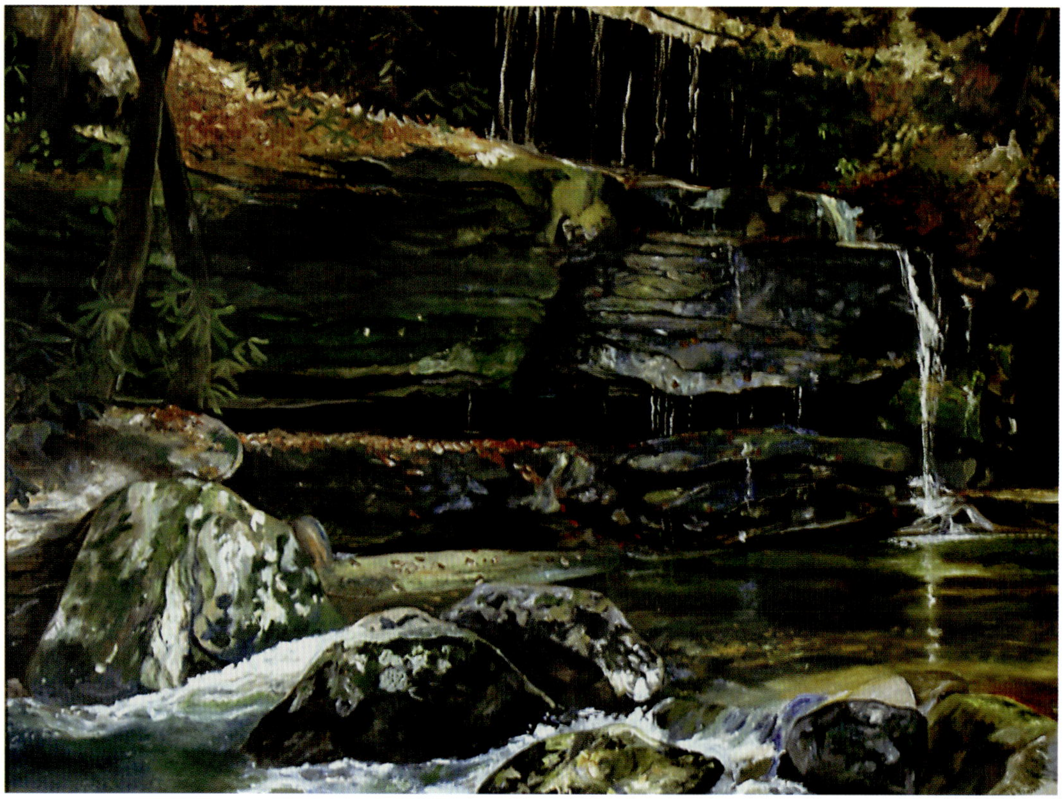

On The Way
Oil on canvas
24" X 48"

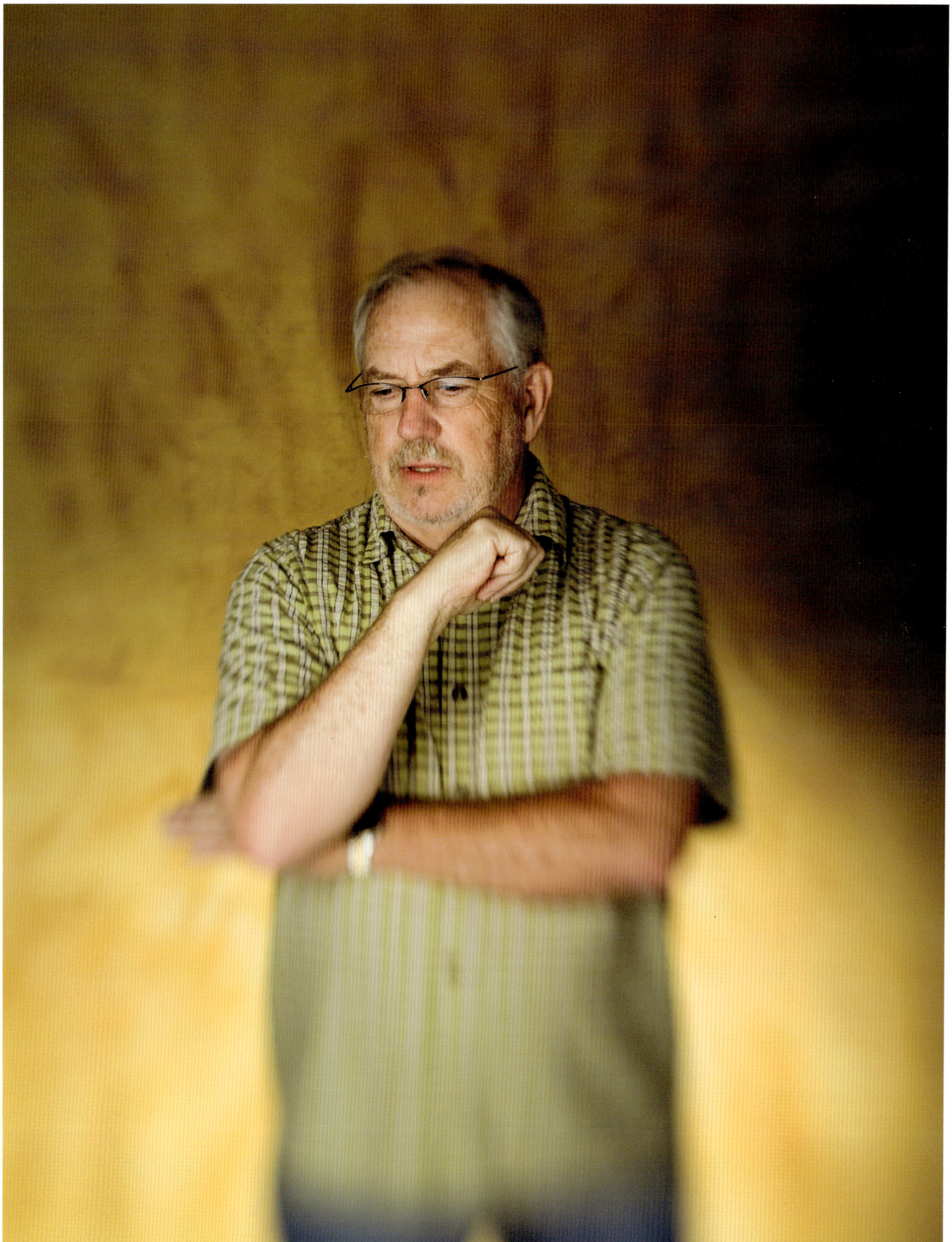

I am a painter of landscapes, but not in a traditional sense. My art primarily reflects the ongoing struggle between nature and humankind to coexist. This is my effort to create a sense of meaning from the world: order from chaos and chaos from order.

This is revealed through numerous layers in my works that build up over time, much like the layers that create our lives. These layers are added and then removed through various methods. Thus, my theme of opposition is represented in the artistic process itself—creation and destruction. The layering process I use when I paint is evolutionary; I never quite know exactly where it will take me visually or conceptually. The idea and the artwork grow, sometimes over several weeks, depending on the size I'm working on, as I create the image. This way of working creates an element of surprise, which I find exciting.

Nature provides ample motivation for my creative pursuits. A landscape setting I have visited will usually be the initial inspiration for an artwork, or possibly a whole series of pieces. Personal interactions within the environment—a bike ride, hike, trail run, park visit, or some other outing in nature—often serve as my muse. Lately, it has been bicycle rides in the countryside of Spartanburg County that serve as reflective time and give me the ability to look inward while taking in the beauty of the landscape. I have begun taking a camera on these rides, and I will stop and shoot photographs along the route I am cycling. These images are often used as starting points for a work.

Depicting the beauty of nature, even in a non-traditional way, reflects an obvious appreciation for what the natural world offers to us. Environmental concerns for Earth affected by human interaction remain just below the surface of each artwork I create.

A Just Cause

Acrylic with mixed media on panel

16" X 48"

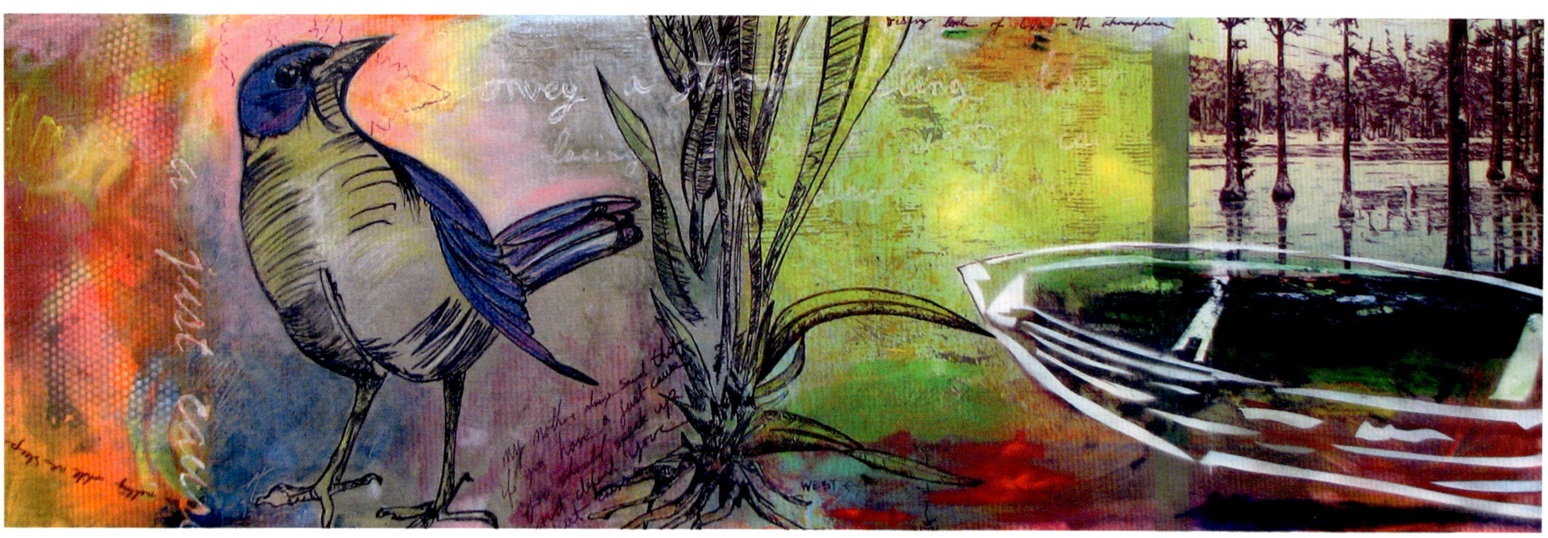

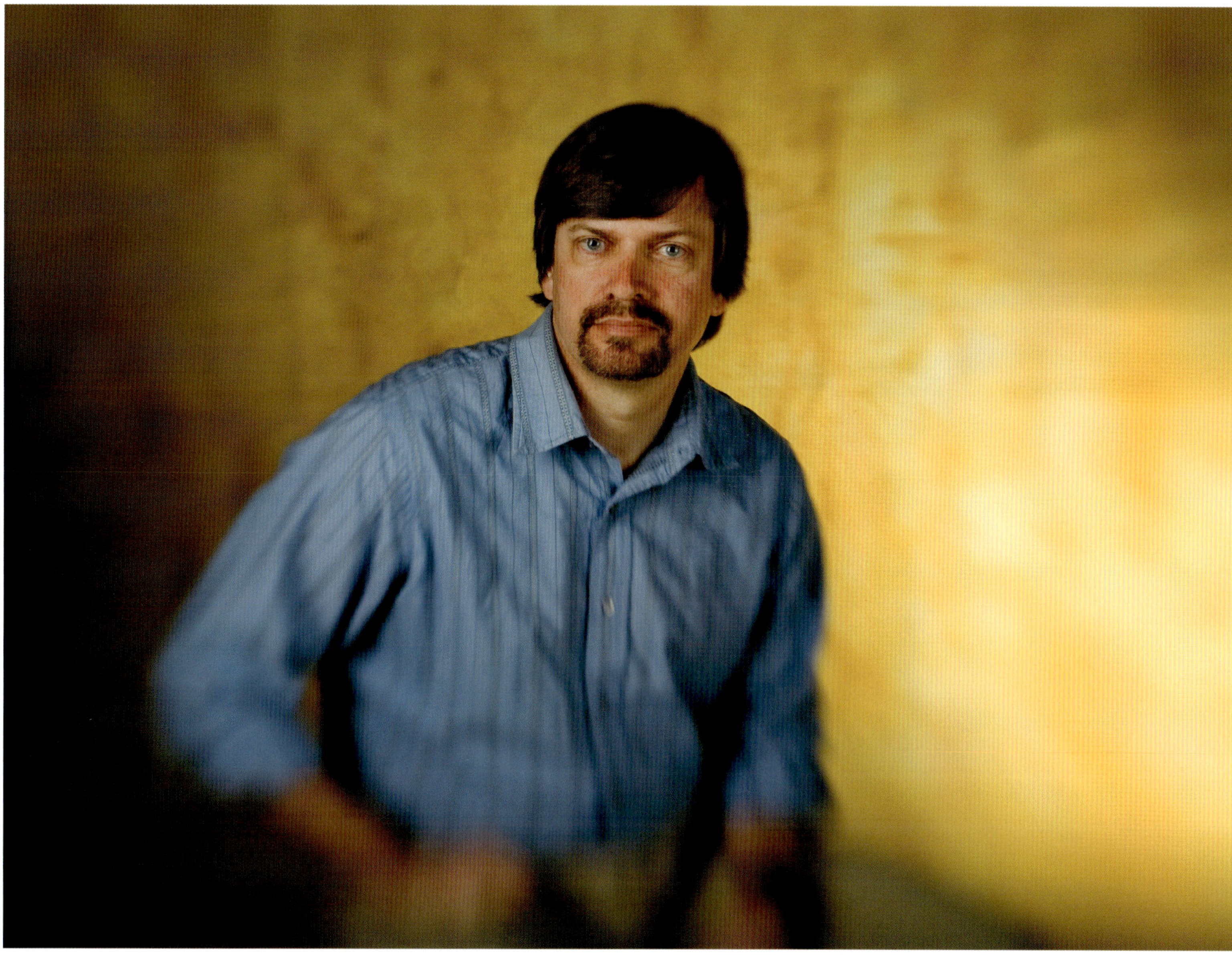

Robert M. Urban

Lalage Warrington

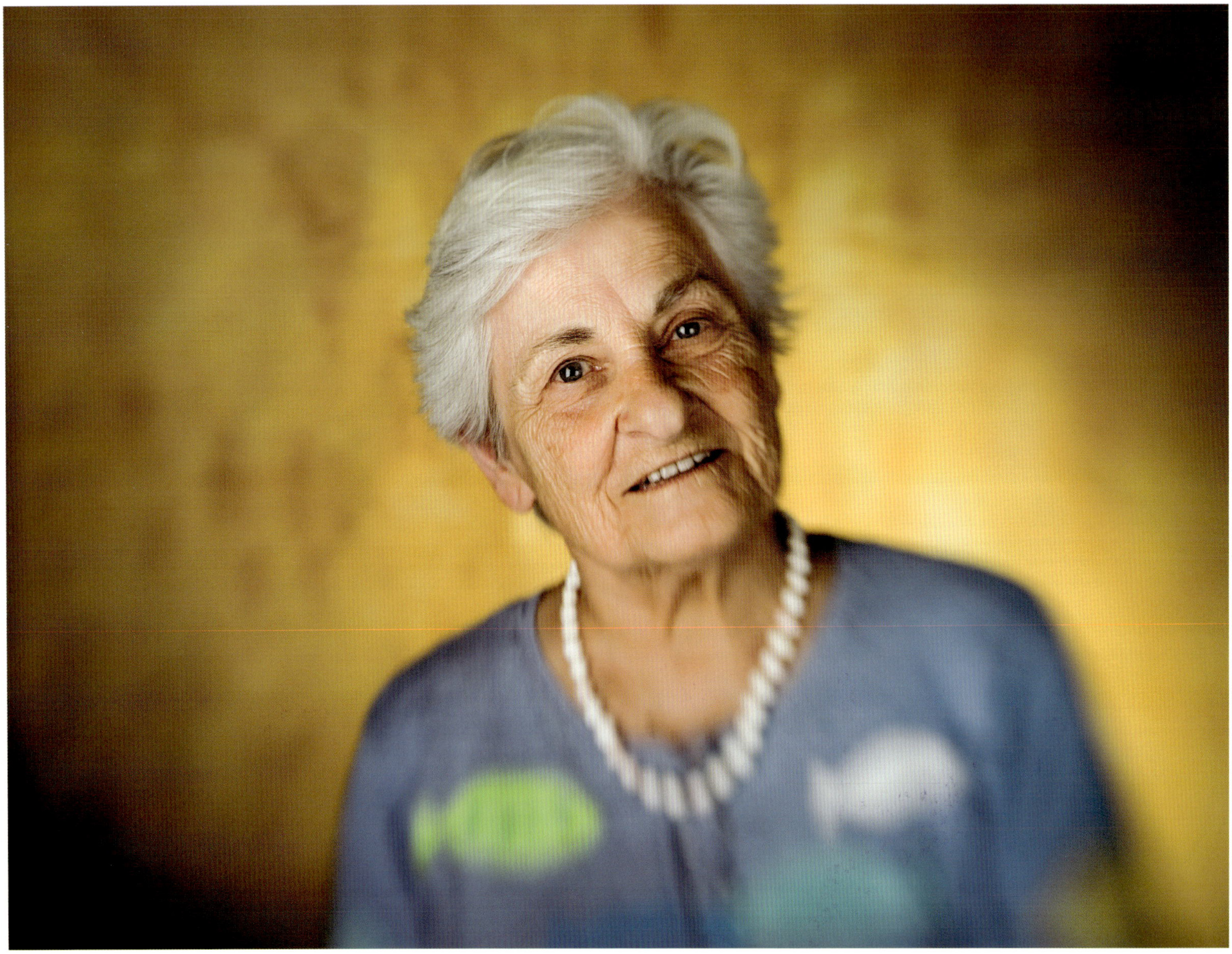

Prosecutor

Clay

20" X 10" X 10"

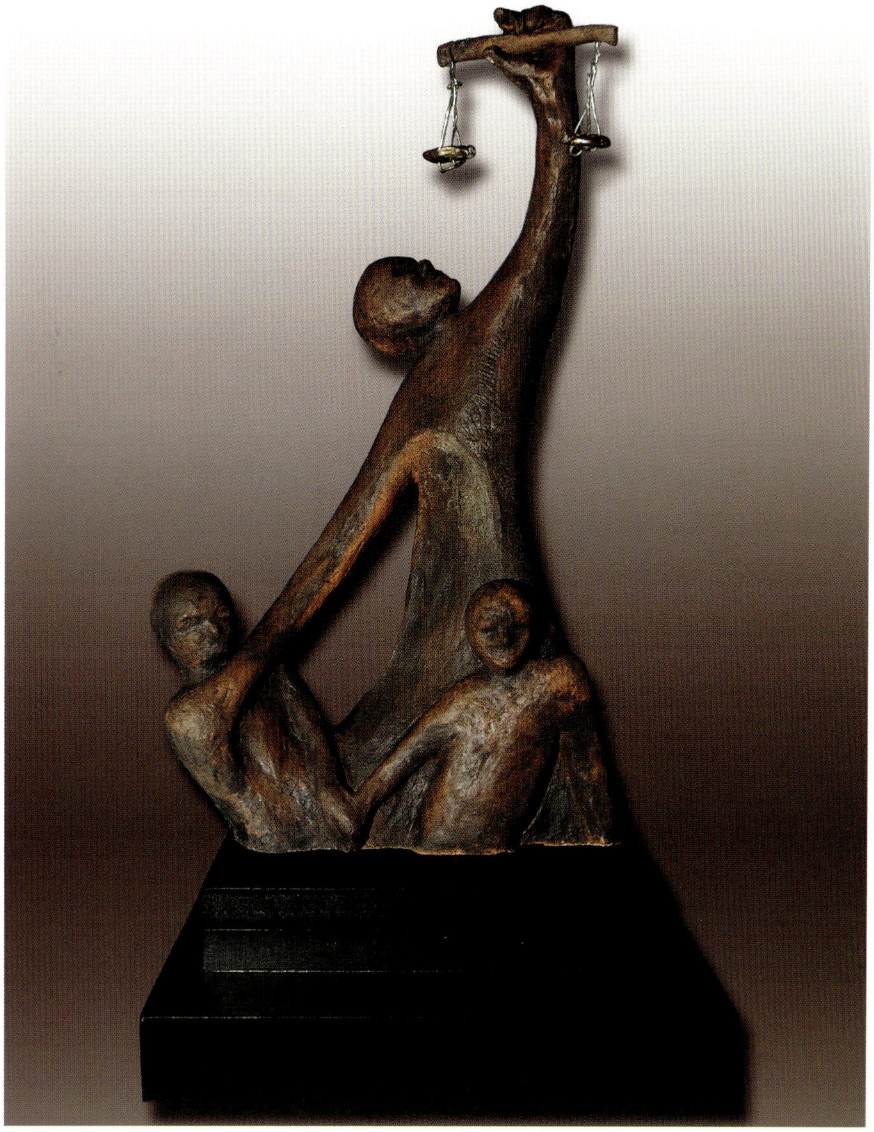

Visual arts became a part of me early in life—watching my grandmother paint, creating clay pieces at summer camp, making pipe cleaner animals, and of course receiving praise for my efforts. After art studies of the 1950s, I found myself trying to explain "modern art" to my friends here in Spartanburg.

Clay sculptures became my choice medium, and the arrival of my children led to a flurry of portrait busts. Classes with Dr. Davidson at Converse polished this change in direction. In addition to commissions within the community, I worked with law enforcement forensic teams, creating facial reconstructions.

Today I strive for arrested movement in my work, for, as William Faulkner said, "Motion is life." I strive to accomplish this by directing the viewer's eye in, around, and up with the piece. I am less concerned with real detail and instead focus on minimalism in shape, form, and line. The emphasis is on producing feeling. If I can add humor, even better!

I find much satisfaction teaching at our Chapman Cultural Center—the Spartanburg Art Museum staff is tops! We are all dedicated to sharing both formal and learned lessons with our students—opening eyes with the joy of creating.

In present-day sculpture, available materials are almost endless. From "found objects" to polymers to old standbys of rock, metal, and clay, sculpture has become very versatile. Clay continues being popularized by pottery, and sculpture focuses more on "public art." Various disciplines form teams of welders, architects, landscapists, visual artists, and community leaders to visually beautify public places. Spartanburg's leaders continue to guide our city into the thriving land of opportunity it has become. There is no better place in the southeastern United States to live as an aspiring artist needing access to inspiration!

Ann Wenz

My earliest memories of weaving are of a neighbor in my native Paw Paw, Michigan. She had a large floor loom and would often give my family gifts of placemats and pot holders. I still have some of them.

In college, as an art education major, I enrolled in a textile course and experienced weaving on a floor loom for the first time. Having always been interested in fashion, clothing construction, and textiles, it was exciting to create woven goods. Since college, I have been enrolled in graduate courses and workshops focusing on many techniques and styles of weaving. Each learning experience has influenced my style and led to new ideas. For the most part, my style and subject matter tend to be based on geometrics and abstractions.

Moving to Spartanburg, the heart of the textile industry, in 1975 was exciting. There were hand-weaving guilds and exhibit opportunities in the Upstate area. The Artists' Guild of Spartanburg and the Spartanburg County Museum of Art (now SAM) provided opportunities for artists as they continue to do today.

Creating a piece of art is a process. One idea leads to another. A mistake turns into an unexpected idea, and problems lead to creative solutions. My ideas stem from the artwork of others, new materials, new technology, and the environment.

In creating a weaving I am always aware of the elements and principles of design: the shape, color, texture, space, line, and value. Repetition of shapes, colors, and materials, in addition to variety and visual rhythm, leads to a cohesive, unified composition.

Although I hope the viewer enjoys the finished product, it is ultimately the process that I enjoy. Thinking of an idea, working with the materials, weaving to a completed work, and then planning for the next piece makes the work worth the effort.

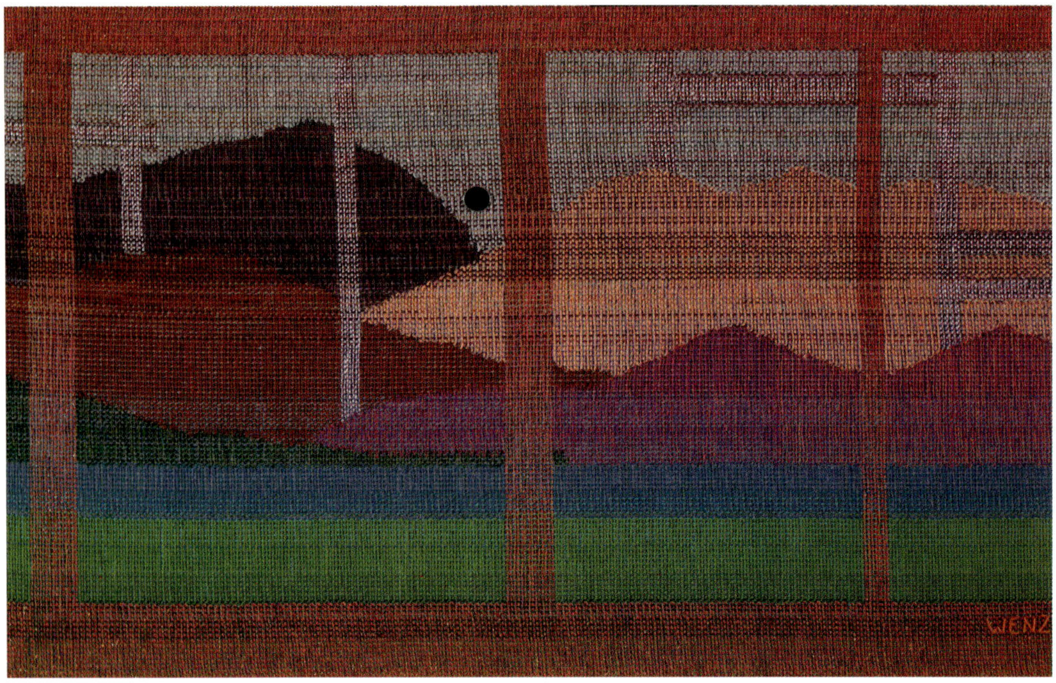

View From My Window

Weaving

25" X 35"

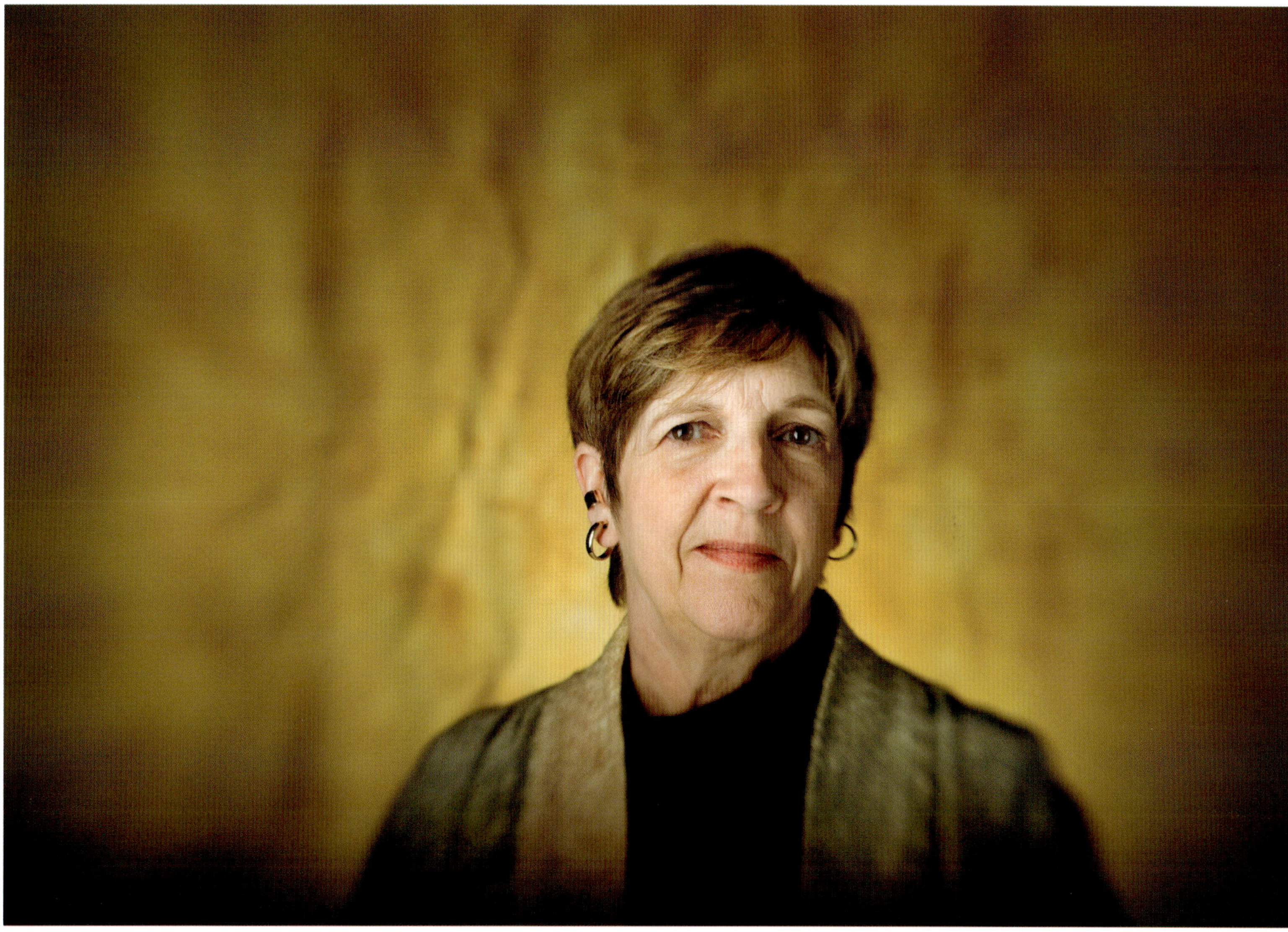

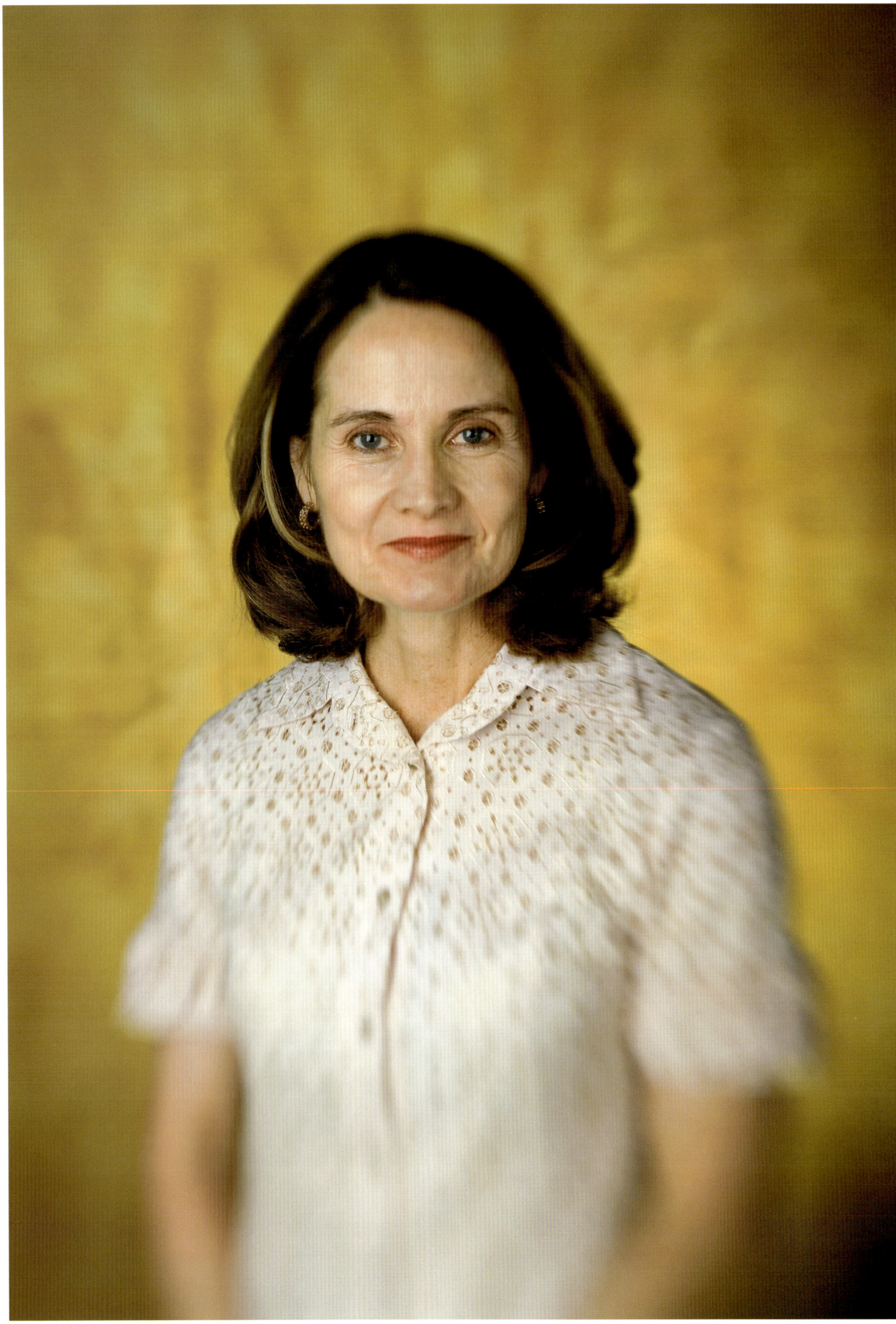

Karen White

I was born in Spartanburg. My mother painted—mainly portraits—one of which is of my grandfather with his favorite dog, Spot, which I treasure. My memories of my mother at her easel are very strong. Luckily I still have her beat-up paint box and wooden pallet. She gave me a love of any and all creative expression—from a first childish sketchbook, to a pre-teen lesson on "the birds and the bees" using an eye-popping picture of Michelangelo's *David*, to regular trips to the public library and required piano lessons, even to sharing her favorite movies with Fred Astaire and Ginger Rogers. All of these got me started on this path.

I went to Converse College, where I received a grand liberal arts education. Professor Melba Long taught art appreciation and opened the door to all the old masters via a slide show extraordinaire. I will never forget her passion. Marriage and six daughters intervened, and the paint brush stayed in the box for a number of years. Eight years ago I returned to serious painting. Once again I felt the delighted pleasure of a child just drawing pictures and exploring light and color, subject and technique.

The arts community in Spartanburg amazes me with all its enthusiastic people, resources, and activities. We have public galleries at the Chapman Cultural Center and HUB-BUB, and generous artists who gladly share their love of the work and the joy of just creating something.

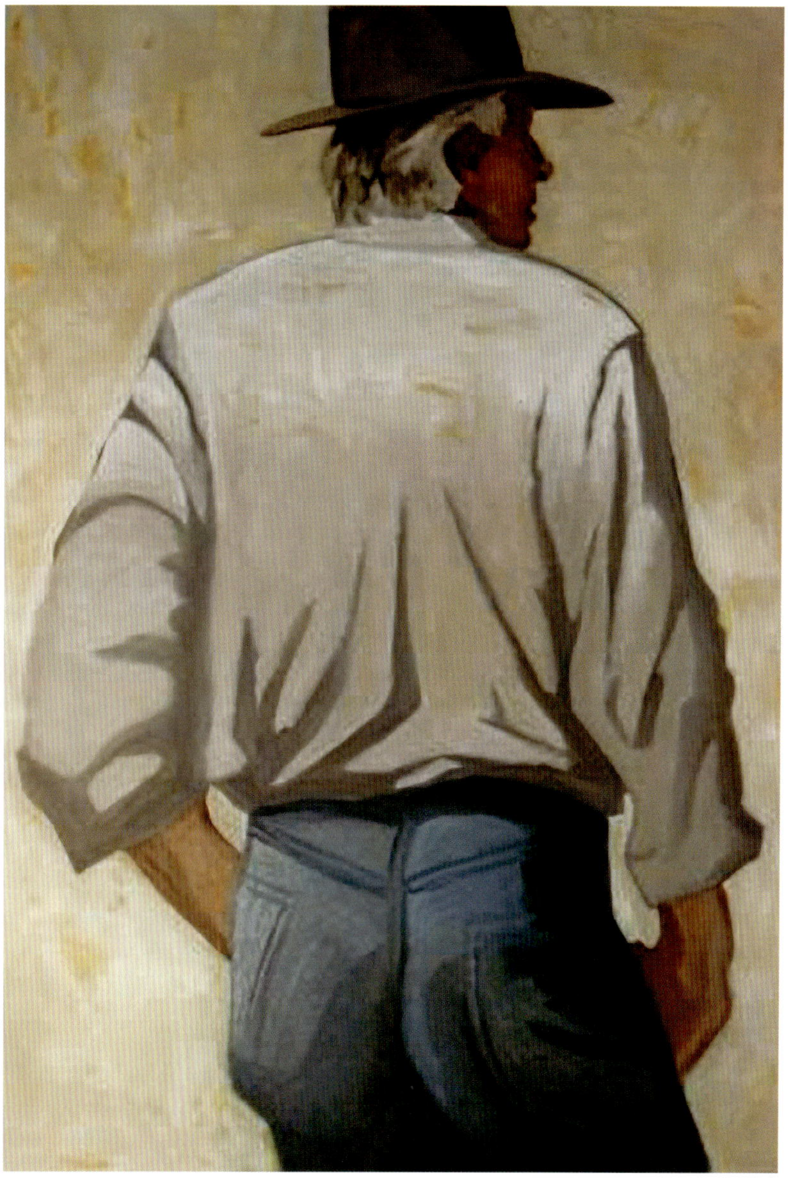

The High Road
Oil on canvas
11" X 14"

I am mainly self-taught but have had the opportunity to attend some excellent workshops around the country with worthy instructors. Supportive artists/friends have also encouraged me. Oil is my medium, and my paintings are a bit narrative, which makes sense because I've always loved a good story. Each work becomes a jump-off into a story-land, some imagined place or moment in time, a whimsical glimpse. Dogs, being a big part of my life, also seem to find their way into many settings, happily participating.

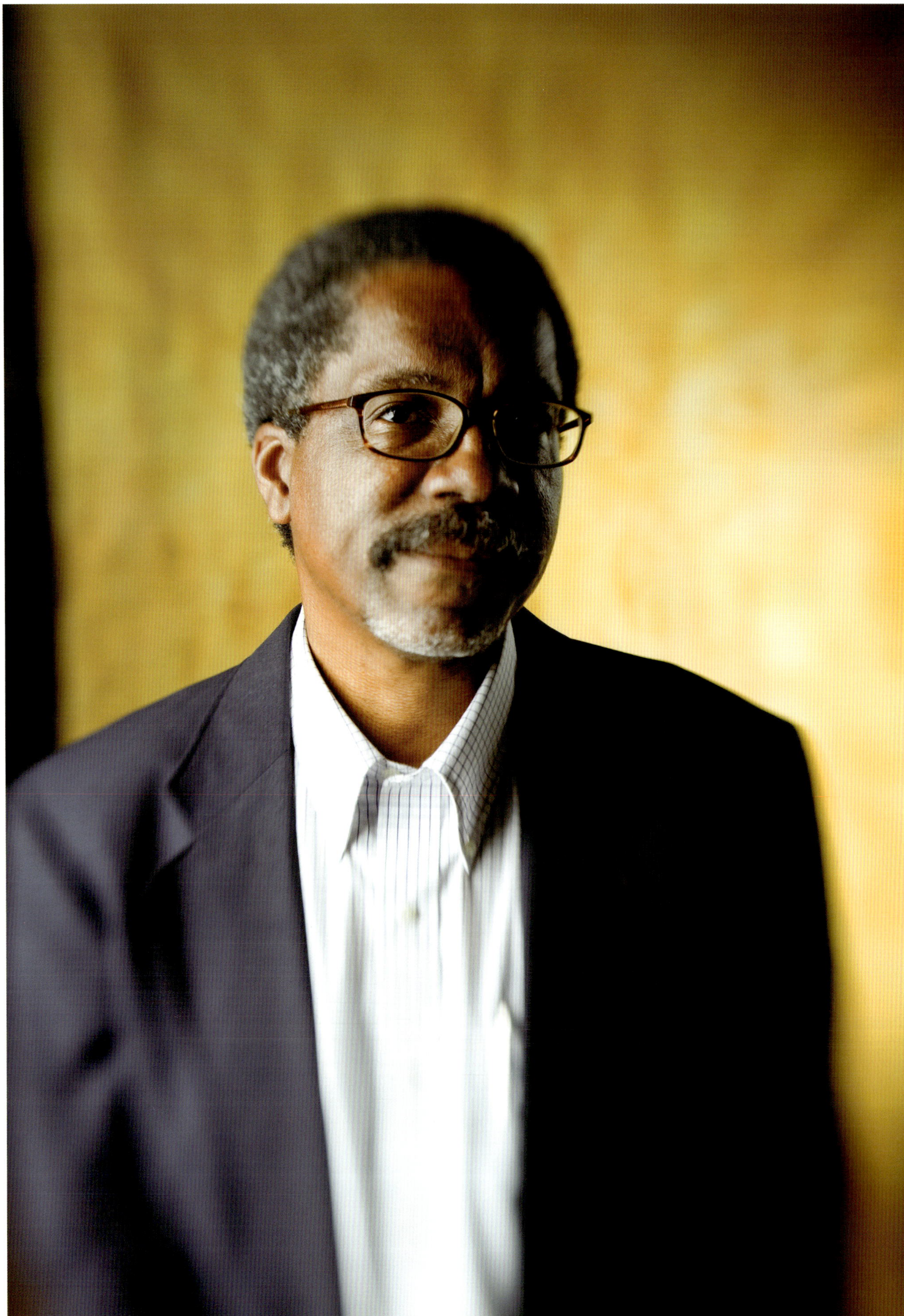

Winston Wingo

My sculptures reflect my interest in surface as it relates to human and organic forms, focusing on the integration of man and the impact of our technological society. In my work human and tooled marks contrast with smoothed, machined and organic surfaces that employ the concepts of Futurism as seen through biomorphic images with geometric shapes. My bronzes are cast using the lost wax process, employing a ceramic shell procedure for bronze casting. I do my casting in Pietrasanta, Italy, where I studied marble carving with Italian sculptor Robert Bertola.

I was born in Spartanburg and was encouraged and inspired to pursue sculpture by Brooks Huggins, the art teacher at Jenkins Junior High School. I received a BA in Art Education from Claflin University in Orangeburg and an MFA in sculpture/painting from Clemson University. My post-graduate studies at in Italy at the Instituto Statute D'Arte , the Luigi Tammasi Foundry and the Artistica Mariani Foundry. My home and studio are in a historic house on South Spring Street in Spartanburg that wowed me the first time I stepped inside. Built in 1922, I have found artistic inspiration here since 1984.

As a painter, sculptor, and art educator, I teach in the Spartanburg public school system. I am currently teaching at Carver Junior High and have taught at Claflin University, Converse College, South Carolina State University, and USC Upstate. I am represented by the Ward-Nasse Gallery in New York as well as Mason Murer Gallery in Atlanta.

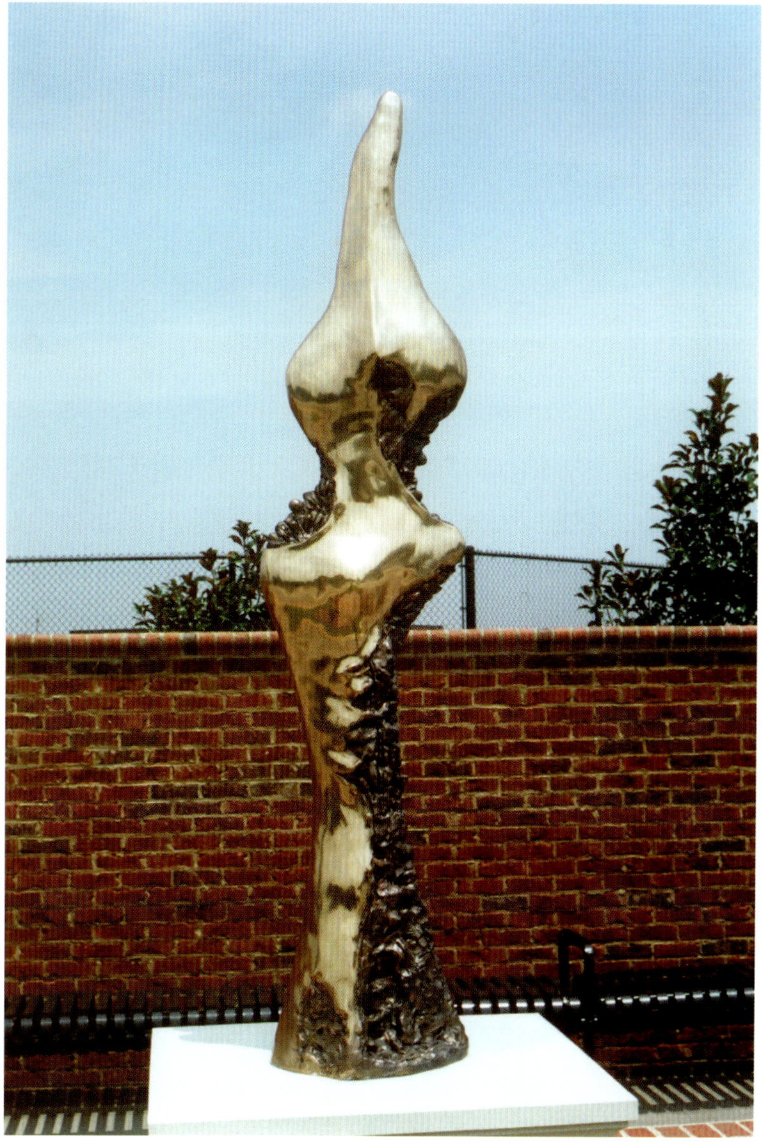

Harmony

Cast Bronze on marble

12' X 1.5' X 1.5'

Edythe S. Wise

Gone Fishin
Watercolor
21" X 30"

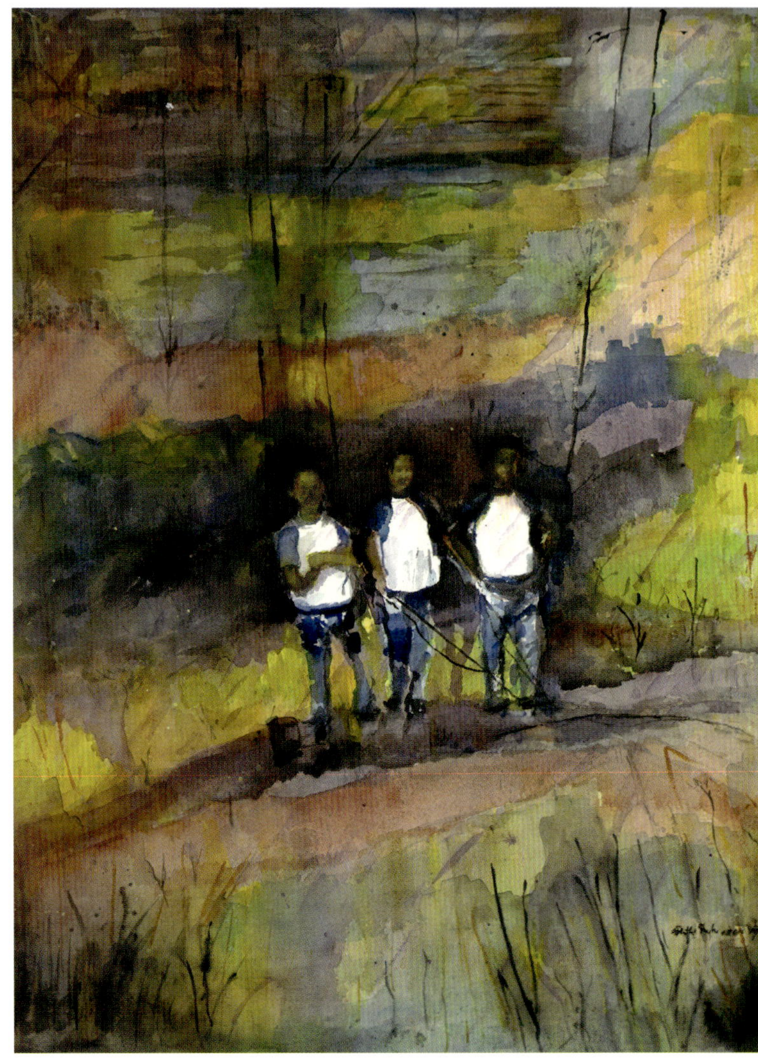

I was born in Sheridan, Wyoming, with an artist brush in one hand and a palette of colors in the other! I have been interested in and active in art ever since.

Upon graduation from Savannah High School, I was employed by E.I. DuPont and Company in Alabama as an illustrator for its safety magazine. After marriage I pursued my art education with outstanding artists in various continuing education programs. Foremost among these were the Famous Artists School in Westport, Connecticut; Armstrong College and Savannah College of Art and Design in Georgia; and Converse College II in Spartanburg. In addition I attended seminars in Scottsdale, Arizona; Callaway Gardens, Georgia; Ruidoso, New Mexico; and Atlanta, and I was a frequent attendee at Springmaid Art sessions.

During this period I published *Color Historic Spartanburg* (two printings) with a grant from the National Endowment for the Arts. I later published *Color the Church of the Advent* to help celebrate its sesquicentennial.

I have participated in numerous juried art shows and won various awards. My work also hangs in Spartanburg Regional Hospital, Mary Black Minor Care Center, and Piedmont Internal Medicine. I am a member of the South Carolina Watercolor Society, The Artists' Guild of Spartanburg, and American Pen Women.

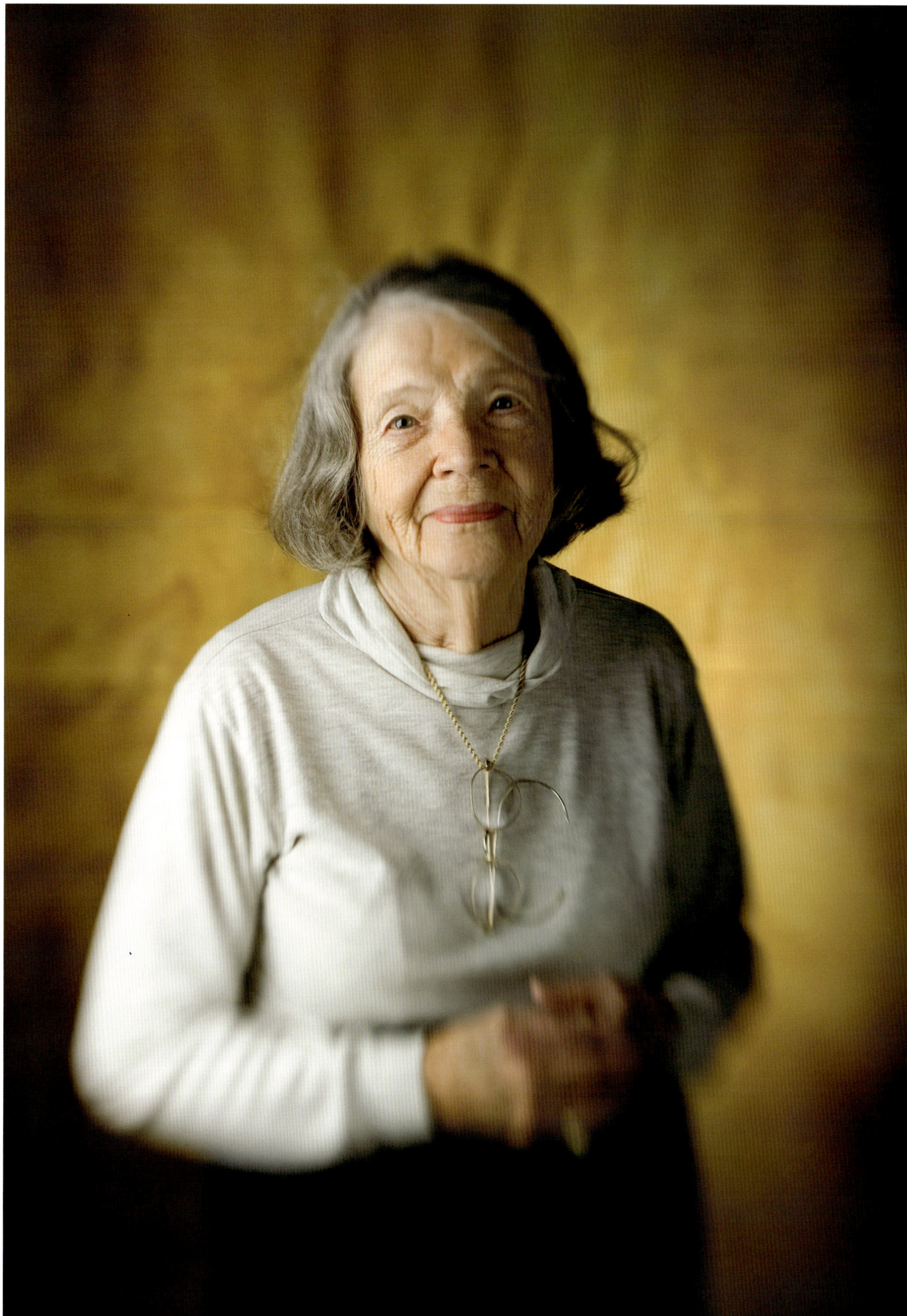

I was born in Philadelphia to Swiss parents, and due to the concentration of textile companies here, my father picked Spartanburg as the town to settle in and start his textile manufacturing company when I was four years old.

My parents were always patrons of the arts, and through our travels they exposed me to many wonderful cultures, places, and museums that sparked a lifelong love of the visual arts. This interest grew slowly though, as I preferred to be outside playing in the woods and creeks surrounding our home. Little did I know that building castles of mud and pebbles in the creek or elaborate wooden forts would be the gateway to studying ceramics and sculpture at Converse College.

At first glance, the natural elements might not be glaringly evident in my work. However, when you look more closely, it becomes apparent that the natural world was my inspiration. The shapes, textures, and colors that I create in my minimalist and abstracted forms are directly inspired by the tree bark, marbled pebbles, and foliage that I am constantly photographing and collecting.

My artwork is tactile. It is meant to be touched, rubbed, and experienced. If someone—especially a child—picks up a bowl I created and says, "Wow, the outside is all bumpy and rough like a rock, but the inside is soft and smooth like when you open a shell at the beach!" then I know I have created a successful piece.

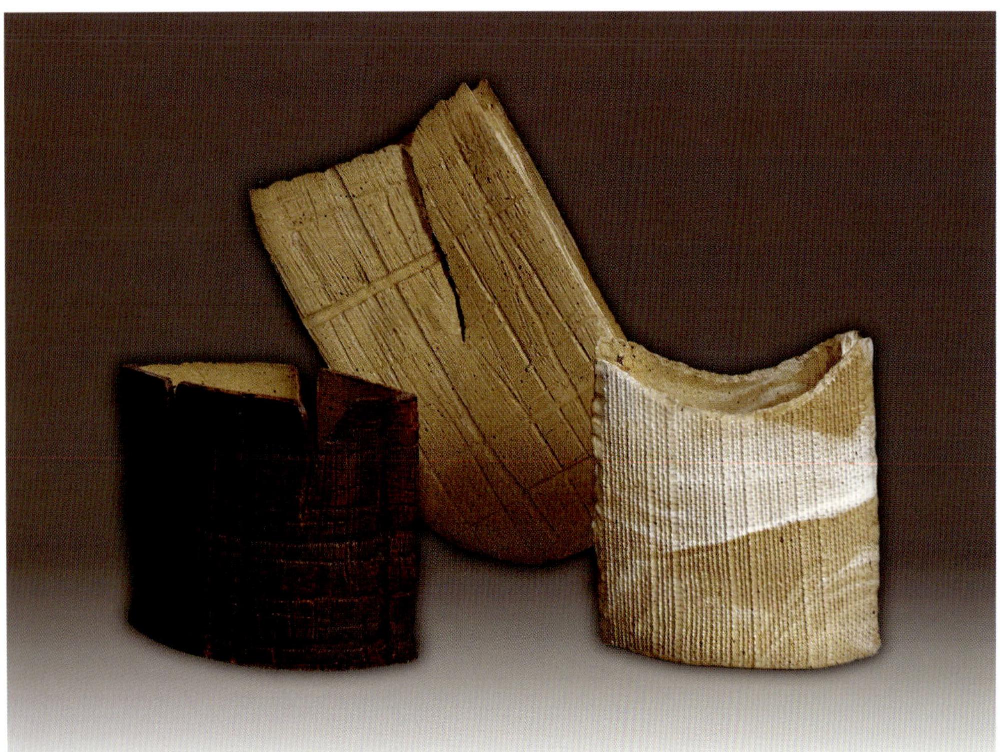

In the Woods

Porcelain and stoneware

12.5" X 8" X 3"

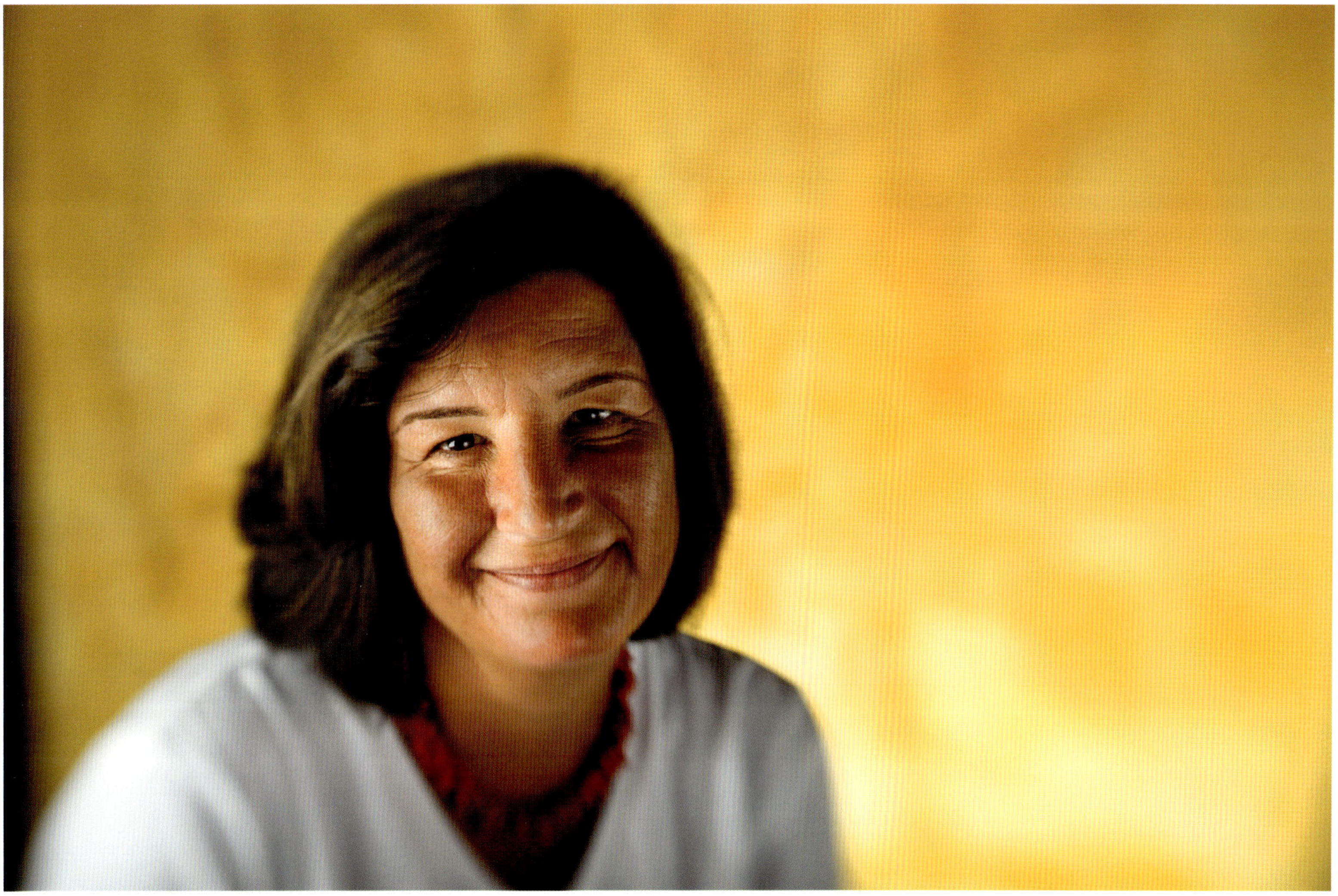

Kathy Zimmerli Wofford

David Zacharias

Everybody knows me as Zach. In 1950 I was born in Beaver Falls, Pennsylvania. I grew up outside of Philadelphia, the son of a railroad-civil-engineer father and a secretary-housewife mother. After high school, I left home for sights unseen and ended up at Clemson University, first majoring in pre-veterinary medicine. A year later, at Clemson's School of Architecture, I took my first art classes and enjoyed them. I changed my major to studio art, transferred to the University of South Carolina and never looked back.

At Carolina I finished a BFA in December 1972 and thought I was ready to make a mark in the art world. That didn't happen, so I applied to graduate school at Carolina in 1974 and completed an MFA in 1979. My first job after that accomplishment was tying steel with a swimming pool construction company in Columbia, South Carolina, the hottest place on the planet during summer. For twelve years I held blue-collar jobs in construction, renovation, furniture making, cabinetry, pipe fitting, ditch digging, and numerous related activities. From time to time, I held part-time teaching positions at USC, USC-Aiken, and at Converse College. At no time during those lean years did I stop making art. If I couldn't make ceramic art, I sculpted or painted, but I always produced. In 1991 I started a full-time teaching position at Converse and have received three different awards for teaching excellence.

Since 1972, I have had twenty-two one-person exhibitions, been in ninety group exhibitions and sixty-eight juried exhibitions. Juried exhibitions have been local, state, regional, national, and international in nature. My work is currently carried in two galleries in South Carolina and one in North Carolina.

The ceramic art that I have produced in the last two years is primarily functional. The outsides of my pieces are covered with 2-D images of fishes incised into the clay. Recently, some of the 2-D fish images have translated into 3-D forms. As long as I smile and chuckle while constructing these pieces, I intend to keep making them.

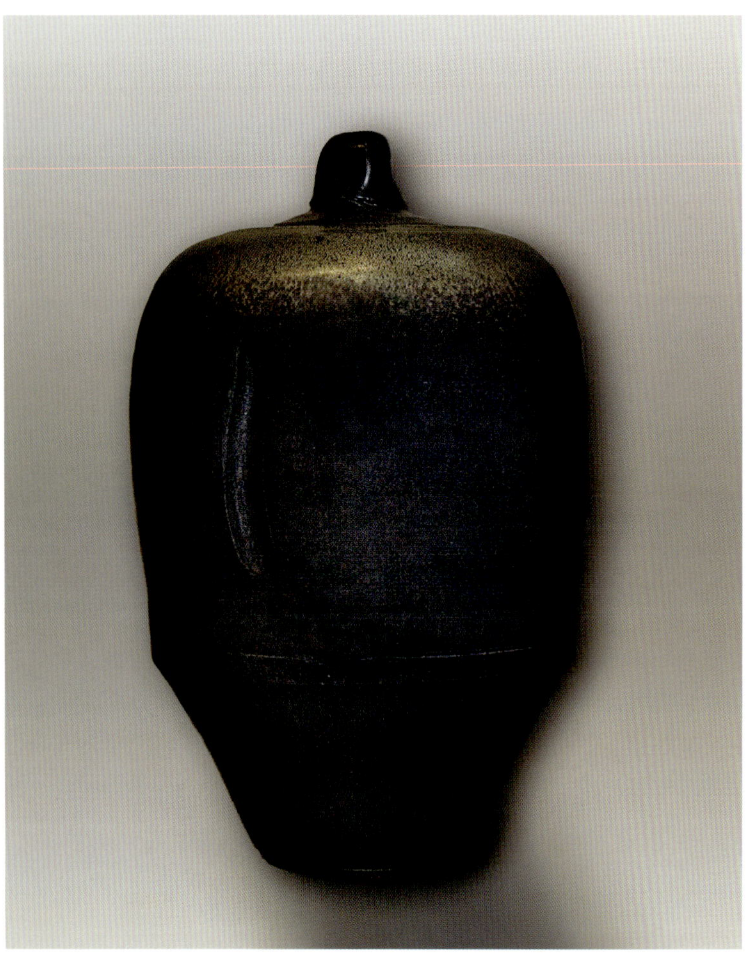

Pickle Jar

Stoneware

22.5" X 15" X 15"

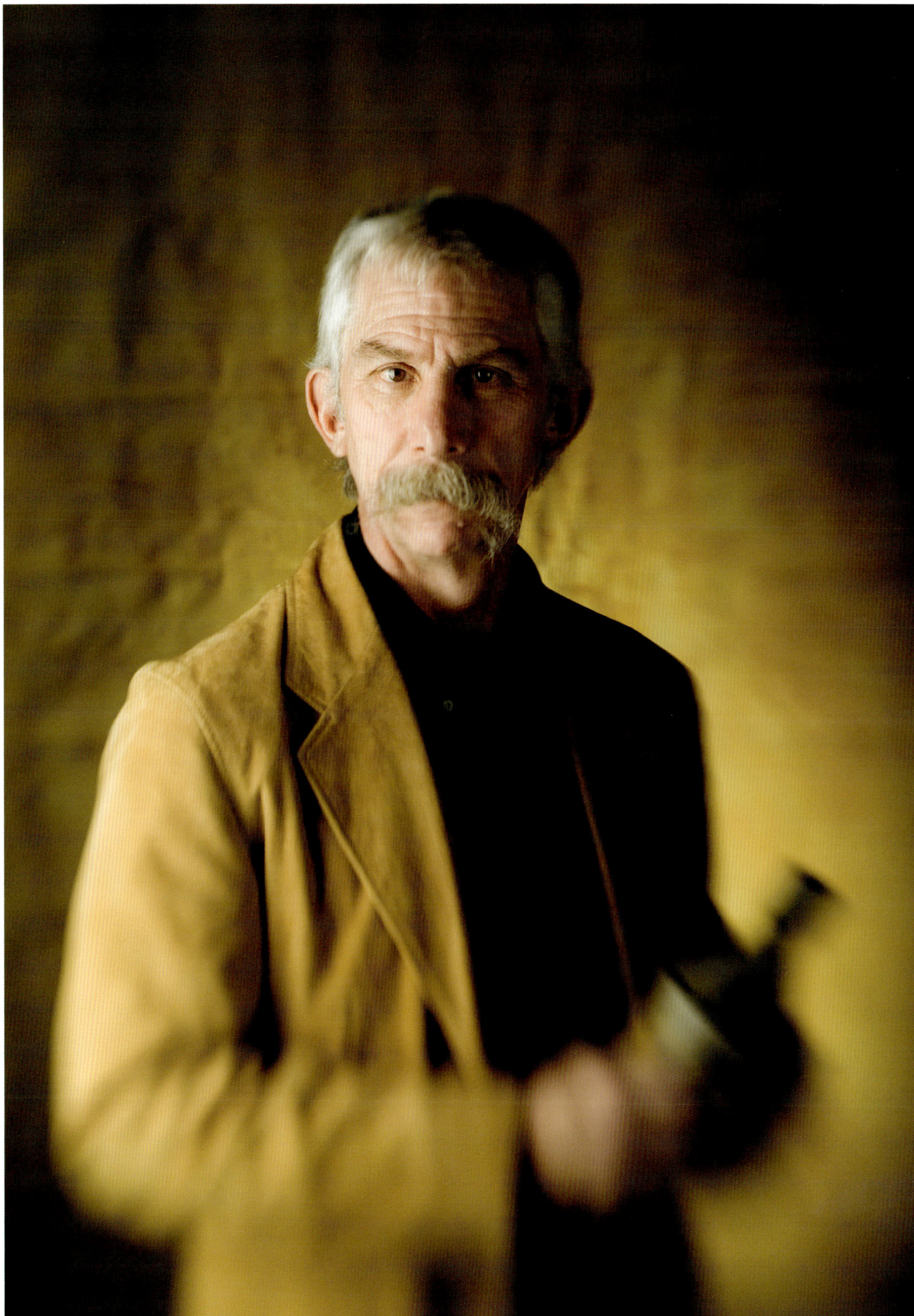

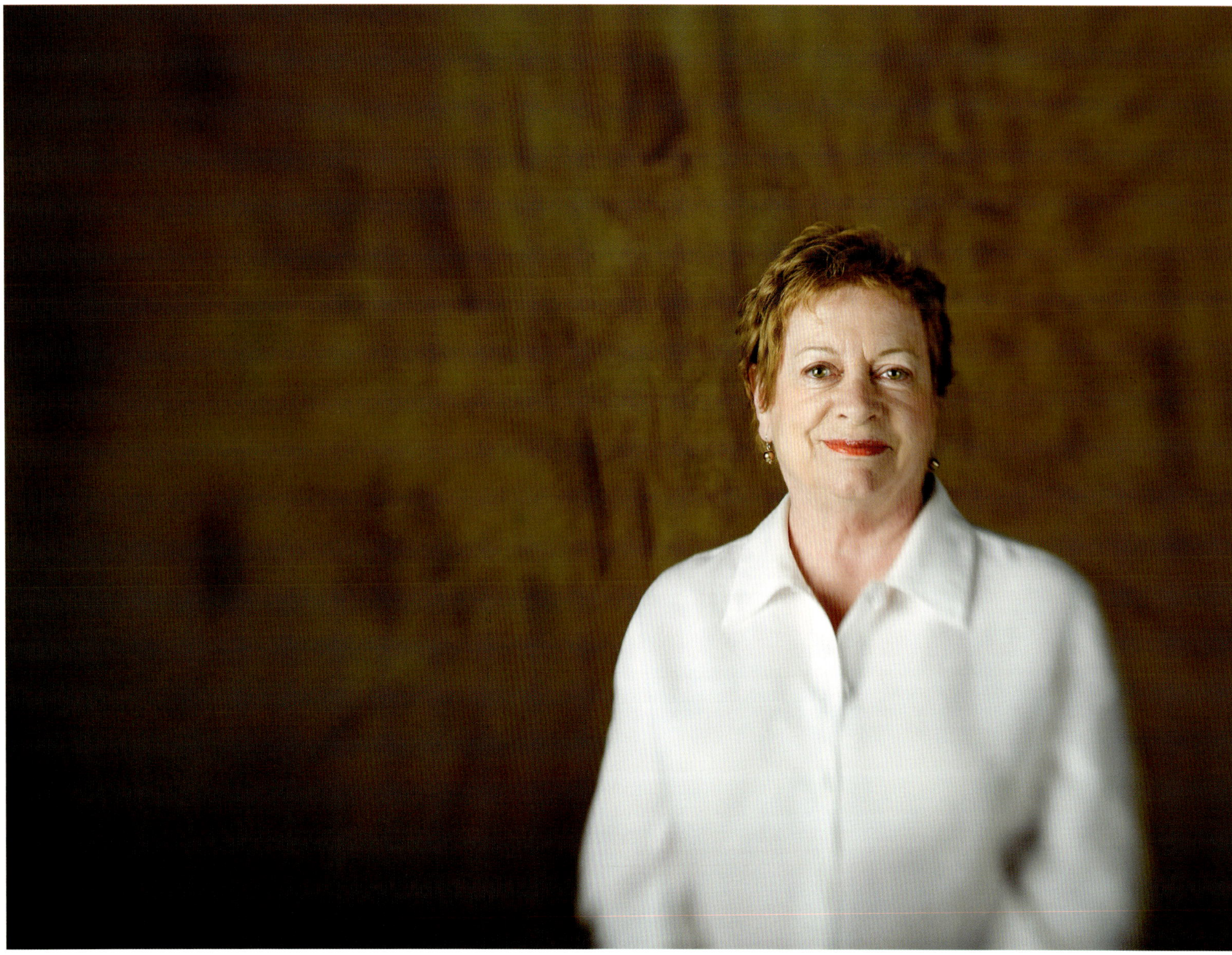

Suzanne Zoole

Life began in Georgia, followed by formative years in Minnesota, New Jersey, and Connecticut. As an adult I spent time in Germany, then Dallas, and finally reclaimed my Southern roots with a fortuitous move to Spartanburg. My development as an artist occurred here, where we have a very supportive and unified visual arts community.

My interest in art was born out of a love for art as a student in Europe, where I was caught up with the work of van Gogh and Matisse. I particularly admired the vivid colors, flat style, and straightforward composition. My parents were indirectly influential in my development as an artist, in unconventional ways. My chemist father was a creative sort who took on various artistic projects with poise and patience. His ability to embrace the role of beginner (with any new pursuit) had a great impact on my motivation. My mother has always had a good sense of space, proportion, and taste that also influenced me. As I took up painting seriously, she became my patron by paying for an out-of-town workshop every year. When I decided to become an artist, I sought out the best instruction I could find, completed the assignments, listened to the critiques, found a mentor, and honed the skills.

My usual medium is acrylic paint on paper and canvas. My style is abstracted realism. I am known for my interiors and am also drawn to paint landscapes and other subject matter. Positive and personal feelings for the subject matter are behind each piece of my work. I love what I am painting. The other ingredient in my choices of subject matter has to do with composition. I am often excited and drawn to a well-composed scene. My camera is a handy tool if I am without my sketchbook.

It pleases me when a viewer sees beyond the surface image to another layer of meaning, whether I intended it or not. I hope the viewer experiences enjoyment of the composition and color, as well as the sheer pleasure that was involved in creating the work.

Back Porch

Acrylic on canvas

40" X 30"

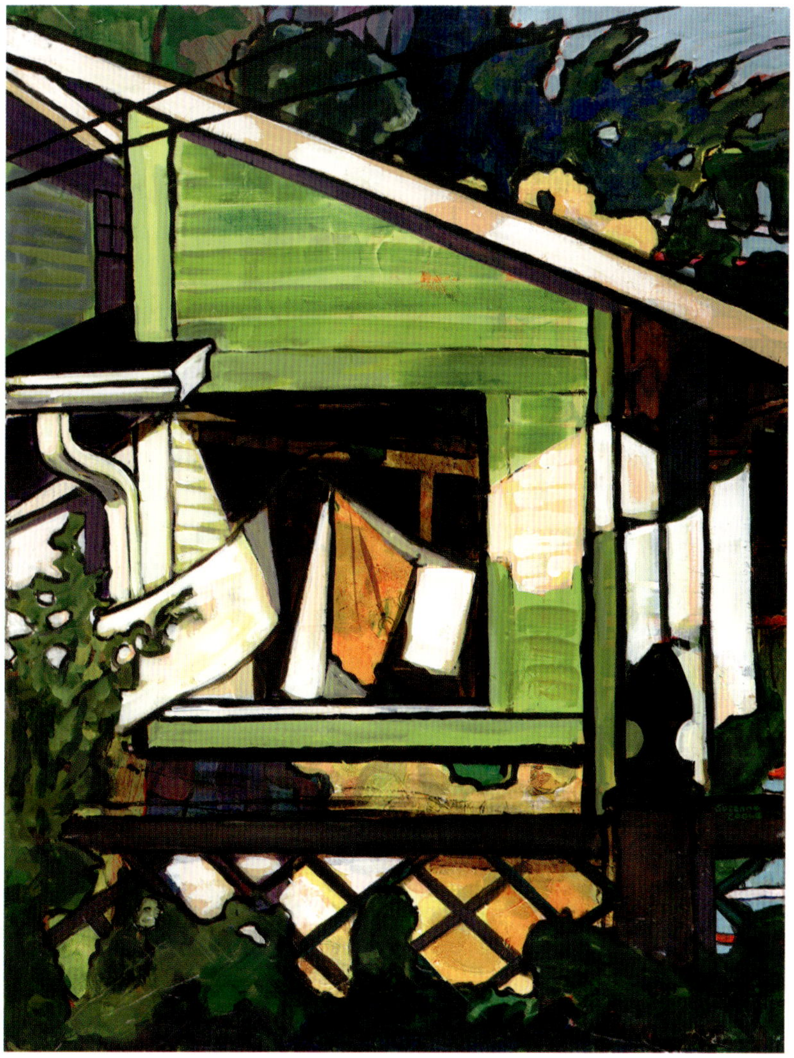

Edward Emory

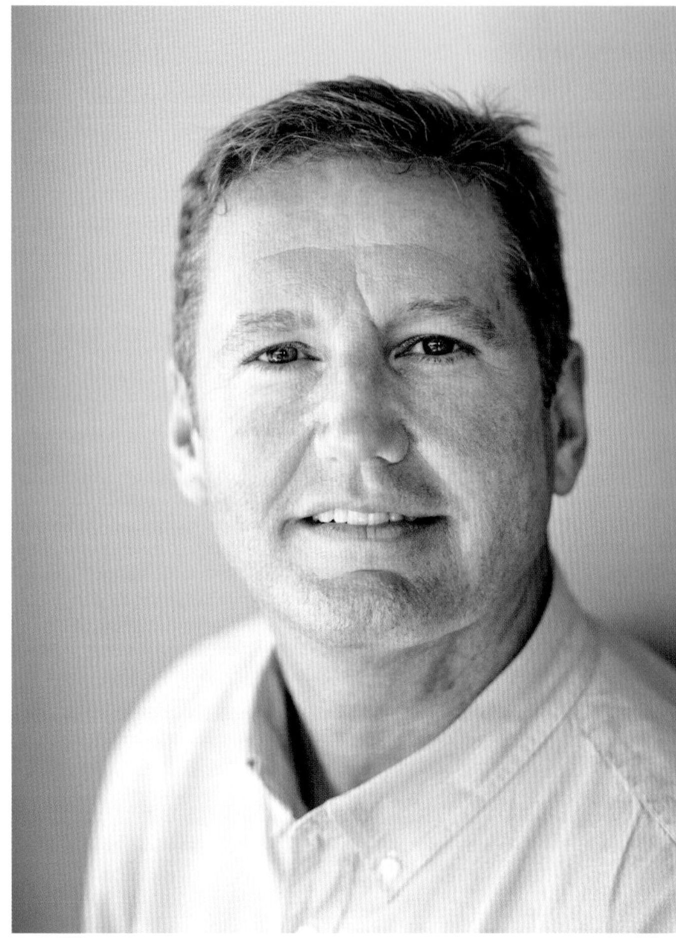

STEPHEN STINSON

Edward Emory has spent the past thirty-four years working with, employing, and promoting artists. His love of visual arts began as a child and has continued throughout his professional career. He and his wife, Shannon, operate one of the largest original fine art galleries in South Carolina. In the 1980s Emory was among the first to embrace digital technology used to produce what eventually became known as "Giclee" prints. His expertise in this technology led to strong personal relationships with artists from all over the United States. He has juried numerous fine arts exhibits, served two terms as president of the Spartanburg Artists' Guild, is a current board member of the Healing Arts Foundation, and is the co-founder of Spartanburg's monthly art walk. Emory regularly speaks to various art groups and artists about the business of marketing and promoting their artwork. He continues to be a devoted supporter of visual arts in his community and the region.

Stephen Stinson

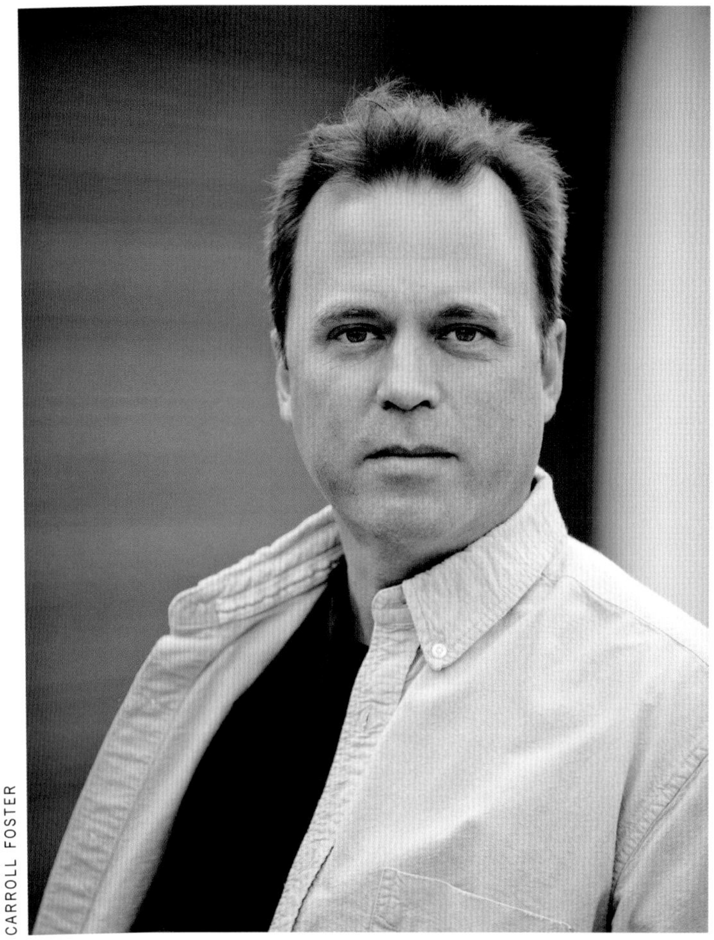

CARROLL FOSTER

If you had asked Stephen Stinson where his life was going at age seventeen, he would never have imagined photography as a full-time career. When he was in high school all he wanted to do was play his Fender bass with his pals in their band, Jericho. Eventually he attended and graduated from the Art Institute of Atlanta with a degree in photography before returning to Spartanburg and working with Olencki Graphics (Mark Olencki) for eight years. He ventured out on his own in 1993 and today he is still producing images for a wide variety of clients, photographing people, food, architecture, and the world around him for advertising, editorial, and corporate assignments. He lives in Spartanburg, married to his high school sweetheart, Patty, and they have one son, Lane, who is now in college.

Hub City Press

is an independent press in Spartanburg, South Carolina, that publishes well-crafted, high-quality works by new and established authors, with an emphasis on the Southern experience. We are committed to high-caliber novels, short stories, poetry, plays, memoir, and works emphasizing regional culture and history. We are particularly interested in books with a strong sense of place.

Hub City Press is an imprint of the non-profit Hub City Writers Project, founded in 1995 to foster a sense of community through the literary arts. Our metaphor of organization purposely looks backward to the nineteenth century when Spartanburg was known as the "hub city," a place where railroads converged and departed.

Spartanburg titles

Hub City Anthology ■ John Lane and Betsy Wakefield Teter, editors

Hub City Music Makers ■ Peter Cooper

Hub City Christmas ■ John Lane and Betsy Wakefield Teter, editors

Seeing Spartanburg ■ Philip Racine

Family Trees ■ Mike Corbin

The Seasons of Harold Hatcher ■ Mike Hembree

The Lawson's Fork ■ David Taylor and Gary Henderson

Hub City Anthology 2 ■ Betsy Wakefield Teter, editor

In Morgan's Shadow ■ The Hub City Writers Project

The Place I Live ■ The Children of Spartanburg County

Textile Town ■ Betsy Wakefield Teter, editor

Come to the Cow Pens! ■ Christine Swager

Magical Places ■ Marion Peter Holt

When the Soldiers Came to Town ■ Susan Turpin, Carolyn Creal, Ron Crawley, and James Crocker

South of Main ■ Beatrice Hill and Brenda Lee

Cottonwood Trail ■ Thomas Webster, G.R. Davis, and Peter Schmunk

Wofford ■ Doyle Boggs, JoAnn Mitchell Brasington, Phillip Stone, editors

Courageous Kate ■ Sheila Ingle

Spartanburg Revisited ■ Emily Smith, Carroll Foster, and Mark Olencki

Common Ties ■ Katherine Davis Cann

Still Home ■ Rachel Harkai, editor

Stars Fell on Spartanburg ■ Jeremy Jones and Betsy Wakefield Teter, editors

For Here or To Go ■ Brandy Lindsey

Expecting Goodness ■ C. Michael Curtis, editor

Because Memory Isn't Eternal ■ Deno Trakas